Battles East

A History of the Eastern Front of the First World War

G. Irving Root

PublishAmerica
Baltimore

First printing

ISBN: 1-4241-6800-7
PUBLISHED BY PUBLISHAMERICA, LLLP
www.publishamerica.com
Baltimore

Printed in the United States of America

Table of Contents

List of Maps

Foreword

In recent decades, a very great deal has been written on the subject of military history. The World Wars, in particular, have been extensively covered. Here in the West, that coverage has not unnaturally been much more complete regarding operations in which Western troops were engaged. Stories of the Western and Italian Fronts, Naval Campaigns, and the Pacific Theater have been told and retold, and today we have a wealth of detailed information available to those of us who are fascinated by the subject as a whole and who enjoy studying it. Moreover, there are few Americans Englishmen, or Frenchmen, those nationalities most easily flushed with pride by the thought of being the great victors of a titanic struggle, who have not at one time or another listened to a veteran's recollection of some famous battle in one or the other World War. For altogether too many people, the wars symbolize a victory of democracy over militarism; a victory of the United States, Britain, and France over Germany and Japan.

All this is quite understandable. On the other hand, however, there occurred gigantic struggles in the vast expanses of Eastern Europe with which the West seems scarcely to have been familiar. Within the last three decades or so a fairly substantial amount of information has been put to print regarding the Eastern Front in the Second World War. There should be by now, at least, a widespread opinion that the Eastern Theater was the main one in the Second War. Hopefully such revelations will ensure that the fighting in the East in the First World War will no longer be regarded as a mere sideshow.

I had always heard that the Eastern campaign consisted of indecisive battles in an equally indecisive war. Were not Russia's efforts, however valiant to begin with, completely annulled by the catastrophic spectacle of the Russian Revolution? And hadn't the Second War eclipsed any decision there reached? In struggling along against this mode of thinking, I was sure there was a definite need to tell the story of the Eastern Front in World War One. I was well aware of the fact that attitudes in the West were in no way similar to those of the average German or Russian feeling toward the subject. If, when during the Second War a German spoke of the "War" he was immediately understood as meaning the war in the East. Then I wondered how true was the claim that in the First War the Western Front was far and away the main theater. For the Russian's part, the Second World War, or at least their defense of the motherland in it, has taken an almost holy or sacred symbolism. Yet there is no First War counterpart to the *History of the Great Patriotic War.* There is no official Russian history of that earlier conflict, which had it claimed even half as many lives as the second, would have been a far more ruinous war than is imaginable for Western peoples. Such was, in fact, the case.

The thought of the specter of huge armies fighting it out over great distances on a giant bleak Eastern European landscape had always captivated my imagination. I wanted to know what actually did happen. But it had annoyed me to examine, say, a single volume history of the war only to find that two-thirds of the book was devoted to the Western Front. Then there are the multi-volume histories. One notable such work, in ten volumes, allots only one single volume to the War in the East. Another drawback is that what information is available generally describes the same few battles in the same old context. It is genuinely difficult to find books devoted solely to the subject, excluding memoirs. But by the nineteen seventies, considerable information had surfaced, generally in bits and pieces. It became my purpose to splice together the story of the fighting from the war's outbreak to the final peace.

I have drawn on sources published from 1916 to present. I do not share the belief that newer references are generally more desirable than older ones, since it seems to me that accounts given closer in time to an event are more apt to accurately depict it and capture the mood of the times. Of course it must be said that much of what was written on the war at the time carried a distinct bias toward the nation it originated from. In Allied Nations especially, this anti-German bias was to prevent otherwise good works from being truly objective ones, and this condition was to last for decades, traces of it even today being noticeable. More recently written sources may not suffer such shortcomings and are often more thoroughly researched. These I have found most useful, if often disappointingly incomplete. Personal memoirs are indispensable for any such research as I have done, yet I have found these to be of relatively small value, as these are necessarily subjective in nature and can at times be evidently self-serving. They do, of course, lend insight to the inclination of the authors, and this in itself can be helpful to the researcher.

It was not long before I noticed the same book titles listed again and again in bibliographies of works on the subject. I began to see the pattern. The same information representing the same broad view of the significance of the Eastern Front was simply being rewritten by different persons, perhaps sprinkled with a few new interpretations or another new source to enforce the old conclusions. This is not to say that a fact can or should be disputed for the sake of presenting a new conclusion. But precious few accounts of the war seemed to me to be realistic. Admittedly, I have spent much time reading these same books and the time has not been ill-spent in my opinion, since in view of the fact that no great wealth of alternative sources are available, they do lend to a general understanding of the subject and are useful for obtaining some details. One good example worth mentioning here is the Ludendorff Memoirs. Many books written on World War I contain quotations from the famous General, yet Ludendorff himself was to fall victim to the misguided belief that only by forcing the issue on the Western Front could the war be won. He too would in the end fail to see the potential for success that had been gained in the East, brought about by the very campaigns he had helped to unleash.

Another point that needs to be made regards casualty figures. I can scarcely remember ever seeing the same figure from any two different sources describing losses for any given single battle. The Russian figures, in particular, vary at anywhere between 3½ and 11 million, a remarkable discrepancy in numbers of human lives! The key word is estimated. Unless an official Russian history appears, perhaps even if it does, we will probably never have any even remotely accurate figures, but as we shall see, arriving at a reasonably good understanding of the losses is by no means impossible. In all cases I suspect that the actual number of Germans, Austro-Hungarians, or Russians killed, wounded, or missing will forever be unknown, but their sacrifices must never be forgotten.

For the reader wishing to consult maps and thus take full advantage of the geographic descriptions in this text, I should like to mention that all place names are as of 1914. That is, cities and towns, provinces, rivers and other topographic features are referred to as they had been in pre-1918 Europe. This may be confusing to some, because sometimes the names have changed more than once. For example, Czernowitz, the Austrian capital of the Bukovina, was incorporated into Romania after the war and called Cernauti. Following the Second World War, the city became part of the Soviet Union, and was known as Chernovtsy. Today it is part of Ukraine, and appears on modern maps as Chernivtsi. The Eastern German territories have all disappeared from the map, some being taken by Poland in 1918, the remainder by Poland and Russia in 1945. Poland, part of Russia in 1914, pushed its boundaries eastward and became independent in 1920. In 1945 its boundaries were pushed far to the west. Galicia, an Austrian province in 1914, became Polish in 1920 and is now divided between Poland and the Ukraine. The Bukovina is divided between Romania and the Ukraine, while Transylvania is now Romanian. The list goes on and on, and the issue is further confused by the Polish and German "W" being pronounced as "V"; hence Lvov vs. Lwow; Zlozov vs. Zlozow, Narev vs. Narew, etc. Such inconveniences are really minor though, especially if the reader can obtain access to fairly detailed maps of the general area perhaps of different time periods.

The following story is intended to be a narration of the military events that occurred on the Eastern Front during World War I. It was not my intention to be dragged into considering political issues. This proved to be just about impossible because of the very close link of the war's impact upon Russia to the perpetration of the Revolution. This latter monumental event would require a book, or books, of its own to be properly described, and such books do exist for the readers whose interests lead them in this direction. For my part I have tried to present only a general picture of the power struggle within Russia and then only as it affected or was affected by the war. Also, I felt it necessary to explain briefly the tragic coming of the war, the background and immediate prelude to hostilities in the East.

Another matter which bears explanation here is my choice for description of the hostile camps. Most history books mention the grouping of the European powers, pre-1914, into two distinctly rival coalitions, the Triple Alliance and the Triple Entente. Yet once the war begins it becomes a matter of Allies versus Central Powers. I must admit that I am not content to use either designation and have consistently referred to the English/French/Russian coalition and the nations which supported it, as the *Entente*, and the German/Austro-Hungarian side, with its adherents, as the *Alliance*. To me, this is more logical, as not all nations which joined the former referred to themselves as "Allied" (the United States, for example) powers. Ludendorff, for example, uses the term "confederated" when writing of his allies in the war, and Hoffmann wrote of the "Allied" troops when doing the same. The term "Central Powers" is a corruption of the German desire for a *MittelEuropa* (Central Europe), a vast bloc of closely linked states in east-central Europe, a dream shattered when both Italy and Romania refused to fight for it, and indeed later joined the other side. Many *Entente* leaders initially called their enemies the Teutonic Empires, later the Central Empires, and at some point the designation Central Powers was used, and stuck. I believe my use of terms is less confusing.

The reader will notice another difference in this book from most other histories in that I have tried to describe the events chronologically, a practice which has fallen out of favor in recent decades. To some, it might be easier to detail the events of the East Prussian Campaign in 1914 separately from those of the Galician Campaign of the same time, and indeed most if not all accounts of the war follow this pattern. But to me it is more logical and much easier to keep the times in perspective by describing the actions in the order that they occurred, even if this necessarily means that our attention must frequently shift from one geographic location to another. For example, if one were to hear a sports game described by first hearing of all the scoring of one side, later to learn of all the scoring of the other side, the whole essence of the excitement of the contest would be lost. Of course, for the sake of the narrative, a purely chronological story is impractical, but I have adhered to a day-by-day style as closely as the events have allowed, and I hope the reader will agree that a less confusing grasp of the history is the result.

I have deliberately neglected to relate repetitious, if detailed, accounts of the few better-known battles in the East, such as the first Russian invasion of East Prussia in August/September 1914, which culminated in the so-called battles of Tannenberg and the Masurian Lakes; several decent works old and new are devoted exclusively to this campaign. Instead, I have tried to highlight other less publicized actions and can only hope that the reader will gain new insight for the First World War and realize that there was much more to that conflict than the mud of Flanders or the wooded hills of Lorraine.

In the twenty-first century it may be fashionable to view World War I as the culmination of a commercial rivalry between Britain and Germany or the results of a long Franco-German vendetta. A closer examination of the facts, however, will reveal a contest for superpower status between Germany and Russia, a status that one would hold briefly a generation later, and the other would seize as the result of a later war, only to lose again when the verdict of the first war was re-imposed upon it.

All dates listed in this work are of the Gregorian calendar which has long been in use in the West but was only adopted in Russia following the Bolshevik Revolution. Even today many other sources dealing with this or similar subjects have not converted the older Julian dates, so the reader is cautioned when engaged in cross-referencing.

Most sincere thanks go out to all those who participated directly or indirectly in the creation of this work over the past forty years. Any errors within are mine alone. Special thanks are due my wife and family, whose encouragement inspired me to continue during times of frustration. They ungrudgingly assisted me in an effort which necessarily denied us much desired time together.

Chapter One
Drawing the Frontiers

During the years immediately preceding the outbreak of the First World War a thorough examination of a contemporary map of Europe would have yielded the existence of twenty-seven sovereign states, of which six were so diminutive as to be smaller than the tiny Kingdom of Montenegro. Nor would any of the others have appeared impressively large, save one giant realm which dominated the entire right half of the paper and ran off the map's edge to an unseen distance to the east. This huge state would have been represented as the Russian Empire, a domain so vast it will inevitably be mentioned in any discussion of history's largest realms. Nor would it have been alone at that time in that distinction. Another representation on the map, the United Kingdom of Great Britain and Ireland possessed an even larger share of the world's real estate, though one would have required a World Map to appreciate it. A third state, France, held lands around the world as well. These three European Nations alone disposed of something like 70,448,000 square kilometers (27,200,000 square miles) of territory globally. If we consider five other European states which also held vast overseas possessions—Germany, Italy, Belgium, The Netherlands, and Portugal—the figure becomes in excess of 82,103,000 square kilometers (31,700,000 square miles). By adding the area of all the other European states to this unbelievable total, the grand total becomes of course even more impressive. Considering this state of affairs at the time, then, it is little wonder that Europeans considered that theirs was the highest civilization of human history, that their culture was destined to achieve predominance on a global scale.

All this may have seemed very logical at the time. What Europeans did not own outright (which was most of the world) they influenced very heavily. Europe was the center of the universe. Europeans, through their initiative, hard work, and efficiency, and propelled by their inventiveness, would create a new and better world for all humankind, however slowly the more primitive non-Europeans might eventually be persuaded to embrace it. But within two generations this image would be shattered; Europe would lose its world leadership (and ownership), much of the continent would have been devastated by war, pestilence and depression, and national treasuries bankrupted. Whatever could have caused such a colossal change over such a relatively short period? Obviously a cataclysmic event or events had occurred.

Fast-forward to the present. Our map of Europe now lists not twenty-seven but forty-five sovereign states, and our diminutive six has only increased by one to seven. It is amazing that any of these have survived. Even more remarkable is that most of the larger states have become a patchwork of small—and smaller—entities. The eastern giant no longer dominates the continent. It is perhaps needless to relate that most sovereign states do not generally surrender territory willingly.

Since the beginnings of recorded history the trend had long been to unify lands under an increasingly powerful authority, be it a king, emperor, pope or any other. Take the British Isles as a case in point. Centuries of almost constant warfare were required to unify various tribes, clans, and fiefdoms into anything resembling a central government. Rebellions and civil wars had to be dealt with. Foreign invasions needed to be repelled. Adjacent kingdoms would eventually be conquered or by skillful political moves be joined with their more powerful neighbor. By the early 18th century the isles enjoyed (or suffered) a single government. By the early 20th century a second government had emerged and by the early 21st there were rumblings in Scotland and Wales that suggested the two may someday become four again. But to return to our map of Europe, we see that something had reversed the centralizing process and that something had created an entirely new look for east-central Europe where the proliferation of new states was most apparent.

Of course, we are aware today of the significant territorial changes that occurred following the First World War. Other such changes rocked the inter-war years and followed the end of the Second World War. Another significant wave of change resulted from the collapse of Communist regimes throughout the Soviet Bloc. Even today no one can be sure that European borders will now remain static. Some will no doubt argue that with the advent of a common currency the European Union will someday bear witness to a true unification of many if not most of the nations of the Continent. They would argue that the 20th Century process of decentralization was only a necessary ripple in the overall process of eventual unity.

Whatever the future of Europe may be, we must not forget its past. There exist today only a relatively few miles of international boundary which correspond with the frontiers of the warring nations of 1914. The greater part has been erased, and redrawn. But for us to consider our story of largely forgotten battlefields in a now largely forgotten war we must take ourselves back in time to an era rapidly disappearing into the shadows of history, to an era when ways of life and human values were vastly different. To do so we must re-create the old map of Europe, understand how it came to be, and also understand where it went.

Inasmuch as our story takes place in east-central Europe, we will begin just there at a time roughly corresponding to the American Revolution. At that time, the largest state in east-central Europe was Poland, the successor state to the large land mass created centuries earlier by the union of old Poland and Lithuania. This state, like all great states, had grown in size, peaked, and then settled into a slow decay. It suffered its first major reverse in 1667 when a growing neighbor to the east, Russia, lopped off a huge chunk of real estate from Poland as a result of a favorable war, and annexed it. This, the Peace of Andrussof, was not in any way fatal to Poland but coming as it did only a few years after the loss of Livonia to Sweden signaled that the old, large kingdom had indeed settled into decline.

Yet the kingdom endured, almost unchanged, for over a century. Then came the fatal year of 1772. The King of Prussia, Frederick the Great, having had a chance to recover from his near disastrous series of wars with many of the powers of Europe which finally ended in the year 1763, was casting covetous glances at Polish territory by the early 1770s. Ever since the acquisition of the Duchy of Prussia by the Elector of Brandenburg, the Duchy had been geographically separated from its sister provinces to the west. And following the successful conclusion of Frederick's wars by which Prussia had gained so much territory and prestige, the time seemed to the King most appropriate to apply the newfound prestige to the business of politics at which he had become most skillful. Frederick had no intention of attacking Poland; he was still in a poor financial condition from the late wars, but he knew the Poles were very weak militarily and he had another card to play. Although he had as recently as ten years before been at war with both Austria and Russia, one power—Russia—had experienced the death of its monarch only to be replaced by a sovereign friendly to Frederick. The other power Frederick now courted, offering it a share of the spoils. Because Austria could hardly have prevented the Russians and Prussians from despoiling Poland, it finally consented to a three-way partition. On August 5, 1772, a Treaty of Partition was signed at the Russian capital of St. Petersburg. By this act Russia received all Polish lands east of the Dvina and Dnieper Rivers, thus creating a cleaner more rounded frontier, Austria received Galicia and Lodomeiria, a convenient glacis for her Carpathian defenses. Frederick, the instigator, received the Bishopric of Ermeland, that annoying tongue of land that so misshaped the Duchy of Prussia, Pomerelia (thereafter called West Prussia) and the Netze District. The cities of Danzig and Thorn were to remain Polish. Danzig, at the mouth of the Vistula River, was considered to be necessary for Polish river traffic though it was now cut off from the rest of the country.

Prussia's share of the partition was by far the smallest and least populated of the three and contained no major cities. Nevertheless, it may have been the most advantageous to its host of the three, as now for the first time the eastern territories of Brandenburg-Prussia were geographically linked; the old Prussian city of Königsberg where the first Prussian King had been crowned was now accessible by land from Berlin, the capital of the Kingdom.

Poland for her part was infinitely worse off than before. The Russian frontier had been simplified along the rivers mentioned above, but she had lost her mountain frontier with Austria and her border with Prussia now resembled a prone letter "V" stabbing due west directly at Berlin, the flanks of which were of course Prussian property. The Prussians could be expected to want to eventually blunt the "V" by acquiring at least its tip, which extended to within 85 kilometers (50 miles) of the center of Berlin, if not the whole salient, and they were known to be scheming to annex Danzig and Thorn—the latter truly a thorn in Prussia's side. Within two decades, allegations of unstable government in Warsaw emboldened the new Russian and Prussian monarchs, Catherine II and Frederick William II, to resolve to make a new partition. Austria, distracted by a war in the west, was bought off and the other interested nations of the continent were placated by clever diplomacy and on April 9, 1793, the Second Partition of Poland was announced publicly.

This Second Partition was a land grab of the first magnitude. Catherine seized a gigantic share, advancing her frontiers from the Dnieper to the

Dniester Rivers, and the border of eastern Galicia. From there the new line ran due north through the middle of the Pripet Marshes, and continued on to the Dvina, curiously enough, a line roughly corresponding to the Eastern Front after the Russian retreat of 1915. Both Pinsk and Minsk were now Russian along with most of Bylorussia (White Russia) and Ukraine (Little Russia) up to the Austrian share of the First Partition. Prussia anxiously received Danzig and Thorn and the entire wedge of Polish territory extending westward from the Bzura and upper Pilica Rivers. It was a gain only a fraction of the size of the Russian, but it shortened Prussia's eastern border considerably.

The Poles were under no illusions now as to their ultimate fate, having lost something like 70% of their land to foreign predators without so much as a skirmish in its defense. The king, Poniatowski, looked askance while Kosciusko led a rebellion against this rape of Poland, but it soon provoked invasion by Russia and Prussia. What was left of the country was now occupied, Warsaw being among the last locations to submit. The three original partitioners now announced that the only way to keep peace in Poland was to divide it amongst them, and on October 24, 1795, the third and final partition was signed, the king pensioned off, and the remnant of the country distributed.

Once again Russia took the largest piece of the pie; the remainder of Volhynia, Polesia, and White Russia as well as Lithuania and Courland brought the Russian border to the Bug and Niemen Rivers. Austria got all the real estate between the Pilica and Bug Rivers, excluding a tiny wedge opposite Warsaw but including Cracow, a University City and Poland's second largest. Prussia took the remainder: east to the Niemen, south to the Bug and Pilica, plus a small patch east of Silesia and north of Cracow. This relatively small share did, however, include Warsaw.

The rape of Poland was complete. Once the largest European state in size it had now disappeared from the map completely. The rapists, naturally enough, had no intention of allowing any allusions to its existence and they appropriately renamed their new provinces "South Prussia," "New East Prussia" "West Galicia," "Kovno," "Grodno," and the like. Russia had advanced from east of the Dnieper to a line along the Niemen, Bug, and Dniester, that is to a very advantageous line at the edge of central Europe and the shortest line between the Baltic and Black Seas, moreover, most of her annexations were peopled by Ukrainians and Bylorussians, Slavic peoples who like the Slavic Russians were generally adherents of the Eastern Orthodox faith. This is to suggest that Russia had greatly strengthened her position in east central Europe. Only in the north had she annexed some alien peoples, Balts, the Latvians and the Lithuanians, who were mostly Protestants and Catholics respectively. But these were comparatively few in number and had the Russian leaders elected to stop their westward advance on the very defensible line they now held, a good deal of history would no doubt have been written quite differently.

Austria, having participated in only two of the partitions, had gained about the same amount of ground as had the Prussians. But her new frontiers were most irregular and although mostly drawn along rivers were very vulnerable. Galicia was one thing; it did provide an excellent upland glacis for the Carpathian Mountain barrier. The "West Galicia" bulge was quite another. The city of Lublin was hardly worth its defense. By participating in the partitions Austria had involved herself with yet another nationality, the Poles, and had increased her Ukrainian population tenfold. Prussia, like Austria, had come away with approximately 20% of old Poland. She too had absorbed two nationalities, the Poles and Lithuanians, though the latter were in fairly small numbers. The first two partitions had unquestionably improved her strategic situation but the third was superfluous. Past Prussian experiences in attempting to assimilate Slavic peoples such as Sorbs, Kassubes, and Masurians had not worked well. How could she assimilate millions of Poles? Mixing Germanic Protestant Prussians and Slavic Catholic Poles was akin to mixing oil and water and unless another ingredient could be added to the mix it was bound to fail.

The peace of Europe was by now failing as well. It may be recalled that the wars of Revolutionary France had begun in 1792. This unsettled period would continue with some interludes until 1815. Once the great Napoleon had become virtual dictator of France the warfare increased in frequency and intensity. Four times did he defeat the Austrian Empire and force it to peace on his terms. Surprisingly, he was at first quite lenient with the Austrians. Not so the Prussians who only once made the mistake of taking the field against him, but who with one defeat were more roughly handled than the Austrians had been after a fourth. Napoleon despised the Prussians and their king and said so. After a one-day battle and defeat at Jena, Prussia was stripped of over half of its territory: Everything west of the Elbe and all it had gained in the partitions of Poland, except about one half of its first partition gains, Ermeland

and Pomerelia. Russia, following several battles with Napoleon on Prussian soil, decided to make peace, and the *Czar* met the French Emperor on a raft upon the Niemen River, the boundary between Russian and Prussian Poland. The two Emperors agreed to pursue a friendly course, which was much to the advantage of both. With all Europe in turmoil the Russian *Czar* was allowed to annex a small piece of Polish territory about Bialystok and two years later another small piece of Austrian land around Tarnopol. Alexander was now adding Prussian and Austrian pieces to his lion's share of Poland. Nor did he stop at that. Provoking wars on the periphery of East Europe, he defeated the Swedes and annexed Finland, then fell upon the Turks and seized Bessarabia. Meanwhile, Napoleon was organizing a sort of new Polish state, probably at the behest of his latest mistress, a Polish noblewoman. For this "Duchy of Warsaw" he relegated the Prussian (except the piece he had given to Alexander) and Austrian shares of the third partition, the Prussian share of the second partition and about half of the Prussian share of the first partition, and a rather small piece of the Austrian share of the first partition. This Duchy of Warsaw was equally despised by Prussians, Austrians, and Russians alike and had no chance of surviving Napoleon for long.

Thus we have the situation as it had evolved when following the final defeat of Napoleon, the representatives of the states of Europe sat down together at the Congress of Vienna to redraw the map of the continent. The British and Russians enjoyed the most prestige, they representing nations which had never been defeated by the French. The Prussians were next on the ladder; they had been defeated only the once and had been major contributors to the final defeat of the French Emperor. Austria probably ranked next; she was the host country for the Congress and had generally been a staunch adversary of Napoleon. The Congress was more concerned with containing France, that is to say Western Europe, than affairs in Eastern Europe, but the Russians were flexing their muscles and both Prussia and Austria wanted to regain what they had lost during the period of the wars. The wrangling of the delegates at Vienna are a remarkable story and indeed have been the subject of entire books, but for our purposes we need only remember that the Russians, above all others, needed to be compensated, or more simply put, aggrandized. Eventually it was decided to allow Russia to obtain the Duchy of Warsaw; it would be elevated to a kingdom and enjoy self-government, but within the framework of the Russian Empire. As expected, both Prussia and Austria protested sharply. The

Austrians, with the weaker voice, were silenced by being allowed to regain most of their other territory in Europe, including the Tarnopol strip lost to Russia in 1809, and by being granted the neutralization of Cracow, which in effect became an independent republic. They were well aware that to regain any more Polish territory was strategically unsound. The same could hardly be said for Prussia, now faced once more with the prospect of the wedge of Polish land pointing westward and creating a horribly irregular frontier. But Prussia was being heavily compensated in the west. Besides regaining most of her former possessions in western Germany she received some new provinces west of the Rhine in order to give her a common border with France. France, it was reasoned, needed a powerful neighbor to help keep it in check. Since the decline of Spain it had never had one, save a few detached Austrian possessions, but now a Prussian frontier might just help contain any further expansionism. After further complaints about the irregular eastern border, Prussia was finally granted the return of all her first partition gains and a rounding off of the "wedge" by a portion—nearly half—of her second partition gains. With everyone more or less satisfied, the Congress of Vienna adjourned, and passed into history.

In retrospect it must be granted that the Congress of Vienna fairly well accomplished what it had gathered for, to assure the peace of Europe for the foreseeable future, and to establish a sort of "Concert of Europe" whereby each of the Great Powers would not act unilaterally without consulting the others first. It has often been denounced as an exercise in Reaction, a conspiratorial effort to smother the forces let loose by the French Revolution, and return to Absolute Despotism. In fact, few individuals alive at the time could have understood or even recognized the symptoms of by far the most powerful of the new forces released during the Revolutionary Period, that of Nationalism. It was a force which would dominate the 19th and 20th centuries but in 1815 was still in its infancy. The Congress had achieved a settlement, and in the east it was a lasting one.

For over a century the boundaries of Eastern Europe remained unchanged. This is a remarkable statement considering how many times they had changed in the prior century or how many times were to change in the next one. Not that there were no problems. In 1830 the Poles revolted against their Russian patrons and were rewarded by being bloodily suppressed and having their "Kingdom" abolished and absorbed directly into the Russian Empire. An entire library at Warsaw was confiscated and sent to the Russian capital of St. Petersburg. In 1860 the Poles rose again, this second insurrection being far more serious than the first, and several years were required to stamp it out completely. This time the unfortunate Poles would be subjected to an intensive campaign of Russification, all teaching and legal activity now being required in the Russian language. Somehow the Poles persevered, however, and all attempts to Russify their language and faith proved illusory.

Within Austria and Prussia, the situation was somewhat different. The Austrian Empire had long been a realm of multiple nationalities and inclusion of the Poles of Galicia was, for the most part, without incident. The Austrian aristocracy was staunchly Roman Catholic and could be expected to understand the Poles religious needs. In 1846 Austria was allowed to annex the Republic of Cracow and thereafter the city became the center of Polish culture within the Empire. Of the three partitioners Austria was certainly the least resented. Although Prussia disposed of the smallest number of Poles, they were never assimilated into German culture. We have already mentioned the religious and racial differences. Perhaps more importantly loomed the attitude of many Prussians, who looked down at the Poles as an inferior race, and pointed to their considerably lower living standards as proof. The Prussian government tried various methods to "Germanize" the populace, including repressive measures similar to those the Russians adopted after 1860 and a policy of purchasing Polish lands in order to resettle German speakers there. The Poles resisted passively and subtly but firmly and eventually their higher birth rate prevented them being submerged in the Prussian sea.

After 1815 then the eastern frontiers remained unchanged for 104 years until the chaos following the World War swept them away for good. Unfortunately for Europe and the world, the political settlement of 1815 would not be so long lived. Once they had recovered from the wars of 1792-1815, the Great Powers would become restless again. This time, moreover, they would need to be ever more cautious; by having absorbed the weaker states which had separated them, they now faced each other over common frontiers. France now bordered Prussia and after 1860 Italy as well. Austria bordered Russia, Prussia, and later Italy. Prussia now had three powerful neighbors and Russia two. It is easy to understand that there was now much less room to maneuver, politically or militarily. But as we have seen, the settlement in the east left long and irregular boundaries between the three Great Powers.

"Congress Poland," as it was often called, protruded deep into the flanks of old Prussia to the north and Austrian Galicia, and behind it Hungary, to the south. Nor was the new frontier advantageous from the Russian perspective; Congress Poland could easily be cut off by Prussians and Austrians acting in cooperation from the flanks. And behind the Polish bulge lay the vast Pripet Marshes region or Polesie, a roadless wasteland which helped bar access to the salient and might reasonably be compared to a tree standing opposite a doorway and only a few feet distant. Congress Poland then created an extremely difficult strategic situation for those entrusted with the defense of the realms. As we shall see it was to affect military thinking in the most profound manner.

The Partitions
of Poland 1772-1795

International Frontiers, 1772
Lands seized, 1772
Prussian and Russian
Seizures, 1793 ++++++++++
New International Frontiers,
1795 — — — — —

MAP 1A

The Partitions of Poland 1772-1795

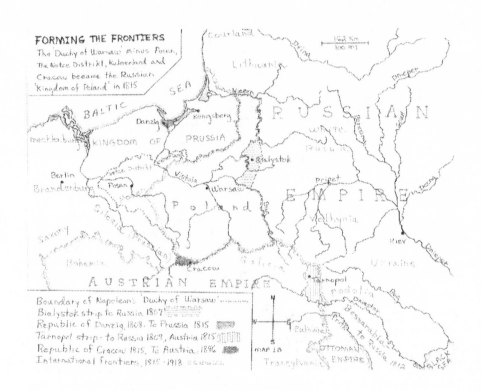

Forming the Frontiers

Chapter Two
Paving the Road to Conflict

The Congress of Vienna had created a continent of five Great Powers—Britain, France, Austria, Prussia and Russia—all of which had agreed to work together to control the inevitable periodic convulsions which had long disturbed the peace of Europe. Our concern here is for the latter three nations who as we have seen now shared common frontiers. Of the three the Austrian Empire was the most mature and its conservative leadership could be counted on to maintain the status quo. The Kingdom of Prussia was somewhat more restless; although conservatively governed it still suffered non-contiguous possessions and was with difficulty trying to assimilate its Poles in West Prussia and Posen. The Russian Empire, like a swaggering juvenile aware of its newfound strength and presence yet unaware of its endurance or impression, alone could be counted upon to pursue an aggressive foreign policy. It counted now only four neighbors on its western borders. The two Great Powers Austria and Prussia it was by commitment to cooperate with. Then there was Sweden, still smarting from its loss of Finland, the border of which was now nearly to the Arctic Circle at the far northern head of the Gulf of Bothnia. Nothing was to be gained there; Russia already possessed enough frozen wasteland. Lastly, there lay the Ottoman Empire, and it was here that extended the path of least resistance—or so the Russians believed.

As the largest contiguous landmass in the world, the Russian Empire contained thousands of miles of seacoast but most of it facing the Arctic Ocean and therefore unusable except for a small port on the White Sea, a southward arm of the Arctic, and this too was ice-bound for half the year. A similar situation existed on the Pacific with only one port, thousands of kilometers distant. Even the northern half of the Baltic was frozen in winter, and of course, all shipping via that inland sea necessarily passed through narrow straits between Denmark and Sweden and into the North Sea, an area closely watched by the British Navy. But if the Baltic was not an ideal waterway, where could one be found? There were only two possibilities: a drive southward through Central Asia to the Indian Ocean or a push to the Mediterranean. The Asian idea was attractive but bound to lead to war with Britain and the world's largest navy, possibly France and Portugal as well. In fact, the Russians did pursue an aggressive policy in Central Asia throughout the 19th Century and a distinct rivalry with Britain resulted, but though Russia would annex much territory over the years, a heavy British military presence would in the end deter war between the two Powers. The Mediterranean scheme was another matter. Two narrow straits separate the Black and Mediterranean Seas, separate Europe from Asia. They are called the Bosporus and the Dardanelles and they constitute one of the most desirable locations on earth from a political, economic, or military point of view, a crossroads of the four points of the compass and the economy of three continents. Truly a bridge between cultures and a focal point of inestimable value, these waterways had been in possession of the Ottoman Turks since 1453. The Ottomans had slumped into a slow but steady decline at about the beginning of the 18th century and during the latter decades had lost the northern littoral of the Black Sea to the Russians. As we have seen, more ground was lost during the Napoleonic period and still more in the 1828-29 war. By the time of the Crimean war (1854-56) Europeans were well aware of Russian intentions, and on that occasion the British and French joined the Turks in order to ward off further Russian predation. The Russian *Czar*, Nicholas I, appealed to his fellow Prussian and Austrian monarchs for help, and when they failed to act, the Russians made no secret of their displeasure. The Prussians had at least maintained friendly neutrality, but the Austrians seemed to prefer the enemy coalition and this was the beginning of a serious Austrian-Russian antagonism which the passage of time gradually exacerbated. The Russians had expected at least diplomatic support, and reminded the Austrians that only by the assistance of Russian troops had the Austrians put down the serious Hungarian revolt of 1848-49. The Austrian Emperor Franz Joseph vainly pointed to the fact that he had returned the favor by sending Austrian troops to suppress the Poles in 1863, but for St. Petersburg this was too little and much too late.

While the Russians fumed over their Crimean setback matters in Central Europe were coming to a head. In 1862 Otto von Bismarck had been appointed

Prussian Chancellor. He would prove to be as able a head of state as any on record; his very name would soon dominate European diplomacy for years to come. Within four years he had engineered wars with Denmark and Austria, watched them both defeated and expelled from German affairs, and witnessed his Prussia annex the provinces of Schleswig and Holstein and the independent states of Hanover, Hesse-Kassel, and Hesse-Nassau. Prussian territory was contiguous for the first time ever. He then formed alliances with the remaining German States and provoked a war with France in which they all participated. Within six months France was defeated, her German-speaking lands—and a little more—annexed and all the allied states united into a single German Empire under Prussian leadership. Thus within the space of nine years Bismarck had fulfilled the dreams of German nationalists which had brewed since the days of Napoleon: A united Germany with the Prussian king as German Emperor *(Kaiser)*. He, of course, retained his preeminent position in the new empire, but having used war as a means to attain his ends, now settled in to a new policy of preserving the peace.

His new policy was one of necessity. He was well aware that though his country had won three wars; three other countries had lost them and might likely be vengeful, Denmark he worried little about, it was a minor power and unlikely to risk war to regain two provinces of which only one was less than half Danish. Austria he had demanded nothing of, save her expulsion from German affairs, a motive now unlikely to provoke retaliation. France was another matter, however; the French never lost an opportunity to bemoan the injustice of their "lost provinces." Forgetting how much more harshly they had treated Prussia the last time roles had been reversed, they determined to never seek reconciliation with Germany as long as the latter held the "despoiled sisters." In vain did reasonable Germans point out that neither Alsace nor Lorraine had been annexed in their entirety, that 90% of the Alsatians were German speakers and something like 50% of the Lorrainers. No, Germany had gained an implacable new foe, and all of Bismarck's skill would be needed to contain it. Nothing short of the return of Alsace-Lorraine could extinguish it.

As a result of the unhappy consequences of the 1866 war with Prussia, Austria was meanwhile experiencing some convulsions. The defeat had emboldened the long-suppressed Hungarians to demand new concessions and at last the Hungarian desires were met not with force but compromise. The *Ausgleich* of 1867 created a separate Hungarian kingdom within the Austrian

Empire; henceforth the realm consisted of two fairly equal halves, each with self government but a common foreign policy and the Emperor, Franz Joseph, would have King of Hungary added to his long list of titles. After 1867 the Austrian Empire is more properly referred to as the Empire of Austria and Hungary or simply Austria-Hungary. Needless to relate, the other nationalities within the empire were envious of the Hungarians, and decided that they too should enjoy self-government. Those unfortunate enough to reside in the Hungarian half were suppressed; those in the Austrian half more like ignored.

By the middle of the century the forces of Nationalism had been gaining momentum everywhere in Europe. The German unification of 1864-71 was, at bottom, a nationalist movement, the recognition of Hungary another. Two less tangible forces had come into being; these would be referred to as Pan-Germanism and Pan-Slavism. Advocates of the first had seen a partial realization of their dreams with the Unification of 1871 and were thus pleased with Bismarck's policies; after the founding of the empire they were more of a problem for him. As the Pan-Germans worked for the unity of all German speakers in Europe, after 1871 their gaze was limited to a few directions. One was Switzerland where two-thirds of the population spoke German but no one expected to lure the Swiss into a German state. Another was Austria-Hungary where the largest bloc of Germans outside the Empire resided, and these in districts mostly contiguous to Germany. But Bismarck's policy towards Austria-Hungary was one of friendship—now that the two monarchs were equals, that is Emperors, there was no reason for further conflict. Lastly there was Russia where large numbers of Germans had settled for various reasons, usually relating to available land for settlement. But nowhere in Russia was a large community of Germans to be found—at least nowhere near the German border. There were large numbers of Germans in the Baltic lands, it was true, numbering up to 10% of the total population, but these were widely scattered— descendents of the Teutonic Knights who settled the area in the Middle Ages to spread the good word of Christianity. Clearly, there was no one logical location in Russia for the Pan-Germans to covet, and most turned their attention to Austria-Hungary, hoping someday for its breakup following which the German lands were sure to seek union with the *Reich* (German Empire).

If the Pan-Germans were increasingly frustrated after 1871, the Pan-Slavs were just getting started. They only needed to glance westward to notice fertile fields to sow. The Poles and Sorbs of Prussia, Ukrainians, Czechs, Poles,

Slovaks, Slovenes and Croats in Austria-Hungary, and Serbs, Bulgars, Croats and Macedonians in the Ottoman Empire. Never mind that Russia had huge numbers of non-Slavic peoples within her borders—and who may have welcomed a liberation of their own—she was the only truly independent Slavic state in the world and a Great Power at that. Russia, they reasoned, must carry the banner of Pan-Slavism, to serve as a sort of protector of all Slavs everywhere. They would not long be disappointed.

In 1877, after alleged mistreatment of Balkan peoples (Slavs), Russia declared war on Turkey and for the second time in half a century defeated it after a hard fight, imposing once again a peace favorable to Russia. More territory in the Caucasus area was annexed (as in 1829), and this time the Ottoman's European territorial block crumbled into pieces of various nationalities demanding independence. Romania was freed, Greece was later enlarged, and three Slavic states made completely or partially independent: Serbia, Montenegro, and Bulgaria. The Russians were confident they could control the latter three if not the former two as all were Orthodox in religion, and all hated and feared the Turks. But then the other Great Powers demanded a say. Evoking the Concert of Europe they met at the Congress of Berlin in 1878 with Bismarck as host. Bismarck asked nothing for Germany, and he wanted to maintain friendly relations with Russia, but realized that the other Powers would not tolerate Russian hegemony in the Balkans. Boundaries were redrawn. Austria-Hungary was allowed to occupy three former Ottoman provinces and Turkey was allowed to keep a considerable area in Europe. The Russians were frustrated and never forgave Bismarck, who they had hoped would support them. The Pan-Slavs were furious with the Austro-Hungarian occupation of three mostly Slavic provinces. Isolated, the Russians yielded; privately, they determined to break their isolation and were still determined to someday smash the Turks for good and seize the straits. When the *Czar* privately asked Bismarck for a free hand to attack Austria-Hungary, he was quietly discouraged from doing so and may possibly have been informed of Bismarck's impending deal with Vienna. The Austro-German understanding was finalized in 1879. Referred to as the Dual Alliance, it bound each country to come to the aid of the other with all its strength if one or the other was attacked by a third power. Both knew very well that the "third power" was France for Germany and Russia for Austria. The alliance was therefore strictly defensive in nature, but Bismarck was taking no chances on

Russia's attitude and playing his hand like a master. He refused a Japanese offer of an alliance which might have hurt his relations with Russia and let it leak back to St. Petersburg that he was urging the Austrians to let Russia take Constantinople (and therefore the straits) because he knew this attitude was sure to cause alarm in Britain. He also reassured the Russians while sending a subtle message to Vienna by declaring that all of the Balkans were "not worth the bones of a single (German) grenadier." This was typical Bismarckian diplomacy at its very best, always playing one Power off against another, never slamming the door to any, but never opening it too wide either.

In the end the German Chancellor had calculated properly; Russia, fearful of isolation from an Austro-German bloc, a nervous Britain, a potentially hostile Japan, was asking for an alliance. Within a year the *Dreikaiserbund* (Three Emperor's League) had been negotiated. Its terms provided for each of the three contracting parties to remain neutral in a war in which any one of them was attacked by a fourth power. In practical terms it meant that Germany need not fear for her back if France attacked; Russia could count on Austro-German neutrality if a war with Britain occurred. Austria need not fear Italy. As it happened Austria need not have worried; soon the Italians were proposing to join the Dual Alliance, and on May 20, 1882, a Triple Alliance was signed. A year later Romania, ever fearful of Russia, signed a defensive alliance with Austria. Soon Serbia was making a similar arrangement, much to the chagrin of the Pan-Slavs. Nor was this all. Still not content, Bismarck helped create a Mediterranean Triple Alliance of sorts among Britain, Austria and Italy very clearly aimed at France. Even Spain joined this latter agreement and its king assured Bismarck of his country's support in any new Franco-German war. When Russia refused to renew the *Dreikaiserbund* in 1887 because of her displeasure over Austria's Balkan Policy, Bismarck intimidated the Russians by approaching the British who were at odds with them over Central Asia and the Straits. The desired effect was achieved and led to the so-called *Reinsurance Treaty* the terms of which were favorable to Russia on paper, but the Chancellor had managed to keep his Russian connection.

By all these arrangements over the years 1871-1890 Bismarck had made war among the Great Powers virtually impossible. By covering his flanks and rear he had forced Germany's only hostile neighbor—France—to face her head on and alone and France clearly could not defeat Germany with her own forces alone. Every other Power was friendly if not allied to the *Reich*. Twenty years of peace had been achieved during which Germany had prospered and grown enormously in industrial strength. She was young, dynamic and with a rapidly increasing population while emigration declined. The Pan-Germans were just sure that she was now the premier power in the world and destined to lead European civilization to ever greater glories. All that was needed now was a powerful German fleet of ocean-worthy vessels.

They might have wished for another Bismarck. The blow fell in March 1890: the young *Kaiser,* Wilhelm II, had dismissed Bismarck! Alarm wracked all the European capitals. Diplomats were aghast. Bond values dropped sharply. Whispers that the peace was endangered grew louder. Who could replace a man of such prestige, such a master of diplomacy who alone fully understood the machinations of his own government and the dreams and anxieties of his contemporaries? Had anyone dared to make such an inquiry of the new monarch his answer would have been simple enough: "Me." The response would have been less born of arrogance than of self-confidence and a deep-seated desire to impress. Wilhelm was sure he could profoundly influence, if not control, Germany's foreign policy. Raised and tutored in a most conservative manner, he believed in the Divine Right of Kings and that his close blood ties to both the British and Russian monarchies were far more important than statesmanship in avoiding international conflict. The French, without a monarchy, would always remain isolated; no self-respecting king or emperor would ever ally himself to such a contemptible republic. Unfortunately for Wilhelm his boisterous, gesturing, self-indulgent manners coupled with his aptitude for subtle threats and his love of everything military were to make him few friends but raise many eyebrows. Although at bottom an honest, religious, and peace-loving man, he tended to rub everyone the wrong way. Perhaps not coincidentally, the Reinsurance Treaty was up for renewal at about the same time as Bismarck's dismissal. The *Kaiser* wavered, and then sided with the new Chancellor, Caprivi, against renewal. The Russians were stunned. Normally, when a Great Power declined to renew such an agreement, the precedent was for it to make counter proposals in order to win more favorable conditions or at least to evade the odium of being solely responsible for non-cooperation. Suspicion abounded in St. Petersburg where it was known that the Germans and British were negotiating. It was feared that Britain might be joining the Triple Alliance, in which case the Russians were the obvious target. The *Czar* ordered more favorable terms be offered the Germans. They were still not interested. Now alarmed, the Russian foreign minister, Giers, who had gotten along well with Bismarck, now offered in desperation even that which the old Chancellor had been unable to achieve three years earlier: a renewal of the *Dreikaiserbund*. Any astute statesman could have grasped the implications of Gier's offer; Russia, apparently terrified at the thought of German-Austrian-Italian-British Alliance, was offering to drop its objections to Austrian Balkan policy and silence the Pan-Slavs in order to escape being isolated. It was a situation which would have elated Bismarck—the British business was all a ruse, and France the implacable foe would remain isolated, while in the east the potential dangers would again be neutralized. Instead, in one of history's most incredible foreign policy blunders, the German response was to inform their Austro-Hungarian allies that thereafter Berlin would be even more closely tied to Vienna and Bismarck had been let go for actions clearly too "pro-Russian' (therefore presumably anti-Austrian). As for the British negotiations—the trump card with which a good player could easily have won the hand—it was announced on July 1st that Germany was exchanging the large island of Zanzibar off the coast of Africa for a tiny protrusion of almost solid rock off the German coast called Heligoland. No one believed in such a one-sided deal and it was generally assumed—especially in St. Petersburg, that an Anglo-German secret deal must have resulted. The heartbreak that Bismarck and his supporters must have felt can only be imagined.

One last carrot was dangled before the eyes of the disbelieving Russians. The young *Kaiser* announced his intention of visiting Russia, and during the occasion in August, the *Czar's* cool reception turned icy when it was finally realized that Wilhelm had not gone to discuss an agreement. When he departed a week later the Russians determined to wash their hands of any restraint against the despised Austrians and the road to war was being rolled smooth for pavement.

Within a year the road was about to be opened for traffic. In July of 1891 a state visit by the *Kaiser* to London seemed to confirm Europe's suspicions; Britain must somehow be associated with the Triple Alliance. Less conspicuous but more significant was, in the same month, a visit by French warships to a Russian naval base near the capital, at one point during which the hitherto unlikely scenario of a Russian monarch standing at attention during a rendition of the revolutionary French national anthem, the *Marseillaise*, was enacted. Clearly, a diplomatic turning point had been reached. Negotiations between the two governments dragged on for months, then years, but in early 1894 a final agreement was reached and signed. It is worth our while to examine the details here. It was as much a political as military arrangement but was classed as a military convention in order to circumvent the French constitution, which required assent of the Chamber of Deputies to international treaties. Like all such diplomacy it was secret, but true secrecy was rare; every power had its network of spies, contacts in other foreign offices, and access to sensitive information by way of bribes, planted mistresses, extortion and the like. The rival powers generally knew what the others were doing most of the time. The terms were: If France was attacked by a Triple Alliance member, Russia would move against Germany. If Russia were so attacked, France would retaliate against Germany. In case any member of the Triple Alliance mobilized its forces, both France and Russia would also mobilize. Other articles specified plans for military action. Standing aback, one notices immediately the aggressiveness of this agreement. *If any member of the Triple Alliance mobilized....*It is also to be noticed that Germany was already recognized as the kingpin of the *Alliance*. The Franco-Russian "Convention" did not make war inevitable—it was in theory a defensive pact—but it did make it far and away more likely.

Most Germans were not unduly worried about the newfound friendship of their eastern and western neighbors; they still had the *Alliance* and it was inconceivable that Britain, now the odd man out, would not support them if need be against its two chief rivals, the ancient enemy France and the expansive Russian colossus. True, Britain had always remained aloof from Continental entanglements, but could she remain isolated forever? Bismarck would have found a way to befriend Britain; indeed, he had once offered an alliance which was fairly well received though not quite accepted. The timing had been a little premature.

Indeed by the late 1890s the British had begun to rethink their long-standing isolationist policy. The door was open for Germany and the story of how the bungling German government managed to kick it closed is another interesting story, but outside our concern here. Anglo-German commercial rivalry, the German attitude during the Boer War, and especially the decision of the *Kaiser's* government to build a powerful battle fleet, to mention just a few reasons, eventually estranged the British and induced them to seek other arrangements. In 1902 an Anglo-Japanese Alliance was signed, and in 1904 came the *Entente* with France. Over the next decade many overtures were pursued between London and Berlin first from one direction, then from another, but Emperor Wilhelm's stubborn, almost illogical, refusal to compromise the rapid growth of "his" fleet would derail them all.

Meanwhile Russia and Japan went to war over issues in the Far East, where Wilhelm had been urging his cousin the *Czar* to expand in order to divert the Russians' attention from the straits and new friction with Austria. The alliance with Britain had effectively covered the Japanese rear, and despite expert opinion the world over that Russia would make short work of the upstart Orientals, it was in fact the Japanese who won a convincing victory. The Germans were ecstatic; the Russian war machine was a joke, the mighty Russian Bear more like a dairy cow—large but harmless. Even before the war's end the *Czar* was approached, the Germans proposing a new deal similar to the old Reinsurance Treaty. The *Czar* hesitated, his advisors reminding him of the necessity of consulting France. Nothing was signed; the Germans believed the door was still ajar.

Now it was Wilhelm's turn. Convinced that his cousin Nicholas II (privately they addressed each other as "Nicky" and "Willy") a gentle, peaceful, soft-spoken man married to a German princess, harbored no animosity towards Germany, he determined to settle Russian-German relations personally. All that was needed was an uninterrupted conversation in good faith between autocrats. Imagining himself to be Chancellor, Foreign Minister, and senior diplomat personified, he contacted his cousin and suggested a summer vacation's visit to each other's yachts. Nicholas, still formally at war, had concerns. Not to worry, assured the *Kaiser*, he would come to Nicky, somewhere quiet but close to St. Petersburg was fine. Nicholas agreed, he needed to escape the summer heat of the capital with its gloomy, (as a result of an apparently unsuccessful war) angry (the abortive revolution suppressed) mood.

At the end of the third week of July, Wilhelm boarded his private yacht the *Hohenzollern*, announced that he was off for a vacation on Goteland, the large Swedish island in the Baltic, and steamed away. Goteland would in fact have been a logical halfway point for the two Emperors to have met, but Wilhelm was going out of his way this time, all the way in fact, to within 105 kilometers (65 miles) of St. Petersburg. Here deep within the Gulf of Finland and Russian waters lay on the forested coastline the quiet town of Björkö, an island of the same name just off the coast, and the bay of the same name in between.[1] Here the *Hohenzollern* dropped anchor within easy distance of its Russian counterpart, the *Polar Star*[2] and soon the usual pleasantries were being exchanged. For once Wilhelm played his part very well and for the first day he was as amiable as he was capable of being, avoiding politics, preaching, or boasting and biding his time to reveal his hand. The following day all was going well. Someone reminded the *Czar* of the war. Immediately showing depression, Nicholas began to disparage the French. Wilhelm agreed and added his own unpleasantries. Nicholas switched to the British and there followed further accusations and insults. Wilhelm parroted and added a few of his own. Slowly, subtly convincing Nicholas that he, Wilhelm, was a true friend of Russia and an unsparing advocate of a Russo-German understanding, the *Kaiser* reminded Nicholas of the treaty which had only recently been suggested by his foreign office. The *Czar* was receptive. Nicholas then sent for Tschirschky of his Foreign Ministry who just happened to be aboard, and asked if a copy of the recent treaty could be produced. When it was, *Kaiser* asked *Czar* to read it. This Nicholas supposedly did several times, each time enjoying it more as his mood improved. Finally the *Kaiser* sprung his trap: He would gladly sign it if Nicky would as well. There was nothing in this agreement which could in any way be construed as injurious to France, Russia's ally. In fact, both monarchs agreed to invite the French to adhere to it. Nicholas, teary eyed, signed. Wilhelm later claimed he wept tears of joy as he signed, invoking the intervention of Deity. Nicholas called his highest ranking guest to countersign, a certain Admiral Birilov his Minister of Marine, while Wilhelm commanded Tschirschky. Soon both yachts were sailing homeward, both Emperors convinced of each other's sincere friendship.

The July 24, 1905, Treaty of Björkö has often been regarded as a worthless, almost adolescent and naïve waste of time by many historians, a testament to the pliability of a weak *Czar* and the misguided foolishness of a delusional *Kaiser*. Others tend to doubt it ever took place but the evidence is too strong for most to seriously doubt it. The *Czar* came away refreshed, his spirits elevated, and certain that at the very least he had done his government no harm and in this regard he was correct. But Nicholas was the type of person who, it was observed, often espoused the opinions of the last individual with whom he had spoken. Easily persuaded, once he had returned to St. Petersburg his ministers had no difficulty convincing him that the Treaty was incompatible with the French Alliance, and that the *Kaiser* had duped him. Angered, he vowed to have no more dealings with "Willy."

For his part the *Kaiser* genuinely believed he had finally neutralized the Franco-Russian threat now a decade old, and scored a success of which even the revered Bismarck would be proud. The problem was that he had appointed no Bismarck who might have exploited the deed and in any case no one in St. Petersburg was being receptive even if there had been one. As the *Czar* had been, the *Kaiser* was told the Treaty was useless, incompatible with German interests. He was further admonished not to meddle in such business as sensitive as foreign affairs issues; he had made some serious messes in his 17-year reign. Confronted with reality Wilhelm backed away, but clung to his belief in the justice of his action.

The Björkö Treaty thus illustrated for any who were in position to see, or cared to look, that neither *Czar* nor *Kaiser* could control the direction of his own government. One might be led while the other needed to be dragged but in both cases the result was similar. Military and financial interests now outweighed the Emperors and when the additional weight of Pan-Slavs and Pan-Germans was added to the military side of the scale (their goals were often compatible if not identical), the balance was predictable. Nicholas, a kind, gentle, peaceable man could be counted on to bend under heavy pressure from his advisors; Wilhelm, who outwardly loved all things military, but who inwardly was terrified of the uncertainties of war and who was intelligent enough to understand that the odds were being constantly stacked against Germany, would have to be watched closely and denied facts if necessary, but he could be more or less controlled.

Germany, unaware of the secret provisions of the *Entente*, was nevertheless troubled by the new Franco-Russian solidarity. A new Chief of the General Staff, Alfred von Schlieffen, had been appointed in 1891. Schlieffen was not a veteran of great campaigns such as Motlke had been, but was purely a professional Staff Officer. His learning had been chiefly of the textbook variety, and he had learnt his lessons well, having a remarkable ability for extremely efficient Staff work. For political issues he had no use or interest. Upon being immediately confronted with the frightening spectacle of a two front war against France and Russia simultaneously, Schlieffen merely grumbled his disapproval of the Austrian alliance, saying that without it

Germany and Russia could live in peace. Then he at once began to work out the details of just such an enterprise. Unfortunately, because of his dislike of the Austrians, there would be no cooperation of planning between the German and Austrian General staffs.

Military doctrine of the nineteenth century, for the most part, revolved around the experiences of the Napoleonic Wars. Germany's most respected disciple of Napoleonic theory had been the great Clausewitz, whose teachings had in turn been carefully followed by Moltke, with outstanding success. With these ideas of quick, decisive victory well in mind, Schlieffen was faced with the thankless task of how to devise a plan by which Germany could hope to win decisively while at once engaged on two major fronts. For him, an attack on Russia, even with Austrian support, was not the answer. Russian territory was too vast, her vital centers too far away from the frontiers to be quickly threatened. Her armed forces, even if defeated repeatedly, could always withdraw eastwards. In fact, this they had done many times in history. And as an invader pressed farther and farther into the inhospitable Russian countryside, his lines of communication and supply would be ever more severely strained and his army weakened. Then, too, there were strong frontier fortifications to be overcome and formidable natural obstacles with which to deal. Decisive victory in the East seemed a remote possibility.

But it was known, or at least believed, that Russia would be extremely slow to mobilize. For this undertaking her own huge size and thinly populated territory, coupled with an underdeveloped road and railway system, would work against her. Schlieffen had reason to believe that six weeks would be required, versus the two weeks Germany needed to mobilize. That left a difference of four weeks or so during which Germany could deal with France. The main blow, then, had to be delivered in the West, and decisive victory there having been achieved, the German forces could be quickly transported East to engage Russia before she could mount a serious threat. With her ally thus defeated, and now confronted with the entire forces of Germany and Austria, Russia was bound to make peace.

Not that defeating France was going to be easy. The France-German frontier was only 240 km. (150 mi) long, and because of topographical obstacles the distance for favorable military operations was only about 65 km. (40 mi). Naturally enough, the French had heavily fortified this area and were quite prepared to deal with any hostile army which attacked there. Schlieffen had no desire to play the enemy's game. His studies convinced him that Germany must outflank France, that is, invade Belgium and Holland, converge on Paris from the North, and envelop the French forces facing east, towards Germany. But after careful calculation the Chief of the General Staff was forced to conclude that the plan would not work. The reason: The city of Paris was too dangerous a fortress to be bypassed, yet the forces needed to reduce it could not be accommodated passage on existing roads. It was an operational impossibility. Besides committing Germany to attack France whether or not Russia was the aggressor, then, the Schieffen Plan, by its author's own admission, was doomed to fail. It was an extremely dubious plan, as one modern historian notices, to have been accepted as the cornerstone of German strategic planning.[3] Incredibly, unbelievably, this is just what in fact did occur. For the next two decades, German preparations were based on deployment according to the plan. Inevitably, as with any military secret, leaks were bound to occur as time passed, and eventually the French were to learn of the plan. A certain German General Staff Officer, in fact, actually sold the details to French agents.[4] But despite the risks to the success of the Grand Strategy, the Germans nonetheless faithfully updated the logistics necessary to implementation of the Plan with each passing year. With the benefit of hindsight, it may easily be concluded that a definite lack of imagination and flexibility prevailed within the General Staff during those critical years. Even Schlieffer's successor failed to scrap the plan in favor of something more realistic. This man, Helmuth von Moltke (often referred to as "the younger"), nephew to the late great strategist of the same name, would contribute little to the insurance of Germany's security. His only modification of the plan was purely politically motivated, insisting as he did that in event of war, Dutch neutrality should not be violated since this would likely bring Britain into league with Germany's enemies.

The ink had hardly dried on the Treaty of Portsmouth ending the Russo-Japanese War than did representatives of the British and Russian Empires sit down to discuss an eventual *Entente*. This was at the behest of the French who were simultaneously engaged in naval and military conversations with Britain as the two pulled closer together. An Anglo-Russian understanding had long been thought impossible by circles in Germany, circles far more extensive than the *Kaiser's* immediate entourage. But by mid 1907 the two giant empires, prodded incessantly by the French, had settled most of their issues. Thereafter the *Dual Entente* had become triple, and a new sinister word crept into German strategic discussions: *Einkreisung* (Encirclement). The mere thought of *Einkreisung* was enough to rattle the coolest military brains. Germany, hemmed in on her eastern and western frontiers, was now blocked access to the open ocean by the world's strongest sea-power. There was only one hole in the ring—one direction still not barred: to the southeast through Austria-Hungary and into the Balkans and hopefully beyond.

The Balkans, of course, had long been a source of friction between Austria and Russia and had precipitated the withdrawal of Russia from the *Dreikaiserbund* as early as 1887. Perhaps the single most decisive issue, other than France's burning desire for revenge against Germany, which led to the Great War can be traced to the year 1903 in this troublesome area. For in that year occurred a dangerous change in Serbian government. Previously, Serbia had looked to Austria-Hungary for guidance and support and had been given such. But Austria-Hungary contained within its borders, particularly in the occupied territory of Bosnia-Herzegovina, large numbers of Serbs and Croats, a related Slavic nationality. In that age of nationalism these peoples were regarded by ardent Serb nationalists as brothers whose lands should be included in a large South Slavic State enjoying complete independence. This attitude was encouraged by many Russians, who saw Russia as the leader and protector of all the Balkan Slavic peoples. On June 10, 1903, the pro-Austrian King and Queen of Serbia were brutally murdered by forces in the employ of rivals to the throne who were pro-Russian and very much anti-Austrian. This change in direction of Serbian policy virtually condemned the whole area to war. Now, Serbian government-encouraged agitators were set to work outside Serbia's borders, inciting Austrian citizens against the Austrian Empire and promoting the cause of a Southern Slavic State under Russian protection. Those who plotted the murders of King Alexander and Queen Draga would continue to plan and undertake many more such vicious acts over the following years, but the most notorious act of all would be the successful conspiracy against the lives of the Austrian Archduke Franz Ferdinand and his wife Sophie. Considering the long years of terror from the regicides of June 10, 1903, to those of June 28, 1914, it is hardly surprising that the Austro-Hungarian government was determined to punish Serbia following the latter action, and the German *Kaiser* was convinced that the government of his cousin the *Czar* would not support a state that "had stained itself by assassination." At least one historian has lamented the unworthiness of the cause for which so many millions of casualties of the First World War were sustained—that of the Serbian government and its ruling House of Karageorgevich.[5] A few years later the whole area was restless and seemed about to explode when a revolution in the Ottoman capital of Constantinople shook the already unstable structure. A group of Turkish nationalists later called the Young Turks were anxious to arrest the decline of the Ottoman Empire, prevent further loss of territory and free it from foreign influence. The Empire was by now but a house of cards, though it did still own real estate astride three continents. They seized effective control of the government, shook up the corrupt bureaucracy and instituted sweeping reforms. Europeans wondered if the "Sick Man of Europe" could possibly be revived on the eve of his anticipated expiration. The two most interested powers, Austria and Russia, were not willing to wait for any such questions to be answered; within a month the respective foreign ministers Aehrenthal and Izvolsky were already dealing—and without waiting to consult their allies. A private arrangement was worked out before the Turks could regain their balance or before the other powers could act in any way which might jeopardize the rare opportunity for easy spoils. The deal was: Austria-Hungary to annex two of the provinces she had been occupying since 1878 (Bosnia and Herzegovina) and withdraw from the third (Novibazaar); Russia to secure passage of the Straits for her warships (one step away from ownership). The terms were to be announced soon, at a date acceptable to both powers, who would then have achieved a *fait accompli*.

Of the two schemers, Aehrenthal had the far easier task to perform. The Germans were not likely to object to the annexation of two remote provinces which for three decades had been under occupation anyway and they had long since—after the reckless snub to Russia in 1890—assured their closest ally of full support. The Italians were drifting away from the *Triple Alliance* regardless; indeed their positions were constantly becoming more estranged. They could eat *fait*. Izvolsky, on the other hand, faced the delicate task of convincing his French and especially his British partners in the *Entente* that Russian control of the vital Straits was in their best interests. They had, after all, gone to war with Russia over basically the same issue only five decades earlier. At any rate, Izvolsky never got the chance.

He had just begun his approach to the French when suddenly Bulgaria—nominally an Ottoman dependency—declared full independence. Aehrenthal knew now he had to act fast. With the Turks reeling and all eyes now turning to the Balkans there was no time to lose. He sent notice to the Russian, now in Paris, that he was taking action, which he promptly did, and before Izvolsky could reply in protest. Bosnia and Herzegovina were officially annexed on October 6, 1908. It was an action that may have aroused more emotion among Europeans than anything since the Congress of Berlin. At least after the latter there was Bismarck to smooth things over. Now there was nothing but rage, and when it was finally restrained, it continued to boil beneath the surface like bubbling magma building up pressure for the inevitable explosion.

The Serbs and Montenegrins were furious. The now-Austrian provinces were peopled by their kinsmen in race, speech, and custom. Bosnia-Herzegovina was for them to expand into, to unite with. How dare those Germans and Hungarians think they could appropriately govern Serbs and Croats? No—matters were now completely unacceptable. The Pan-Slavs, of course, demanded war on Austria. The Turks were also more than displeased: the annexation violated earlier agreements and large numbers of Islamics were being absorbed into an alien realm. The Russians fumed. Besides the tumult caused by its Pan-Slavs the government would have to deal with an immense loss of prestige. Austria had gained something in an area of intense Russian interest while Russia had gained nothing—it appeared as though Russia had been duped! The whole mess was most embarrassing.

No one was more embarrassed, or angry, than Izvolsky. He tried hard to salvage something of the situation. Racing from capital to capital he found the French hesitant and cool, the British negative and cooler; ironically, only the Germans made no objection if they, too, were compensated. But the Russian had nothing to offer, and in the end he was forced to himself accept the *fait accompli*. It was a classic case of the proverbial possession and law: Austria had Bosnia-Herzegovina in her possession pre-annexation; Russia did not have the straits. Embarrassed, his credibility eroded, his allies disgusted, Izvolsky grasped at straws for weeks, then retreated in exhaustion.

After Bosnia, the Pan-Slavs redoubled their efforts to undermine Austria-Hungary. When the heir to the Imperial throne let it be known that he favored a future Triple Monarchy, an Austria-Hungary-Slavia of sorts, a gesture intended to secure some support among moderate Slavic people, it only provoked the fanatics to determine to kill him. No number of concessions could appease them, no amount of compromise however well intended was tolerable. As for the Russian leaders, even the peaceable *Czar* was annoyed with Aehrenthal and Austria. They vowed to never again back down from an Austrian challenge. The road to war was by now bearing traffic. The safety net that Bismarck had woven around Germany had now unraveled; all that remained was the Triple Alliance, not inconsiderable, had it at least been sound. But Italy continued to drift away and by the end of the first decade of the new century neither Berlin nor Vienna was entertaining any illusions as to its loyalty. Then in the autumn of 1911, without any prior consultations with its "allies," Italy announced it was annexing the Ottoman province of Tripoli, and made war on Turkey. Besides displeasing every other power—especially Germany whose advisors were hastily attempting to modernize the Turkish military— this action led to another dangerous development. With Turkish hands now tied to the Italian war, four Balkan states—Serbia, Montenegro, Greece and Bulgaria—joined forces and fell on what was left of European Turkey, each promised a certain share by mutual prior agreement. In this the First Balkan War the Turks were overwhelmed and driven back to Constantinople and the Straits. But before the capital could be taken by the Bulgarians (whose army was closest), Russia intervened by warning Bulgaria not to advance to the Straits. Somewhat later Austria warned the Serbs and Montenegrins to give up some of their gains in order to assign them to a new state of Albania. No one was happy. Then the small states fell out with each other. The Bulgarians, frustrated that the Serbs and Greeks would not turn over territory promised to them, and hurt that the Russians seemed to have abandoned them, suddenly turned on their former allies and the Second Balkan War was on. At first the Bulgarians held their own. Then the Turks and even the Romanians took advantage of the situation to fall upon their rear. Bulgaria was resoundingly defeated and lost ground to all four of its neighbors (the Turks of course were only retaking what had recently been theirs).

The effects of the Balkan Wars are significant to our story because of the resentment that the Bulgarians now held for the Russians. Far from being the big Slavic brother Russia purported to be, she had instead apparently supported the Greeks and Romanians (non-Slav) and the Serbs (with whom Bulgaria had already fought a war, in 1885). The Serbs and Montenegrins, reigned in by the hated Austrians, had been denied access to the sea by the purposeful insistence of Austria to create the new state of Albania to which both had been obliged to yield ground. Turkey lost 90% of its European lands and was nearly expelled from the continent. Romania, by her jealous action, had gained some territory and with it a new enemy. Bulgaria felt cheated, betrayed, and stabbed in the back and burned for revenge. The others had not gotten all they wanted. And into this Balkan volcano, without much of a cooling-off period, soon stepped the Austrian heir to the throne.

Military thinking in Austria-Hungary was dominated by one man: Field Marshall Baron Franz Conrad von Hötzendorf, Chief of the General Staff. An able commander, Hötzendorf realized that with the bulk of Germany's strength directed initially westward, it would be Austria's assignment to bolster the fortunes of the Teutonic Powers in the East. But he would have preferred an offensive strategy designed, in cooperation with the German Eighth Army, to pinch off Russian Poland before the Russians could mobilize sufficient force to prevent it. The problems Austria-Hungary faced, however, were similar to those of Germany. In event of war she would no doubt have to fight on two fronts, against Serbia and Russia. Would the six armies available upon mobilization be equal to the task? Eventually two plans were worked out. In event of war with Serbia only, three armies would crush the small nation while the other three guarded the border with Russia. If war did come on two fronts, then two armies were allotted for Serbia, four for Russia. Later the second plan was revised. Assured of German support, Hötzendorf allowed only seven divisions for Serbia, the remainder (forty-one divisions) would take the offensive against Russia. But Hötzendorf still wavered, being unable to decide whether or not to allot a second army for the Serbian Front, or to keep the forces opposing Russia as strong as possible. With the Austro-Hungarian railway system neither as complete nor as efficient as that of Germany, it was imperative that logistics for entraining troops be worked out carefully and deliberately, which meant that a firm plan was needed. The vacillation at Hötzendorf's level meant that Germany's chief ally would enter the war ill prepared for quick, decisive action and would thus risk losing any advantage of a mobilization speedier than Russia's.

Russia, for her part, had not stood idly by while the rest of Europe prepared for war. Her humiliating defeat at the hands of the Japanese in 1906 had led to a series of political and economic reforms which gave rise to an unprecedented prosperity. The following years, up to the outbreak of the Great War, witnessed a general strengthening of Russian military power, much to the alarm of the Germans. By 1914 Russia was spending more on defense than

Germany. She possessed a larger army, more railway mileage and rolling stock on which to move it[6], and an elaborate network of frontier fortifications. Her army disposed of more cavalry and artillery. And she was hotly engaged in constructing a powerful, modern navy.

Perhaps more importantly, outcome of the Japanese War had forced the government to recognize the need for an independent Army General Staff. Previously, the Staff had been a department of the War Ministry, and had been ineffective in war, filling for the most part an administrative need. Now, it became independent, answerable only to the *Czar*, and hence a much more effective weapon if handled properly. In 1908, the initial Chief of the General Staff was replaced by V. A. Sukhomlinov, who would more or less write the book of Russian preparedness for war. Sukhomlinov was a fairly able strategist who realized that Russia must, in event of war, mount an offensive against Germany as rapidly as possible to take some of the pressure off the French. He therefore altered basic Russian planning which had hitherto been essentially defensive. Of the six armies which mobilization would initially produce, four would be thrown against Germany, while the other two guarded the Austrian border.

But Sukhomlinov soon ran into stiff opposition to his plans. Many of his contemporaries believed that Russia should strike at Austria-Hungary with most of her strength instead of Germany. The reasons most often forwarded were that Austria had been the real adversary in recent crises, and that Austria being weaker than Germany would be easier to quickly knock out of the war so that full attention could be turned on the stronger opponent. In the end, a compromise was worked out, and like most compromises, it was a very poor substitute for either point of view. This new plan called for two armies to invade Germany, while four armies tackled the Austrians. The promise to throw eight hundred thousand men at once against Germany, which was the letter of the Treaty of the *Dual Entente*, was conveniently forgotten, and Russian strategic planning was undeniably split between those who favored a northern and those a southern, strategy. Nevertheless, military preparation commenced. In 1914 began the "Great Programme," designed to boost army strength to a level that would considerably overshadow that of Germany. It was believed that Russia would be "ready" by 1916. Unfortunately, political events would not wait for that date before they prompted her to commit her forces to war.

Perhaps no other historical development has been so intensely studied, scrutinized, and been the subject of so many millions of written words than has the beginning of the Great War. The haunting questions of how it could have happened and why have been answered from a multitude of perspectives. The Serbian terrorist organization The Black Hand, which successfully planned and executed the murder of Archduke Francis Ferdinand and his wife on that fateful summer day in Bosnia, has itself justly been the subject of much microscopic-like attention. The diplomatic exchanges, the statements of leading personalities, the military interference is a sequence of events like a countdown to a demolition by explosives which has been replayed again and again in the hope that some obscure but critical key might be found which would tend to explain the entire process. Even today it remains a fascinating study, but it is beyond the scope of our concern here. For our purposes, we will focus on a few points of incontestable historic fact.

First, Austria-Hungary had been the victim of Pan-Slav terrorism for a long time, but by 1914 it was increasing in tempo and the murder of the Archduke heir shocked the nation much like 9/11 shocked the United States 87 years later. The Austrians felt some kind of response was necessary to preserve their prestige and self-respect, and virtually all of Europe tended to agree. A military response—a sort of punitive expedition—was decided upon. When consulted the Germans agreed; the so called "blank check" is an inferred myth. Unfortunately the Russians had secretly committed to support Serbia, though they later let it be known they might tolerate some mild Austrian punitive measures. Of the three Emperors, none wanted, expected, or would have permitted, a general European war. But they were deliberately misled by information withheld or at least delayed until its relevancy had been overtaken by events. Nicholas, ever unsure of himself, could be molded like soft clay. Franz Joseph, always peaceable but by now very elderly and easily misled, believed to the last moments of peace that he was making war on Serbia only. Wilhelm, who had been on vacation sailing in Norwegian waters, was assured it was not necessary for him to return to Berlin. Intelligent enough to suspect he was being circumvented, he returned anyway but the information then fed him was stale until it was too late. In vain did he and Nicholas exchange the famous Willy-Nicky telegrams; behind the scenes the military people were preparing to mobilize their armed forces. For years before the war the phrase "Mobilization means War" had haunted the capitals of Europe. What it meant was that no power could allow a potential opponent to mobilize—and therefore get a head start—in a situation in which war was likely, even possible. Should one power fail to do so, another could invade its territory before it could even respond. Since most of the "secret" treaties were well known in rival capitals there can now be little doubt that the mobilization clause in the Franco-Russian alliance contributed to, or even instigated the "Mobilization means War" mentality. At any rate, *without* first mobilizing, Austria-Hungary declared war on Serbia on July 28, 1914, exactly one month after the murders in Bosnia. The measure was intended as another *fait accompli* and meant little; the extent of Austrian action being a half-hearted bombardment of the Serbian capital of Belgrade by Austrian monitors in the Danube River. The mad scramble was on. The military men chaffed for mobilization, the diplomats urged restraint, and the ambassadors received and delivered notes. First the French, then the Russians, pleaded with the British to declare their solidarity; if they did so the *Alliance* would back down. The British, a people long accused of never saying what they mean, gave non-committal responses to the inquires of both sides. The *Czar* ordered mobilization on July 29th, rescinded it some hours later, and then ordered it again the next day. The Germans, convinced the British were not going to act, sent an ultimatum to St. Petersburg on July 31st demanding cessation of Russian preparations opposite the German frontier. Its time limit was 12 hours. Austria mobilized. Germany inquired of France what it would do in the event of a Russo-German war. The next day the Germans had their answer: France would do what its interests required it to do. The Russians made no reply and later that day both France and Germany mobilized. Then at 7:00 pm the *Kaiser 's* government declared war on Russia. Everyone knew this meant war with France as well. The British finally said what they meant on the 4th, by declaring war on Germany. Two days later, Austria finally got around to declaring war on Russia. In the meantime, Italy informed its partners in the *Triple Alliance* that as they had been the "aggressors" (presumably by that she meant the first to declare war?) she had no obligation to support them. By August 6, 1914, the German and Austro-Hungarian Empires were at war with the Russian and British Empires, France, Belgium, Serbia and Montenegro. The first two will be referred to as Nations of the *Alliance*, the latter as the *Entente*. On August 23rd Japan declared war on Germany and thus joined the *Entente*. The unthinkable, the unspeakable, and the unimaginable had occurred. Much of the world was at war.

Chapter Three
The Contestants

War had come to Eastern Europe. It had long been anticipated but scarcely desired. At last the frontiers of 1815—now 99 years old—were in serious jeopardy. The Pan-Slavs expected to witness the fulfillment of their dreams; Austria-Hungary would be pushed beyond the Carpathians, Germany relieved of her stewardship of the ancient Slavic lands east of the Elbe. The Pan-Germans for their part anticipated the destruction of semi-oriental Muscovite power on the eastern frontiers and a re-conquest of all of Congress Poland. But these issues would now have to be settled—as Bismarck had once remarked—by "iron and blood." Before we examine the course of the fighting in the east, let us first have a look at the contestants in this match.

The Russian Empire was in 1914 the largest contiguous political entity in the world. Atlases of the day list its size at about 22,403,500 sq. km. (8,650,000 sq. mi.) but the numbers vary widely and this is only a median figure. Doubtless, no one really knew how large the Empire was; it contained vast tundras, taigas, swamplands, and deserts that had never been surveyed and could scarcely be traversed given the available means. Everyone knew it was big and disposed of over half of European soil and not far short of half of Asia. Because of its latitude it was thinly populated when taken as a whole; in general, the farther east one traveled the thinner the populace became. Estimating the total population of this gargantuan state usually produced figures suspiciously round; the birth rate differed widely among the scattered, far-flung peoples within its borders. Books and atlases forwarded numbers from 165 million to 180 million, but whatever the true number it was at least 50 million in excess of Germany and Austria-Hungary combined. Over one hundred ethnic strains were to be found but many of these were small groups of nomadic or semi-nomadic peoples widely distributed in the sprawling, underdeveloped east. Slavs probably constituted two-thirds of the total and these—Russians (or

Great Russians), Ukrainians (or Little Russians), and Bylo-Russians (or White Russians)—were mostly in cities located in the European portion. Small numbers of Great Russians fanned out along the southern reaches of Siberia to the Pacific, mostly in cities and towns along the newly completed Trans-Siberian Railroad. Most of the Central Asian peoples and many in the Trans-Caucasus region were Islamic; most of the Slavs and the Romanians in Bessarabra were Orthodox. The Poles and Lithuanians were generally Roman Catholics and the Finns, Estonians and Latvians often Protestants. In the latter areas were found the highest standards of living in the Empire, and in general most Russian industries developed in the western provinces. Still, by 1914 fewer than 5% of the population lived in cities of 100,000 or more, a sure indication that the Industrial Revolution had not quite yet gotten a firm foothold in the *Czar's* realm.

Of the 5,440,000 sq. km. (2,100,000 sq. mi.) of European Russia roughly 20% was good arable land, some of it amongst the best wheat producing regions on earth. And while an estimated 70% of the populace made its living in some sort of agriculture, woefully little of this activity was in any way mechanized, and much of it occurred without the use of commercial fertilizers. It was, compared to Western Europe, a primitive society, and estimates as to the prevalence of illiteracy run as high as 60%.[7] Much of the problem could be traced to an extremely poor transportation net and such vast distances for one to serve. Even European Russia was 2700 kilometers (1700 mi.) north to south and nearly as broad east to west. Traversing this vast landscape were a scanty 240 miles of railroad for every million people. Contrast this with 600 miles for every million Germans and 555 miles for every million Austro-Hungarians or 2720 for every million Americans! The situation regarding roads was even worse; they were few, were unpaved, and became bottomless morasses during periods of prolonged rain and during the period when the frozen ground thawed in the springtime. Of course there were the waterways; such a large landmass can be expected to possess some large rivers, but the geography of Eastern Europe is such that most Russian rivers, European and Siberian, flow north/south and at any rate would be frozen for a good portion of the year and flooded at other times. This serious transportation issue would bedevil Russia throughout the war: There were never enough rail lines and the existing ones were incapable of transporting the millions of troops, thousands of horses, and mountains of equipment and supplies to the battle zones, supply them there or switch them to other sectors as needed, plus evacuate dead and wounded men to say nothing of refugees. An enormous strain was soon placed upon the locomotives and rolling stock, always inadequate, and slowly repaired or replaced when necessary. Trained railroad personnel were lacking and no provisions had been made to instruct others, and every technician would be needed in the factories anyway.

That is, what few factories existed in Russia. Pig iron production—long one measure of a nation's strength—in 1910 had amounted to a paltry 3,040,000 tons for a country containing one sixth of the planet's land surface! By contrast, Germany had produced 13,100,000 tons in the same year, the United States 27,700,000. Even Austria-Hungary, with a tiny fraction of the necessary natural resources, produced two thirds as much at 2,002,000 tons. The state of other manufacturers was much the same. Yet neither most Russians nor their western allies of the *Entente* were much concerned. Russia was rich in resources. There were vast forests to be exploited. Most important minerals were found in abundance; the empire was second only to the United States in production of petroleum and like the latter was a major exporter of grains. But most exciting of all considerations was its endless supply of manpower. Optimistic voices everywhere had millions upon millions of Russian soldiers trained, outfitted, armed and marching resistlessly westward, rolling over anything in their path. Thus was born the myth of the Russian Steamroller, the unstoppable war machine certain to crush whatever barrier the hapless nations of the *Alliance* might erect in the way.

Such wishful thinking was not entirely without substance. European Russia and the Caucasus areas embraced 16 provinces, some as large as any other European state, plus Poland and Finland. The Empire was further divided into 12 military districts for the purpose of organization and mobilization for defense, or in the event, offense. The standing peacetime army alone numbered 1.4 million which would be raised to 5 million in war. Between 1914 and the Revolution, Russia mobilized some 12 million men, raised 248 infantry divisions of various types and 46 cavalry divisions including Cossacks. She also had to man her not inconsiderable navy. Like most nations, some of this was accomplished with smoke and mirrors: during the winter of 1916-17 the divisions were reduced by four battalions, from 16 to 12. This enabled the creation of some 60 "new" divisions—all short of artillery because the reduced units were not about to part with much. Nevertheless, if nothing else, Russia could surely produce conscripts.

She could have produced far more but for an archaic recruiting policy. The armed forces consisted of mostly Russian Christians. The Empire's large Islamic population went untapped; men paid a tax in lieu of service. The non-Slavic peoples in the far north, in Siberia, and in the Caucasus were also exempted, as were the Finns, recent immigrants, and clergymen. Educators and certain classes of students, unless they switched careers before the age of thirty, were likewise exempt. Roughly half of all men were exempted for family reasons. Students able to pass the officers' examination and students of medicine or pharmacy would have their active duty reduced to one half or one third of the norm (this little stipulation would have serious consequences in the years to come when a crippling officer shortage resulted). In addition, there were "conditional" exemptions such as men with siblings serving or secondary breadwinners (primary breadwinners were exempted for family reasons) who might be called up if the army was shorthanded and enrolled in the reserve. Although military service was officially compulsory the only records kept pertained to men who had come forward in the first place, and it can only be imagined how many young Russians slipped through the would-be net. In a country which did not even know its own population it could not have been difficult. At any rate, for those not exempted by decree or design, a further 17% were rejected for reasons of health.[8]

Service for those who were recruited was three years for infantry and four for cavalry. Infantry then passed into the reserve for another seven years, then a second class of reserve for eight more. Finally they ended service in the *Opolchenie* (Imperial Militia) or at age 43 whichever came first. *Opolchenie* were classed into two groups, the first of which were theoretically combatants, the second, not. Thus upon mobilization 35 reserve divisions were counted upon although these would initially not be equipped with modern ordnance.

A Russian army regiment consisted of about 4000 men with eight machine guns, and 14 messengers on horseback, 21 telephone specialists and five dozen advance scouts, some on bicycles. An infantry division contained four regiments of four battalions plus an artillery brigade of six batteries of eight guns apiece. Included would be two brigades of two regiments each and one to three squadrons of cavalry. Divisions became the smallest integral units fairly early in the war; in prior times the Corps or Field army had been.[9] This is to say that as the circumstances of wartime necessity dictated a smaller self-contained unit than previous experience had required. As time passed the divisions in every warring nation's armies became more self-sufficient by the addition of specialized troops hitherto reserved for larger units. Soon Russian divisions also included sappers, telegraph troops, railway troops, wireless, searchlight, engineer, pontoon and supply (four days' rations) troops. In all about 20,000 men, 5,000 horses, 48 field pieces and 32 machine guns. The human total sometimes reached 22,000 though both it and the quantity of artillery was reduced in the autumn of 1916.

The Russian infantryman was issued a Moisin-Nagant bolt action rifle with a fixed five round magazine and a bore of 7.62 mm. Most of these weapons were of the 1891 model, or the 1901 upgrade and expelled a bullet at 620 meters/second (2035 feet /second) {2660/811 upgrade}. 120 rounds were carried with 56 per man more in the company reserve. A 43 cm (17 inch) bayonet was fixed as standard practice on campaign. With the bayonet the weapon weighed about 5.44kg (12 pounds). Also carried were an entrenching tool, a haversack, a water bottle and, most conspicuously, the tent cloth and greatcoat which were rolled up together and slung over one shoulder in a horseshoe around the body with the ends stuffed into a mess tin. His uniform consisted of gray-green trousers, a khaki short-visored cap, and a baggy light brown tunic. Black leather knee boots rounded out his distinctly brown, earthy appearance. A heavier version of the same outfit would be worn in cold weather, as well as brown woolen greatcoat, tall fur or fleece cap, and a beige wool hood designed to cover the head, with cap, and neck. As the war progressed, most soldiers also carried one or more hand grenades and a gas mask folded into a rectangular metal box. At this point each man was groaning under a burden of 30 kilos (65 pounds) before his superiors realized his headgear was inadequate.

Steel helmets began to appear in 1916, first used by the Imperial Guard. These were of the French type, only colored brown and with the Imperial Eagle badge attached as a distinguishing feature. The French agreed to supply their Russian allies with 2 million of these, but nowhere near this number ever reached the front, and the Russian effort to produce homegrown helmets never got off the ground. A factory was set up near the capital, which eventually stamped out ten thousand of the Russian version (ballistically superior and simpler in design than, but similar to the French model), a second facility in Finland may have produced as many as a half-million but few of these were ever worn in combat, the Revolution having meanwhile intervened. At bottom, the Russian soldier was alone among troops of the Great Powers in that his general appearance and equipment changed little during the war.

Russian Cavalry were armed with the shorter carbine version of the infantry rifle with 40 rounds of ammunition issued per man. Officers carried a six-shot revolver as opposed to the infantry officers' seven-shot pistol. Instead of a bayonet, horsemen carried a curved saber. A typical cavalry regiment consisted of 850 men, 8 machine guns and the same specialist troops as in infantry regiment. At division level this rose to 4500-4850 men, 4800-5400 horses, and two eight-gun batteries of artillery. In late 1916 all cavalry (including Cossack) regiments were reduced from six to four squadrons. Artillery was also reduced at divisional level but the number of machine guns was increased. By that time most cavalry units were being increasingly ordered to dismount and being used as infantry.

Cossacks were a unique type of cavalry found in no other army in the world. Typically between 20 and 38 years of age, they spent one year training, then four years active duty. This was followed by four years on call during which they were required to train for a month annually; then they passed into a four-year period of no annual training, then into reserve. Cossacks were a free-spirited, hard-riding people generally from the non-Slavic areas of the Empire namely the Caucasus area, the Steppes of the north Caspian area and western Siberia. Many were Islamic and these were allowed to form voluntary units known as "alien" troops. Cossacks made excellent scouts and reconnaissance troops and were very effective in pursuing a beaten enemy, but their value as defensive fighters was negligible. At any rate, by the addition of large numbers of Cossacks, Russia's cavalry establishment far exceeded that of any other nation in 1914.

Artillery was another matter. As we have seen Russian infantry divisions were fairly well allotted with field pieces. These were Pulitov-made 76.2 mm (10 times the infantrymen's rifle bore) weapons of 1902 vintage. A shorter, lighter, so-called mountain gun of the same caliber but made by the French firm of Schneider was issued to the cavalry. Schneider made M1909 122mm howitzers were allotted twelve per Corps. Krupp also supplied a similar (120mm) weapon before the war, as well as its 105 mm gun. Both firms built a few M1910 152 mm howitzers; Schneider also supplied a 152 mm gun,[10] and there were a number of old M1884 Schneider 150mm howitzers still in use. In general though the Russians were always lacking in heavy artillery. Once the usefulness of mortars had been established, a 58 mm 1915 model was developed and the British provided some of their own by 1917. During the war, all the major powers were forced to rapidly expand their production capabilities and Russia was no exception. Ironically, she never matched her enemies' production, though by the advent of the year 1917 she outpaced both the British and the French in the monthly production of field guns.[11]

The ammunition to feed the guns could also be a problem, as it was with all the nations at war. In September 1914 the Russian armies in the field required one and a half million shells; the very next month the requirement leaped to 3.5 million. The average daily expenditure for the first three months of war was calculated at 45,000 rounds. By November, in a frantic effort to conserve, batteries were reduced from 8 to 6 guns, and by the beginning of the new year the war ministry had ordered 14 million shells and 3.6 million rifles from foreign concerns.[12] Most of these and other foreign orders would never be received owing to shipping and other transportation problems. But the Empire solved its own problems in the end. Given time it would meet the challenge. Rifle production increased tenfold in two years, as did artillery production; shell production ballooned to nearly 30 times the 1914 level![13]

The soldiers in the field could of course be forgiven for their impatience while the shortages were made good. Infantrymen without rifles often constituted 30% of a units' personnel; some reports claim figures as high as 50%. In such cases the unarmed men suffered the unenviable task of waiting for an armed comrade to fall in order to secure his rifle. With small arms initially at such a premium, emphasis was placed on repair and salvage and at one point the authorities proclaimed a bounty on both Russian and enemy rifles which, however was observed to have "no useful results."[14]

The Russian machine gun was a Maxim M1910, 7.62 mm belt-fed, water-cooled weapon mounted on a two-wheeled Sokolov carriage. It used the same ammunition as did the Infantry rifle, and it was used with or without an armored shield designed to protect the shooter. A solid, reliable weapon, it long outlived many foreign models and was still in service a generation later. It was never produced in sufficient numbers before the war, so the Russian army would have yet another shortage to deal with once the nature of modern warfare had been recognized. Unfortunately the shortage of rifle ammunition apparent by autumn 1914 meant that the stutter of the Maxim would be heard less frequently than was desirable. At the time of the war's beginning, only three factories in all Russia produced small arms ammunition; these were immediately overwhelmed with orders and the initial deficiencies were never really made good, at least until the Revolution.

Another frustrating shortage that Russian troops were suffered to endure was a serious deficiency of boots. Virtually every account of wartime Russia mentions this problem, none quite as colorfully as General Brusilov wrote of the winter of 1916-17: "Practically the whole population of Russia was shod with army boots."[15] He went on to suggest that the soldiers were selling their boots to civilians, then returning to the army depots behind the front to plead necessity and be issued another pair. As usual, the lack of local industry induced the people responsible for supply to place huge foreign orders; as usual, most failed to materialize. Probably an entire account could be written about Russian technical shortcomings during the war, but at bottom was the underdeveloped, backward state of Russian industry at that time.

Not all the news was bad. One area in which Russians certainly had taken a lead was in the design and construction of armored fighting vehicles. The nature of the fighting in the east differed considerably from that in the west and wheeled vehicles were not considered impractical. At least 20 different firms produced some sort of armored car; some of these mounted machine guns, others medium artillery. In 1916 the first half-tracks appeared. Far and away the largest producer was Aleksei Pulitov, whose massive armaments complex in St. Petersburg eventually produced 250 various armored cars and half-tracks. Another player was the Russo-Balt Wagon Factory in Riga. This facility had to be moved upon the approach of the enemy in 1915, to Taganrog. According to one source, more than thirty different models[16] of these machines served the Russians during the war; by late 1917 over 200 were in service. Armored trains were another innovation seen mostly in the east; they could move in all but the deepest snows. Easily armed heavily, they could bring a lot of firepower to bear at a given point and quickly withdraw, often before enemy artillery could get the range. The Germans and Austrians usually made good use of any such Russian equipment they captured, a testament to its effectiveness.

The Russian Empire's only attempt at tank construction was a less than effective machine. Before the war was a year old a gigantic 10 meter tall two wheeled vehicle was under construction. A roller-like 2 meter high device at the rear gave it a tricycle-like balance point. Each of the two massive main wheels were powered by its own engine and the unfinished prototype weighed 36 metric tons (40 tons).[17] The only enclosure for weapons paralleled the axle to the rear so presumably its own wheels would be in its line of fire. Needless to relate, the project was abandoned and no tanks would see service on the Eastern Front.

Accounts of Russian Naval strength in 1914 vary considerably, but it certainly embraced at least 10 older battleships, 6 armored cruisers, 8 light cruisers, 40 destroyers, 75 torpedo boats, 12 light gunboats and 25 submarines, most of which were older units. Total tonnage certainly exceeded a half million and probably was closer to a full million. While this fleet can in no respect compare to a larger more modern one such as the British or Germans possessed, it could by no means be despised. As we shall see it was to play a not inconsiderable role in the war.

Russia had not been slow to show interest in an air fleet; as early as 1910 an Imperial Air Service was established which had been fairly well organized when war broke out. As many as 950 planes may by then have existed in the Empire, but scarcely more than 200 were ready for action. Like all other hardware, the number decreased in the first months of the conflict, but within six months had leveled off, then began to rise. As with other armaments, aircraft totals peaked just before the Revolution, at about 1000 serviceable units; thereafter the numbers declined. In addition, a bomber squadron of two dozen or so aircraft were available for special missions. The Imperial Navy also possessed seaplanes, which operated in both the Baltic and Black Seas. The total of seaplanes in use may have reached 225 or so with the majority operating in the Black Sea area. In the matter of airships most sources are silent; one account states that 16 were in service in the spring of 1914.[18]

Thus was a vast military machine available for the Russian leaders upon its mobilization. How it was to be used was another matter; the *Czar's* government had nothing to compare to the German General Staff, no definite plan of action (several had been considered). It was known that Germany was the more formidable opponent and that its war plans called for an invasion of France by the bulk of its army while the Austro-Hungarians held off the eastern foe. But it was also readily apparent to anyone who could read a map that the salient created by Congress Poland could easily be lopped off the Russian hinterland by enemy forces operating south out of East Prussia and north from Galicia. Nearly half of the peacetime Army, quartered there, would be lost.

Clearly, Russia needed a plan to be adopted; more importantly, a command to see it through.

The *Czar* quickly appointed a supreme command (*Stavka*). For its symbolic head—an aristocrat was always chosen to head up any government organization—he chose his second cousin, the fifty-eight-year-old Grand Duke Nicholas Nicholaievitch, hitherto Inspector General of Cavalry. The Chief of Staff (actual commander) would be General Yanushkevitch, the Quartermaster (real commander) General Danilov. Imperial Russia was often sarcastically referred to as a bureaucracy instead of a government, alluding to how painfully slow matters of state were handled; now, as his armies assembled on the western frontiers, Danilov and his staff somehow needed to organize an offensive, to help take the heat off the French. They opted for a pre-war contingency to advance against both flanks, both opponents simultaneously. All that was needed was for the railway network to assemble the units in the proper places at the proper time.

It had been no secret that in the event of war between the Austro-Germans and the *Entente*, the Russians would have a considerable numerical superiority on the Eastern Front. The population of the vast Russian Empire, at nearly 170 million, was far larger than that of Germany and Austria-Hungary combined, whose peoples numbered about 115 million. And with Austrian forces split, and the bulk of the German army in the West, the discrepancy of military force, it would seem, would be enormous. But Russia was never able to take full advantage of her manpower resources, and her huge size coupled with her underdeveloped rail system, made the problem hard to correct. Under the terms of the agreement with France, Russia was obliged to send 800,000 men, within three weeks of the announcement of mobilization, against Germany. This would have meant that virtually all the forces she could initially mobilize would have to assemble on the German frontier. For Russia this was not only an operational impossibility, owing to transport and supply considerations, but a political impossibility. Those forces within the government favoring the "southern" or Austro-Hungarian solution were not going to allow the Dual Monarchy an opportunity to overwhelm Serbia. So it was that the First and Second Armies only would invade Germany. Between them they numbered about 400,000 men or only one-half the number that had been promised the French. The Third, Fourth, Fifth, Eighth and Ninth armies would tackle the Austrians. What worried the Germans most in the East was not numerical inferiority. They had long since accepted this as an inevitable if bothersome fact. But the Schlieffen Plan and all German preparations revolved around the expectation of a slow Russian mobilization to give them the needed time to reckon with the French. By 1914, as many voices had warned, they could no longer count on such an expediency. In the event, the Russian First and Second armies invading Germany were ready to move by August 15th or only two weeks after mobilization had commenced. The Schlieffen Plan was based on a six-week Russian mobilization, which allowed the Germans barely enough time for all their plans. In retrospect then, the Schlieffen Plan was even worse strategy than its opponents feared it would be. It certainly was a doomed strategy. Russia's "Great Programme" and her economic strengthening since the Japanese War, all of which generally helped speed and smooth her mobilization, had seen to that.

The Empire of Austria-Hungary at 676,250 sq km (261,100 sq mi) was, behind Russia, the second largest state in Europe. In population it ranked third at 49.9 to 51.1 million in 1914. As we have seen it was composed to two roughly equal halves each of which enjoyed its own parliamentary and administrative apparatus but both recognizing the Hapsburg Emperor Franz Joseph. The Austrian half consisted of 15 provinces as widespread as Voralberg on the Swiss frontier to Bukovina beyond the Carpathians. Its lack of national consciousness may be illustrated by its speech: German predominated in seven provinces and was an important minority in six others, Czech in two and one, Slovene in two and two, Polish in one and one, Croatian in one, Ruthenian in one and one; Romanians were a minority in one and Italians in two. Hungary, on the other hand, included just two provinces, Hungary proper and Croatia-Slavonia, which had its own Diet and governor. Large numbers of Germans, Slovaks, Romanians, Ruthenes and Serbs resided in Hungary; Croatia-Slavonia at least was mostly Croatian. The newly annexed provinces of Bosnia and Herzegovina were a third piece of empire and belonged to neither Austria or Hungary. They were peopled by Serbs and Croats and enjoyed their own self-government though limited in nature it was.

Only 24% of the people were Germans and 20% Magyars, the two dominant races of the Empire. The remainder were Slavs (including Czech, Slovaks, Poles, Ruthenians, Slovenes, Serbs, and Croats 46%), Romanians (6%), Jews (4%), Italians (1½%), and Gypsies. These peoples had little enthusiasm for the war, which they believed was being fought for German and Magyar interests. Moreover they would be pitted against their racial kindred in Serbia and Russia, and later in Romania and Italy. Most would have preferred to join these nations rather than do battle with them. To be sure, they were somewhat better educated and lived a little more comfortably than the average Serb or Russian, but their real desire was for more political and economic freedom.

Not surprisingly then, the Austro-Hungarian Army was comprised of large numbers of troops lacking any real enthusiasm for battle. To make matters worse, few of these men could understand their officers' orders, as over 90% of the officers were either German or Magyar. Some genuine efforts had been made before the war to overcome such obstacles; Conrad von Hötzendorf himself spoke seven languages, for example, and many lesser officers similarly attempted to better understand the men they would command. Most of these leaders, however, became casualties within the first eight months of the war, and their replacements were rarely so concerned, through no fault of their own. The initial military disasters put tremendous strain on the whole Austro-Hungarian Army, the discipline and training of which had never been on the same level as that of the German Army. In early 1915 the first mass desertions began. By April, several Czech regiments had gone over to the enemy; it was a trend which would continue to grow throughout the war. To the end of 1916 roughly 300,000 Czechs had deserted, and the Russians found that about half of these troops were willing to fight for them, against the *Alliance*.[19] Ruthenian troops also deserted in great numbers. They could perhaps be forgiven in that by language, religion, geography, and culture they were very closely linked to the Russians, while having nothing in common with Austrians or Hungarians. Later, Ruthenian insurgency would cause some serious problems in Galicia. The story was much the same regarding Serbs and Croats, who hesitated to fight against their cousins over the border.

This large, complex state bordered eight different neighbors along several thousand kilometers of frontier—the longest in Europe. When war came it immediately faced the handicap of having to fight on two fronts simultaneously. The border with Russia was 800 km (500 mi) long, that with Serbia and Montenegro only somewhat less lengthy. The Monarchy's peace time army had been 450,000 strong; in the event of war it could be raised to 3.35 million. Eventually a total of 7.8 million men would be called up during the war years.

Like most European nations of the day, Austria-Hungary based its armed forces on universal conscription. There were of course exceptions, teachers and priests were exempted, as were men with dependant families who were attached to the *Ersatz* (substitute) Reserve which included training but no active duty. Army service plus active reserve service (*Landwehr*) encompassed the years 18-33; beyond this came the inactive reserve (*Landsturm*) for those 34-55 years of age. Infantry served two years active with 10 in reserves, cavalry served three active, seven reserve. All fit men not called up were automatically considered *Landsturm* from age 19 to 37; the unfit paid a tax in lieu of service. Men with the necessary educational requirements could serve only one year active if they volunteered, before passing into the reserve. These men often went on to become officers of the reserves. For the regular army special schools had been set up to train under-age males for officers and non-commissioned officers to lead the majority of men whose careers were often only the required two years. In general, Austro-Hungarian officers were well schooled, patriotic, and devoted to their *Kaiser*.

The typical Austro-Hungarian infantryman of 1914 wore an all "pike gray" uniform distinguishable by its distinctly light bluish appearance. His boots, belt, and straps were natural brown leather, as was the visor of his cap. Bosnian troops often wore a "pike gray" fez. Personal equipment included four ammunition pouches, a bayonet, an entrenching tool and a haversack attached to the belt, and a knapsack, greatcoat, tent section, and eating utensils slung over the shoulders. Later, a gas mask and grenades were often carried as well. Armed with a rifle he was ready to march, carrying about 28 kilos (62 lbs). The rifle was usually a Mannlicher M1895 8mm 5-shot piece, though in 1914 there were still many older M88/90s and M90s in service. All these used a steel core bullet with a steel lubricated jacket. Cavalry used the shorter carbine version of these weapons. They compared quite favorably to most infantry weapons of the day. Large numbers of Mausers, domestically produced (under license) for export and other types were used as well.[20]

Officers were often armed with handguns. A wide variety of these were available, everything from small bore automatics to large bore revolvers. Many, especially early in the war, still carried swords as side arms. This practice—like so many others—was soon discontinued. For example, the ancient art of the drummer was an early casualty; at the end of the second month of war drummers surrendered their instruments and were issued rifles.[21]

The old uniform also was discarded. In September 1915 the "pike gray" was replaced by a "field green" model closely resembling the color used by the Germans. After Karl became Emperor in late 1916 he pushed for yet another color—khaki—to be adopted; probably he desired some measure of distinction for his troops who were increasingly mixed with German units and under German command. The initiative was quietly ignored. By that time the Empire had begun to produce its own steel helmet, a design unlike any other then in use. But before long it too was discontinued and production shifted to the German model. Officially this was done to ease production; unofficially German pressure was suspected. The helmet's color at least remained Karl's desired khaki.

A typical Austro-Hungarian infantry division numbered about 15,000 men with 42 to 46 pieces of artillery. As with the forces of other nations it tended to add more specialized troops as time went by so that transfers of this smaller unit might be undertaken with the assurance that it was self-contained, as opposed to having to move a larger unit (Corps, Army) for the same assurance. One source lists a 1918 division as containing 21,765 men, 7281 horses, 112 machine guns, 68 mortars, 46 guns, 34 howitzers and 20 heavy guns/howitzers.[22] Some of the areas of greatest expansion included pioneers (engineers) telegraph, railway, air service, and automobile troops.

Cavalrymen wore more colorful uniforms in the early stages of the war, sported various types of headgear, and still carried swords and lances typical of their particular formations, be they heavy or light cavalry or scouts and reconnaissance troops. A 1914 cavalry division fielded about 7000 men and horses with only one drawn vehicle for every 10 or 11 animals. It also carried a small number of machine guns and dragged 2 dozen or so mostly light artillery pieces.

As did all the war's combatants, Austria-Hungary soon recognized the importance of artillery in the nature of the fighting that developed shortly after the opening shots. From a 1914 compliment of perhaps 2600 pieces the numbers were increased as steadily as industrial output would allow. In this regard the Austrians were not as lacking as it is often believed; their inventory had climbed to well over 4000 within two years and continued to rise until 1918 when serious economic pressures and wartime shortages took their toll. Even so firms like Steyr in upper Austria and Skoda in Bohemia served their Emperor well.

Unique to the Empire's artillery arm was its much higher percentage of mountain guns than any of the other belligerents. These shorter and lighter weapons were often assigned to the cavalry. One excellent model of 75mm weighed only 620 kilos (1365 lbs) but could throw a 6.3 kilo (13.9 lb) shell 7 kilometers (4.3mi). Another 10.4 cm model shot a 15.5 kilo (34.2lb) round 8 kilometers (4.9mi). Regular artillery included 80 and 104 mm field guns and 10 and 15cm field howitzers. Then there were the heavies. A Skoda made 305 mm siege howitzer had to be dismantled and towed in 3 pieces by trucks; a battery of two of these monsters required 20 trucks when all the equipment, supplies, and ammunition were considered. When the 25.5 metric ton (28 ton) weapon was finally on its platform, it could hurl a 384 kilo (846 lb) shell 12 kilometers (7.5 mi)! This "305" was certainly one of the more successful weapons of the war, but Austria produced other, similar ordnance. Nor was she lacking in mortars. Smaller, reasonably portable 12 cm trench types were produced as well as larger units on wheels such as the 22.5 cm and the 24 cm. All in all the artillery, like the rest of the nation's equipment was of good quality.

Austria's choice for a machine gun was the Schwartzlose model 07/12. It was an 8 mm, belt fed, water-cooled device on a tripod mount. Like its Russian counterpart, it could be used with a protective shield, or not. It was a quite reliable weapon, lighter than either the German or Russian models, but slightly less powerful.

In the domain of armored warfare Austria-Hungary contributed the least of any Great Power. No doubt the terrain on two of its three fronts was so unsuitable as to have been a contributing factor in its lack of initiative. But we have seen how involved the Russians became in the manufacture of armored cars, and a similar effort might reasonably have been expected from Vienna/ Budapest. In fact the army had experimented with the idea of armored fighting vehicles in the pre-war years, but no serious production ever resulted. Apparently a few types were built from 1915 on but the numbers must have been very small. No tank production ever materialized either, and it seems that none was ever seriously contemplated. Austria's sole endeavor in the widespread use of armor, then, was limited to outfitting a number of locomotives, as did their enemies, for use on the Eastern Front. These were often armed with naval ordnance[23] and machine guns and could be formidable weapons when not subjected to enemy artillery fire, which could easily destroy the *Ersatz* plate armor.

Naval forces of the Dual Monarchy in 1914 amounted to 6 battleships, 2 armored cruisers, 5 light cruisers, 18 destroyers, 5 dozen torpedo boats and a half-dozen submarines, with a total tonnage of about 350,000. Austria's geographic position precluded its ships engaging those of the Russians.

Not so its air force, which until Italy's intervention was mostly committed in the east. Austria was reported to possess over 350 aircraft in 1914, and 10 dirigibles. However it is unlikely she enjoyed more than 50 planes and one or two airships plus 10 balloons as serviceable when the war began. The air service was organized into Fliegerkompanien (*Flicks*) of eight planes apiece with six active and two in reserve. As the number of *Flicks* increased they began to assume more specialized roles such as reconnaissance, ground attack, bombers and fighters. Gradually the number of *Flicks* in the east increased until early 1918, when the Russian front was ruthlessly denuded of forces for other theaters.

The munitions crisis which so plagued all the warring nations from late 1914 for as much as two years was pretty much under control in Austria-Hungary by autumn 1915; her efficient—if somewhat small—industrial base could fairly well satisfy the needs of the military. Small arms production was only slightly less than Russia's,[24] but hers was the smaller force to equip. And Austria could always expect help from her neighbor-ally. She was also self-sufficient in food, a benefit few others at war enjoyed. All in all, Austria-Hungary was an asset to, and certainly not a liability for, the cause of the *Alliance*. She would raise a total of 78 infantry divisions and twelve cavalry divisions before the war was over. The personnel called to arms reflected the diversity of ethnic groups in the empire: 10% were Latins (Romanians and Italians) the other 90% almost evenly split between the various Slavic groups and the Germans and Hungarians.

All the awesome forces of this great state were formally under the command of Emperor Franz Joseph I but the 84-year-old gentleman had never been a military leader and was well aware that the last two wars his nation had fought with another "Great Power"—while he had been on the throne—ended in defeats. His empire had not won a major battle since 1848 and in some circles was considered to be the next power on the "Sick Man's" list as soon as Ottoman Turkey expired. But he appointed in 1906 a Chief of the General Staff determined to prevent any such eventuality. Franz Conrad von Hötzendorf, a strong advocate of preventative war, had by 1914 eight years in which to plan his nation's strategy and he had done so thoroughly and had even anticipated war against Italy. Now he watched with scarcely concealed delight as his armies mobilized and all the various peoples of the Austro-Hungarian empire enthusiastically demonstrated their support for this defensive war against terrorists and Pan Slavist aggression.

By July 31st mobilization against Russia had become reality, yet only then did von Hötzendorf waiver. He could not decide to which front should be sent the Austrian Second Army. Finally, under pressure from the Emperor and the powerful Hungarian Prime Minister, Count Istvan Tisza, he decided it should go to face the Russians. In the meantime, though, it had already entrained for the Serbian Front in compliance with an earlier order. Because of technical difficulties,[25] it was allowed to complete its journey to the Danube before being sent back to the Russian theater. When it reached its first destination, two of its corps were allowed to be used temporarily against the Serbs while the rest of the Army was sent back north. In the end, only one of the two remaining corps would rejoin the rest of the army, the other remained facing the Serbs. This mishandling of the Second Army was typical of the nature of Austro-Hungarian mobilization. Indeed, it was late August before the Austrian forces to oppose Russia were assembled and organized, and even then their positioning was poor. Anyone looking for a quick move against the Russians before the latter could mobilize was to be sorely disappointed, as they had all in all done a better job than had Hötzendorf. Finally, the Austrian First, Second, Third, and Fourth Armies and some special units were ready to give battle against Russia.

The third Great Power with a major interest in east central Europe was the German Empire. Like Austria-Hungary it shared frontiers with eight other states, and the longest most vulnerable of these with its partner in the Dual Alliance. The only other lengthy border was that with Russia; it too faced a war on two different fronts. But the French border was short and that with Russia about 1000 kilometers (625 miles) of lakes, small rivers, and open plains. Yet, as we have seen, German pre-war planning called for seven-eighths of its army to push westward while the rest, with the Austrians, was expected to hold in the east.

Germany's population by 1914 had reached between 65 and 68 million—second largest behind Russia's in Europe—on a land area of 540,870 sq. km.

65

(208,830 sq mi), third largest on the continent. It was the youngest of the Great Powers and was established only after the French war of 1870-71; even the Kingdom of Prussia dated only from 1701. Germany was a federal state of four Kingdoms, six Grand Duchies, five Duchies, seven principalities, and three free cities plus the *Reichsland* of Alsace-Lorraine which was technically owned by all the others collectively. Prussia was far and away the largest and contained roughly two-thirds of the area and population. It was the only German state to border Russia. By 1914 Germany had become a modern industrial society and a true heavyweight in manufacturing and commerce. Some measure of its strength may be gleaned from the fact that it was one of the only four nations on earth with over 20% of its citizenry living in cities of 100,000 or more residents.[26] We have already seen how it far surpassed Russia and Austria-Hungary in pig iron production and railway mileage per capita. It also possessed the world's second largest navy and a chemical industry second to none. Geographies of the time invariably remark on how clean the streets of the empire were kept, how punctually ran the trains, how conscientiously the laws and rules were obeyed and enforced. It was clearly a nation in step for the common good and it was, unlike Russia or Austria, almost homogenous: at least 93% of the population were proud German speakers. There were relatively small numbers of Danes in North Schleswig, French in Lorraine and Lithuanians around Memel on the Baltic. The largest non-German group were of course the Poles who lived in fairly large numbers in the most easterly provinces, but most of these people were by no means disloyal to the government.

This young, energetic, bustling nation was governed by a *Reichstag* of elected delegates and a *Bundesrat* of representatives of all the Empire's member states which made and approved the laws and could not be vetoed by the Emperor. The latter did, however, appoint the most powerful political figure—the Chancellor—and he was supreme commander of all the armed forces. Germany like Austria was by no means a truly democratic state in the modern sense, but it was certainly not a repressive autocracy like Russia, and most Germans of the time considered themselves to be well governed.

The *Kaiser's* peace time army was 880 thousand strong; on a war footing it could be expected to exceed 4.5 million. During the years 1914-1918 a total of at least 13.5 million men were called to arms and possibly as many as 16 million. Either figure represents a greater military commitment than any other nation. Before she had finished, Germany had raised 246 infantry divisions and 11 cavalry divisions of which 138 and 11, respectively, would see service on the Eastern Front.

Prussia had been the first European state to mandate universal military conscription on her populace and many others had by 1914 long since done so, but in Germany the tradition was unique. Substitution was unknown. It had long been ingrained in the German psyche that service in the armed forces was a privilege and an honor and no self-respecting individual would want to evade it, let along *try* to evade it. As such, criminals and those who had been publicly disgraced were not permitted to serve. Only 2% were exempted for serious family requirements. For the more than one-third who were rejected for health reasons, disappointment or dejection were often the result.

A German male became eligible for service at age 18 (later lowered to 17) and his commitment did not end until age 45. Two years were active—three for cavalry and artillery—and 5 for active Reserve in which he trained for 8 weeks per year (4 years for Cavalry and Artillery). Then he passed into the *Landwehr* for 5 years (three for the others) during which he trained for 2 weeks per year. Then came the second class of *Landwehr* (no training) until age 39, after which he passed into the *Landsturm* until age 45. Untrained men 17-39 were also considered *Landsturm* so they could be trained and used in an emergency. The minimum height for soldiers was 150 cm (5ft. 1 in.), 175 cm (5ft. 7 in.) for elite *Garde* units. Men from well-to-do families often became one year volunteers. They were to equip and clothe themselves and pay for their own lodging and after the year's service passed into the reserve. Medical trainees could do six months active service, then serve as assistant surgeons for six more months. Pharmacists could serve one year or after six months be transferred to the Sanitary Corps (Medical). Naturally many training facilities also existed for careerists, besides the principle Cadet School of the Empire. Located outside Berlin, it and eight others were scattered about Prussia and one more each in Bavaria and Saxony. In addition, there were specialized schools for Cavalrymen and Artillerymen and General Staff including the Great or Imperial General Staff.

All horses within the nation were inspected every 18 months to serve as a basis for requisitions in times of emergency and facilities for such action were numerous: 19 in Prussia, 4 in Bavaria, 3 in Saxony and 1 in Württemberg. In similar fashion, a count of all motor vehicles was kept. The army paid a certain stipend to owners for several years into the life of each vehicle in order to reserve it in case of need. If the need arose within those years, the owner forfeited his machine to the military. In the last full year of peace, 1913, 50,000 autos and light trucks were reported and 7700 heavy trucks. At the beginning of the war 1500 were in reserve.[27]

The typical German infantryman of 1914 wore brown leather boots, calf high, and a *Feldgrau* (Field gray or gray-green) uniform. His headpiece was a black leather spiked helmet with brass trim which identified his home *Land*. He carried the usual slung leather ammunition pouches—120 rounds total—and a knapsack of personal items with a mess tin and greatcoat attached. Attached to his belt were an entrenching tool and bayonet, a water bottle, and a haversack. His weapon was an M1898 Mauser bolt-action 5-shot rifle of 7.92 mm caliber, which fired a steel-core bullet with a copper/nickel alloy jacket. The total burden then borne amounted to about 31 kilos (68 lbs). After the passage of some months, he would also be expected to carry a gas mask and a grenade or two.

As was the case with all his contemporaries, the appearance of the German soldier changed as the war dragged on. From September 1915 the brass on his helmet and belt buckle had been replaced with less scarce metal, six months beyond that he was being issued a modern steel helmet and a new all-arms campaign tunic. The high boots would tend to disappear later, to be replaced by ankle boots with leggings. In 1915 a new Zeiss 3 power scope became available, in limited quantities, for the Mauser. It enabled the German troops to dominate no-mans-land for awhile until the enemy caught on. The Mauser, a sturdy, reliable and powerful weapon also had a shorter carbine version which was used by the cavalry; they, in addition, still carried either a saber or a 225 cm (7ft. 4 in.) steel lance, depending on the type of troops.

A German infantry division of 1914 involved 17,500 men with 3900 horses and 500 wagons, 24 machine guns and 72 field pieces, at least on paper. As battalions per regiment were reduced and new priorities emphasized, these numbers declined and by 1918 were often more like 12,000 men, 1500 horses with 350 vehicles, and perhaps 3 dozen light and one dozen heavy guns, but with 6 dozen mortars and 250 machine guns. The usual transportation and communication as well as several types of engineering formations would of course also have been included. New units such as flame-throwing and tunneling troops also grew out of the engineers.

A cavalry division was necessarily much smaller and in 1914 consisted of 5000-5500 men, perhaps 5500-6000 horses, 80-85 machine guns and 12 field guns.

Germany entered the war with a single machine gun in service, as did most other countries. Her weapon of choice was an M1908 Maxim water-cooled design; its great weight (64 kg, 140 lbs) precluded its use as an offensive tool, but it used the same ammunition as the Mauser rifle and was an excellent, reliable defensive weapon. A later version was much lighter (20 kg, 44 lbs) but was not available until 1917. Meanwhile the Germans had captured large numbers of Danish-made Madsens from the Russians and made extensive use of them. Finally in 1918 there appeared the Schmeisser MP18—the world's first widely used submachine gun—but it arrived too late to be put to general use before the war's end.

Probably the dominant weapon on the battlefields of the Great War was the artillery piece, and it was in the area of artillery that the Germans excelled, and had excelled, since the days of the Franco-Prussian War. "Strong as Krupp steel" was an everyday expression and the premier cannon maker in the world was not going to disappoint. The "French 75" had gotten all the press but Krupp's 7.7mm answer was a better weapon. A newer design, it was lighter—one metric ton to 1.1—and it easily outranged the "75," 9200 yards to 7440.[28] These guns were available in large numbers from early on; each was issued 96 rounds of shrapnel and 42 of high explosive. Also in great quantity were the 105 mm howitzers and these types would soon prove more valuable than field guns when the fighting became static. The 105 was initially issued 90 rounds but the allotment was quickly increased. Germany also possessed a number of big 21 cm howitzers (often referred to as a mortar) and gigantic 42 cm howitzers, the latter the largest non-naval ordnance then in use, nicknamed "Fat Bertha" (fat was the barrel, Bertha the Krupp family matriarch), it weighed 68 metric tons (75 tons) and hurled a one ton shell for 14.2km (8.8 mi). Needless to relate, no fortification could withstand this monster. A 17cm naval gun mounted on a wheeled carriage could also be called upon. Its range: 23.5 kilometers (14.6 miles)! Anti-aircraft units included a modified 77mm field piece and 88mm weapon on a four-wheeled mount.

But the Germans were not just hypnotized by a bigger-is-better mentality; some of their most effective bombardment came from a variety of small and easy to produce devices. A grenade launcher (*Granatenwerfer*) was the product of war-time expediency. The *Minenwerfer* (bomb thrower) was produced before the war and by its outbreak was available in three versions. A light, 7.6cm light mortar hurled a 4.7kg projectile for 1,050 meters; a medium 17cm weapon delivered a 49.5kg projectile to 900 meters; a heavy, 21cm version was capable of firing a 100kg projectile 550 meters. Within two years all three sizes had been updated, their range increased, and were capable of firing chemical ordnance.[29] Enemy troops were often terrorized by the horrific sound of incoming Minenwerfer rounds. Russia had nothing comparable to these weapons. They did constitute wheeled artillery, but were often dismounted and set in trenches.

As a final note on artillery as it pertains to our story, it should be remembered that the traditional battery of 6-77mm guns or 4-105mm howitzers had been reduced in most formations within a year of the war's outbreak to provide units for the burgeoning number of new army subdivisions. It was, of course, a classic example of robbing Peter to pay Paul. Hence within the calendar year of 1916, new field artillery batteries numbering 801-915 were raised and sent to bolster the existing divisional weaponry on the Eastern Front.[30]

To feed the chambers of an ever growing number of weapons large and small, Germany's industries, greatest in Europe, were by 1916 straining and sputtering to meet the demand. With every able-bodied male needed at the front and the British naval blockage barring importation of necessary raw materials, serious manpower and material shortages constantly bedeviled the Germans, who also were expected to materially assist the other nations of the *Alliance*. By making use of available labor in occupied districts and by developing a whole host of *Ersatz* products to replace those previously made from unavailable materials, the German economy somehow staggered through crisis after crisis. Non-military production was curtailed and living standards suffered, but the necessary war material was churned out in generally increasing quantities. Krupp alone made exemplary efforts to replace ammunition. According to one serious study of the firm, it replaced more than 900 field guns and 200 light howitzers in the first year of war. A new munitions plant delivered 8,000,000 shells during the second year, and by the third, an astonishing 9,000,000 shells and 3000 guns were being produced. And all this was achieved, it claims, without a reduction of quality in the products.[31] Every German soldier carried or had access to, in the company or regimental pool, almost 400 rounds for his rifle; machine guns disposed of 12,000 rounds each, artillery pieces 470 and howitzers 305 shells each (including divisional pool). It was not a steady, sustained growth—most target figures were never attained—but the armed forces were well served until the last year of the war when food and munitions shortages began to markedly affect morale.

Lack of a powerful navy was no issue for Germany; hers was second only to Britain's in 1914. With 37 battleships, 5 battle cruisers, 40 light or armored cruisers, 90 destroyers, well over 100 torpedo boats and 30 submarines it was a force to reckon with. Total tonnage afloat or in construction exceeded 1.3 million tons. Her strategic position dictated Germany remain on the defensive in the west, but no fleet was going to sail the Baltic if she disapproved; by making use of the Kiel Canal the Jutland Peninsula could be bypassed and a German force in the North Sea would become a Baltic threat within hours. And it was on an arm of the Baltic where lay the Russian capital.

Well before the war the Germans had recognized the value of military aircraft and had organized flying sections at major towns and cities near the potentially hostile frontiers. Numerical strength is much disputed; as many as 40 dirigibles and 1000 airplanes have been claimed. Serviceable aircraft in use is of course another matter. One source listing combat-ready airplanes shows: 250 in 8/14, 800 in 10/15, 1550 in 10/16, 2270 in 3/17, 3970 in 3/18, and 2710 in 11/18.[32] At first, aircraft were used only for observation of the enemy, but soon enough, as in all other countries, fighter sections appeared. Other types of groups created included liaison, artillery spotters, reconnaissance, ground attack, pursuit, and others. Naval aviation was similarly expanded and specialized.

As we have seen, once war was declared seven eighths of German military might was loaded onto trains—thousands of them—and sent to the western frontiers to assemble for the attack upon France. With this huge force traveled Count Helmuth von Moltke, the Chief of the Imperial General Staff. Only one army, the 8th, railed eastward to stall the "Russian steamroller" while the projected six-week campaign was undertaken. Moltke may have been facing westward, but like a wary pedestrian on a dark street he could not contain a frequent backward glance. The danger was obvious. His doubts, and those of all concerned Germans that August could be summed up as two burning questions: How soon would the Russians attack? Could 8th army hold them? The answers were about to be delivered.

Chapter Four
The Initial Battles

So it had come to war. Three of the world's greatest powers now faced off along a sprawling, irregular line across eastern Europe. Even as the crow flies, the distance along the Russo-German seam was 885km (550mi), another 725km (450mi) were exposed along the Austro-Russian portion. This vast landscape would now have to be defended, or at least watched, lest an enemy force burst through and stab at the vital points.

The vital points were, naturally, major population centers or industrial locations and the transportation facilities by which they connected with, and were tied into, the economy of the nation. Disruption or occupation of an enemy's source of strength is a cardinal mission of military strategy. In 1914 this meant, in effect, controlling or destroying the railroads, that intricate network of steel which linked all cities and important towns with sources of goods and raw materials and with seaports or waterways. It was by rail that most urban and manufacturing areas—and armies—were fed and supplied.

As early as the 1850s rail transportation had superceded the horse and wagon as the primary means of movement on land, and in every conflict since the American Civil War the rail had figured in the decision. Railroad expansion finally peaked in the first decade of the 20th century. Then the rails settled into a slow decline as they were gradually replaced by rubber tires driven by an internal combustion engine. Nevertheless, in 1914 the automobile was still too unreliable, too underpowered. The locomotive was still supreme.

It is hardly surprising, then, that railroads became, and remained, primary objects of military strategy throughout the war. They alone were capable of supplying armies or of quickly transferring units to sectors where they were most needed. From the moment of the war's outbreak they were to figure immeasurably in its conduct. The Austro-Hungarians, and especially the Germans, possessed an intricate rail network constructed with the thoroughness of a spider web, so as to leave no areas without service. Many lines deliberately followed the frontier—but at a safe distance behind—as to serve a military purpose. Nothing of the sort existed in Russia, where the border areas were deliberately neglected in a backward-looking effort to discourage invasion.

Moreover, few railways crossed the frontier. For one thing the gauge was different; Russian rails were wider apart than the rest of Europe. Another reason was the pitifully low Russian living standards and subsequent lack of low level commerce. Only three main lines crossed into East Prussia, one into Posen and one into upper Silesia. A mere three more crossed into Austrian Galicia. These and all border crossings were sealed off as soon as the telegrams announcing the declaration of war arrived, but no one on either side of the line doubted that any serious enemy action would easily sweep aside the border guards.

In the event, it was the Russians who struck first. Squadron-sized and larger groups of Russian cavalry, eager for action, mounted and galloped to the frontier, scattering German sentries. One group at the extreme western tip of Congress Poland—and the closest location in all Russia to Berlin at 290km (180mi)—forded the border stream the Prosna River, and reached the railway bridge over the Warthe on a main north-south line. This structure they duly attacked, but were driven off. On the same day, August 2nd, another group clashed with defenders at Prostken, a border town near the southeastern tip of East Prussia, but were reversed before they could destroy any of the track of that, the Königsberg-Bialystok line. A third force of Russians made for the Johannisburg/Bialla area where a main line runs close to the border and cut communications with Lyck to the east and began ripping up rails.

The German response was hardly slower. Already during the night of the 2nd/3rd a command of Uhlans (light cavalry) under a young officer occupied the town of Kieltze, Russian Poland. The officer's name was Manfred von Richtofen and his deed would not be his most notorious in this war. Then, on the morning of the 3rd, *Landwehr* troops advanced into Poland and seized the city of Kalisz on the Russian side of the Prosna, and the railroad junction towns of Czestochowa and Bendzin near the industrial district of upper Silesia. The Russians tried to neutralize the effect of the latter action by blowing up the bridge over the Brinitze River which formed the border at that point, connecting German Schoponitz with Russian Sosnowice. They also advanced along the

Warsaw-Danzig line past Illowo and along the line which paralleled the Vistula towards Thorn. Russians further north entered Eydkuhnen and Bildeweitschen inflicting damage and causing considerable alarm.

At sea the Germans drew first blood when the cruiser *Magdeburg*, sailing off Courland, turned landward and shelled the port city of Libau, Russia's southernmost on the Baltic. Having set fire to the docking facilities, *Magdeburg* desisted while another cruiser, *Augsburg*, laid mines in the vicinity.[33] This occurred early on the 2nd, and was probably the first action of the war.

By the 5th Russian cavalry were again harassing Prussian localities; in the east Lyck was attacked; farther west it was the turn of Soldau, both on major railroads. The latter place was outflanked when the Russians swam yet another border stream and took Grotken, but without sufficient forces the invaders could not succeed, and withdrew. The next day a stiff fight developed at Eydkuhnen again; it lay on the single most important railroad in the province: the main line from Königsberg and the seacoast to Kovno and the Russian hinterland. The town was successfully defended.

Meanwhile the primary forces were hastily assembling. The Russian 9th army, at the eleventh hour ordered to Warsaw, began detraining there on August 7th. Along the periphery of East Prussia, the first hysterical reports of Russian behavior were coming in; these predated the Belgian stories by a week or so and may have in fact inspired them, or at least some of them. Enemy soldiers were behaving outrageously, burning, looting, raping. Many of the Belgian cases were later disproved; most of the East Prussian cases were not. At any rate, after the first week or so of war Prussian civilians would regularly flee at the approach of the enemy, willingly accepting the uncertain plight of refugees to what they believed was certain mistreatment at the hands of the Russians. While East Prussia burned and quivered under the realities of war, thousands of fleeing residents clogged the roads with wagonloads of possessions and multitudes of livestock.

Perhaps nowhere else in the world in 1914 could one cross an international boundary and step into such a different atmosphere. On the German side of the border were cozy, tidy farmhouses amidst well-drained, well-worked fields. Neat, clean little villages and towns were connected by smooth, graveled roads. Waterways were often channeled; woods were well pruned and devoid of deadwood and undergrowth. Both small farms and larger estates abounded; larger towns and cities appeared completely modern, totally functional. On the Russian side, the opposite prevailed. Roads were often simply wagon tracks on the ground, not negotiable in muddy conditions. Woods were tangled, trackless growths lacking wood roads. Small streams might appear many meters wide in swampy, sluggish courses. Farmhouses had no floors; dwellings in towns and villages were often dilapidated, unpainted structures. When Russian troops advanced into East Prussia that summer and autumn they could hardly believe what they saw: A hitching post in front of every house, a well in the yard, perhaps a piano in the parlor! Some wanted to loot, others wanted to destroy that which they envied, but mostly they came away with a feeling that the enemy represented a wealthy, advanced society of plenty. From out of the first weeks of war grew the ominous feelings of inferiority of *materiel.*

The probing continued by both sides until mid-August. The Germans were more concerned with covering the open spaces in Poland—they occupied Wielun beyond the upper Prosna on the 5th—and concentrated on repairing the railways that had been damaged early on. The Russians still had their gaze fixed on Prussia. On the 9th they pushed over the border again, this time from the east at mid-province. Marggrabowa was taken then burned and evacuated three days later under German pressure. In the Baltic, the cruiser *Magdeburg* shelled a lighthouse on Dägo Island on the same day. All these were minor actions, but behind the scenes *Stavka* was assembling four entire armies which could be used against East Prussia: The one mentioned at Warsaw plus the Second along the Narew, the First due east of the frontier and the Sixth along the Baltic Coast.

Four more were forming about Galicia where the Austrians were already stirring. The Eighth (Brusilov) would face the Zbruch, the Third (Ruski) at Rovno/Lutsk, the Fifth (Plehve) around the upper Bug, and the Fourth (Zalts) around Lublin. Command of this powerful Army Group—the Southwest Front[34]—was entrusted to General Ivanov. A roughly equivalent force under the Archduke Frederick was assembling to oppose it. First army (Dankl) collected behind the lower San, Fourth Army (Auffenberg) along the upper San, and Third Army (Brudermann) around Lemberg. Two other "Groups" of about corps strength and named for their commanders assembled on the flanks. The Kövess Group covered the Zbruch and the Kummer Group guarded the Cracow area. Kummer sent a force raiding into Russian Poland;

elements of it had penetrated nearly as far as the city of Kielce, when on the 15th, following a brief but bitter engagement, they were turned back.

The problem for the *Alliance* with regards to Galicia was, as a glance at the map could reveal, that the province formed a sort of partial circle facing northeast. Any advance from the circle in more than one direction would tend to separate the advancing forces even farther apart as they proceeded. By contrast, forces moving in from the far side of the circle would tend to converge as they moved in, thus favoring the Russians. As East Prussia presented a similar problem, the Germans had long since shelved the idea of any movement in cooperation with their allies designed to sever Poland from Russia, a decision which annoyed von Hötzendorf. Undeterred, he remained committed to the right hook from Galicia even without cooperation. By August 11th Dankl reported he was ready to move and his vanguard crossed the frontier near the lower San River. To divert the enemy's attention, Kövess was instructed to raid far to the east. Deploying along the border stream—the river Zbruch—with infantry, he threw his cavalry across the river and attacked the Russian town of Gorodok several kilometers distant. This attack was beaten off, but a larger force splashed through the stream and advanced on the small city of KamenetsPodolsk, which was taken on August 17th. The commander of the Russian Eighth Army later wrote that he declined to parry this thrust in the belief that he would simply outflank it when he began his own advance a day later. KamenetsPodolsk was indeed abandoned by the Austrians on the 19th, but not before they returned the entire ransom they had coerced from its citizens.[35] Meanwhile, Dankl, having advanced only a few miles, halted and waited for his neighbor Auffenberg to move.

In East Prussia events were now moving quickly. The Russian First (Rennenkampf) and Second (Samsonov) Armies were ready for action. Grouped into the Northwest Front under General Zhilinsky, their task was to pinch off the exposed German province from the east and south. Rennenkampf was ready first. Urged on by Zhilinsky who was being prodded by *Stavka*, which in turn was being bombarded with frantic appeals from the French for quick action, he began his march on the 16th.

For far longer than anyone could remember the frontiers of East Prussia had remained constant. The Polish borders might change like the seasons but the outline of East Prussia outdated the oldest geographies or historical atlases. It had survived Polish overlordship and the demise of the Teutonic Order without having wide rivers or mountain ranges to set it apart from the surrounding countryside. Yet as we have seen it was a distinct social entity and from the air its outline could be detected. Covered fairly well by small streams which did not appear on most maps, the remaining line was etched into the earth in the form of a ditch: the German farmers would channel the edges of their fields to provide excellent drainage; therefore the ditches extended only to the edge of German-owned land. Where the line traversed a forest it was still recognizable by a forester's path or wood road on the Prussian side, and a difference in the size and quality of the trees was usually noticeable. Only a few kilometers east of this manmade and natural divide the Russian First Army had detrained and fanned out on a 65km (40mi) front. The center, of course, spanned the Königsberg railroad. Its three infantry corps spanned three-quarters of its front, with cavalry on both flanks extending from the Forest of Rominten in the south to the Schshuppe River in the north. During the night of August 16/17th, the advance scouts crossed the ancient Prussian frontier.

By now the main body of the German Eighth Army was in position astride the railroad in the Gumbinnen area, only a short distance in advance of the *Angerapp Stellung*, a prepared series of fortifications along the river of that name which flowed north out of the main Masurian Lakes to the city of Insterburg on the railroad. Its commander, Lieutenant General Max von Prittwitz und Gaffron, intended to fight an initial battle in advance of the defensive positions and then withdraw behind them, but the commander of his left wing was eager for a fight and moved his troops as far east as Pilkallen where it came into contact with elements of the Russian right on the 17th.

The Russian cavalry on First Army's right had in the early morning hours crossed the streams which formed the border, the Schshuppe and the Schirwindt, captured the town at their junction[36] and ridden off into the countryside. They might have flanked the exposed Germans in Pilkallen but in fact played little part in the main action of the 17th, the so-called Battle of Stallupönen, during which the gung-ho commander of the German left, General Hermann von Francois, satisfied his need to engage the enemy. The whole affair was a confused, undisciplined action as a war's first battle is apt to be, but the Germans in the end withdrew, though they claimed 3,000 prisoners.

Both army commanders were somewhat shaken by events on the 17th. Rennenkampf appealed to Zhilinsky to prod Samsonov; the former had already instructed the latter to have Second Army cross the border on the 19th.

Prittwitz, for his part, decided to order an attack on the 20th; if one of his Corps could slow the Russians, perhaps the whole army could stop them. The next two days were pretty much wasted as Rennenkampf inched forward and Prittwitz perused constant reports from aviators, scouts, reconnaissance troops, and intelligence reports. The Russians could afford to waste time. The Germans could not; everyday brought the Russian Second Army nearer their supply lines to the west.

The German attack of August 20th took the Russians by surprise, partly due to a night movement through woods, partly because Rennenkampf's intelligence was faulty and his cavalry were not keeping in routine contact. The result was an initial German success, Francois again playing the role he relished, but by midday the steadfast Russian infantry were holding their own. Mackensen's Corps was roughly handled in a frontal assault; the German right, attacking only at noon, achieved little. Sporadic fighting went on until darkness stopped it. Russian losses reached 17,000 men. German losses were comparable, they having suffered terribly at the hands of the Russian artillery. Most importantly for Rennenkampf, he had won the field, forced the enemy to retreat and taken 2,000 prisoners and a number of artillery pieces.

Perhaps the most significant casualty of this Battle of Gumbinnen was the nervous system of Prittwitz. Having been forced to endure the breakup of his attack he now received the ominous news he had been dreading: Samsonov's army, aiming at his rear, would begin crossing the frontier on the 21st. Before long he was informing the high command of his predicament and decision: withdrawal to the lower Vistula which itself, he claimed, might not be able to be defended.

Moltke was aghast. To withdraw to the Vistula meant to abandon all of East Prussia and part of West Prussia too, abandon tens of thousands of square kilometers with all their resources to say nothing of the population, most of whom would become helpless refugees. Moltke's response was to sack Prittwitz and appoint Ludendorff, a talented officer who had already made somewhat of a name for himself on the Western Front, to replace him. A retired member of the nobility, General Paul von Hindenburg und von Beneckendorf would become the figurehead commander of Eighth Army. Rennenkampf decided to regroup after Gumbinnen, and by the time he began to move again—on the 23rd—the new duo had arrived on the scene and Eighth Army's Chief Operations Officer had already conceived a new plan with which to greet them.

Samsonov's Second Army had begun to advance at the same time as the First Army, but its railheads were much farther from the frontier, on the Narew River. His left had the farthest to march; high right-hand Corps had been put under First Army command. It faced the main Masurian Lakes and would need to force the narrow fortified defiles between them in order to make contact with its comrades to the west. But after Gumbinnen it was ordered north to skirt the north edge of Lake Mauer and thus left the flank of First Army far removed from the Second. At least the left wing had the Warsaw/Danzig railroad to advance along; the right and center traversed an area of sandy, stunted pine woods with few roads. Even so, the Russian right began to cross the border on August 21st.

While the Russian Northwest Front was about to do or die in Prussia, Southwest Front was receiving mixed signals. Brusilov's Eighth Army began its crossing of the Zbruch on the 18th; under Austro-Hungarian fire, the maneuver would take three days. Russki's Third Army, advancing from the Lutsk/Dubno area first reached Galician soil on the 20th. Hitherto Galicia had been spared the early cavalry raids Prussia had been subjected to. Austria's decision to delay her declaration of war played some part, the knowledge that Galicia would be well defended, another. On Russki's extreme left the Russian Tenth Cavalry Division was advancing when it was suddenly struck by the Fourth Austro-Hungarian Cavalry Division of Brudermann's Army as it approached the Tarnopol-Lemberg Railroad east of Zborov at a small Galician town called Jaroslawice. In a day-long, wild, old-fashioned slash and stab engagement, on August 21st, both sides acquitted themselves well until the appearance of Russian infantry compelled the Austrians to withdraw. A decade and a half later this Battle of Jaroslawice would be remembered as the "Last Cavalry Battle of World History"[37] by two European authors.

At this time both sides were about equally strong. Hötzendorf's decision to push north with his left (First and Fourth Armies) upset the applecart; they were advancing into two Russian Armies (Fourth and Fifth). Once Auffenberg's Fourth had moved up to cover his right, Dankl and First Army moved out of the wooded hills of the border area and pushed north onto the open plain beyond. On August 23rd, Dankl crashed headlong into Zalt's Fourth Army thus beginning a three-day slugfest centering on the city of Krasnik. In the melee that ensued, the Austrians, somewhat more numerous and enjoying more accurate artillery support, finally broke Zalt's will and he retreated to the north. This prudent action cost him his job; Ivanov replaced him with General Evert, who was told to defend Lublin and promised assistance from Ninth Army. Dankl's drive finally was halted by the 26th, only 17.5 kilometers (11 mi) south of Lublin and both sides, exhausted in the heat and dust, warily surveyed each other. On the same day began an engagement between Auffenberg's Fourth Austrian Army and the Russian Fifth under Plehve only a short distance to the east. Auffenberg had been much slower to move than Dankl; consequently his opponent was pretty much ready for him as he crossed the border, although Plehve had been ordered to pivot to the west to support Zalts and did not expect an army-strength opponent. The resulting battle around Tomaszow was a confused, uncoordinated fight amongst untested troops in wooded country. By the 27th fighting had spread as far east as the River Bug; an Austrian cavalry division was scattered, and an infantry division broken near Laszczow. Heavy battles developed in the center of the line around the town of Komorow, from which the whole mess was named. Before it was over the most westerly Corps of Brudermann's Army had to be diverted to the Sokal area to take Plehve in his left flank (August 28th); the strategy was foiled when the Corps commander, after two days of relative success, pulled back his forces, fearful of a threat to his own flank. Auffenberg's left had been preparing to wheel east to join with the troops driving west, but when the latter halted the former also quit, and instead reached out toward First Army in order to create a continuous front between the Vistula and the Bug. An opportunity to surround Fifth Army was thus lost. Instead, Brudermann, weakened by the loss of his left hand Corps, was now in trouble.

The Austro-Hungarian Third Army formed up around the provincial capital of Lemberg. With Kovess defending the border area, General Brudermann had no intention of advancing beyond the most convenient defensive position to the east. Here, a series of small rivers flow due north-south to the Dniester at fairly regular intervals to the Zbruch and beyond. From Lemberg east there flowed the Gnila Lipa, Zlota Lipa, Strypa, and Seret before the frontier line. All these gouged out deep trenches in the plateau, and all were separated by rows of hills; in sum, Galicia was defensible from an eastern attack by simply making good use of the natural obstacles. Brudermann chose to defend the line of the Zlota Lipa, perhaps the best defile of the bunch, and was in good position long before Brusilov approached from due east. The problem after his left Corps had been sent west was that now his own left flank was exposed. The semicircle of Galicia now figured in the campaign: Into the gaping hole between Third and Fourth Armies now marched General Russki's Third Russian Army.

Russki moved very slowly at first but as we have seen crossed the border on the 20th and captured Brody on the railroad to Lemberg after a minor engagement with weak enemy forces on the 22nd. By now Brusilov had routed Kovess's widely dispersed troops and entered the important city of Tarnopol on the 23rd. A running battle then developed as the defenders contested the broken terrain of east Galicia back to the main defense line at Brzezany on the Zlota Lipa. The hard battle for this river line commenced on the 26th. Next day the Russian commanders received good news: elements of the Third and Eighth Armies had linked up on the Tarnopol-Lemberg railroad after defeating the enemy in the Zloczow-Zborow area. On the 28th, Brudermann's army, outnumbered badly and terribly battered on the Zlota Lipa, fell back to the Gnila Lipa. Third Army reached Busk on the upper Bug. If Lemberg were to be defended, Brudermann could retreat no more. If the Austrians could boast of victories at Krasnik and Komorow, they had paid a heavy price—eastern Galicia—to achieve them. While the enemy had been chased off the front porch, the side door had been kicked in.

Meanwhile, out on the Baltic *Magdeburg* and *Augsburg* continued their devilish duties. Once it was realized that the Russians would not contest the coast of Courland, the German cruisers moved north and were joined by some smaller craft torpedo boats and minelayers. This small fleet received a scare on August 17th when two Russian cruisers were detected emerging from the Gulf of Riga. But the Russians apparently wanted no confrontation, and withdrew whereupon the Germans continued on. They intended to mine areas of the Gulf of Finland and help bottle up the main Russian Baltic Fleet there. All went well until the 26th when *Magdeburg* ran aground, in heavy fog, off Odensholm Island near the Estonian coast. Despite desperate efforts to free it, *Magdeburg* had to be abandoned: the surrounding waters were too treacherous for larger vessels to close properly. The crew hastily destroyed what they could and were taken aboard an accompanying destroyer under Russian naval fire. A seemingly minor episode, this event was actually very important for the *Entente*. A search of the ship discovered, undestroyed, the code books of the German Admiralty. Soon in the hands of British cryptanalysts, they would play a critical role in the naval war against the *Alliance*.

While critical events were unfolding in the Baltic and in Galicia, events in East Prussia came to a head during the last week in August. We left Samsonov crossing the frontier against generally light opposition; only one German Corps defended the entire line from the main Masurian Lakes to the River Drewenz. The Germans made good use of aircraft and were well informed of enemy movements. When Russians encountered more than token resistance they brought up artillery and opened fire and many Prussian towns were destroyed this way. Often buildings would catch afire after a few rounds and in the dry August heat the flames spread easily. By the day's end on August 22nd, Russian soldiers patrolled Niedenburg, Ortelsburg, Soldau, and Willenburg and dozens of smaller towns and villages. Thousands of German refugees fled towards larger cities still beyond the reach of the enemy.

Long before the arrival—on the evening of the 23rd—of Hindenburg and Ludendorff, the Executive Operations Officer of Eighth Army had devised a new set of priorities for the defense of the province. His plan called for disengaging the cautious Rennenkampf at the *Angerapp Stellung* and moving the bulk of Eighth Army far to the southwest, to engage Samsonov, who now represented the greater threat. The officer was Colonel Max Hoffmann, a tall, stiff, poker-faced very Prussian-looking presence. He was a pure professional and not prone to excitement. He had been acquainted with Ludendorff and was able to persuade the latter to concur with his plan. Immediately the efficient German railway network was working overtime, as unit by unit Eighth Army was carried to confront Second Army. Now only a thin cavalry screen remained to shadow Rennenkampf, who finally began to move forward again, taking Insterburg—and thus forcing the *Angerapp*—on the 23rd. Rennenkampf would continue to advance now every day for a week without serious opposition. He moved cautiously, many have said too cautiously, but he had been attacked twice already and he was not well served with intelligence reports. By the 27th he had made contact with the outer defenses of the "fortress" of Königsberg but bypassed these and continued east for two more days before events to the south forced his halt. By then he had reached Bartenstein and his forward cavalry had ridden as far as Wormditt, 38km (24mi) beyond!

Once Rennenkampf began advancing into a vacuum, Zhilinski urged Samsonov on and suggested that Second Army begin to move more northerly instead of northwesterly in order to take the obviously retreating Germans in flank before they could escape behind the Vistula. Samsonov disliked this idea—the Vistula lay to the west—but he agreed that Allenstein needed to be taken; two of his five Corps would head north. One reached Bischofsburg on the 25th and a day or so later the other fought its way into Allenstein. This was the closest the two armies of Northwest Front would be to each other and had they only known how little was the distance the entire Masurian Lakes area might have been encircled by a juncture near Rastenburg within a day or two. But Samsonov had just paid a heavy price to smash through the defenses around Orlau/Frankenau and he believed the enemy to be beaten. A line Gilgenburg-Lautenburg was reached before he realized his mistake.

As early as the morning of the 24th. Francois's Corps was already detraining at Deutsch Eylau. Ludendorff ordered an attack for the 25th but the usually rambunctious Francois chose to stall while more of his artillery could arrive. Following a visit by Eighth Army command he half-heartedly attacked on the 26th, a day the entire Second Army was on the move. By this time Mackensen's and Below's Corps had completed a 32km (20mi) march to join battle near Bischofsburg and August 26th was a day of heavy fighting all along the line amidst the lakes, woods, and potato fields of the morainic *Masurenland*. German artillery tended to outclass its Russian opponent; in close fighting the Russian infantry tended to prevail. Ludendorff feared his hard pressed line would be penetrated in the center where the original defenders were by now tiring after several days of combat. The remainder of Eighth Army could not arrive too soon.

There was other help on the way. On the 25th, Moltke at supreme headquarters had made an historic decision: reinforce the east from the west. Under great pressure considering the plight of thousands of refugees, the energetic pleas for salvation from the owners of the large estates, and an appeal from the president of the East Prussian Bundesrat to defend his homeland,[38] as one historian relates, Moltke detached two Corps and a cavalry division from the French campaign for the Russian Front. Eighth Army was notified by telephone. The war in the east was already affecting that in the west. Of course, these reinforcements would not arrive in time to affect the desperate fighting in Masuria or Galicia. But by the morning of August 27th Samsonov's army had reached its maximum penetration of Prussian territory.

At 4:00am on the morning of the 27th the roar of artillery on the Russian left heralded the commencement of Francois's main attack, directed primarily at

Usdau on the main railroad running due north. Other attacks pinned the Russian center and drove in the right. Counterattacks faltered in the smoke-and-dust shrouded forests. The seesaw fighting favored the Germans; they were fighting on their own soil and enjoyed better artillery and at least some air support. Mackensen and Below closed in from the northeast. Before the day was done Soldau and Neidenburg were German again. Ludendorff wanted Francois to limit his right hook but the aggressive Francois once again displayed a knack for a liberal interpretation of orders and pressed on. A day later the whole confused issue had basically been decided; the Germans had cut off the Russian retreat. Francois's thin line was at first very vulnerable and some hard fighting was yet to be done, but when the Germans reached Willenburg on the 29th, the outcome was bound to be bad for Samsonov. Over the next two days frantic attempts by the Russian center to fight its way out weakened, then faltered altogether. Mackensen closed in on the Russian right and although a relieving force temporarily recaptured Niedenburg on the 30th, a day later it had been driven off.

For the encircled Russians existed only two alternatives: surrender or try to escape through the woods in small groups. For those selecting the latter, some were successful, others not. Samsonov himself chose death[39] to surrender. Some Russians surrendered after a token fight, others without one. Sporadic shooting echoed throughout the broken countryside on the 31st, but when the dust finally settled and the smoke cleared German forces counted over 90,000 prisoners and 350 artillery pieces. Thousands more bodies were strewn everywhere; some even floated among the numerous lakes and ponds. Eighth Army admitted a loss of 13,500 men—a figure no doubt deliberately low—but there could be no doubt Germany had won a spectacular victory.

Once the German commanders had given the battle a suitable name—Hoffmann was probably most responsible—an explosion of publicity echoed all over Germany and thus the legends of Tannenburg were born in the minds of the imaginative and repeated as with the dutiful routine of the patriot. Most of these myths have thankfully since been dispelled: Hindenburg, having made a lifelong study of the topography of East Prussia, had preplanned the battle to the last detail; Second Army had perished in the marshes with entire battalions drowning in the awful quicksands; the despoiled sacred soil of the Teutonic Knights had been cleared of the Asiatic hordes. But other more serious misconceptions were born of Tannenburg (the Russians called the battle Allenstein). Russian personnel, especially at the senior level, began to develop an inferiority complex that would eventually trickle down to the lowest levels. On the other hand Ludendorff, as one historian has noted, became convinced of his own military genius and discovered that large numbers of Germans were ready to agree with him.[40] At the beginning of the month of September, as the remnants of the Russian Second Army staggered back to the Narew, the Germans could now turn on Rennenkampf, who was slowly closing in from the northeast.

Even as the German press whipped the nation into a frenzy over the new savior Hindenburg and the outcome of the fighting in Masuria, the issue in Galicia was still in doubt. As we have seen, the Austrian Fourth Army missed its own opportunity for an encirclement of the Russian Fifth Army at the very same time that the initiative of Francois and Mackensen was yielding great results. If the movement around Krasnik and Komorow had stalled the Austrians they were at least content in the knowledge that Kummer's group on their extreme left was advancing, mostly without opposition, into the vast no-man's-land beyond the Vistula. Kummer's force was small and mostly cavalry, and it easily penetrated the void of central Poland and took the larger localities of Kielce and Radom by month's end.

By now the principal force in Galicia, the linked Russian Third/Eighth Armies, had advanced to the main Austrian defense line on the Gnila Lipa. Brudermann's force was daily being augmented by piecemeal arrivals of Second Army units from beyond the Carpathians. By an efficient act of indecision, Hötzendorf at the beginning of the war had initially sent Second Army to the Balkan Front, and then reversed himself when he realized the force in Galicia was inadequate. Most of the month of August had therefore been a train ride for Second Army, and at last its units would see action. They would soon wish they had not.

Ordered to attack from the Gnila Lipa position the fresh (and green) troops advanced into a hail of artillery and small arms fire on the 29th. Next day it was the Russians' turn; the hills littered with thousands of blue-uniformed Austrian dead and hundreds of horses were negotiated by the soldiers of the *Czar* who then broke through the river line behind a powerful bombardment. Many defenders fled to the west but others—as many as 20 or more thousand—were captured, with 75 field pieces.

The road to Lemberg, the Galician capital, was now wide open. Brudermann had no intention of trying to defend it; he would retreat to the

Grodek position, a chain of lakes along another Dniester tributary west of Lemberg. Hötzendorf did not interfere; he would trade Lemberg for time to execute yet another scheme, a flank attack by Fourth Army which would set things straight. When Russki's troops, spread out in an arc from the upper Gnila Lipa to the volcanic hills west of Busk, began to advance, they encountered no resistance but rear guard actions. Brusilov, for his part, arrived on the Dniester at the confluence of the Gnila Lipa at Halicz on August 31ˢᵗ and prepared to cross the stream and seize the town. The Austrians made a stubborn resistance around the village of Botszonce. Following the battle the condition of the tortured, churned-up earth, which was littered with shell fragments, human fragments and all sorts of military debris was testimony to how awful the conflict had been.[41] A day later the Austrian line broke and the remnants fled over the steel-girder bridge which was destroyed before the Russians could prevent it. The latter had already begun to prepare a pontoon crossing; before it could be used the Austrians had evacuated Halicz, and by the time of the fall of Lemberg, Brusilov was over the Dniester.

Lemberg was an important political and strategic prize. Fourth largest city in all Austria-Hungary it was a rail center and a munitions depot. Founded in 1259 it had generally been governed by Poles until the 1772 partition transferred it to Austria. Since that time an influx of Germans had somewhat transformed its character, but the population for the most part was Ukrainian. An occupation by Russia was an idea not particularly upsetting to the inhabitants who were in the event rather courted by the Russian policy. Russki reached the outskirts of the place on September 1ˢᵗ then reconnoitered an abandoned defense for 36 hours before cautiously approaching. On the 3ʳᵈ, Grand Duke Nicholas reported to the *Czar*. "With extreme joy and thanking God, I announce to your Majesty that the victorious army under General Russki captured Lemberg at eleven o'clock this morning."[42] The Grand Duke would appoint a certain General Count Bobrinsky governor-general of the "reunited" (with Russia[?]) province who in turn renamed the capital (Lvov) and subjected the citizenry to a host of speeches designed to convince them that they were really Russians.

Only now did Russki respond—with any enthusiasm—to Ivanov's demands that he turn his army to the northwest, to assist Fifth Army. Now a situation had developed in which Russki's army was directed, unknowingly, into the path of Auffenberg's Fourth Army, which had been ordered by Hötzendorf to take the conquerors of Lemberg in flank.

In the north Dankl had been reinforced with a German *Landwehr* Corps. He made one last effort to break through to Lublin in the early days of the month, only to be stopped cold; the Russian Ninth Army had arrived to reinforce the Fourth and replace the departing Fifth. Now Ivanov launched an offensive of his own, on September 4th, and for the next few days the towns of Tomaszow, Krasnostaw, and Sukhodoly so recently taken by Austrians were back in the news as locations of bitter fighting and Russian breakthroughs. Ninth Army overwhelmed the *Landwehr* Corps and forced its rout over the Vistula and battered Dankl's men as well. Fourth Army advanced too, and only with the greatest difficulty was Dankl able to prevent the ensuing retreat from becoming a panic-stricken rout.

While this action commenced north of the San, Auffenberg and Russki collided northwest of Lemberg, beginning a series of engagements known as the Battle of Rawa-Russka. A more confusing series of maneuvers is hard to imagine. Both commanders lacked worthwhile intelligence, but in the event it probably would not have mattered; neither had a plan, neither had expected a major struggle here. Enormous clouds of dust, churned up by hundreds of thousands of feet and hooves added to the misery of the heat and the smothering effect of smoke from millions of discharged rounds of ammunition and hundreds of structures in flames. The fires in turn lit up the night sky sufficiently for the fighting to continue after dark. No doubt Auffenberg was loath to lose the town as it was home to large railroad facilities and warehouses. Plehve, encouraged by good news from his neighbors north and south, kept up his attacks. Indeed it was events on the flanks that decided the battle after several days of mayhem; the Austrians were obliged to withdraw by the 11th. Thus the engagement in which Austrians shuddered to remember such locales as the Valley of Death, Hell's Ten Acres, and the Leaden Stubble Field, was over. But it left another, bitter memory. Many Austro-Hungarians were captured at Rawa-Russka, including a large number of Czech troops, who, it was alleged, had surrendered without a fight—deserted really—to the Russians in large, still organized, formations. The details are still murky; we do know the captures were real enough, we do not know how much was premeditated or simply circumstance regarding the attitude behind this action. Whatever the case, this occurrence would bedevil the *Alliance* for the rest of the war.

To return to our story, we can understand the sheer volume of military activity during those September days only by contemplating the larger picture:

All Russian and Austro-Hungarian forces in Galicia were heavily engaged at this time—a time for huge maneuvers in the west as well. Five Russian and the equivalent of five Austrian armies were simultaneously grappling in huge set-piece battles in which their casualties were enormous. Two more were struggling in Prussia and others were rushing to join the fray. Nothing quite like the movements of September 1914 had even been seen before nor would it be again.

As early as the 5th, the Austrian defenders of the Grodek positions had sortied as far as Kurnicki to probe the preparations of the expected attack. Brusilov had diverted much of his strength to the left flank and Russki could be relied on to move methodically, and it was not until the 6th that the Russian's began to close up to the defenses. The first energetic attacks were pressed on the 8th and renewed on the 10th. Then next day Hötzendorf ordered a general retreat all along the line; he was by now well aware that his forces were disseminated, exhausted, and demoralized. Dankl began to cross the San River, the projected new defense line on the 12th, then the rains arrived; steady, soaking precipitation which soon dampened the energies of all the troops whatever their uniform.

It was during those September days that the war added a new dimension to fighting. Austrian and Russian aviators, hovering over the battlefields, began to shoot at one another with rifles and handguns; before long aircraft were being armed with machine guns, and airplanes became offensive weapons. A remarkable incident occurred on the 8th. It may have been the first instance on the Eastern Front of one airplane bringing down another. A Russian captain named Nesterov was determined to prevent a group of Austrian planes from dropping bombs at Sholkiv, and he deliberately rammed his airplane into that of the leader of the enemy group, a certain Baron von Rosenthal. Both machines were destroyed and both pilots killed.[43]

Following the *Magdeburg* incident, the Russian Baltic Fleet became more active when it was determined that the Germans retained rather weak forces in the area. But the German commitment, though second rate, was by no means negligible. When the latter sent a 35-ship fleet to sweep the inland sea for a week early in September, the Russian patrols fled to the relative safety of the Gulf of Finland, from which the main Russian battle fleet emerged on the 8th. This was a day too late; having sunk a merchant ship on the 7th, the Germans had sailed away.

In order to cover the port of Memel from Russian troops retreating out of East Prussia, the Germans also sent a cruiser and a torpedo boat there at mid-month. The only other important naval action of the month took place off the port of Windau in Courland, where the Germans contemplated a landing of 700 troops to destroy the facilities there. From the 23rd to the 25th, a 38-ship fleet was reported by jittery Russians, but it inflicted very little damage to the coastline and withdrew without incident.[44] The whole operation may have been merely a feint; whatever the case it hardly seems to have been worthwhile.

After the rout of the Russian Second Army in the last days of August, the Germans of the Eighth Army were free to deal with First Army, which had halted its advance and appealed for reinforcement upon learning of Samsonov's defeat. Ludendorff wasted no time in regrouping; in less than a week he was ready to strike again. Leaving only token forces along the southern frontier, he now directed his forces—swelled by the five divisions from Belgium on September 2nd—against Rennenkampf. The first of the fighting began on September 7th, and within two days it was general all along the line. General Francois was attempting a new right hook through the heavy woods of the main Masurian Lakes area.

By the 8th, Bialla and Arys had fallen, each yielding large numbers of prisoners. Next day a heavy battle in the forests near Lyck raged; initially the Russian lines stood firm, but later they retired and the town was abandoned on the 10th. That very day a battle east of the Lötzen gap near Soltmahnen was a German success, netting 5,000 prisoners and 60 guns. In the center Rennenkampf counterattacked toward Rastenburg with two divisions, roughing up German 20th Corps and delaying its advance considerably. Francois now wanted to pass east of the Rominten Forest and cut off the Russian retreat, but Ludendorff ordered him to pass it to the west, a less risky maneuver. For once, Francois was not disposed to disobey, as his men were tired and his supplies lagging. Goldap with 1,000 more prisoners was taken on the 11th, the same day Rennenkampf evacuated Insterburg. The two sides became involved in heavy fighting in the Forest on the 12th just as Ludendorff was urging on Francois in the hopes of another grand encirclement. But First Army headquarters crossed the frontier on the 13th and the bulk of the army did likewise, minus a couple thousand more casualties in the Forest of Rominten. On the 15th Hindenburg proudly announced that all German territory had been cleared of enemy troops.

Had the campaign ended at this time the Germans could well have claimed an impressive defensive victory after a month of heavy fighting. They had inflicted something like 165,000 casualties on the Russian Second Army, of whom 100,000 were prisoners, and perhaps 105,000 on First Army, of whom 40,000 were captives. They had captured at least 350 and 150 artillery pieces, respectively, to say nothing of those destroyed. For the remarkable total of at least 265,000 enemy casualties and 500 of his guns they had suffered perhaps 75,000 dead, wounded, and missing. Since they occupied the battlefields, much of their own equipment could be salvaged. Germany badly needed this victory, coming as it did at the same time that the campaign in France had stalled. The question on the mind of strategists ever since has been whether the transfers of troops from West to East during the French campaign had affected its outcome.

What is absolutely certain is that events in the East were affecting events in the West, and the reverse could be assumed to be valid as well. Moltke became an early scapegoat of indecision in the West; on September 14th, he was replaced as Chief of the General Staff by General Erich von Falkenhayn, another man committed to success in the West. By now the necessity of assisting the Austrians was paramount; within two days the new Chief had approved a Ludendorff plan to send most of Eighth Army's units to Silesia—the new force would be called Ninth Army—where cooperation with the Austrians was possible. He also directed Ludendorff to consult with Hötzendorf regarding strategy; the two sat down on the 18th. By then Austria-Hungary was reeling, having lost 325,000 men and nearly 300 artillery pieces to Russia's 225,000 and 100, and her armies were still retreating.

Stavka on the Russian side was also shaking up the commands; Zhilinski of the crippled Northwest Front was replaced by General Russki of the Third Army, the leadership of which passed to General Radko-Dmitriev. The Grand Duke then called for a discussion with his Front commanders for September 13th at Cholm. Russki, whose new command was in no condition to advance, argued for defense along the Niemen. Ivanov, whose troops were still moving forward, wanted reinforcement for success. He was to be disappointed. Nicholas Nicholaevich ordered Fifth Army to move north of Warsaw to cover Russki's left and Fourth Army on its left to form a link with Ninth Army on the Vistula, Third and Eighth Armies could remain in Galicia, First and Tenth would watch East Prussia, Sixth and Seventh would remain on the Baltic and Black

Sea Coasts, respectively. A few days later the Duke's decision appeared to be correct when the Russians recovered from the body of a German officer papers which revealed German intentions (September 17).[45] It now seemed that both sides had finally decided to concentrate on the great bulge of Congress Poland after a month of relative neglect. Both the Austrians and the Germans had sent weak, unsupported units into this level, open area; Austrian cavalry had penetrated as far as Kielce and almost unnoticed, Germans had occupied Lodz on September 3rd. Now, as Ninth Army began detraining here, the Russians prepared to push on across the plains and into Silesia.

We have now reached a point at which to wrap up our look at the campaigns on the flanks, which after mid September had fallen out of favor with both commands. In the north, the Germans decided to pursue the enemy into his own country. In Galicia the heavy rains and subsequent troop transfers spoiled the Russian pursuit of the badly defeated Austrians. Following the battle of the Grodek line of lakes, the Austrians retreated to the river San. Mosciska was taken on the 14th, then the mud slowed the Russian advance to a crawl. It was not until the 20th that their artillery began to bombard Jaroslav and a weak cordon around Przemsyl was established. All along the line of the San retreating Austrian engineers tried to destroy every bridge over the river, but the Russians nabbed one at Kreszov near Tarnograd and only bad weather prevented disaster for the Austrians. Sandomierz, on the Vistula, fell on the 14th and the extended Austrian line west of the river quickly fell back, only sporadic clashes in the uplands lingered until the 20th. Jaroslav began to be evacuated on the 21st and two days later it was in the hands of the Russians, and by which time Dankl was already crossing the Wislocka. Przemsyl was another matter. This ancient citadel, a city of 50,000 or so inhabitants in 1914, was perhaps the strongest fortress in all Galicia. Besides possessing a remarkably strong perimeter of many well-placed forts, the stronghold had been lavishly equipped with stores and provisions of all kinds in quantity, and preparations had been made for a long resistance. It was believed that sufficient supplies were on hand for a defense of eight months or more, and the commander, General Kusmanek, was inclined to do just that if necessary. When the Russian ring about the city was complete on the 22nd, the place was packed with troops, horses, guns, wagons, and military implements of all sorts; it had been directly on the line of retreat for the Third Army, and had therefore inherited much of the latter force, exhausted by a hurried retreat through the mire, and overtaken by the enemy. Ivanov locked a powerful ring around the fortress within a few days and began to shell it with light artillery, a hail which turned out to be a costly mistake; the Russians settled down to await the arrival by rail of the heavy siege guns necessary to reduce such a fortress. For the moment, Przemsyl stood firm, like an island amid a turbulent sea.

With the Austrians retreating west by southwest there was now no considerable force to prevent Brusilov from fanning his army out to the south, toward the Carpathian Mountains. Stryj, an important rail junction town at the edge of the uplands, was taken along with Sambor on the 18th. Czernowitz, capital of Bukovina, was evacuated as indefensible as all of eastern Galicia became Russian by default. Most painful for Austria was the loss of the Galician oilfield around Boryslaw-Drohobycz. The Russians pushed on to the crest of the Carpathians and by month's end had captured three of the passes leading into Hungary including the Dukla, which was taken on the 28th . Chyrow, on the railroad to Przemysl, fell on the 24th.

Hötzendorf, meanwhile, had finally found a line he felt he could defend, along the lower Dunajec River, a northward flowing stream which rose deep in the mountains and joined the Vistula some 70km (44mi) east of Cracow. No further retreat could be tolerated; it would be do or die on the Dunajec and its tributary, the Biala. The pursuing Russians, advancing into an ever-narrowing strip of land between the mountains and the Vistula, were in no condition to press on and finally the line in the east stabilized.

It would take a little longer on the German end of the line, where Ludendorff was determined to pursue Rennenkampf into Russian territory. Both commanders saw the river Niemen as the immediate objective; it lay some 80km (50mi) distant. The Russian Tenth Army, now on the Narew, would be prevented from intervening on the German right flank by a diversionary attack on the fortress of Osowiec; this was carried out with the greatest difficulty as the German bombarding force struggled in the marshy environs of the well-sighted fortress. Although the shelling commenced for several days it was to little effect and the whole episode is noteworthy only in the fact that both the *Kaiser* and *Czar* made appearances at the site during the barrages,[46] but it does not appear that they had been there simultaneously.

Once the Germans had crossed into Russia they began to experience the inevitable problems of transport. The railroad gauge could be converted simply by removing one side of rails and spiking them closer, to the desired width, but this was labor intensive and time consuming. The roads, as we have seen, were mostly unimproved and in the autumn rains became rutted ribbons of mire. On both the northern and southern extremities of the Niemen objective sat the fortress cities of Kovno and Grodno, likely to be stubbornly defended. In the center was a secondary position at Olita and it was here that Ludendorff proposed to cross the river and split the opposing forces, then possibly fall on either Kovno or Grodno from the rear.

The Niemen River below Grodno is a formidable stream of 200 meters width or so; worse still for the Germans, its western bank is low with swampy environs, while the east bank constitutes a high bluff. Russki had deployed his troops along this natural defensive position by the 23rd. They allowed the advancing Germans to construct two pontoon bridges south of Olita by the 25th, only to destroy both with artillery fire as infantry began to cross. Somewhat of a repeat performance was staged on the 27th with the same results. By this time the transfer of the German Ninth Army was complete and the Hindenburg/Ludendorff team departed to take command of the new force. The Niemen operation was called off and a general retreat began on September 28th.

It was during these late September battles amidst the brilliant colors of the deciduous trees that the Romanov dynasty suffered the loss of one it its own. Prince Oleg, son of Grand Duke Constantine (who was the *Czar's* cousin), was mortally wounded in action against German cavalry. He was the first, and only, battle casualty of the dynasty in the war.[47]

General von Schubert, the new boss of Eighth Army, inherited a difficult situation. The Russian Tenth Army to his right began to advance to cut off the German retreat. By October 1st it had forced back the enemy at Osowiec and captured Augustovo. Beyond the town it collided with the retreating Germans in the forest of the same name, initiating several days fighting in trackless woods extending north to Suwalki. Reports of major actions in this area continued until the 5th, both sides claiming victory and large numbers of prisoners. In fact it was the Russians who advanced and when unopposed entered East Prussian territory again. It was not until the 8th that they were stopped in the south, having captured the town of Lyck once more. On the northern end of the line, a German counterattack drove them out of Schirwindt on the 11th. And in the center the line finally stabilized near the border at Wirballen after several days of savage fighting. An American observer who witnessed the battle at Wirballen wrote a graphic account of a Russian attack on the freshly dug German defenses. Artillery shattered the brown waves of men as they attacked, and German machine guns cut down those who survived the shells, the gunners coolly doing their duty as though attending to normal business. Individual Russians were observed to be hurled back by the impact of the bullets striking them. Yet the determined Russians tried again and again to reach the German line; the seemingly endless battle was characterized by successive assaults, not one of which reached its intended objective. Bursting shrapnel took a terrible toll on the aggressors, and those who eluded the rain of steel from above were mown down by the scythe-like sweeps of the rapid-fire weapons. Smoke, dust and the screams of men added to the confusion. Finally it was over. The dead were everywhere, erratically strewn about over many acres, and lying in every conceivable position the human body is capable of achieving. He then examined the battlefield through field glasses, and observed, to his horror, "squirming, tossing, and writhing figures everywhere."[48] Then came the pitiful cries of the wounded.

The above is an excellent account of the newly accepted value of entrenchments and represents one of the first instances on the Eastern Front of trench fighting. As the Germans dug in along the Prussian frontier, the Russian advance was halted, and for the time being, both sides paused to lick their wounds.

Thus ended the opening moves and initial battles on the Eastern Front. The action, of course continued, but the events set in motion by the opposing forces upon mobilization had run their course. By the end of August Germany had moved 22 divisions to the eastern theater with two more arriving, Austria had 49, Russia 130½. At the end of September the totals were 24 with two more arriving for Germany, 50 with one departing for Austria, and 126½ with one arriving for Russia. These units had been thinned by 80,000 or so German and nearly 400,000 Austro-Hungarian casualties. Total Russian losses reached 520,000 more or less; two entire divisions destroyed at Tannenberg were never rebuilt, and two more mauled at the Masurian Lakes were disbanded. Russia and Germany might be able to replace their losses, but Austria-Hungary never really recovered from the 1914 fighting. She had lost much of her German and Hungarian cadre and the better part of two provinces from which to draw resources: Galicia and Bukovina. And another large force was surrounded in Przemysl. From September there could be no doubt in the minds of the Germans but that their ally would need a good deal of support. In the minds of the Russians there was no doubt as to which of her enemies was the more formidable. For Austria-Hungary the goal might be simply to survive. But for Germany the question arose as to which theater priority should be given: reinforce failure in the west or a despairing ally in the east? And the Russians would continue to debate the wisdom of concentrating against a stronger, versus a weaker, opponent.

East Prussia in 1914

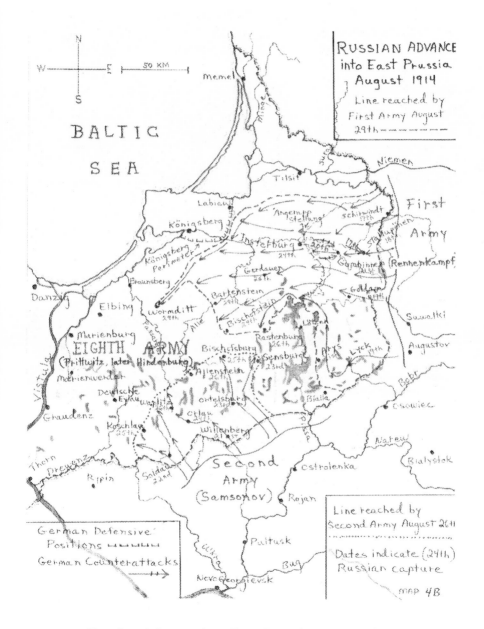

Russian Advance into East Prussia August 1914

German Advance Out of East Prussia September 1914

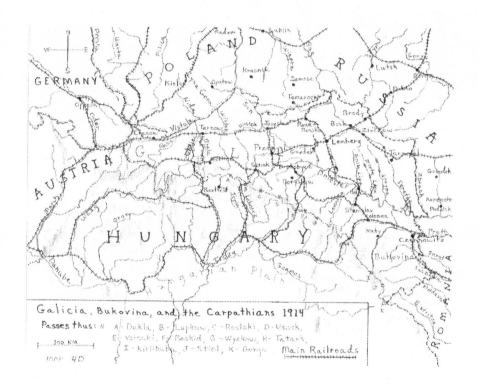

Galicia, Bukovina, and The Carpathians 1914

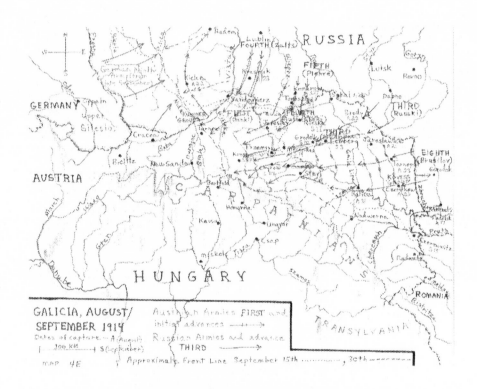

Galicia, August-September 1914

Chapter Five
Drawing the Line

Even before the Russian offensive in Galicia had spent itself on the Dunajec and Biala Rivers, new friction within the High Command had surfaced and threatened to squander away Russia's hard-won opportunity to gain the strategic advantage. Ivanov and his Chief of Staff, Alexiev, determined to push on against the Austrians, capture Cracow, and maybe even invade Hungary. But they were strongly opposed by those influenced by General Russki, who had recently been given command of North-West Front, replacing Zhilinsky. Russki argued that the German's rout of Zhilinsky might tempt them to attack in the direction of Warsaw, a movement which would necessarily preempt any further advance of South-West Front. Although Hindenburg had insufficient forces for such an undertaking, the idea did worry Ivanov, who had no way of knowing German dispositions. He despised the idea of sacrificing Cracow as a prize, for it lay only 55km (35mi) from the German frontier, just beyond which was the vital industrial region of upper Silesia. Less than 160km (100mi) to the west, the Tatra Mountains break down to plains through which the River March flows on its way to the Danube. These plains, between the Carpathian and Bohemian mountain chains, constitute the famous Moravian Gap, an historical invasion route, and gateway to Vienna. To sacrifice Cracow as an objective was equivalent to sacrificing a golden opportunity to strike at the hearts of the German and/or Austrian Empires. In the event, the appearance of the Ninth Army on his northern flank meant that Ivanov would have to divert forces to confront it. This in itself would not have presented much of a problem, since the Russians vastly outnumbered their foe, but the High Command had by now other ideas. Under constant pressure from the French, and having built up a tremendous superiority of numbers, it had resurrected its old plan of an invasion of Germany from the central Polish plains. A regrouping of the Russian armies was therefore undertaken, as the center of gravity shifted to the north. Eighth Army and Third Army remained in Galicia while the new Eleventh Army began arriving to carry out the siege of Przemsyl. Ninth, Fourth, Fifth, and Second Armies were to stretch north across Poland in that order, as far as the fortress of Novogeorgievsk on the Vistula. First Army was to be moved south to cover the gap between the river and the Prussian frontier.

The *Alliance* was also busy regrouping. Austrian First Army was shuttled over the Vistula to the western bank and three armies to its right—Fourth, Third, and Second, west to east—shifted westward slightly to fill the gap. At this time neither side possessed any appreciable force from the Uszok Pass all the way to the Romanian border, a circumstance which was exploited by neither as well. But the gaping hole in the center of the front which had existed since the war's outbreak was being plugged at last. Previously only a single Corps of German Landwehr under General Woyrsch had been stationed here, and as we have seen, had pushed some distance inside Poland. With Ninth Army now in place, Woyrsch could concentrate on a much shorter line—the northern portion—than before.

Ninth Army had begun to move forward into the vacuum of Central Poland as early as September 29th. Austrian First Army, hampered at once by the marshy ground along the Nida River, struggled ahead until by October 4th the two formed a front from Opatow to Tomasow, along which the first combat of the campaign occurred. At Opatow over 8000 Russians became casualties when their formations broke; at Radom the Austrians were clearly losing when the arrival of German troops turned the tide, their artillery alone causing 8000 of the enemy to litter the fields. Within a few days the armies of the *Alliance* had reached the Vistula along a broad front; only a bridgehead opposite Ivangorod remained to the Russians, who now found themselves unable to cross the river for their own deployment.

Further south, the other Austrian armies advanced once again to the San. Already, on October 2nd Russian forces surrounding Przemysl had demanded its surrender, after several days of bombardment. General Kusmanek had declined; he had fought off several attacks among the outer forts already and would do so again when a major assault was made beginning on the 5th, which lasted several days. The effort was completely unsuccessful. Austrian cavalry reached the fortress city on the 9th, and elements of Second Army fought their way through the Russian ring on the very next day. For several days the garrison was free to escape, yet it made no determined effort to do so, believing that the greater safety lay within the city, the abandoning of which might create more problems than it solved. Certainly huge quantities of war material would have fallen into Russian hands. But Austria-Hungary desperately needed manpower by that time, and the failure of the High Command to order a speedy escape from Przemysl was an omission which it would soon regret. Jaroslav was also retaken but the Austrians did not advance beyond the San. They did however counterattack the Russian left near Sambor and began to collect all available resources for a new move farther east along the long, weakly manned front in the Carpathians.

The Germans too were now throwing every available unit into the space between Ninth Army and the Vistula in an easterly drive to meet Ludendorff's men approaching from the south. On October 9th, German troops had found documents on the body of a dead Russian officer which revealed the alarming strength of the enemy. The same day Ivangorod came under shell fire; two days later the Germans had reached the Bzura River and for the first time in the war, the sounds of battle could be detected in Warsaw. Knowing the danger he faced, but reluctant to stop the advancing left under Mackensen or discourage the Austrians before Ivangood, Ludendorff was slow to give the order to halt, much less retreat. He allowed Mackensen to grind it out for several more days; fighting raged on the Blonie defensive position—the last one west of Warsaw—for several days between the 13th and the 17th. It was of a seesaw nature, and created somewhat of a panic in the city, where refugees had recently sheltered. An eyewitness reported that the German advance had caused a lot of suffering. He was heartbroken to watch the cartloads of families moving eastward as the Russians retreated. These pitiful refugees often packed all their belongings into their primitive Polish farm carts and took to the roads, exposed to the rain and cold. He also noted that the population did not flee the Austrian advances.[49] At its height, the German tide reached within 11km (7mi) of Warsaw to the west, 30km (19mi) to the south. Russian strength continued to mount as the regrouping progressed, albeit at a snail's pace, and finally on the 18th a general order to withdraw was issued from the German command.

Hötzendorf needed more convincing. He allowed the Russians to cross the Vistula at Ivangorod in hopes of wreaking havoc amidst the confusion, while at the same time ordering his own crossing of the stream at Josefov, to take them in flank. Both schemes were resounding defeats and cost Austria a further 50,000 casualties. Once the Russians were over the river in strength First Army had not the means to stop them, and in dozens of minor actions amidst the spruce woods of the uplands of the great Vistula bend, the Austrians were gradually forced back to the southwest. The major town of Radom fell on the 28th, Kielce, after an especially bitter fight,[50] including a savage action at Leszczica, where Austrian and Russian Poles found themselves engaged in an unwilling war between brothers,[51] changed hands November 3rd. The story on the San was much the same, where Radko- Dmitriev and Brusilov encountered stubborn, but not prolonged, resistance. Hötzendorf was reluctant to yield Jaroslav and other good defensive positions a second time, in the end he was compelled to do so and retired once more to the Dunajec-Biala line by early November.

Further east the Austrians enjoyed their only true successes. In a series of engagements east and southeast of Przemysl they defeated persistent Russian attempts to re-encircle the city. Their artillery was particularly effective during some of these, which enabled them to carry out several counterthrusts which gained some ground in the Chyrow-Sambor area and north of Nizankovice, a town on the very border of today's Poland and Ukraine. Another group of cavalry seized the Tatar's Pass on October 20th and rode as far as Czernowitz to wrest it from the Russians two days later. Still others burst through the Uszok Pass and pushed into the enemy flank beyond Turka; that same day, the 31st, a Russian column at Kuty near the Romanian border was driven off. Both sides were slow to reinforce this long, mountainous section of front.

Ludendorff, meanwhile, was having trouble disengaging his foe. Having shelled and bombed Warsaw as late as the 17th, he now ordered all roads, railways, bridges and anything else of possible use to the Russians to be destroyed as his forces fell back. This meant tons upon tons of supplies had to be moved and livestock driven off and a host of other duties which required time to perform. The Russians pursued, and series of rear-guard actions were ordered which further devastated the unfortunate countryside. Woods were smashed by artillery fire; houses were left as blackened ruins. Several German divisions which made a stand on the river Pilica became separated from the army and were forced to retreat due west, while the main body headed for Czestochowa to the southwest. The latter was reached November 2nd. Kalisz became the destination for the Pilica force, and those in the extreme north made for Posen. They were back at Lowicz by the 23rd and delayed the

Russians by a sharp rearguard action on the 26th, then retreated quickly. Two days later even Lodz was Russian again. The German provinces of Silesia and Posen were now very vulnerable to invasion.

In East Prussia very little activity followed the suspension of the second invasion on the 9th. Marggrabowa was retaken that very day, and German counterattacks continued until about the 12th. A minor distraction occurred on the 14th, when Germans advanced from Soldau along the railroad and captured Mlava inside Poland, at the height of the Battle for Warsaw. Otherwise both sides preferred to entrench before the onset of bad weather made digging much more difficult.

October hosted some action in the Baltic Sea. German submarines were by now patrolling Russian waters and on the 11th one sank the Russian armored cruiser *Pallada*. This act would soon be avenged. At the end of the month three Russian destroyers laid over 100 mines in the waters off the northernmost German port, Memel, and a few days later they floated nearly 200 more between Memel and the outer port of Königsberg. Within 10 days more a German armored cruiser plus a merchant ship had become victims of these mines, and sank.[52]

On October 29, 1914, the Ottoman Empire declared war on Russia. The announcement was not exactly a surprise to anyone; most circles in both *Entente* and *Alliance* nations had long anticipated such an eventuality. But Turkey's entry would have far-reaching effects on the course of the war, especially the war on the Eastern Front. The Black Sea—site of Russia's only warm water ports—was now sealed off by a hostile power. With the Baltic sealed by Germany, the arctic frozen much of the year and without major ports, the flimsy, single-track, 11,000km long (6800mi) Trans-Siberian Railroad to the Pacific port of Vladivostok remained. Russia was thus effectively isolated. In addition, she now had to defend a second front as well; Turkey and Russia shared a common frontier at the eastern end of the Black Sea. Russian resources would have to be diverted from the Austro-German front (now known to the Russians as the West front). For their part, the Turks mobilized an entire army for an early strike against Russia. As soon as war was declared, Turkish warships shelled several Russian Black Sea ports and torpedoed two gunboats at Odessa.

A week earlier (October 23rd) Romania had closed its borders to German provisions bound for Constantinople. Now the *Alliance* could entertain no illusions as to the attitude of the Bucharest government; it had abandoned them, just as the Italians had. But the entry of Turkey went a long way towards evening the odds between the two warring camps. It was probably more important for the *Alliance* than would Italian solidarity have been, as it created three more fronts for the *Entente* to supply (geographically only two, but the British decided to create a third in Mesopotmia, and for a time a fourth at the Dardanelles), and threatened to attract the Islamic world to the cause of the *Alliance*. But there had never been much chance that Turkey might have joined the *Entente*; her fear of Russia was too deep-seated. And the Turkish leaders were certainly correct in believing that Russia meant to seize the Straits during or after the war, and probably regardless of circumstances. An *Entente* Russia probably assured an *Alliance* Turkey.

Following the unsuccessful bid to capture Warsaw and the subsequent retreat of Ninth Army, the Germans scrambled to devise a means to save face for Hindenburg, the newly made national hero. Ludendorff had no difficulty in finding scapegoats, he ranted about lack of support from Falkenhayn and raved over the incompetence of the Austrians, with whom he suddenly disliked cooperating. Falkenhayn relented somewhat and reluctantly agreed to Hindenburg's appointment as commander-in-chief of the German forces in the East, and promised new support from the Western Front. Mackensen was given command of Ninth Army, which would be allowed no respite. Before it had completed its withdrawal, Ludendorff had for it a new mission: it was to entrain in the upper Silesia area and be railed north across Posen to be redeployed between the Warthe and Vistula Rivers along the frontier. From there it would take the Russians, who were now known to be pressing an invasion of Silesia, in flank. Owing to remarkably efficient railroad personnel and machinery, alerted at the eleventh hour, the whole movement was completed by November 10th.

Ludendorff knew the Austrians would be incapable of serious assistance in the coming battle. Already on the 4th they had been defeated at Jaroslav and forced to abandon Sandomierz a day later. Przemysl was in danger of being reinvested from the same day, and battles all around the city, especially to the south, raged on for a solid week. November 12th was not a good day for Franz Conrad von Hötzendorf: the Russians crossed the Nida River and took Miechow, practically within sight of Cracow, and they completed their second encirclement of Przemysl. Clearly, Austria could offer no help to the Germans.

Trouble was also brewing in East Prussia. The Russian First Army advanced, took Mlawa by the 5th, and pushed beyond the border. Soldau, scene of such awful fighting in August, was in Russian hands again by November 10th, Tenth Army to the east began a general invasion on the 7th. The German defenders had been expecting just such an event and had strongly fortified the old positions extending from the two main Masurian Lakes, Mauer and Spirding, north along the Angerapp River and beyond to the northern border. After short, skillful defensive engagements designed to slow and punish the enemy, they fell back to the *Stellung*. Tenth Army made only one major attack thereafter, a fairly heated affair on the last day of the month at Darkehnen. It was bloodily repulsed, then the weather worsened and the fighting subsided as both sides prepared the ground before it froze too solidly.

Russki of Northwest Front could be forgiven for not bothering too much about the third invasion of East Prussia; he had been given command of Second, Fifth, and Fourth armies as well as the First and Tenth. These three, north to south in that order, were to spearhead the Grand Duke's invasion of Germany, of which the Germans were well aware. But in a typical act of command inefficiency, the Ninth Army of Ivanov's Southwest Front was also to participate, and given the friction between the Front commanders, the invasion was likely to be ill-coordinated.

The first Russian penetration of German soil occurred on November 9th when cavalry raided the area around Pleshen for a day or two; on the 10th the Silesian frontier was violated to a depth of a few kilometers. Then on the 11th, Mackensen struck. A furious artillery barrage preceded the German Ninth Army's attack; its breakthrough was swift and deep. Within three days, the very day the Russian invasion had been scheduled to begin, battles at Kutno and Wroclawek were raging and a wedge was being driven in between First and Second armies. Rennenkampf's First Army was in the worst position; divided by the wide Vistula its left was mauled and its right was being harassed by enemy troops in East Prussia, and Rennenkampf refused to send any strength over the river to what seemed certain destruction. Second Army, its right in shreds, could not stop the German drive. The Grand Duke ordered Fifth Army to pivot northward to reinforce it; that left only two armies to continue the invasion and it was cancelled on the 16th, by which time Mackensen was advancing on Lodz and Lowicz. And he was about to be reinforced by some *Landwehr* units which had repulsed a Russian attack on Kalisz on the 12th and were moving up from the southwest. His left wing encountered an enemy force defending the Piontek Causeway, a recently constructed passage of the marshes along the upper Bzura River suitable for heavy traffic, but without great difficulty drove it off and held the road by the 19th.

The main battle was now centered around Lodz, a manufacturing city of some importance, and also the supply center for Second and Fifth Armies. Perhaps because of this fact, these two formations managed to reach the site in strength before Mackensen did so, after a notably rapid two-day march. Their orders were to move to Lowicz, and take the Germans in flank, but these were soon prudently altered to allow for simply a defense of Lodz. Mackensen's ambition was a straightforward one: encircle the enemy forces and seize the town. To this end he ordered three of the six Corps to frontally push back Second Army, while one guarded against any possible action from Rennenkampf, and the other two bypassed the town to the northeast in order to swing around and attack it from the east. The *Landwehr* units pressed in from the west. Fierce fighting raged along the perimeter of town the from 18th, the result being that the Germans were unable to overcome the defense, and their attacks gradually petered out. It was during these actions that the Russians made their first widespread use of armored cars, which proved their worth.

To the northeast, the story was different. Here, the two Corps sent to outflank the Russians from the east had no particular difficulty penetrating that thinly-held sector of the line, and driving around the right of Second Army. With this accomplished, First Cavalry Corps dispersed to a screen of detachments for the purpose of guarding against any possible enemy activity originating from the Lowicz-Skierniewice area, while XXV Corps, supported by the 3rd Guard Division, continued the movement into the weak flank. But by the 21st, this force was stopped in its tracks by Russian units which had been rushed east to meet the danger. Suddenly, it was the Germans who were now in danger. Their path blocked to the east, south, and west, they could only hope that escape to the north would be possible before a reviving First Army could prevent it. In fact, Rennenkampf had somehow managed to assemble a force of 3½ divisions by the 20th, and sent it marching southwest to frustrate the enemy. It easily brushed aside the thin line of cavalry in its way, and captured the town of Brzeziny, on the Germans' route of escape, on the 22nd. After further successes the next day, at Strykow, and elsewhere, it must have appeared that the three encircled German divisions were doomed, and the Russian command actually ordered up 18 trains to cart away the expected bag of prisoners!

Indeed, a more irresolute commander might well have lost his nerve and offered surrender, for the cold was getting bitter and the troops were almost exhausted and were low on munitions. But the German General Scheffer of XXV Corps was equal to the task. Along poor roads and under difficult weather conditions—by now it was snowing—he withdrew as far as the Lodz-Koluszki railway line, where he ran into a crack Siberian division of First Army's relief force, which had dug in along it. Scheffer decided to fight his way out, and launched a heavy attack against the Russians on the 24th. After a bloody battle, the Siberians were all but destroyed; following this action the rest of the relief force withdrew towards Lowicz. The 3rd Guard Division captured Brzeziny presently, allowing for a German escape from the potential trap. Scheffer's force retired to a more practical position on the line, bringing with it 16,000 prisoners and 64 guns, for a loss of only 4,300 men of its own,[53] by the 26th of November.

At last the Austrians began to move when on the 18th they launched a drive heading northeast from Cracow. It was not a moment too soon; Russian cavalry were in the very suburbs of the city as late as the 20th. They advanced nearly as far as Kielce before being stopped by the 28th. The Przemysl garrison attempted a breakout which was defeated on the 15th. Artillery duels characterized the action around the beleaguered city for the rest of the month; they were particularly fierce on the 25th.

In the only other notable action at sea during November, the German battle cruiser *Goeben* and escorts—now flying the Turkish flag—engaged a more numerous Russian battle fleet off the southern tip of the Crimean Peninsula on the 18th. In a short, sharp exchange hampered by fog and mist, both sides drew blood, but neither could prevail. *Goeben* was the most powerful *Alliance* ship in the Black Sea and her loss could not be risked. The Russians, with older, slower, and less well-armed vessels had no desire for a decisive showdown. The "battle" was therefore uneventful and indecisive.

While the fighting around Lodz temporarily subsided during the last week of November the Grand Duke Nicholas called a *Stavka* conference for the 29th. Once there both Russki and Ivanov pleaded a case for their respective Fronts to be reinforced and considered the main national effort. Both ends of the line still had gaping holes beckoning, tempting an attack. But the more tempting of the two was to the south, where it was believed a new push might traverse the mountains into Hungary, might capture Przemysl, or perhaps take Cracow. The latter was particularly attractive; its capture would tend to split the two foes, and would open the doorway to the Moravian Gate, a natural feature through which armies had invaded central Europe for centuries. Vienna would be accessible and the heavy industry of upper Silesia rendered extremely vulnerable. And if Austria-Hungary was knocked out of the war, her ally could not possibly survive alone for long. The meeting adjourned with the orders of the day as defense in the north, but push on in the south. The only consolation for Russki was when his insistence on sacking Rennenkampf for his failure to assist Second Army at Lodz led to the appointment of General Litvinov to command First Army.

Across Poland *Stavka's* counterpart *Ober-Ost* (Hindenburg's supreme command in the East) was also being called to confer, at Posen on December 1st. With both Falkenhayn and the *Kaiser* present Hindenburg was made a Field Marshall and Ludendorff a Lieutenant General. Falkenhayn, who had only recently—and grudgingly—sent three more Corps from the Western Front, lost no opportunity to remind everyone that such dilutions of strength on the "main" front could in no way force a decision in the East. Ludendorff countered by stating that grandiose mobile operations might still be feasible in the East, but no longer in the West. Therefore all new reserves should be used to eliminate Russia from the war; besides the Austrians needed massive reinforcement. In the end all that resulted from Posen was an intensification of the dislike between the personalities that dominated *Ober-Ost* and *OHL* (Falkenhayn's command).

Russki, who had wanted to entrench behind the wide Vistula, now needed to find another, more westerly line. He selected the most logical one from a topographic standpoint. The Bzura River is a sizeable tributary of the Vistula and enters it on a south to north course which is extended in a fairly straight line along its tributary, the Rawka. Somewhat to the south along roughly the same longitude flows the Pilica, which rises not far north of Cracow and flows generally northward to Tomasow, due south of the Bzura/Rawka trench. These waterways were made to order for Russki's needs at the beginning of December; the Grand Duke had ordered defense west of the Vistula, and here was the best location for it. The men of Northwest Front dug in while struggling with the bitter cold and frozen earth. They would soon be glad they did.

Ludendorff, having been reinforced with troops from *OHL*, decided they needed to be used in another attack. He had thus far been fortunate; the Ninth Army attack in November might have been disastrous if not for Russian blundering. Now he proposed to assault a wary foe, still far superior in number, in a head-on attack in winter weather. Nor would there be any worthwhile support on either flank.

Things went well enough for the Germans at first; they did not know the enemy plan this time. Lodz came under shellfire on December 5th, and German troops entered the city the very next day. It was to be the last relatively easy conquest, being west of the projected Russian defense line. But for the next three weeks central Poland was the scene of combat as heavy, determined, or desperate as any of the war. The German advance smashed headlong into the brick wall of the Russian defense. All along the line from the Vistula to the Pilica fighting went on day and night; the ground trembled under the constant rumble of the big guns. Tales of the action have some villages changing ownership several times as attack was followed by counterattack. The largest town in the area—Lowicz—finally fell to the Germans on the 15th, but this was still west of the river line. For ten more days Ludendorff persisted while the German press reported the capture of any tiny village as though some significant point had been won. In the end Ludendorff had to admit that Ninth Army would not enjoy winter quarters in Warsaw; no scapegoat could be found—Mackensen had protested the attacks after Lodz's fall—so the weather suddenly was declared unsuitable. The "Second Battle of Warsaw" was over. German casualties were far heavier than in any previous operation since August, and estimates run as high as 100,000 from mid November to year's end. Christmas for the men at *Ober-Ost* could not have been merry.

At least someone was celebrating. On the very day of the much more publicized truce on the Western Front, Russian and Austro-Hungarian troops in the lines around Przemysl were meeting in no-man's-land to exchange handshakes, good wishes, and gifts to the sounds of musical instruments.[54] One man wrote of finding three Christmas trees in no-man's-land, left deliberately by the Russians, who included notes with holiday good will and a desire for an early settlement to the fighting. A cease-fire prevailed on Chirstmas Day.[55] The Austrian garrison had thrice in the month mounted breakout attempts—the latest and most powerful on the 22nd—but all had failed. Incredibly, the number of troops in the city had increased during the interval between the two encirclements, at a time when all could have escaped; the total complement was now 127,000 men, twice what the fortresses had been designed to require. Clearly, a force this size needed to be relieved.

Hötzendorf had every intention of relieving Przemysl; his main problem by the end of November was Cracow, an even more important city which by then was itself in danger of falling to the Russian advance. His Second Army he had sent north to fill the gap vacated by German Ninth Army when the latter was transferred to the Vistula-Warthe area. First Army was also north of the lower Vistula. That left only Fourth Army on the Dunajec/Biala and Third Army in the Carpathians with which to contemplate any relief effort, but both these armies were seriously under strength and were already involved in heavy defensive battles.

Ivanov, meanwhile, was urging on his armies. Already on November 25th, Brusilov had taken the Lupkow Pass, one of the few with a railroad. Radko-Dmitriev took Neu-Sandec, a railroad junction on the upper Dunajec, then forced the lower stream as well, and advanced to the Raba, the last river line before Cracow, by early December. Lechitsky of the Ninth Army, not to be outdone, had closed to within 19km (12mi) of Cracow from the north. Almost in desperation, Hötzendorf ordered a counterattack north of the city by Fourth Army in the Miechow/Wolbrum area. Fortunately, it was successful—yielding 29,000 prisoners—and he withdrew a force of seven divisions under an able general (Roth) and railed them with all haste on a roundabout trip south of the mountains from which they could be turned north, against the flank of Radko's forces. It could not be sent too far to the east, as Brusilov had pushed on to Hammona on the Hungarian side of the mountain ridge. This did not seem to be a problem when, after fighting his way across the Raba, Radko turned his main forces northwest, directly on Cracow. The latter captured the salt mining center of Wieliczkov, almost in the suburbs of the city, on December 4th. Ludendorff, well aware of the dangers inherent in a fall of Cracow, sent a full-strength German division to join Roth, and another for the direct defense of Cracow. The latter was in place by the 6th and helped stop Ninth Army. The former, with its Austrian comrades, joined battle in the rugged, wooded area on the north slope of the Beskids. Roth's men took Radko on his weak left flank in a series of engagements beginning December 3rd near a rail town called Limanowa. The rugged terrain favored the attackers, whose movements were shielded by the hills and forests. Roth was able to recapture Neu-Sandec, Grybow and Gorlice, a considerable forward movement which compelled

Radko to retreat all the way to the Dunajec/Bialla lines by the 17th, when the battle fizzled out. Brusilov was obliged to withdraw strong portions of his Eighth Army to stop Roth; when Boroevic (Austrian Third Army) noticed this movement he attacked and recaptured the Dukla, Lupkow, and Uszok Passes by mid-month. The Austrians were able to push down the north slope of the mountains and seize most of the railroad east of Gorlice, as far as Sanok and Lisko on the San; at this time they were tantalizingly close to Przemysl, inspiring the breakout attempts of the 19th and 22nd, but Boroevic had no reserves to spare for an all-out effort to lift the seige. By Christmas day it was the Russians who were regaining bits and pieces of ground in local counterattacks amongst the snowy foothills and icy streams. North of the Vistula, Fourth Army attempted to take some pressure off its neighbors by attacking from the Cracow area to the northeast. Here, an Austro-German force reached the Nida before it was reversed on the 28th trying to cross the stream. By year's end, fighting had subsided all along the Eastern Front.

Conspicuous by its absence was the war at sea during the waning days of the year. The Germans had contented themselves with mine laying in the remote Gulf of Bothnia early in December. What they hoped to achieve is difficult to imagine. The Russians were up to similar schemes, though far to the south, in heavy traffic areas. These plans were delayed in midmonth when accidental detonations sank two of the minelayers near where *Magdeburg* had been destroyed. The atrocious winter weather in the Baltic should have been sufficient reason to cancel most activity.

The 1914 campaign was over. After five months of furious fighting a line had been drawn, finally, between the opposing armies. From the Niemen River in the north to the Carpathian Mountains in the south hastily dug trenches cut across the scarred landscape. In the mountains themselves the front consisted of mostly wooden barricades and strongpoints between the occasional dugouts; all the wood was of course from the local forests. Only in the extreme north and in Bukovina near the Romanian frontier were found no definite front lines. These areas had yet to figure in the campaigning and were still relegated third-line troops to watch for enemy action. In the center the great armies attempted to settle in for the winter. But this war had already brought so many surprises that it was probably only a minor shock for the participants to learn that the snows would bring no relief; the fighting would continue irregardless of weather. In earlier wars such conduct had always been regarded as impractical, if not unthinkable. But this war had become so propagandized as an uncompromising struggle for national survival that few personalities in the warring governments were much concerned anymore about its direct, or even indirect causes. Now the only talk among its directors revolved on how best to win it, and by whatever means.

Once the troops could be convinced to get over the early prophesies that the war would certainly be over by Christmas, they dutifully and stoically prepared to endure further exertions. One description of the German lines reported that German baggage trains and artillery pieces were mounted on runners to better negotiate the ice and snow, and frozen rivers became arteries of movement. New types of motorized sledges were employed, and scouting groups on foot were often outfitted with skis. The infantry began to wear heavy garments without color and therefore were invisible against the snow. The eastern German cities of Posen and Thorn became huge supply depots; captured cities such as Lodz and Lowicz were partially torn down to obtain building material for forts and defensive fortifications.[56] On sections of the line that followed streams or cut across lakes, soldiers on both sides were ordered to constantly break the ice that quickly formed in order to deprive the enemy of an easy means of crossing the water barrier. The entire line appeared as though combat was in progress from the thick smoke of thousands of bonfires fed with mostly green wood as soldiers strove to keep from suffering frostbite or general exposure. Burying the dead was usually impossible; even given the time and energy necessary, the ground was frosted deeply and the fuel needed to melt it often unavailable. Injuries and light wounds became serious in many cases at low temperatures, and serious wounds were often fatal. Against the backdrop of such miserable conditions, the High Commands of all three Empires prepared to continue the struggle unabated.

By New Year's Day 1915 the Germans controlled a wide swath of Congress Poland for a large net gain of ground; only a small strip of East Prussia was in Russian hands. As if to offset this, Russia had conquered most of Galicia for only a tiny piece of Poland in Austrian hands. Of the combatants, Austria was by far in the worst shape. It seemed that only the Carpathians had prevented a full-scale invasion of Hungary, an act which could be renewed at any time. Cracow had been saved but Przemysl was still isolated. Worse still, Italy, Austria's former partner in the Triple Alliance, was demanding a cession of territory along the common frontier, and Romania, another former ally, was following the Italian lead. The implication was that these former allies would remain neutral if Austria complied; would join the *Entente* if she did not. In a precarious position, the Austrians pretended to be conciliatory, and stalled for time.

As for the questions of grand strategy, it will be remembered that the war had begun with a declaration by Austria-Hungary against Serbia, in order to force the suspension of terrorist activities against the empire. Russian intervention had thus far prevented Austria from achieving her goal; in that regard it could be maintained that the Russians had been successful; they had also drawn much German strength away from France. The larger question of whether Russian strategy had prevented the early Conquest of France is one which has never been, and of course can never be, definitively answered. Would the five divisions transferred from the west to the east in late August have made the difference at the Marne? It seems unlikely. Would the rout of Rennenkampf at the so-called Battle of the Masurian Lakes in September been successful without them? Possibly, but not certainly. The war was like a living organism; to affect any one organ was to affect the performance of the whole unit.

Austria-Hungary had begun the war on the Eastern Front with 49 divisions, and by year's end had committed 53, nearly all under-strength by that time. Germany fielded 22 divisions by the end of August; by the end of December the number was 38. To oppose these 91, Russia now possessed 143, up from 130½ in August despite the Turkish intervention which drew off several more. This truly was war on a colossal scale over a vast landscape: Nine Russian armies facing six along a 1125km (700mi) front. At least half a million Austro-Hungarians were casualties by now, and probably 140,000 Germans. Losses to the Russian Empire were at least 700,000, and quite possibly three quarters of a million. All these figures are totals of dead, seriously wounded, prisoners of war, and deserters.

The Eastern Front, then, had claimed at least 1,340,000 men's lives terminated or seriously disrupted, possibly 1,420,000, in five months. For the survivors there was only the assurance of yet more battles to come. As the cruel winds whipped over the snow-covered plains of Poland, and blizzards raged in the Carpathians, men on both sides of the line contemplated the future with anxiety.

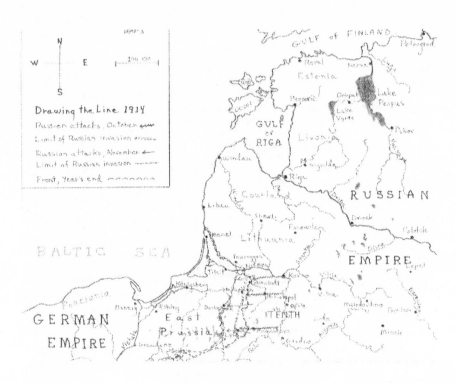

Drawing the Line 1914

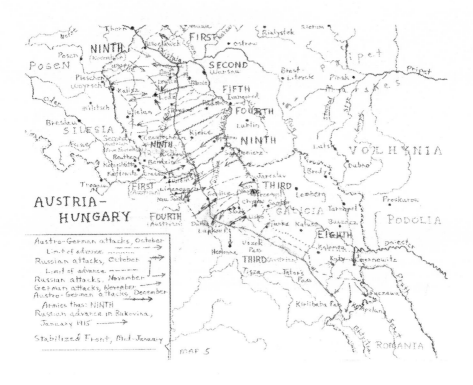

MAP 5

Chapter Six
Nightmare in the Snow

New Year's Day 1915 dawned clear and cold on much of the newly drawn Eastern Front. The *Kaiser* was in East Prussia, his visit to the front on January 1st would be the first of four such, designed to improve morale amongst the troops. Falkenhayn, Hötzendorf, and Ludendorff were meeting in Berlin, in an effort to address the Austro-Hungarian emergency. Three new Corps had been raised in Germany, and the two commanders of the East insisted that they were needed against the far more numerous Russians. Such exhortations could not impress Falkenhayn, a committed Western Front exponent, but his prestige had recently been lowered by his failure to deliver success in the West. As against this, Hindenburg still retained enormous popularity—a product of the German press—which was somewhat curious considering the equal lack of success in the east since the defeat of the first invasion of East Prussia. It was agreed that Falkenhayn visit Hindenburg's headquarters in Posen on the 12th to discuss strategy. Hötzendorf, for his part, seems to have convinced Falkenhayn of the necessity of reinforcing the East as one means of deterring the wavering neutral nations, whose hostile intervention at that moment would certainly have been catastrophic for the *Alliance*.

He had good reason to be worried. Already on January 1st, the Russians had captured the Uszok Pass and were steadily reinforcing the hitherto thin line in the Mountains. Some idea of how porous the "front" in the eastern Carpathians had been may be gleaned by considering the status of the capital city of Bukovina, the easternmost Austrian province. We have seen how Czernowitz fell to Russia early in the war. A town of 70,000 or so, the only major one for many kilometers in any direction, it was worth holding, and the Austrians soon recaptured the place. On October 30th it was Russian again, for two weeks only. Its most recent change of flag had been on November 29th, after Ivanov's renewal of the offensive had been officially sanctioned. Soon practically the whole of Bukovina was Russian, which meant that the *Czar's* troops were moving into areas coveted by the Romanians.

The Austrian response was uncharacteristically swift. On the 13th the Foreign Minister Count Berchtold resigned and was replaced by a protégé of the Hungarian Premier Count Tisza, Baron Stephen Burian. The message was, or should have been, clear: Hungary would be defended at all costs. A new Seventh Army was being formed for the eastern Carpathians. Ludendorff, of his own accord, had offered 3½ German divisions; these would be joined with an equal number of Austrians to form yet another force for the central Carpathians. No time could be lost. The Russians had taken Kimpolung on the Romanian frontier on the 6th and had seized the Kirlibaba Pass, leading into Hungary, on the 17th. Soon, it was learned that the Bank of England had advanced a five-million-pound loan to Romania.

Although Falkenhayn had not agreed to send the three new German Corps to the East as a result of the Posen Conference, he was soon overruled by the *Kaiser* who supported the popular Hindenburg/Ludendorff team. In addition, a fourth Corps was also on the way, comprised as it was of mostly French-speaking Lorrainers and therefore not considered reliable for the Western Front.[57] Ludendorff insisted that the four new Corps should form a new Army (Tenth) and be used for an offensive out of East Prussia. Falkenhayn, enraged, appointed one of his own favorites to command the middle Carpathian army—now called the German (despite its being half Austrian) South Army—and directed Ludendorff as the Chief of Staff. This move would not only split up the Hindenburg/Ludendorff team, it would force the latter to work closely with the despised Austrians and their incohesive Empire, which he had already referred to as a "corpse." Hindenburg, uneasy without his ambitious lieutenant, offered to resign; Ludendorff protested loudly. In the end the duo were reunited and free to pursue their East Prussian scheme. Falkenhayn seethed, half-hoping failure in the East would vindicate him in his belief of an eastern dead-end, yet anxious that his appointee at South Army—Linsingen—should not be burdened with probable defeat.

While the Germans engaged in high-level infighting, their opponents were also shifting gears, and not without a grind. For reasons not entirely clear the Grand Duke suddenly withdrew his support for the effort of Southwest Front and announced that it would instead now be Northwest Front, which would now receive massive reinforcement. Perhaps his intelligence had discovered enemy troop movements into Prussia, or more likely, he had gotten word that the Romanians were not ready to intervene. An entire army—the Twelfth—was created along the southern frontier of East Prussia and put under command of the redoubtable Plehve and Tenth Army (Sievers) was brought up to full strength. Even the shell shortage which had so handicapped the Russians since September was somewhat alleviated; reserves per gun were considered adequate. It appeared that a repetition of the August strategy was in the making.

The quicker moves of the *Alliance* would upset the Russian plans. It was the Austrians in the mountains who were first to move, on January 23rd, and the long struggle for control of the Carpathian Passes was underway. A more difficult battleground in the dead of winter is difficult to imagine. The mountains themselves are not terribly high—the peaks average 1500-2500m (5000-8000ft)—but are characterized by multiple ridges running parallel at a depth of 48-175km (30-110mi). The range covers the entire area from the Moravian Gate to the Iron Gate and it affects the weather on both sides. Warmer breezes from the south collide with cold winds off the northern plains and create strange and sudden atmospheric conditions along the divide. In the west the treeless tops of the High Tatra give way to heavily forested conditions on all but the highest peaks to the southeast. On the Hungarian side streams have gouged out countless defiles leading to the main ridges; on the Galician side the slope is generally far more abrupt with fewer foothills. Thus a defense of the mountain barrier is more practical from the south side, and a much more difficult undertaking from the north. Should the Russians succeed in penetrating this natural barrier, there would be nothing to stop them from overrunning the plains of Hungary beyond. Unfortunately for the defenders, a series of passes had long been in use to cross the rugged uplands, and some were gentle enough to have allowed the construction of railroads. From the Dunajec/Biala lines eastward were: Dukla Pass (road), Lupkow (road and railroad though these were separated by a ridge), Rostoki (road), Uszok (road and railroad), Verecki (road and railroad), Beskid (road), Wyzkow (road), Tatar or Delatyn (road and railroad), Kirlibaba (road), Stiol (road), and Borgo (road) on the Romanian border. In winter these passes were apt to be buried in several feet of snow and any military movement without their use completely unthinkable. Blizzards were frequent, and unpredictable. And within this dark, frozen, and snowbound landscape two mighty opponents were about to grapple.

Ivanov's forces had generally closed up to the mountain spine—the line of the passes—in early January, and as we have seen, captured a few of them. On the 23rd it was Hötzendorf's turn as he hurled General Boroevic's reinforced Third Army against the western passes. The Uszok was somehow captured almost immediately, but for the most part the "offensive" stalled for lack of mobility. Low-hanging clouds obscured visibility; artillery shells disappeared into the snow or at best shook it from the boughs of the evergreens. Farther east, Linsingen's South Army attacked the middle passes on the 26th and advanced slightly from the Verecki and Beskid into a blinding arctic nightmare; weapons froze, flesh froze. Seventh Army on the extreme right was only slightly more successful but only because it faced weaker resistance; it drove the Russians off the ridges and began a slow re-conquest of the Bukovina, losing more men to exposure than to enemy action. Appeals by the three Austrian armies to Hötzendorf came to nothing; his staff, as one historian wrote, were comfortably housed in accommodations with their wives in the town of Teschen, where they scoffed at any protests from the front.[58]

While thousands of men vanished into the Carpathian snows, others were trying to avoid a swim in the icy Baltic Sea. For three days in mid January an undetected force of Russian vessels had floated hundreds of mines designed to catch German ships hugging the Baltic shore in order to use the Kiel Canal. The effort paid off by the 24th when the cruiser *Gazelle* was seriously damaged and a day later the *Augsburg* was, as well. The latter was eventually repaired, the former, not. At the same time another German cruiser, *Prince Adalbert*, ran aground north of Libau as it steamed to shell the Russian seaport. And on the 26th, Libau was spared again when a German airship, about to bomb it, crashed into the sea some 11.5km (7mi) distant. It was the first loss of the war for the Naval Airship Division.[59] Icing was determined to be the cause.

By the end of January both sides were about ready to launch their respective East Prussian operations. Ludendorff wanted a secondary or diversionary attack to pin down the enemy and distract his attention and ordered Mackenson's Ninth Army to undertake it. At the same time, the attack would serve to test a new sort of weapon. Chemists at Germany's Kaiser Wilhelm Institute for the Advancement of Science had developed a substance which caused irritation to the eyes and nose of those present when it vaporized. This chemical, Xylyl bromide, was a tear gas; it was not poisonous and therefore not technically in violation of the Hague Convention or so the Germans reasoned. It could be carried to the enemy by means of artillery shells. After some hesitation, Hindenberg was persuaded to allow its use, and 18,000 15cm artillery shells had been prepared for use. In all, the attack force consisted of seven divisions with 600 field pieces on an eleven-kilometer front, a density of 8,000 men and 55 guns per kilometer or one gun and 152 men every 19 meters. This was one of the first instances of intense concentration on the Eastern Front, and for the first time the big guns would throw three types of shell: high explosive, shrapnel, and chemical.

From the bluffs on the western side of the river Rawka, the German guns thundered on the last day of January. The bombardment was renewed briefly but intensely the following morning, after which the German infantry attacked, with the high ground between the Rawka and a parallel stream, the Sucha, as the first objective. This was duly reached and the Russians retreated into woods; there they turned on their attackers and inflicted grievous losses. By February 3rd the attack had spent itself five to ten kilometers from the start line; deep snow and low temperatures had exhausted the attack divisions. Two days later the Russians, reinforced with Siberian troops, countered, and a day later were back on the original positions, more or less. About 20,000 Germans and nearly twice as many Russians were casualties, but none of the latter had been caused by the chemical shells; apparently no one had considered the fact that the extreme low temperature would prevent the chemical from vaporizing. If the Germans were disappointed, the Russians seemed indifferent. For years it was assumed that they simply did not know they had been the victims of the war's first chemical attack. But as they ended up holding the battlefield, someone certainly noticed that something was up. Perhaps the information, kicked upstairs, was disregarded. At any rate no press releases contained it, nor was it passed on to Russia's *Entente* allies. All in all the battle at Bolimow—as the action is remembered—was uneventful, but it did achieve its purpose of distracting Russki and *Stavka*.

Ludendorff had completed the regrouping of his forces in East Prussia by late January. Eighth Army was commanded by General von Below of Tannenberg fame, and the new Tenth Army by General von Eichhorn, a Hindenburg selection. The two groups disposed of 17 divisions, about equal in total numbers, to the 13 divisions of Siever's Tenth Army. Their task was to drive in Tenth Army's flanks, encircle it, then push southeast towards

Bialystok and the rear of the enemy forces north of the Vistula. Exceptionally poor weather cloaked the German preparations, at any rate, Front command was more concerned with completing the assembly of Twelfth Army in Masovia which was assigned to invade Prussia within a fortnight, than with Siever's pleas of lack of reserves. Not until February 5th did the Russians learn that East Prussia had been heavily reinforced. Then the weather broke; a blizzard swept out of the plains on the 6th, but the German leaders decided to stick to the schedule irregardless. Eighth Army opened its attack on the morning of the 7th in heavy snowfall which effectively blinded the defenders. Litzmann's Corps surged over the Pissa at Wrobeln and took Bialla, isolating Johannisburg and smaller Russian units strung out along the lakes. On the 8th, Tenth Army smashed in the Russian right beyond Insterburg, as far as Tilsit, and in quick succession occupied Lauenstein, Pillkallen, and Schirwindt. In the center, another German group struck east from Lötzen. To the south, Gallwitz pinned the enemy before Przasnysz. All along the line bewildered Russians, most of whom were in any case not first line troops, surrendered or fled.

By February 12th the front was irreparably broken. On that day Eichhorn was over the frontier, his advance guard as far as Mariampol. When orders for retreat were finally issued on the 14th, it was already too late. Eighth Army had taken Lyck and was nearing Augustov, while Tenth Army had already reached the forest of that name. The German advance was greatly facilitated by the capture of large quantities of food and winter clothing at Wirballen. It was also helped by the Russians exhausting themselves trudging through deep snow while the pursuers were able to make good use of the trampled-down, ready-made routes, with much less expenditure of energy.

Sievers had attempted to make a stand at Eydtkuhnen on the 10th; he now tried again at Suwalki on the 12th with the same results. A citizen of the Polish town remembered the morning of the 14th when the streets grew quiet. Soon she saw her first "pickelhaube" come around a corner, warily on the lookout for snipers. Soon others appeared, then came larger bodies of soldiers, with officers.[60] Front command ordered retreat that very day; it was of course too late. Eighth Army had entered the forest by now, that huge, marshy, lake-dotted wilderness of few good roads.

Between the 16th and 21st of February, Tenth Army from the north and Eighth Army from the west compressed Siever's command into a pocket from which escape was possible only to the southeast. The Russians could be forgiven for not knowing what direction to withdraw towards, in trackless, snowy forest and without even the sun as a guide. One Corps was isolated and destroyed; all others were roughly handled, and Siever's command ceased to be an army but in name only. It was scattered, with most groups seeking the safety of the fortresses of the Niemen and Bobr. Eichhorn's Tenth German Army had used the Niemen as left flank protection during the drive on Augustov and now it turned east to close up to the stream. On the 20th a bridgehead had been won in the north at Tauroggen, and now the Germans tried to force the river at other points as well, but it was only a replay of the efforts in September. Soon, Russian counterattacks had retaken the few bridgeheads and once again Ludendorff called for retreat to the frontier, or a line just outside it.

Eighth Army had also turned ninety degrees to attack the Bobr line, particularly the fortress of Osowiec, another prize which had eluded capture in the autumn campaign. The *Kaiser* had made another appearance behind the lines at Lötzen and Lyck on the 13th and 14th, giving short speeches and thanking his soldiers for their efforts in clearing the "sacred soil" of East Prussia. With all German territory once again inviolate, every effort should be made to expel the enemy from his jump-off points. Osowiec must be taken. But if the marshes of the Bobr had plagued the attackers in September, they would plague them in February; soon German artillerists were wondering if floundering in semi-warm swamp water was any worse than slipping on, or breaking through, swamp ice. The bombardment of Osowiec finally commenced on February 25th and desisted ten days later. The result was another replay of September, plus additional losses to exposure. Not that the Russians were without problems either. An English observer wrote of the anxiety caused by the shell shortage. Officers complained that struggling with the Germans was quite a different experience from fighting Austrians. The Germans were more accurate with their artillery fire and the amount of shell they used was "extraordinary." Infantry complained of being unsupported, and the gunners complained that the weapons had become inaccurate because of wear to the recoil systems.[61]

Mining continued to be the order of the day in the Baltic; on the 12th the Russians floated many in the Gulf of Danzig. In the far-off Gulf of Finland, the Russian cruiser *Rurik* struck a German mine and was badly damaged. It was soon run aground to avoid sinking.

Back in the Carpathians, men were still freezing and dying. Hötzendorf was getting desperate to relieve Przemysl with its large garrison and huge stock of war material. Boroevic had long been stalled north of Uszok Pass, the nearest point of relief for the fortress. Worse still, the ever-aggressive Brusilov had advanced on Dukla and Lupkow passes back in late January and had taken the former. And on February 5th, he had forced the railway side of the Lupkow and seized the town of Mesölaborcz. A ten-day battle for the road side ensued; it was winter war at its worst as thousands of starving, frostbitten men perished in the elements or were taken prisoner, often willingly. Artillery, when it could be moved, was ineffective, except at causing snow slides which could bury friend or foe. Boroevic, protesting too often or too loudly, was moved with his headquarters to the west and a scraped-up force called Second Army was inserted in the line and given every man Hötzendorf could spare. Its commander, General Böhm-Ermolli, was ordered to attack, and according to one writer "could be trusted to be more sparing with recognition of reality."[62] He opened his offensive on the 17th from the Uszok and Rostoki passes but the net gain was a few small villages on the north slope of the mountains. Farther east, South Army had inched forward from the Verecki and Beskid passes to try to link up in the valley of the Opor. To accomplish this it had to pass the ridge at Koziowa, an excellent defensive position for the Russians and one which they intended to retain. First contact was made on the 6th when the Russians commenced a withering fire from well-concealed positions on the forested slopes and in the ravines. One account has "twenty-two furious bayonet charges"[63] occurring on the 7th without result for the attackers. Pike grey and field gray—as well as blood red—now littered the otherwise nearly all-white snowscape.

Only on the extreme eastern end of the line could the Austrians claim any success. Kimpolung in the far Bukovina was recaptured February 7th and the province systematically cleared of Russians. By throwing an entire army into the area, this persistent hole in the front was finally plugged. On the 18th of the month, Czernowitz was Austrian again, for the fourth time in the war. Without serious opposition General Pflanzer-Baltin decided to press on to the northwest, into the Russian flank. Kolomea was taken then Stanislav three days later; Seventh Army was now in position to move against the troops opposing Linsingen's South Army, and perhaps link up with the latter well in advance of the mountains. It was not to be. The Austrian vanguard reached the Dniester at Halicz and encountered a stubborn resistance which finally threw them back by March 1st. For the next two weeks fighting was sporadic in the valley of the Dniester, but after the Russian re-conquest of Stanislav on March 4th it was indecisive. Still, Pflanzer-Baltin had gained much ground and probably prevented the Romanians from seriously considering entering the war.

Elsewhere the news was all bad for Austria-Hungary. Despite a final effort to overcome both the elements and the enemy on February 27th, Linsingen and Böhm-Ermolli were stuck deep in the Carpathian snow. The Russians even succeeded in forcing the Rostoki Pass in early March, further isolating the two. Nothing now could save Przemysl. Hötzendorf's reckless use of his armies in the mountains in the dead of winter had cost him 250,000 casualties, probably half of these from exposure. What was left of the forces along the Carpathian Front were plagued by illness and low morale, and this meant desertion had become all too frequent. Long-persistent rumors that the Slav troops of the Empire were disloyal began to get louder and more open. The Czechs and Ruthenes (Ukrainians) in particular were suspected of treachery. But where the Austrians saw only problems, their allies saw inefficiency. Increasingly after the Carpathian disasters, the Germans would at first suggest, later insist, that German commanders control Austrian troops. The Dual Monarchy would resist this trend to the bitter end, but after the first winter of war it was practically helpless, its prestige seriously undermined.

Other action had meanwhile commenced on the other end of the front. Filling the gap between Eighth Army in East Prussia and Ninth Army in Central Poland was the German XX Corps, on the line opposite where the new Russian Twelfth Army was forming. Ludendorff decided that some effort should be made to upset the deployment of this fresh enemy force, before it became a serious threat to the southern border of Masuria. XX Corps was thus ordered ahead, reinforced with some *Landwehr* and Reserve Divisions, on 22nd February. Twelfth Army, though disorganized, resisted well enough to force the Germans to try to outflank their foe instead of plowing their way through the ill-prepared defensive positions. Swinging well to the east, the invaders bypassed a Russian force defending the town of Przasnysz then wheeled around and surrounded it. 10,000 bewildered Russians surrendered here on the 24th as a result, a disaster which seems to have shaken the Russian Command to a considerable degree.

Ludendorff's victory was short-lived. Frustrated and desperate, the Grand Duke ordered every available battle-worthy unit in the area to engage the enemy and expel him from Poland. The result was a confused yet savage battle, notable in that the Russians made use of a number of armored cars equipped with machine guns. Krasnosielce, a village at an important crossing of the Orjits River, was the scene of a heavy fight; the Russians finally carried the day and pushed on toward Przasnysz. Both sides waged a fierce, desperate struggle for a relatively meaningless strip of real estate. One account of the action has men engaged in close quarters, where grenades and even swords were used to good effect. Many of the Russians, otherwise unarmed, were anxious to close with the enemy, wielding bayonets, knives, and primitive weapons which they were quite adept at using, when they got the chance to do so.[64] Usual German advantages in firepower were of course nullified in hand-to-hand combat, a practice the soldiers of the *Kaiser* tried always to avoid. Finally, the arrival of the IV Siberian Corps turned the tide, and by the 26th, the Germans began to retreat. Przasnysz and the surrounding countryside was lost, and with it nearly as many prisoners as the Germans had taken not a week earlier. The Russian counter had indeed been a praiseworthy undertaking, but the obvious reference to the chronic lack of small arms is telling.

On March 9th, a reinforced, regrouped German force advanced once more, down the Orjits and Omulew Rivers, with its objectives Przasnysz and Ostrolenka. The Orjits formed for a ways the boundary between Prussia and Poland, then curved south passing east of Przasnysz before emptying into the Narew, while the Omulew flowed from Willenberg directly southeast to the fortress of Ostrolenka on the Narew. Though the terrain was thus suitable for such an advance, weather conditions became unsuitable, alternately freezing and thawing, and making the movement most difficult. Heavy Russian resistance also became a factor. For two weeks, indecisive fighting commenced; Ludendorff then called off the whole operation, and withdrew nearly to the frontiers, but taking care that the battle line should remain on Polish soil. For the whole Mazovian campaign, he claimed 43,000 Russian prisoners and 25,000 killed. The Russians countered by insisting they had taken 30,000 Germans and killed nearly as many.

While Plehve and Gallwitz wrestled in northern Poland, Sievers felt strong enough by early March to once again threaten East Prussia from the east, and he began to move from his base at Grodno toward the border. For a few days he advanced to contact with the enemy, but was himself countered beginning on the 8th, and bested in two days of fighting after which he gave an order for general retreat. The Germans gave chase until they too ran into determined resistance and were stopped. Once again the weather dominated the action, as described in one account which tells of sub-freezing temperatures and roads so slippery with ice that exhausted horses fell by the dozens, and foot soldiers could march only three kilometers per hour at best.[65] The episode was over by mid-month.

Barely had the bullets all fallen west of the Niemen, when they began to fly again on the flanks. At the stubborn fortress of Osowiec the bombardment, which had never completely stopped but only subsided, began again in earnest. The Russians reported the appearance of German 28- and 42-centimeter guns, and the 30.5cm Austrian weapon. This type of firepower should have been enough to smash the strongest of forts—it had done so many times thus far in the war—and the easy survival of Osowiec is testament to the lack of stable gun-emplacement in winter and in the surrounding marshes, and also the weather. German gunners reported their shots as ineffective and inaccurate, a curious tale in this war, but Russian reports continually confirmed that damage caused by enemy shelling was minimal, and failed even to destroy the outer earthworks. Two more major efforts were made by the attackers on March 27th and April 11th before the spring thaw rendered the ground too spongy for military operations.

Only one hole in the line now still existed and it was about to be filled. Thus far no notable events had occurred at the extreme northern end of the front, along the Baltic coast. But on March 17th, two Russian groups of brigade size struck simultaneously at Tauroggen and Memel, Germany's northernmost city. Conquest of the small strip of German territory north of the Niemen was the obvious intent; the whole area was patrolled only by *Landsturm* troops. These resisted as best they could but were driven off and the Russians took both localities. Memel was looted and partially burned, but the rampage was short-lived. After some street fighting, the city was cleared on the 21st by German troops who included one of the *Kaiser's* six sons, Prince Joachim, within their group. One of the Russian withdrawal routes was the coast road; it was shelled at the town of Polangen, just over the frontier, by German warships in the Baltic. A few days later another force of Germans counterattacked north along the Jura River and took the town of Laugszargen on the border, then crossed the ice on the stream and recaptured Tauroggen. No one could know it yet, but before the onset of April 1915, the last Russian soldier had been expelled from German soil for the rest of the war.

No sooner had Prussian soil been cleared of the enemy than the German press was presented with ammunition of its own. On April 3rd a special correspondent of the *Chicago Daily News* published an account of Russian "outrages" in East Prussia, claiming he had carefully investigated every charge he made. His accusations included the burning, deliberately, of hundreds of villages which were left uninhabitable, and the rape of thousands of Prussian women by Russian troops.[66] Russian actions during 1914-15 were tame compared to what would happen in 1944-45, but in both cases the attitude of the Russian government ever since has been one of official denial. Even the collapse of Communism did nothing to shake this stance; it still refuses to acknowledge history. But to return to our story, the confirmation of the tales of the refugees, by a neutral source, only served to convince the average German that he was indeed fighting in the east against a savage, barbarous foe.

Whatever horrors the population of East Prussia may have endured, human opinion was by no means sympathetic to them. One Polish woman, fed up with the German occupation wrote that although she tried not to allow feelings of hatred to overtake her, to hear the words "East Prussia" spoken aroused "something akin to that feeling" in her. She went on to complain that East Prussia was the German excuse to ravage Poland, to requisition everything from furniture to agricultural implements. Even the trees were all cut down![67]

At about the same time, on March 15th, another Pole, having escaped to Switzerland, related that one hundred thousand of the 127,500 square kilometers of Poland had by that time been devastated by the fighting. He claimed 15,000 villages had been destroyed, burnt, or damaged, and 1,000 churches or chapels ruined. More than a million horses and two million head of cattle had been seized by the armies and "not a grain of corn, a scrap of meat, nor a drop of milk" remained to nourish the civilian population. At least 400,000 individuals had lost their means of subsistence. Galicia, he continued, was no better off; all but 5,000 of the 75,000 square kilometers of the province were in Russian hands. The invaders had grabbed 900,000 horses, 200,000 cows, all the grain, the oilfields, and part of the salt-producing area of that unhappy land. More than one million displaced persons had sought shelter in other areas of

Austria, where they lived "in sheer destitution."[68] The larger towns and cities had long been destinations for many hapless, panic-stricken refugees; the belief was that they could at least provide some shelter from the elements and possessed some rudimentary food distribution system. But this was a different kind of war. Aircraft could now reach locations which even the largest naval gun could not, and a new form of terror was soon introduced to urban populations. On March 18th a German Zeppelin raid on Warsaw caused little material damage, but sent crowds of terrified residents and refugees alike scattering in all directions. On the 31st, Libau was again shelled from the sea. The message was clear: only flight into the depths of the interior of the country could ensure safety. The question became: could it ensure survival? For many in the path of war, there seemed no alternative, and a great exodus was in the making.

There would be no escape for the doomed garrison of Przemysl. A half-hearted Russian attack on the 13th had breached the outer defenses; clearly the defenders were losing hope. General Kusmanek ordered a last desperate breakout attempt which commenced on the 18th and was soon bloodily repulsed. Kusmanek harbored no further illusions; he had nothing to be ashamed of, having conducted a long skillful defense that had suffered relatively few casualties—except during the breakout attempts—while inflicting many on General Selivanov's Eleventh Army. His troops had not suffered much except for some belt-tightening and a monotonous diet, and his officers had enjoyed every sort of luxury. But provisions had run out and the failure of Hötzendorf's winter offensives meant no help could now be expected. Accordingly, he ordered the systematic destruction of anything and everything that might have been useful to the Russians for military purposes. The remaining explosives were thrown into the San River. More than 1,000 artillery pieces large and small, and many of the small-arms too, were rendered useless by removing essential parts and destroying them. Any horses that had not been killed for food were shot. All day long on the 21st the Russians could hear the explosions and commotion and knew what it meant; they were not surprised when on Monday morning, March 22nd, Austrian officers waving flags of truce appeared, emerging from the city by automobile. The Russians were surprised to learn of the spoils when they took 120,000 prisoners and huge quantities of ammunition of all calibers which could not be disposed of. For the next two weeks, 10,000 men per day were sent to the railheads to begin a long journey to the frozen prisoner-of-war camps in Siberia, places so remote as to need no fences, because any attempted escape would only ensure death from exposure.

The plight of the prisoner of war was at first not so very bad. Russians believed that officers, as gentlemen, should not have to be subjected to interrogation and of course no labor. They were generally well treated by both sides. For the rank and file the biggest challenge was always proper nutrition, a problem that would only get worse for both camps as the war dragged on. Prisoners of the *Alliance* were often pressed into service as agricultural workers, and invariably under guard. The Russians used a different approach. Their internment areas were so isolated that they usually allowed prisoners complete freedom of movement by day and warned them to return by a certain hour after which they would be locked out, with no hope of shelter. It was not unusual for Germans and Austro-Hungarians to obtain employment if any was available in the local economy.

Even before the fall of Przemysl, one more drama had begun which needed to be enacted before the snow melted at the front. After the failure of Hötzendorf's winter offensives, Ivanov wanted to strike back hard, believing the Austrians, so terribly weakened, might crack. He accordingly reinforced his armies there and urged his commanders ahead, promising further support as soon as Eleventh Army was finished at Przemysl. The rather weak forces in Bukovina attacked first, on March 15th beginning a series of minor actions which would last for a month without significant result. Brusilov pushed off on the 19th against the western passes or beyond them as the case might be. A minor success was scored near Bartfeld on the 23rd; mopping up around the southern exit of the Lupkow was complete by the 26th, and the Uszok was being threatened by the 29th. On March 27th Brusilov announced that he had pushed seven miles south of the Hungarian frontier. In reality, the Russians were now experiencing many of the same problems of weather that had bedeviled the Austrians so recently. On April 2nd the fighting south of the passes was undertaken in deep snow which slowed all movement to a crawl. Cisna and the Rostoki Pass were reported as captured on the 4th, but this was the last Russian success. Within a few days, German troops were appearing on the line; a new *Beskidenkorps* had been created to assist the Austrians[69], and it went right into action south of Lupkow Pass. On the 10th, Ivanov called off the offensive in the mountains. A few more actions rounded out the fighting;

an Austrian attack north of Uszok Pass gained some ground on the 14th, but stalled three days later despite a renewed effort.

Mercifully, the first winter of war was over, its snows now swelled the streams of east-central Europe, its frosts loosened their grip on the tortured, blood-soaked soil. The strategies of the generals had been tested and been found wanting; all life forms in the battle zones had been sacrificed. But no one could foresee an end to the fighting. Indeed, there was no talk of peace, only greater sacrifice. And the scope of the war was expected to soon be widened. As early as March 6th, Hötzendorf had informed Hindenburg that he believed war with Italy to be inevitable. In the eyes of the Austrians, a bad military situation was about to become much worse.

Austria-Hungary had suffered 750,000 casualties since the beginning of the year, a staggering rate of attrition, which, unless diminished drastically, would certainly mean complete defeat within the year. Already overtaxed on two fronts how could the Empire possibly survive a third against Italy, perhaps a fourth if Romania followed Italy's lead? For many, the answers were too bitter to contemplate. The first whisperings of a separate peace with Russia were heard. Morale in the army was very low, especially among the 50% of the troops who were neither German nor Hungarian, and desertion began to be a problem, especially in the case of Slav soldiers facing the Russians. Material deficiencies had become another handicap; huge losses such as were borne in Przemysl could not quickly be made good. Clearly, Austria faced a crisis of the first magnitude, in large part due to the obstinate offensive policies of Hötzendorf, who was once again forced to appeal to his more powerful ally for help.

Falkenhayn could take no pleasure from the fact that he had predicted failure of the winter offensives; he was, in effect, now being presented with the bill. Ludendorff was also screaming for more troops, but at least he had delivered a tactical success in the "Winter Battle of Masuria"—a typical Ludendorff (or Hoffmann) misnomer—and German soil had been cleared of the enemy. Clearly, Austria-Hungary needed more support and would collapse without it. Reluctantly, Falkenhayn tabled his western strategy and agreed to send substantial reinforcements to the East. The *Kaiser* had also been won over to the new planning, and by mid-April it was decided to form two new German armies on the Eastern Front. Falkenhayn would send eight divisions from the Western Front to the Cracow area where they would form the

Eleventh Army and be commanded by General August von Mackensen (formerly of Ninth Army). A further three infantry and three cavalry divisions were sent to the far north and became *Armergruppe Lauenstein*, to be launched into Courland to distract the Russians. Later, the group was doubled in size and subsequently became known as Niemen Army. German losses since New Year's had not been inconsiderable—perhaps 50-60,000—and it was only with the greatest efforts that the nation could maintain its armies with anything like full strength. There were now the equivalent of four armies facing the Russians with yet another about to be created. The German commitment had risen from 39 divisions in January to 57 by May. Austria-Hungary had retained, on paper at least, 58 divisions since mid January. It transferred two into the line, one away, and incredibly had lost only one at Przemysl.[70] Already a trend had begun which would last throughout the war: the Germans would frequently transfer units up and down the line or between the major fronts; the Austrians preferred to leave troops and equipment in place, and if need be, transfer headquarters only.

On the Russian side no one was terribly pleased with the outcome of the winter fighting either. Shortages of small arms, ammunition, and especially heavy artillery were affecting strategy; the fortress of Przemysl had held out so long simply because the besiegers lacked the heavy artillery which alone could have ensured its early fall. Troops were facing combat conditions without firearms. Desertion was not uncommon. Rumors of corruption in the highest levels of government were gaining credibility, at least among the peasant, often illiterate, soldiers. A whispering campaign against "Germans" in their midst was begun; there were plenty of targets, from the Empress on down through the bureaucracy, Russia had long been home to a large "German" aristocracy. And then there were the Generals—Rennenkampf, Plehve, Sievers, Evert, and Pflug to name just a few—and numberless junior officers with suspicious-sounding names. Even Russia's *Entente* allies were suspected of reneging on contract-orders and failing to properly support the war effort. Scapegoats such as Sukhomlinov could be found for material shortages but who could stop the subversion? Such questions could only aversely affect morale, and the Grand Duke decided to abandon all offensive schemes for the moment and improve upon his front line defenses. Russki complained, claiming the front was far too long to be properly defended everywhere, and that no reserve could be created as a result. He was overruled and then resigned, stating health problems as the reason; his replacement was General Alexiev, former Chief of Staff to Southwest Front.

Russian commitment to the front against the Austro-Germans now included ten armies with two more still stationed on the flanks, the Baltic and Black Sea coasts. By April, 148 divisions were available to oppose the 115 enemy divisions, which were smaller in numbers to begin with. Material deficiencies were slowly being made good, and most Russian leaders were still confident, given that the army be allowed a breathing spell, of victory. Russian casualties during the winter are unknown and difficult to estimate, but the Germans had accounted for nearly 100,000 and the Austro-Hungarians, probably half that many. Still, no one in either camp doubted Russia's ability to make good manpower losses. They were still less concerned with whether or not that manpower was used efficiently and effectively.

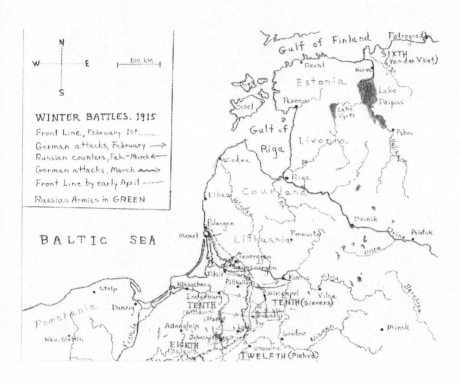

Winter Battles, 1915

Chapter Seven
The Front Moves East

By April 1915 the military situation of the Empire of Austria-Hungary seemed untenable. It had failed to defeat the small Kingdom of Serbia on its southern border and had sustained a series of catastrophic defeats at the hands of the Russians all of which had cost it a loss of one and a half million men. Only a quarter million remained on the line to face the Russians, who were threatening to pour over the mountains into Hungary. Of these, fewer than half spoke German or Hungarian, the two languages of command, and gone were most of the multi-lingual officers with whom the army had begun the war. Franz Conrad von Hötzendorf himself spoke seven of the Empire's ten major languages, but few of his junior colleagues were as well trained. It is easy to understand how a Ukrainian, Polish, or Slovak soldier could relate far easier to the speech of his Russian enemy than to his Hungarian master, once the original cadre of leaders with whom the men could relate had become casualties, such a basic function as language of command had become a worrying problem. And with the entry of Italy and Romania into the hostile camp seemingly imminent, the loyalty of the Latin-speaking troops would presumably be severely tested. Nor were Austria's woes limited to personnel considerations; communications and supply were often as inefficient as Russia's, and without the sheer volume. The artillery were so diverse as to require several dozen different types of shells, and the weapons were in short supply, as were small arms. It seemed that nothing save massive reinforcement from Germany could prevent an early collapse of the old Empire.

Falkenhayn and *OHL* were well aware of the problem in the southeast, bombarded as they were by Ludendorff and *Ober Ost* for increased resources for the Eastern Front. By spring 1915 even the skeptical Chief of the General Staff had to admit that Germany needed to make her main effort in the East that year, if only to prop up her main ally. He predictably disliked Ludendorff's plan for an offensive from East Prussia; Hötzendorf's plan made more sense to him, besides, by agreeing to it he could wring some concessions out of the Austrians. What he wanted, what all the German leaders wanted really, was for Austro-Hungarian troops to be placed under German command. They saw Austrian weaknesses more as failures of leadership, less as failures of soldiers or weapons. In the event, the agreement more or less satisfied both Chiefs: Mackensen's new Eleventh Army was to be inserted into the line between the Austrian Third and Fourth Armies and be given control of both of the latter. Falkenhayn also reinforced Ludendorff and agreed to a "diversionary" attack on the left wing, and Hötzendorf promised his own right wing distraction. Mackensen's group would be backed by an unprecedented amount of artillery; estimates reach as high as 1700 guns and mortars, with one gun in five a heavy.[71]

As early as April 21st, reports of enemy activity opposite the Dunajec/Biala front were reaching Southwest Front headquarters. Staff officers there, perhaps Ivanov himself, preferred not to deal with such annoyances; they were anxious to renew the Carpathian offensive and had the Grand Duke's support. When a more serious warning came in on the 26th, it too was waved off. The Russians would concede the Germans "surprise," without their actually having achieved it. All available reserves were now being sent to the extreme south for an attack on Bukovina.

On April 19th, the Germans were first off the mark when they sent their cavalry divisions of Lauenstein's group into the thinly defended Lithuanian countryside. To cause further confusion, available aircraft were sent on various missions; ten planes bombed the provincial town of Bialystok on the 20th and a small group of Zeppelins raided Warsaw a day later. Ludendorff's diversion was underway. Southwest Courland was rapidly overrun by the German horses; Shavli on the Libau railroad was entered on the 30th, its citizens stunned to find themselves so suddenly hosts to an alien army. Slower-moving columns of infantry were far behind, and some were marching up the Baltic Coast. Two German cruisers shelled the hapless port of Libau once again on the 27th, then returned two days later for a repeat performance. Thus far in the war no other city had been so heavily bombarded by naval guns. The German navy continued to support its ground forces in Courland for another two weeks. On May 2nd it mined the waters of the Irben Strait (north of Courland) and again shelled suspected Russian positions, as the army closed in on Libau, all along the coastline. On May 8th the Germans entered the blasted port, but lost a destroyer to a mine in the harbor.

The right-wing pinning attack came on April 25th, when Austrian Seventh Army and South Army attacked all along the front from Bukovina to the Koziowa position, as it turned out, the very area where Ivanov was planning to move against them. Four days later Second Army struck at the Rostoki Pass. These strikes gained little ground, as was expected, but they did upset Russian planning and tie down units, and thereby prevent their transfer to the area farther west, where they would be sorely needed. The Russians scored a significant local success at Gorodenka on the 27th/28th, stopping Seventh Army from pushing westward along the Dniester to the rear of units deep in the mountains.

At about this time on April 26, 1915, Field Marshal Moritz von Auffenberg was arrested after a search of his residence uncovered irrefutable evidence of his involvement in a plot to sell Austrian and German military secrets to the Russians. Apparently even the enormous sum Auffenberg was to receive in money for his information was discovered. His first contact with the foreigners occurred after 1911, when he had become War Minister; he was only one, although the highest-ranking, of several figures investigated by the Austrian Secret Service. It may be recalled that he was commanding the Fourth Army in Galicia early in the war, when his "victory" at Komorow motivated Franz Joseph to confer upon him the title of Baron. The arrest tended to raise morale in the Austro-Hungarian Army; the Empire's defeats could easily be explained away as treachery.

Radko-Dmitriev's Third Russian Army held a front extending from the Vistula along the Dunajec and Biala Rivers to a point where it turned east from the latter stream and continued over the East Beskids west of the Dukla Pass and on to beyond the Lupkow. It was a long frontage for an army which straddled a major mountain range and was expected to hold two Passes. It did have the advantage of possession of both Gorlice and Tarnow, rail towns immediately behind it, but Radko had not fortified the line, preferring to let the rivers account for the first line of defense, with one trench line behind. Even this was by all accounts poorly constructed, too shallow, and often not connected to any communications network or supporting positions. This was not unusual for the Russian side of the Eastern Front at this time; *Stavka* had no comparable experience to that of *OHL* on the Western Front. What Radko did have was a force of over 200,000 men with well over 600 artillery pieces, though none of the latter were of the heavy variety. Mackensen's preparations for the coming offensive were thorough. He insisted on, and received, adequate munitions and supply services. With the Austrians on his flanks, he commanded over 300,000 soldiers and concentrated along a narrow section of front. The Austrians brought forward a number of armored trains with which to exploit the expected breakthrough.

Despite Ivanov's complacency, the Russians knew pretty much what was coming. A nurse with the army at Gorlice recorded in her diary for April 28th that the soldiers related how they were well-fed and reasonably well supplied at the front, but that they were all apprehensive with the appearance of German forces on their sections of line. They entertained no such fears of the Austrians, but believed that with the coming of the Germans, an enemy offensive was certain to be imminent.[72] When Austrian deserters in the last days of April revealed even greater details of the coming attack, Third Army was finally put on alert, but by then it was too late to do anything worthwhile to stop it. The Russians could be excused for any deficiency of munitions, as all their armies were at this time complaining of material shortages.[73]

On the 28th Mackensen allowed his right wing to advance in the foothills of the mountains, along the upper Ropa River. Two days later the left was waved off, up to the Vistula. Both were probes designed to divert enemy attention from the center, where the breakthrough was planned.

A quick rundown of the order of battle on the Eastern Front in May 1915 is indicative of the importance with which the *Alliance* regarded its Gorlice-Tarnow offensive. In the far north "Niemen Army" under General von Below was forming; across the remainder of East Prussia lay Tenth Army (Eichhorn) and Eighth Army, now commanded by von Scholtz. Just north of the Vistula a force of several divisions was being organized into yet another army (Twelfth) under the hitherto Corps commander Gallwitz. Stretching across the Polish Plains were Ninth Army (Prince Leopold of Bavaria), the so-called Woyrsch Detachment, and First Austrian Army (Archduke Friedrich). Then came Mackensen's group south of the Vistula, Fourth Austrian Army (Archduke Joseph Ferdinand), Eleventh Army (Mackensen), and Third Austrian Army (Boroevic). Three more armies covered the line to the Romanian border, Second Austrian Army (Boehm-Ermolli), South Army

(Linsingen), and Seventh Austrian Army (Pflanzer-Baltin). In other words, "Army Group Mackensen" comprised roughly one-quarter of the total strength of the *Alliance* in the East at that time. For the Russians, the deployment north to south was as follows: Fifth Army, Tenth Army (now Radkevitch), Twelfth Army (Churin), First Army (Litvinov), Second Army (Smirnov), Fourth Army (Evert), Third Army (Radko-Dmitriev), Eighth Army (Brusilov), Eleventh Army (Shcherbachev) and Ninth Army (Lechitski). Out of ten Armies on the line, therefore, only one would absorb the coming blow. One lone army, and the one perhaps the most thinly stretched, at that.

Unfortunately for the Russians, they were also to be the victims of new, more effective tactics. Mackensen's Chief of Staff, von Seekt, proposed a heavy bombardment using guns of the largest caliber in order to demoralize the enemy. The front line thus shattered, the three armies should advance, using the powerful German Eleventh Army as a spearhead, while the Austrian armies on either side gave support by rolling up the flanks and attacking secondary objectives. This was the birth of the famous "phalanx" system of advance, which Mackensen was to use to great advantage in the coming months. Had Radko-Dmitriev disposed of significant reserve forces, he might certainly have defeated the "phalanx" as easily as any other offensive tactic, but a single Caucasian Corps was all he could count for an appreciable unit not committed to the front line. To his lasting credit as a commander, he placed this Corps behind the Gorlice sector of front, as he suspected there might be trouble brewing at that point.

And trouble there was. On May 1st, hundreds of guns and mortars positioned in the hills between the upper Dunajec and the Biala belched forth destruction. All along the line between Tarnow and Grybow the steel rained down on the Russian trenches, burying men alive, destroying barbed wire and communications, and smashing gun emplacements and strongpoints. The carnage continued for hours, then stopped and was renewed for four hours the following morning, from 6:00 to 10:00am. Huge Austrian Skoda mortars helped obliterate what was left of the front line; by the time the infantry attacked there existed almost no evidence of it. Tarnow and what was left of the village of Ciezkowice were taken that day. Russian resistance was minimal; those who could, fled, those that survived the shelling tended to surrender quickly, having been reduced to a state of shock and left isolated in the churned-up wasteland that had earlier been a defensive position. Reserves, few enough in number, soon disappeared into the smoke-ridden, dust choked hills, never to be seen again by their commanders. Many of these men were made prisoners, lacking as they did alternative positions to which to retire when routed.

Within two days Mackensen had taken Gorlice, turned the Dunajec/Biala line, and crippled the Russian Third Army. On the 4th, Radko hurled the Third Caucasus Corps, his only sizeable reserve, at Eleventh Army at Biecz and slowed the German advance along the railroad to Sanok, but farther north the fighting had already reached the watershed between the Dunajec and the Wisloka. The latter stream was crossed on the 5th, secured on the 6th. The nurse who had heard rumors of the impending attack was now swept up in the retreat. She recalled, painfully, the cries of the wounded begging not to be left behind, but her unit was ordered to flee. They had hoped to stop in Biecz for a rest, but in the event were unable to do so as enemy artillery shells were falling nearby, causing many casualties, and turning the withdrawal into somewhat of a rout. By the time her unit reached Yaslo, it was being swept along with huge masses of retreating men and vehicles moving "ever eastwards."[74]

By counterattacking at Biecz, Radko hoped to gain time to extricate the troops on the far side of the mountain passes before their escape routes were cut off by Mackensen's advance. He was partially successful; only one division, under General Kornilov was trapped near Dukla and forced to surrender, after a rear guard action on the 7th. That very day Jaslo was lost and with it any hope of stopping the Germans west of the upper San. Even so the Grand Duke was reluctant to order a general retreat; he still dreamed of an invasion of Hungary by Eighth Army. In fact the last Russian was driven out of Hungary by May 9th, and by ordering Third Army to hold its "positions" he had ensured its destruction. By the time the Russian command realized the seriousness of Eleventh Army's offensive, Radko's force had practically ceased to be as an effective fighting unit. On the 10th Third Army was finally given permission to retire behind the San, two days after the capture, intact, of the railroad bridge at Rymanov which threatened to dislocate the entire Carpathian Front. A Russian counterattack in Bukovina on the 9th/10th was ineffective and at any rate could hardly have affected events in western Galicia. The Austrians were forced back to the Pruth by the 12th, but all eyes were on the San, over which the remnants of Third Army fled on the 11th and 12th. Sanok on the upper stream fell to Second Army at the same time, as did Turka to Linsingen. A day later even Jaroslav was in sight of the fast-moving armies of the *Alliance.*

With the collapse of the center, the Russian forces on both flanks were obliged to withdraw or they would occupy a dangerous salient. As the Austrian Fourth Army rolled up the flank on the Vistula, it took thousands of prisoners and fulfilled its intended purpose well. Evert, to the north of the stream, needed no urging to pull back from the Nida; he abandoned Kielce on the 12th and was back at Opatow by the 14th. To the south Eighth and Eleventh Armies' positions had become untenable and they began to fall back toward the Dniester. Only the newly placed Ninth Army in the Bukovina was full of fight and took Nadworna on the outer approaches to the Tatars Pass, on May 15th. It was to be the last Russian success in Galicia that spring.

Elsewhere along the front events went almost unnoticed, overshadowed as they were by the Gorlice/Tarnow breakthrough. On May 3rd, the German Ninth Army once again launched a gas attack on the Bzura and Rawka lines; its outcome was just as disappointing as the original in January had been despite the release of 263 tons of chlorine, which caused 6000 Russian casualties. Lauenstein's drive in the far north had gained a lot of ground—cavalry had penetrated as far as Mitau—but the Russians had finally put their Sixth Army to good use and soon shoved back the Germans, retaking Shavli on the 11th and advancing to a general line Windau/Dubissa River a few days later. Here the front stabilized, as both sides collected additional strength. And Evert, responding to an Austrian crossing of the Vistula near Baranow, countered half-heartedly on the 15th. But the main drama had now shifted to the San.

The San River rises in the mountains near the Uzhok Pass and flows in a northwesterly direction to its junction with the Vistula. From a few kilometers beyond Przemysl its course is fairly straight all the way to its mouth, and it is on this stretch that the Russians, as the Austrians had done in September, planned to make a determined stand and halt their enemies. Mackensen's advance units had first sighted the stream on the 14th and had crossed it the next day, somewhat north of Jaroslav. By then Radko had been sent a few divisions from Northwest Front and he counterattacked on the 16th, beginning a five-day battle around Sieniawa/Jaroslav, as the Austro-Germans struggled to cross the river and establish bridgeheads on the northeast side. The Russians fought hard to maintain the line of the river and would have preferred to retain some bridgeheads of their own on the opposite bank. Apparently the *Kaiser* was present to witness one crossing made on the 17th; he then presented Mackensen's Chief of Staff, Colonel von Seeckt, with the *pour le merite*[75],

Germany's most prestigious decoration, for the great successes of the prior two weeks. Soon the Germans were over the river in force and could not be dislodged. Once they had brought up their artillery they systematically destroyed the Russian bridgeheads; thousands of men were killed as they tried to escape beyond the stream. Jaroslav was next, and by the 20th the *Alliance* had built, or were building, 15 bridges over the San. Mackensen knew his troops were tired by now; he wanted only to establish good positions, take Przemysl, and pause for a rest and resupply before moving on.

Ivanov had other ideas. Scraping up every bit of strength he could muster, he loosed several powerful local attacks against his antagonists. One of these allowed for an evacuation of Przemysl which was begun on the 20th. Austrian and German troops had nearly surrounded the city after the former took Dobromil and Sambor on the 15th and the latter closed in from the northwest. In the event the counters stopped both advances, and a corridor of escape was held open for ten days. By the 25th the Russian aggression around Przemysl was spent,, but two days later another well-executed thrust recaptured the crossing town of Sieniawa and carried the Russians over the river once more. However, Radymno, another crossing nearer Przemysl, was lost on the 24th and a day later long-range Austrian guns were shelling the place from the south. The city was now at the head of a dangerous salient.

Elsewhere along the front Russian commanders were doing what they could to distract the enemy. Evert's army, still west of the Vistula, surprised its pursuers in the Lysa Gora, the highest hills in central Poland, when it turned and fought for three days (May 15th-17th), halting the Austrian advance. The Russians claimed to have inflicted 7,000 casualties in this ambush-like action. For his part, Alexiev prodded Second and Tenth Armies into action from Grodno and Kovno respectively, against the defenses outside the Prussian frontier, but these attacks were not pressed with determination; the Russian officers had already developed an inferiority complex with relation to the Germans. The latter countered May 17th to the 20th, threw back the attackers, and even gained some ground. Fifth Army obligingly also struck on the Dubissa, and a mixed force of cavalry and infantry penetrated to within sight of Rossiney, a road junction of some importance, on the 22nd. This group was flanked the next day and driven back across the river in such confusion that many of its wounded were lost, and drowned, in the stream. Far to the south, Linsingen and South Army were moving forward through a scene of horror, the burning oil fields of Galicia. All the wells had been fired by the retreating Russians and the entire area from Drohobycz to Kolomea—150 kilometers (90mi)—was ablaze with burning crude, creating a panorama of hundreds of columns of black smoke rising hundreds of feet high and forming an umbrella of gloom that blocked out the sun. As the men of South Army passed this smelly, depressing piece of countryside their breathing became labored and they were subjected to a thick pall of soot which settled upon them; they must have felt as though they had been transported back to prehistoric times when constant volcanic activity was shaping the face of the planet. On June 1st, South Army entered Stryj, and no doubt hoping to leave the "black country" behind, headed on to the Dniester.

By contrast, at the same time but a relatively short distance to the east, an American correspondent was entering the war zone at the point where Russia, Romania, and Austrian Bukovina came together. He reported that on the Austrian side of the border were well-maintained roads, kempt little towns, and impressive private estates, the look of "order and prosperity." On the Russian side were muddy dirt-tracks for roads, dirty-looking thatched huts, and run-down groups of "shacks" for villages, a depressing panorama.[76] He was soon describing some prisoners of war who represented most of the various ethnic groups of the Austro-Hungarian Empire. He claimed to notice a distinct dislike of the Croats for the Magyars, of the Magyars for the Germans, and of all the groups for the Czechs, who refused to speak any other language but their own. Moreover, all nationalities were divided along a clearly defined line of social status with the higher grades inclined to snub those of the lower classes. He wrote of his belief that the larger group represented a fair sample of the Imperial army.[77]

The merits, rather than the shortcomings, of Austro-Hungarian citizenship were on the minds of most of its soldiers when on May 23rd, the announcement was made that Italy had declared war on her former partner in the *Triple Alliance*. The news was not so much shocking as it was infuriating, and even the marginally loyal Slavs of the Empire had no qualms about fighting the treacherous, despised Italians. Hötzendorf had wanted to attack Italy for years in one of his pet "preventative wars," and now he certainly would have liked to have been the first to strike in the Alps. But Falkenhayn would not provide the support necessary for such an operation, and offered instead to send a few German divisions to replace the Austrian Third Army of Army Group

Mackensen. Before this could be ordered, however, the Army would have to complete the re-conquest of Przemysl; in the event very few division-sized units were actually transferred to Italy from the Eastern Front, as the Austrian Command continued its policy of reluctance to clog its railway network with thousands of troops shuttling from one theater to another. It is not an exaggeration to say that Italy's entry into the war did not at that time affect operations against the Russians. Nothing could now prevent the fall of Przemysl to the Austro-Germans. By May 30th German troops, following a heavy barrage, stormed the outer forts and began several days of combat amidst the ruins of forts and city streets. The Austrians closed in from the south fighting for every meter. On June 1st the first of the old forts—now reduced to rubble—fell and a domino effect followed until the city was finally declared secure by the 4th. At last was Mackensen free to pause and rest, regroup, be resupplied, and re-directed.

With the center of the front thus exhausted, the *Alliance* command determined to press hard on the flanks in order to keep the Russian giant, now staggering, off balance. The western-most section of front, the Bzura/Rawka line, was now deemed ripe for collapse, and another attack was ordered for June 1st. This affair was pretty much a repeat of the May assault, but weather conditions were more favorable and this time the 12 or 13,000[78] cylinders of chlorine gas released were used with deadly effect. The Russians should have been prepared for chemical warfare by now, but as Colonel Knox noted, the gas masks sent to the front were still resting at the supply centers at Warsaw, yet to be distributed to the troops. He estimated "over one thousand" men had been fatal victims of the gas.[79] Total Russian losses were actually much higher, probably 30,000 for the months of May and June on those bloodied rivers. The Austrian First Army was meanwhile trying to support the overall plan and duly attacked again near Opatow. The effort was tactically unremarkable; an incident on the Russian side developed that was portentous. Apparently some Russian troops, after an unsuccessful counterattack and finding themselves isolated in no-man's-land, tried to surrender, and were deliberately fired on by their own artillery. The Russian command, tired of defeats, retreats, and surrenders, had begun to take drastic measures to encourage a more resolute defense. It is probably needless to relate that many Russian soldiers, often expected to fight without weapons or ammunition, did not appreciate such attempts to "restore discipline." A dairy entry of June 5th recorded that five of six grenades thrown by a Russian patrol that day at Austrians failed to explode.[80] If Austria-Hungary was the first combatant to endure a crisis of morale, it was soon enjoying the company of Russia in that regard.

On the north wing, the newly created Niemen Army was ready to move by early June. Already a German naval force was making its presence known along the coast and for a few days in the first week of the month tried, unsuccessfully, to enter the Gulf of Riga. Enemy activity had forced this small fleet to retire, but the Russians lost a minelayer to a U-boat in the process. Lauenstein struck on June 5th with about twelve divisions, half of them cavalry, to exploit the maneuverability of the under-defended area. *Stavka* was forced to reinforce the mostly third-line troops covering the line there, after which the defenders easily outnumbered the attackers, ensuring a slow German advance. Shavli was taken again in mid-month but in general this second campaign in Lithuania and Courland stalled. It did, however, achieve its purpose—a further drain on Russian resources.

At the opposite end of the front, Linsingen was still on the move. His first crossing of the Dniester occurred at Zurawno, some distance due east of Stryj and due south of Lemberg, the ultimate prize in all Galicia. Brusilov countered this bridgehead on the 8th, pushing the South Army back over the Dniester. This setback did not unduly worry the German commander; he knew that friendly forces on his flanks would soon make the enemy position untenable. Austrian troops were soon crossing the same river upstream—June 11th—and captured Moscieska on the road to Grodek three days later. Stanislau had fallen on the 9th. Under pressure from Austrian Seventh Army, the Russians completed the evacuation of Bukovina on the 12th. During these actions, an as yet unknown Austrian pilot named Jindra shot down his first two enemy aircraft over the town of Monasterzyska on June 13th. These "kills" would not be his last. Despite success in this area, the *Alliance* had not heavily reinforced Seventh Army; this southern end of the front was to act as a sort of pivot on which the forces farther west would swing, like the motion of a door pushed forward from a right-hand hinge. There were further crossings of the Dniester, especially along its upper course, and the rail crossing town of Halicz was taken on the 28th. But without further resupply, both Seventh and South Armies could not hope to achieve much more.

By contrast Ludendorff was noisily appealing to Falkenhayn to augment the Courland drive where he had become convinced a great success could be achieved. A state of panic had developed in Riga, now only a few days' march from the front. As the center of the Russian steel industry and the second busiest port on the Baltic, its loss would have been unacceptable to the Russians, who accordingly sent further strength to the Northwest Front. The Grand Duke totally rejected suggestions that a general retreat was yet necessary, for political reasons.[81]

In west-central Galicia, the situation continued to deteriorate. Fighting had resumed in the Vistula-San triangle throughout the German pause in their offensive. A meeting of commanders at the *Kaiser's* headquarters in Pless had produced a further dispute between Falkenhayn and Hindenburg/ Ludendorff. The latter team refused further troop transfers for the purpose of exploiting Mackensen's great breakthrough; Ludendorff still entertained grandiose hopes of a great envelopment in the north or a wide sweeping movement from East Prussia to join up with Mackensen in a "super Tannenberg." Falkenhayn disliked the idea of envelopment and pointed to the success of the direct attack system in Galicia. Hindenburg pressed for the idea of a unified command of all *Alliances'* forces on the Eastern Front, that is, that he should be given such command. But the Chief of the Imperial General Staff was secretly glad that Mackensen's Army, let alone the Austrians, were independent of Hindenburg, and at length he won the *Kaiser's* support. "Army Group Mackensen" would continue to deliver the main blow in the East. A new force, named the "Bug Army" was created out of units transferred to Eleventh Army's right, replacing Austrian Third Army, and was under command of Falkenhayn's man, Linsingen. Bavarian General Bothmer took over "South Army."

On June 12th Army Group Mackensen lunged forward again and cleared the Vistula/San triangle for good. The San was crossed on a broad front despite desperate resistance; the Austrians defeating the Sieniawa bridgehead force and crossing in turn. A few Russian units made a good showing during the battles of the river crossings, but there were too few reserves, insufficient munitions, and inadequate artillery support, so once the front line units were decimated, they were forced to retire. Many, exhausted, chose surrender. Once firmly over the river, the Austrian-German army group opened a wide gap between the Russian Third and Eighth Armies, then changed direction and pushed due north, towards the gap between the Vistula and Bug rivers. Tarnograd was taken on the 16th, then Javonovo on the 17th as Russian discipline began to evaporate and resistance began to crumble. An eyewitness to the mayhem at the little Galician town of Molodych described a scene in which Cossacks were plundering peasants' farmyards, looking for pigs and poultry. Presently the witness heard a short noisy scuffle which was punctuated by the scream of a woman and a "gruff voice calling for *veryovka* (rope)." For hours the Russians pleasured themselves while the cries of the woman went unanswered. Later other Cossacks were observed ransacking every hut and house, carrying off all livestock and forcibly taking away all males of military age. The very vocal protests of wives and mothers were so frantic that the witness could not forget the pleas "for many a long hour."[82] So much for the "proper" behavior that the Russian authorities always insisted that the troops exercised in occupied areas, especially Galicia, where the population was claimed to be "Slavic brothers" of the Russians or "Russian in race and sentiment." Apparently the retreating soldiers were not always mutually sentimental. And a few days later, on the Russian frontier, herds of cattle were being driven over the border, as were large numbers of sheep, pigs, and poultry. Many homes and farms were burned, as was anything else that might be of use to the Austro-Germans, such as haystacks or piles of straw.[83]

Almost in desperation did the Grand Duke call for a conference of Army commanders at Cholm, on June 17th. Nothing of essence was decided there save to call for an evacuation of nearly all Galicia, should the Grodek position be lost. It was, in effect, an admission of defeat. Radko-Dmitriev was replaced by General Lesh who attempted to make a stand near Rava-Russka, but the Germans would not be denied and entered the town on the 20th, the same day that the Grodek lines were outflanked by Austrian Second Army from the south, and abandoned. Brusilov's Army was dangerously short of ammunition, and especially shell by now and could not restore the situation. Clearly, Lemberg could not be held, and an evacuation of the city was hurriedly undertaken. As had happened at Przemysl, the garrison was able to remove most of the material of war which had been accumulating there over the months of Russian presence. Aside from rear-guard annoyances, the Austrians did not have to battle for the city, and Boehm-Ermolli's men quietly took possession on June 22nd. The Russian governor had of course departed, and with him the dreams of the Pan-Slavs to Russianize and annex all of Galicia. In general, the populace showed little emotion for either the departure of the Russians or the return of the Austrians; at least neither side in its retreat had destroyed the infrastructure. At least one man was overjoyed at the return of *Alliance* troops: Raoul Stojsavljevic had been piloting an airplane during the winter offensives and was forced to land, by heavy snow, on February 16th after which he and his observer had been taken prisoner. But he had escaped his captors within a week and had been hiding in the Lemberg area ever since, hoping for just such a day as June 22nd.[84] Stojsavljevic would soon be airborne again, flying for the Empire of Austria-Hungary.

While the Austro-Hungarians celebrated the capture of Lemberg, "South Army" and Austrian Seventh Army had rolled up the Russian left, pushing as far as the Gnila Lipa River and a line from Halicz, at its confluence with the Dniester, to the city of Kolomea in south Galicia. Only the northeastern part of the province, then, remained in Russian hands by the end of June. At this point in time, another meeting of the German High Command produced a slight change in *Alliance* strategy. The problem was that with Mackensen's Austrian Fourth, Eleventh, and Bug Armies advancing north from Galicia into the area between the Vistula and Bug Rivers, a huge gap would be opened between them and Austrian Second, "South," and Austrian Seventh Armies to the south, which were driving in a general eastward direction, or almost at right angles to Mackensen. To cover this gap, the Austrian First Army was transferred from the left bank of the Vistula, upon which it had come as a result of the June fighting, and a position from which it would hitherto be strategically useless—considering the path of Mackensen's advance—to Volhynia, that Russian province sandwiched between Galicia and the great Pripet Marshes. From here, it could effectively cover Mackensen's right flank while supporting Boehm-Ermolli to his left. At the same time, it was decided that Ludendorff should attack southward from East Prussia with the intention of forcing the strong Narew line. If this were accomplished, Warsaw, compressed in a salient from both north and south, would become untenable for the Russians, who would then be obliged to surrender all of Poland. Ludendorff at first protested, but finally agreed when assured that his operations in Courland and Lithuania would be allowed to continue.

Four *Alliance* drives therefore commenced: Eastern Galicia, Mackensen's, the Narew offensive, and the northern operations. Falkenhayn's strategy was simple, keeping the meager Russian manpower and ammunition reserves spread as thinly as possible while his own forces smashed the enemy offensive potential. He did not want to push too deeply into

Russian territory, fearing a repetition of the disastrous French 1812 or Swedish 1709 campaigns. Once Russia had been sufficiently crippled and put on the defensive for an indefinite period, Austro-German forces could be transferred to other fronts to knock out Serbia and Italy, or to reinforce the West. On the Russian side it was well agreed that something had to be done to stop Mackensen, and therefore reinforcements were being sent south from the strategic reserve. Both the Grand Duke and his Chief of Staff Alexiev were still opposed to the idea of a general retreat with all its difficulties of morale, abandoning of fortresses, and political implications. They were, however, unaware of the impending offensive against the Narew and continued to belittle the enemy capabilities in the far north. As a result, little was done to prepare for absorption of the coming blows, save a minor tactical withdrawal on the Bzura front, an act which served only to help turn the flank of the line about Radom for the benefit of General Woyrsch.

From late June, fighting raged up and down the front as the *Alliance* attacked, first at one point, then at another. On the 28th Halicz had fallen to Bothmer who then fought a savage battle on the Gnila Lipa; the Russians defending admirably until their flanks were threatened by Pflanzer-Baltin and Boehm-Ermolli. They then retired to the Zlota Lipa line by mid-July. Mackensen, meanwhile, also resumed the offensive, continuing his policy of artillery bombardment in earnest followed by the phalanx system of attack. As usual he was successful, but once over the border into Russia the advance slowed, due to poorer condition of the roads, forests, and the swampy defiles of the upper Wieprz River valley. A participant of the campaign remembered a Russian counterattack of June 27th by recalling the intensity of the bombardment to which the Russians were subjected, and lamented how irresponsible was the enemy leadership to so recklessly sacrifice its men. After hundreds of Russians had been cut down, the defenders allowed them to attend to their wounded. He could never forget that many were left "screaming all day in the wheat field."[85] At Tomaszow the *Czar's* troops again turned and fought, but could not prevent the fall of the town on the 29th. That very day, only a few kilometers distant, was remembered in retreat as a wild and confused movement accompanied by terrifying noise. Infantry, artillery, supply and support troops and wagons were mixed with the inevitable panic-stricken refugees and the galloping cavalry. Cries, shouts and curses mixed with pleas, screams and orders were partially drowned out by dogs barking, horses snorting, geese trumpeting and a host of other noises, both mechanical and organic. A nurse caught up in the mayhem covered her eyes and ears with a blanket to lessen the sensual horror of it all. The next day dawned on a sweaty, dusty, exhausted column of emaciated animals and humans, yet the exodus was far from over.[86] Such pitiful scenes were becoming common across Poland.

The month of June ended just as the month of May had, with troops of the *Alliance* advancing, and in general, the Russians in retreat. There was a minor naval clash off Windau in northern Courland, and sporadic fighting around Shavli, in Lithuania, portents that the Germans were up to something in the north, but the Russians had bigger headaches. The center of the line, and with it Russia's fortresses, was being threatened. The loss of these fortresses into which so much labor, money, and ordnance—to say nothing of faith—had been placed, was unthinkable. According to one historian, of six major fortresses in western Russia, these could account for over 9,000 cannon; Novogeorgievsk alone contained 1,680 artillery pieces with nearly a million rounds of ammunition.[87] Such locations could not easily be evacuated, if at all, so it was decided to try to defend them. This reasoning was all well in line with the Grand Duke's policy of no general retreat; somehow the line must be held. Russia's commitment to her west front for June/July 1915 had risen to 151 divisions spread over 12 armies (counting the 6th, which was not on the line). The *Alliance* now fielded five German, four Austrian, and two mixed (with German commanders) Armies. These eleven contained 55 Austrian and 61 German divisions by July; the German contingent having surpassed that of the Austrian in May. This theater had indeed become quite comparable in terms of numbers of men to the Western Front.

By early July, Mackensen's drive was inevitably running out of steam. A pause would soon be needed, as it had been a month earlier to rest and refit. After the capture of Josefovo on the 1st, the center emerged from the forested region of the river Tanev; the left pushed several kilometers beyond Krasnik and the right was at Sokal. Difficulties with the swampy terrain of the Wieprz valley were then encountered, further tiring the troops. Then on the 5th began several days of Russian counterstrokes. Bug Army was forced to relinquish its gains east of the Bug, including Sokal, while the Austro-Germans on the Vistula were pushed back to Krasnik, and obliged to fight off several more attacks over the next few days. By July 10th all was quiet in south Poland, and

Mackensen gladly accepted the chance to resupply. No doubt, he would have appreciated some time to reflect upon his newfound status: He had been promoted to Field Marshal as a result of his successes since the breakthrough on the Biala.

The relative quiet that descended all along the Eastern Front for a few days around the 10th and 11th of July was about to be shattered, in grand fashion. As a result of the Posen Conference of the 1st/2nd, *OHL* had decided to unleash all of the German armies in the east to try to cripple the Russians to the extent whereby they would be willing to negotiate a ceasefire, perhaps even a separate peace. With the *Alliance* now fighting on eight different fronts it was obvious to all but the most optimistic military minds that if the war was not to be lost, the *Entente* nations would have to be knocked out one by one. The most isolated—Russia—would be a good place to start, and uncharacteristically, Falkenhayn gave his blessing to the eastern strategy for 1915. Instead of being pleased, however, Ludendorff and Hoffmann were upset that their plans—the main effort to be made by Eighth and Tenth Armies—had been passed over in favor of the Falkenhayn plan to strengthen the Eleventh and Twelfth Armies for the main drives. But the *Kaiser* approved Falkenhayn's plan, and the best Ludendorff could salvage was some additional support for the Courland operation.

On July 12th the roar of medium and heavy artillery shattered the relative calm around Przasnysz and Osowiec as the Germans began to rain thousands of shells upon the Russian strongpoints. The next day began the general offensive from Courland to the upper Bug. The most powerful army was Gallwitz's Twelfth, which would have to force the Narew with its string of fortresses. But it was well equipped and had made meticulous preparations, and attacked on a 45 kilometer (29mi) front between the Orjits and Lindinya Rivers. Litvinov's First Army bore the brunt of the blow and was broken through near Przasnysz—which was lost on the night of the 14th/15th—then separated from its neighbor to the east, Churin's Twelfth Army, which was engaged with the German Eighth. Litvinov fought it out for a few days, then ordered retreat to the Narew, but the Germans moved quickly taking Pultusk on the 19th and crossing the river in strength by the next day. On the 23rd a further crossing had been won at the mouth of the Orjits, and Rozan captured. A few of Gallwitz's units had reached the Bug by the 25th, but Litvinov countered the next day, and for two more, and temporarily at least brought Twelfth Army to a halt.

In the far north, the action had begun as early as the 2nd, with naval movements off the coast. A fleet of German minelayers and escorts was engaged by a stronger Russian force, with the subsequent loss of the minelayer *Albatross*. Subsequent activity was supported from the air and on July 15th a Russian two-seater was shot down into the Gulf of Riga and upon impact the bomb it was carrying exploded, killing the observer and maiming the pilot. He would live to fly again, however, and would become an ace before the war was over.[88] Inland, Below's Niemen Army advanced over the Windau River while pinning the Russians along the Dubissa. Resistance was spotty and uncoordinated and easily brushed aside by the Germans. On the 20th, Windau, near the northern tip of the Courland Pennisula, fell, as did Tukkum, a railroad junction on the Windau-Riga line only 55 kilometers (35mi) or so from the latter. Below then concentrated on the Aa River line and Mitau, while his right wing forced the Dubissa and drove on the Swenta, taking Ponievitz on the 25th as it went. It seemed that the whole northern end of the Front was in danger of collapse. Both Eichhorn (Tenth Army) and Scholtz (Eighth) were indirectly supporting Below, by moving east towards Kovno, Olita, and Grodno, but they faced much more serious Russian resistance, and gained little ground.

As early as July 7th, Ninth Army, now under Prince Leopold of Bavaria, had launched a renewed effort on the Bzura/Rawka lines as a diversion for the main offensives. It was called off within two days in expected failure, but it did reveal a problem of its opposite number, the Russian Second Army: a crippling ammunition shortage. This intelligence prompted Leopold to apply pressure on the southern flank near the river Pilica, where his troops linked with those of Woyrsch. Together, the two commanders began a slow push towards the Vistula, an act which in itself served to outflank Warsaw. Woyrsch took Radom by the 20th, and advanced on Pulawy, with thoughts of taking Ivangorod. He was soon crossing the Vistula 15 kilometers south of the fortress. Leopold watched in delight as the outflanked Russians abandoned the Bzura line on the 18th and withdrew to the Blonie position outside Warsaw. With the wings caving in all around, they even evacuated the latter lines on the 24th. Now there was no place to defend west of the city; its fall could not be long delayed.

Mackensen would have preferred to rest his armies for a while longer— the Austrians on his left had lost 20,000 men in the Krasnik battles—but he duly resumed the offensive on the night of the 15th/16th. The decisive engagement occurred at Krasnostaw, where a furious artillery bombardment helped carry the Russian positions; the defenders, dazed and almost helpless, without proper armament, badly deficient in ammunition, retreated leaving 15,000 men to be taken as prisoners. The town itself was taken on the 18th, the day a Russian nurse recorded in her diary that from a recent consignment of 30,000 artillery shells to front-line units, "fewer than 200" were serviceable when put to use. She also reported that hundreds of thousands of small-arms cartridges made by foreign firms and supplied to the troops had failed to fit Russian-made rifles; conversely the large number of Japanese rifles distributed to neighboring divisions would not accept Russian ammunition. Since the inefficiency of Russian supply had once again failed the soldiers, many of them were forced to fight with bayonet only, or as was all too often the case, "hew themselves clubs from the forest."[89] A few kilometers farther north Lesh again attempted a stand, at Trawniki; the story was much the same, with German artillery alone causing the destruction of the best portion of an entire division. In a separate but notable action, the Russian Guard met the Prussian Guard for the first time ever in battle, the two elite formations slugging away until other portions of the Russian line gave way, necessitating a withdrawal by the Guardsmen as well. Nothing now could prevent the capture of Lublin and Cholm, despite frantic efforts by the Russians to hold these cities. They fell to Mackensen on July 31st and August 1st, respectively. Thereafter, Lesh's only concern was to slow the enemy enough to allow evacuation of the salient that was forming about Warsaw, and to this end he constructed a weak line from Vlodava on the Bug to the lower Wieprz and on to the Vistula.

Elsewhere along the front events moved quickly in late July and early August. Below's center finally smashed Plehve's defenses at Shavli, where on the 21st the Germans captured a huge quantity of leather which was earmarked for the manufacture of boots, reportedly worth more than a million rubles.[90] Pushing on to Mitau, they joined the left wing and began a battle for the city by the 30th, which ended in its capture on August 1st. Undeterred by a naval action on the 3rd in which Russian seaplanes shot down a German seaplane and crippled a gunboat near Windau, Below approached the main prize of the north, the port city of Riga. On the Vistula, Woyrsch captured Novo-Alexandria, a "fortress," and a bridgehead on the 21st. The Russians fell back to Ivangorod, another "fortress," two days later; General von Kovess, commanding an Austro-Hungarian force, was ordered to invest and capture the place. After several days of preparation, he attacked behind an artillery barrage. Despite heavy machine-gun fire and persistent Russian bayonet counterattacks, he broke into the city on August 3rd and prepared to reduce the fortress with heavy guns and mortars. But it surrendered the next day, and with it were taken hundreds of big guns with thousands of shells. The Vistula line had been irreparably broken.

It had in fact already been broken on the 28th of July when Woyrsch crossed the stream in strength near the mouth of the Pilica. He was now in position to strike at the rear of enemy forces on the lower Wieprz, or those in Warsaw. Air battles were also becoming more frequent. A Russian pilot with the unlikely name of Thomson shot down a German machine over Kobylniki; northwest of Warsaw, then, noticing an enemy airfield below, swept down and strafed it, scattering dozens of personnel.[91] Another German was somewhat luckier. Flying over the burning town of Wisznice he lost control in the smoke, then was hit by small arms fire, forcing a landing in what he believed to be Russian held ground. The man, Manfred von Richtofen, was relieved to discover the location had just been taken by the Prussian Guard.[92] The world had not heard the last of this man.

For Russian ownership of Warsaw, the end was near. Beginning on July 26th, a frantic evacuation commenced, and increased in fervor as the days went by and the Blonie lines were gradually abandoned. One account mentions how all factories were hastily stripped of their machinery and whatever material could be salvaged, the remainder being dynamited into oblivion. "Every fragment" of metal was removed, especially copper, be it in the form of pipes, fittings, or housewares. Brass and bronze were also targeted, and many churches lost bells and doors lost knobs. Public archives of all types were also evacuated, as were "millions of rubles" in paper currency and of course all coins and gemstones. Communication centers were wrecked and in the outlying countryside un-harvested crops were destroyed and villages burned. Thousands of heavily-laden carts and wagons were driven over the Vistula bridges and to the east, in columns many kilometers long.[93] These processions were hampered by the movements of thousands of fleeing local inhabitants, anxious to avoid a German occupation.

The city was efficiently abandoned during the first days of August, the last of the defenders slipping quietly away over the Vistula on rafts and pontoons under cover of darkness. By the evening of the 4th, every Russian unit was east of the river; all the bridges were subsequently blown up. Next day Leopold's Ninth Army took over the entire city without a struggle. Four days later the suburb of Praga, on the east bank of the Vistula, was captured, thus permitting bridging operations to begin. On the 10th came the news that Mackensen and Woyrsch had linked up, but the Russians were saved from encirclement by the failure of Gallwitz to quickly overcome the Narew positions and drive south to join Mackensen as well, a movement which if successful would have trapped the bulk of the Russian First and Second Armies. As it was, Gallwitz was held up first on the Narew, then on the Bug, while the evacuation of Warsaw and subsequent retreat commenced. Scholtz fared no better. Frustrated at Osowiec, Lomza, and Ostrolenka, all fortresses on the Narev-Bobr, he hurled heavier and heavier attacks against them and finally received the surrender of the latter two, on 10th and 4th August respectively. Osowiec continued to hold out, despite a desperate gas attack made on the 6th. There would be no rapid breakthrough to the south from the Narew front, and by the third week of August the German Eighth and Twelfth Armies had lost a total of some 90,000 men for a return of perhaps 40,000 prisoners.

The Germans did of course have ample reasons to be pleased. Soon, Prince Leopold, who was brother to the Bavarian King Ludwig III and son-in-law of *Kaiser* Franz Joseph, was hosting a who's who of the German High Command in Warsaw. *Kaiser* Wilhelm was present, as was Hindenburg and Falkenhayn and dozens of other officers to inspect the newly won prize of the warm weather campaign. The armies of the *Alliance* were reporting 425,000 Russian prisoners since May 1st and the number of dead and wounded must have been almost as great. The Russians could counter with much smaller totals: 60,000 captives, 85,000 German and perhaps 70,000 Austro-Hungarian killed and injured. But the front was still fluid; the Austro-Germans were still advancing, with no obvious defense line in sight on which they might be stopped. Romanian intervention had once again been discouraged and Italian intervention seemed not to have mattered. Austria-Hungary was still firmly in the war; its troops performing well when under German leadership. Russia was reeling; Poland was all but lost to her. For the moment, the news was all good for the *Alliance*.

Amongst the salutes, proper uniforms, and shiny medals in the Warsaw streets, only Falkenhayn was not visibly moved to joy. A sober, serious, professional, he was pleased enough that his reinforcement of the east had brought good results, but he would have preferred to have been in Paris instead of the Polish capital. Every man sent east was, in his mind, a man who should have been in France, to force the issue there, where the war would be won or lost. The eastern distraction of 1915 meant that nothing of essence could be achieved on the Western Front that year, and time was of the essence for Germany, where already the food and raw material shortages resulting from the *Entente* naval blockade were beginning to be problematic. For Falkenhayn, all the effort in the east could only be worthwhile if the *Czar* could be driven to accept a separate peace, and there was no indication of any such development brewing. Hindenburg and Mackensen could enjoy carrying their Field Marshal's batons; the Chief of the General Staff was losing patience with the whole affair in the east.

While Falkenhayn lost patience, the Grand Duke Nicholas was losing his precious fortresses. Kovno came under artillery fire on August 5th and Novo-Georgievsk was finally isolated on the 9th despite Alexiev's pleading to use all available railroad resources to evacuate its huge stores. Lomja, on the Narew fell on the 10th, and the town of Siedlec, well to the east of Warsaw on the 13th. The Grand Duke still hoped to hold a line, roughly Mitau-Kovno-Grodno-Brest-Zlozow, the greater portion of which was covered by the Niemen and Bug Rivers, his generals thought otherwise, citing manpower, equipment, and ammunition shortages and a crisis of morale. Everyone at least agreed that what was left of the salient now to the east of Warsaw would have to be given up now that it was too late to save Novo-Georgievsk. In the salient near Bialystok on August 14th, a Russian doctor reported that the Russian forces were in retreat all along the line. Thousands of refugees had taken to the countryside and food was becoming scarce and therefore pricey. Ammunition for the front was lacking and the means of transport were breaking down. Many major towns and cities were "seething with unrest."[94]

Eichhorn made his first major attack on the fortress city of Kovno on August 15th, having fought his way through the forests before the city in order to gain suitable emplacements for his big guns. No fewer than eleven forts, three to five kilometers from the Center, guarded Kovno, itself a vital trade, transportation, and communications center at the junction of the Niemen and Viliya Rivers. Its capture would turn the line of the Niemen, but Russian resistance was less than impressive once the bombardment began, and on the 17th it collapsed. The next day the Germans could boast of the spoils: More than

20,000 prisoners, 1300 artillery pieces, and over 850,000 shells to say nothing of the numerous machine guns and war material of all sorts, including millions of tins of preserved meat and other provisions. The "fortress" commander, Grigoriev, fled and was later tried and convicted of deserting his troops.[95] That very day, *Stavka* decided to divide Northwest Front into two separate Army Groups; Alexiev's command would now be known as West Front, and Russki was recalled to take over Northwest Front, now on the most northerly section of the line.

For the Russians the second half of the one-two punch was sustained only a day after the Kovno disaster. On the 19th Novo-Georgievsk surrendered after a ten-day siege characterized by a half-hearted defense. Even the prizes of Kovno were surpassed: 80,000 men taken prisoner, 1500 guns with 950,000 shells, more or less. Five entire infantry divisions—two second line and three third line—were stricken from *Stavka's* order of battle. The shock of the double catastrophe was such that almost no one noticed when, also on the 18th Woyrsch crossed the Bug and Leopold took Bielsk. Only at sea that August did the Russians score anything like a victory; obsessed with the disasters in Poland, few would have noticed. As early as the 8th, German naval forces had tried to force the Irben Strait between the northern tip of Courland and the islands beyond. They were trying to support the drive on Riga by coming into the Gulf of that name and driving away enemy forces which might be used against the invaders. After an encounter on the 10th, the German ships withdrew, only to return six days later to begin four days of intermittent combat in which they lost a minesweeper and a destroyer. Thick fog on the 17th halted these actions for a time; heavy Russian ships had meanwhile entered the Gulf from the north and caused the loss of at least one cruiser, one minelayer, one destroyer, and seven torpedo boats, for the loss of only two or three Russian gunboats on the 18th. Worst of all for the Germans, an enemy submarine torpedoed the battle cruiser *Moltke* on the 19th, the day a diversionary landing at Pernau in Estonia with four troop transports containing 700 men was planned; reports of other enemy subs in the Gulf coupled with the *Moltke* incident caused the operation to be cancelled on the 20th. The next day the Germans evacuated the Gulf and steamed home, escorting the damaged *Moltke*. The whole episode seemed a failure, and the land forces had been stalled outside Riga even before it began. But it did serve to unsettle the Russian command, prompting *Stavka* to order the Guard Army to the Baltic coast on August 15th, at a time when it was desperately needed elsewhere to stem the rising enemy flood tide.

Perhaps the most stubborn fortress of all proved to be Osowiec, which had resisted capture for nearly a year. Topography had something to do with the prolonged resistance; the Bobr marshes had long bedeviled the Germans. But with the front crumbling all around it the defense could not be expected to hold, unless it was willing to be surrounded. When Scholtz's Eighth Army, after some hard fighting, finally seized the junction of the Bobr and Niemen Rivers the opportunity to retreat was taken, lest it soon be lost, and on August 22nd Osowiec finally flew the German flag. Bialystok became the next objective for pursuer and pursued alike. Along the roadside the following scene was witnessed: Some walking wounded were making their way along a thoroughfare when suddenly a general in an automobile drove up and began questioning the men in derogatory tones. The soldiers were unwashed, unkempt and of course with bloody, soiled clothes. The general shouted at one man, demanding to know where his boots were. After the soldier bleated out a weak, apparently unacceptable response, the general struck him in the face with his gloved fist. Not a whimper of protest was audible, and the general drove on, leaving the wounded men to drudge on as best as they could.[96] Such actions did nothing to improve morale, which was ever sinking to new depths.

During the last days of August, the Russians lost what was left to lose of the old Congress Poland. Bialystok, Olita, and Brest-Litovsk were all given up during a three-day period (25th-27th), the latter town was a blazing inferno when the Germans arrived, deliberately torched by the fleeing Russian army. A new phase of the war in the east had arrived: scorched earth. No longer were the Russian commanders willing to fall back and regroup following an enemy success, then take up new positions only to fight it out on the new line. The new strategy was the one on which Russia had traditionally fallen back upon in times of need: retreat willingly into the vast depths of the country, while destroying anything and everything which might be of use to the enemy, along the way. As the *Czar's* forces fell back, they were ordered to turn the countryside into a "desert." All crops and dwellings were destroyed or burnt and the peasants and livestock driven east; the enemy was to be denied any agricultural output from the ground he gained, and denied a labor force to put to work. Efforts were made to even burn the vast forests which characterized the areas into which the armies were moving. Gigantic clouds of smoke and dust rose from the activities of this huge host, military and civilian alike, struggling eastward along the primitive road system of western Russia.

Prince Leopold's men were led into the Forest of Bialowieza, an inhospitable entanglement said to be the last expanse of primeval forest in all Europe. It was the last haunt of the scarce European bison.[97] After blundering about this wilderness for a few days, the Germans emerged to the fire of Russian rearguards. Sometimes, if rarely, the latter did turn and fight; heavy battles were experienced at Orla, a town east of Bielsk, and at Gainowka Station, in the same vicinity.

To Falkenhayn, the days of the grandiose encirclements and the easy captures of large amounts of war material and large numbers of prisoners were over, as he now reminded everyone he had predicted they would be. He had no desire—let alone intention—to be drawn by the enemy into the vast expanse of Russia, which had swallowed the armies of Charles XII and Napoleon, and caused their ultimate defeat. He was well aware of the fact that the farther into Russia one advanced, the longer his lines of supply would become, through a country of forest and marsh with few roads. There were the terrible winters to consider. And to what objectives would his armies advance? What location or locations, if taken, could induce a Russian surrender, or at least deliver a crippling blow? Petrograd and Moscow were too far distant to be realistic goals; capture of the latter had not brought victory to Napoleon. No, he would stick to his original strategy for the east: limited objectives against Russia; support Austria-Hungary. The Russian retreat was to be followed, but only until more defensible lines could be attained. And there was more. Hötzendorf, who had spent most of the summer procrastinating and complaining of exhaustion of his resources, was now pressing for German support for an attack on Italy.

Naturally, Ludendorff was aghast. He still believed good things could be achieved in the east, especially on the northern end of the front which was still the most undermanned, yet had yielded the most territory thus far. When he appealed to the *Kaiser* for support, Falkenhayn in another vengeful gesture further restricted Hindenburg's power in the east by placing the central German forces under independent command—that of Prince Leopold—in a new army group. Ludendorff, never one to take a rebuff well, determined to press his northern operation regardless of support—and of Falkenhayn's wishes. Hötzendorf was told to forget the Italian scheme—Germany was not yet at war with Italy—but that another option was now feasible: the defeat of Serbia. He need only straighten out his southern section of the Eastern Front, thereby freeing up some reserves, and Falkenhayn would provide an entire army—Mackensen's Eleventh—for Serbia. Hötzendorf agreed, and for the first time in the war, German strength on the Eastern Front would decrease (Austrian strength there had decreased slightly after Italy's entry into the war). On September 1st, 1915, 74 German and 55 Austro-Hungarian divisions faced 154 Russian divisions, and the latter were still slowly being increased.

After four months of defeat and retreat the Russians were, of course, looking for scapegoats, that the overall military establishment might somehow save face. The *Czar* himself solved the problem—as only he could have—by relieving his cousin the Grand Duke of supreme command and sending him off to the Turkish Front to boss the Russian forces in that theater. Having feared for their own heads, all the senior commanders could breathe easier until the Emperor announced that he would be the Grand Duke's replacement; then they were stunned. Everyone knew the *Czar* lived in a semi-dream world and had had no training or experience for such a position. His new Chief of Staff Alexiev would in reality be the head of *Stavka*. He in turn handed over his Front command to Evert, who had distinguished himself by his ability to retreat faster than the enemy could advance. All in all, the departure of the well-respected Grand Duke only served to undermine morale even further, as he was well liked by the troops for his reputation for honesty, fairness, and dedication, and his willingness to lead by example. He was not to blame for the terrible deficiencies that the army had experienced in a year of war; he had not been a party to pre-war Russian planning. But he was not totally blameless for the disasters of the summer; after all he had been in overall command of the entire West front, and he had been counted among those who resisted efforts to scrap the nation's "fortresses" as outdated relics. Their retention had cost the Russian Empire at least 125,000 men, 3000 field pieces, and two million precious shells over the summer.

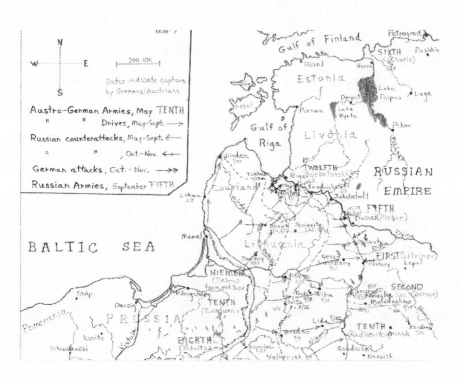

Eastern Front, 1915

EASTERN FRONT, 1915

Chapter Eight
Autumn and Winter 1915/16

Following the loss of Warsaw and the string of fortresses along the river lines of Poland and western Russia, the Emperor of all the Russias, Nicholas Romanov, took the decision to himself assume the Supreme Command of all Russian military forces, the head chair at *Stavka*. It was a move he had wanted to make in August 1914 but had been dissuaded from doing so; now no argument, however eloquent, however persuasive, however logical, could move him to reconsider. To a man, his Cabinet of Ministers tried, first collectively, then one by one to convince the monarch of their profound misgivings towards this the latest twist of the Imperial will. When Nicholas refused to be swayed, the pleadings turned into frank statements of fact, and finally into warnings for the future of the dynasty and even the Empire. The critics pointed out that he had not the necessary experience or training for the post, that his personal safety would be difficult to ensure, that in an autocratic state the autocrat needed to rule from his capital, and that in his absence the Empire would in effect be without a government at precisely the moment in history when it needed a strong, centralized one. The army was in retreat and was decimated, under-equipped, and demoralized; any further defeats would be seen as a defeat to the person of the Emperor, and the nation, already in turmoil, could not afford further trauma. Moreover, the absence of the stabilizing effect of the Imperial presence, might lead to trouble in the already restive capital and other Russian cities.

All this effort was in vain. Nicholas said he needed to make a personal sacrifice for the war effort, needed to somehow offer up himself to the national interest. The generals could only shake their heads. They, as well as the Ministers, knew well how weak and indecisive the Emperor was, how completely ignorant of tactical and strategic understanding, how he tended to assert himself at inappropriate times for irrelevant reasons. No officer was anxious to see the Emperor replace the Grand Duke; most of literate Russia believed the Empress, which in effect meant Rasputin, was behind the change. The average peasant soldier still held the monarch in almost reverential esteem, but he had not been unhappy with the leadership of the Grand Duke; most men were confused by the whole affair, and Nicholas was unwittingly risking their trust. The timing of the Emperor's decision to leave Petrograd for *Stavka* seems suspect. The Russian armies had been in retreat mode since early May and the trend would continue throughout the campaigning season. Why the *Czar* chose to depart the capital in early September may very well have been dictated by nonmilitary considerations, specifically, political unrest. Any time a repressive government is faced with a series of defeats such as suffered by Russia from May 1915, it necessarily begins to feel the paranoia of destabilization. Russia, of course, did have a fledgling parliament—the Duma—but it was only a decade old and was certainly not a true representative body for average Russians, nor was it duly elected, nor did it have any real power and authority. But it was a means by which certain Russians could express certain misgivings about issues that were important to them. Once the war had upset what little comforts the Russian people enjoyed, and particularly after the defeats since May had sent hundreds of thousands of wounded, sick or deserting soldiers streaming into the rear areas, especially the cities, and equal or greater numbers of destitute, helpless, and panic-stricken refugees along with them, Russia's political scene became a hotbed of expression which witnessed the formation of, and rise of, parties all across the political spectrum. Inevitably, the Duma would become the forum for discussions and debates of every sort relating to the new crisis. Some Duma members managed to secure enough support to approach Cabinet members; soon a political agenda was being demanded of the Ministers, many of whom were not unsympathetic to the ideas of the reformers. Just as some of this activity was coming to a head, the *Czar* departed for headquarters at *Stavka*. Once there, he issued orders that the Duma be closed and its members dispersed. The Duma President, Rodzianko, complied, generally suppressing his anger and disappointment. One historian of the time wrote of a two-day strike of all Petrograd factories, and considered that from those days forward a considerable increase in defeatism in Russia was noticeable.[98] With the Duma closed and the *Czar* gone to the front, the Empress assumed control of the government and everyone knew that the Empress was utterly under the influence of Rasputin, whose sentiments were unmistakably anti-war. Most Russians became convinced that this duo, along with countless government officials and military people, were decidedly pro-German. In this they were wrong, at least about the Empress and Rasputin, but the effect was disastrous for the war effort.

In the other *Entente* nations, the *Czar's* decision was much appreciated; they saw it as a sign that Russia would continue to fight on the Eastern Front. Indeed, a few days into his command the Emperor issued a public statement to the effect that his nation would fight on for as long as it took to achieve victory, and would never make a separate peace with the enemy. It was clearly understood by all that his role would be that of a figurehead, that his Chief of Staff would be the real decision-maker. For that post Nicholas chose General Michael Alexiev who, in the words of one writer, compared poorly to the Grand Duke in a physical sense, he being shorter, stouter and lacking a beard.[99] Apparently the two men got along well despite the fact that Alexiev was not a member of the Aristocracy. Honest and unpretentious, the new Chief of Staff was somewhat of a workaholic, spending long hours studying his maps and reports in minute detail. Overall, he was a very unlikely, and a very good, choice for Nicholas to have made.

On September 5th the *Czar* arrived at the city of Mogilev on the upper Dnieper, site of the new headquarters; the late site at Baranovichi was considered to be now endangered by the enemy advance. The new command was faced with the ongoing *Alliance* advance, plus two renewed efforts, one at each end of the Front. The Austrians, at Falkenhayn's urging, had finally decided to clear all Galicia and advance into Volhynia. These new efforts commenced on the 27th of August, behind strong artillery and air support; the Austrian flyer Jindra scored his third victory that day near Czortkow on the lower Seret. The Zlota Lipa was crossed a day later; the advance by Seventh and South Armies would eventually be pushed over the Strypa and beyond. Further north, Kovel, an important railroad center, had been taken by Fourth Army and when Second Army reached Brody on September 2nd, Hötzendorf urged it to support its neighbor in the drive on the "Volhynian Triangle," a fortified area defined by the three fortress cities of Lutsk, Dubno, and Rovno. If this objective could be secured, the Russians could be ejected from all of the province and the Austrians would enjoy excellent winter quarters. While Ivanov pleaded for reinforcement from a *Stavka* in transition, Hötzendorf nervously awaited news which might repair his wounded prestige. Lutsk, the westernmost city of the triangle, fell August 31st; north and south of the city the attackers crossed the Styr. Then came the bad news. The attack on Tarnopol was stalled by heavy Russian resistance; the latter countered the spearheads over the Styr. One last triumph came on September 6th, at Radzivilov on the frontier just beyond Brody, where Second Army scored a local victory which propelled it into Dubno by the 9th. Then the Russians counterattacked from Tarnopol on the 10th and 11th and drove South Army, now under Count Bothmer, back to the Strypa which he crossed, and dug in on the 13th. The *Alliance* offensive had spent itself without having cleared all of Galicia. Persistant attacks led to the recapture of Dubno by Ivanov's men on the 20th; thereafter the fighting in Volhynia/Galicia settled down to positional warfare.

On the northern end of the front, Ludendorff still believed great things could be accomplished, and he was anxious to achieve them before the anticipated order to halt had been received from *OHL*. Accordingly he unleashed Below's Niemen Army on August 28th against the line of the River Dvina. This large stream, on which lay the important cities of Riga and Dvinsk, represented a formidable barrier, and the railroad which connected Riga on the coast to Dvinsk some 200 kilometers (125mi) upstream, was on the right or northern bank, making its seizure a very difficult task. The only river crossings between the two cities were at Friedrichstadt and Jakobstadt, roughly 80 km (50mi) and 130 km (80mi) respectively up the stream from Riga. If the Dvina line could be disrupted though, the whole northern flank would be turned and the road to Petrograd wide open, or so Ludendorff believed. Below made his primary effort towards Friedrichstadt, and brought the town under shellfire during the last days of the month. A sharp Russian counterattack at the village of Linden on the left bank of the river was broken up within a day (September 2nd/3rd) and a 15 kilometer swath of the riverbank secured. The German attack then stalled, but there was bigger news further south. The last Niemen fortress—Grodno—was captured by September 3rd, but with only 2000 prisoners, a far cry from the totals of earlier successes, and an obvious sign that the Russians were not going to risk any more large scale forfeitures. Only stragglers, deserters, and badly wounded men were being taken now, as Alexiev husbanded his remaining strength for a stand on ground more favorable somewhere to the east. There were many rearguard actions, some rather energetic, such as at Volkovysk, east of Bialystok, on the 7th, and at Troki, 15 kilometers west of Vilna on the 8th. The river Zelvianka was crossed on the 9th in an effort to outflank and isolate a stubborn rearguard, but the Germans were by that time pretty much punching at air.

Despite the long-anticipated order from Falkenhayn to stop the eastward movement which was received on September 2nd, Ludendorff was loathe to reign in his army commanders, all of whom seemed to be on the verge of important captures which would certainly improve their positions, especially if the latter were to be maintained through the coming winter. Vilna was far and away the most tempting prize within German reach and it was first attacked on the 10th, beginning a week-long battle. The Vilna-Petrograd railroad was subjected to air attacks the next day, and on the 12th the Germans crossed the Viliya River and seized a few kilometers of track. Farther north on the same line, Eichhorn's army obliterated Russian defensive positions with artillery fire and took Novo-Sventsiany on the 12th, and hurled Lauenstein's cavalry into the breach to gallop off to an eastern unknown. According to one source, elements of this force captured 3000 head of cattle at Smorgon then rode deep into the Russian rear to destroy the Beresina River bridge at Borisov but were prevented from doing so by the timely arrival of Russian troops. The Germans only managed to blow up "a few yards" of track at Zhodino, well to the east of Minsk on September 16th.[100] This minor action represented the extreme easterly point of German penetration into Russia in 1915. Radkevitch's Tenth Army was meanwhile trying to defend a hastily occupied and weak line from Orany to Mosty. Scholtz easily burst through this, while Zeppelins bombed Lida, destroying its facilities. Radkevitch was compelled to withdraw, exposing Vilna from the south, and the largest city of Lithuania finally changed hands on the 18th. Lida fell two days later. Scholtz took about 4000 more prisoners for having cleared yet another salient; the center of the line was now fairly straight except for the cavalry penetration in the Vilecka sector. The Russians now decided to attack this overextension, and on the 20th a series of counters won back Vilecka and Smorgon within a few days, but on the wings the German advance crept ahead. Slonin fell on the 18th and after ten more days of constant harassment, Ludendorff could claim the important rail junction (and former *Stavka* H.Q.) of Baranovichi. On the north wing Niemen army slugged its way to the mouth of the Aa by the 18th, but the main effort was directed at Dvinsk at the juncture of Below's and Eichhorn's forces, and for a while every available reserve was sent there. By the 25th, the Germans were a mere 12 Kilometers from the place, but could advance no farther. Frustrated, Ludendorff ordered the city bombed. He called off the general offensive on the 26th. Two days later his troops reported they had anchored the front lines on Lakes Drisviaty and Postavy. The campaign in the north was over.

We need now consider only one last sector to complete our look at the Front-wide advance of the *Alliance* that followed the spring breakthroughs of 1915. Between the middle courses of the Bug and Dnieper Rivers lies a vast area of high water tables; the entire region was undoubtedly once a large inland sea, a Great Lake of sorts. This is the Polesie, or Pinsk Marshes, usually known as the Pripet Marshes, and by its very nature is perhaps the most primitive swath of ground in all Europe. Located south of White Russia but north of Volhynia, it effectively cut the front neatly in half, once the fighting moved east of the Bug. Only two railroads crossed this nearly impassable wilderness: From Brest-Litovsk due east to Mozyr, a 640 kilometer (400mi) stretch, and from Baranovichi to Sarny, a north-south distance of 320 kilometers (200mi) and all around these two were 125,000 square kilometers (50,000sq mi) of real estate thus described by a Hungarian officer: Shallow lakes extending for miles on end out of which occasionally poke stunted trees which resemble little islands in the gloom. The frequent rains inundate the few poor roads, and a few "miserable cottages" often caught by the rising waters are home to ungroomed natives, who eke out a precarious living from woodcutting and other products of this vast wilderness. These inhabitants stare with bewilderment at Austro-Hungarian and German cavalrymen, and inform them that nearly half of all the immediate ground is covered with weeds and high grasses; there are thousands of acres permanently under water, but some solid, dry ground can occasionally be encountered. The whole area is very sparsely populated, and no accommodations for even small numbers of troops can be expected to be found, but camping in the open is a generally unpleasant experience, owing to the countless insects and snakes, and the "vaporings of the marshes are liable to cause fever and typhoid." The entire district was, under most imaginable circumstances, to be avoided by military forces.[101]

By the third week in August, it was the task of Bug Army to somehow deal with this unforgiving region. Woyrsch's men were skirting the northern fringes, Austrian Fourth Army, the southern. Following the withdrawal of Mackensen and Eleventh Army, a shake-up in command saw Linsingen hand over South

Army to Count Bothmer and assume direction of a new "Group Linsingen," which basically was a renamed Bug Army and much of Woyrsch's strength. Not surprisingly, Linsingen opted to advance along the east/west railroad and take Pinsk, the only small city in all the Marshes. First, his men seized the Horodets Canal, a strategic waterway linking the Bug and Pripet river systems, or in a larger sense, the Baltic and Black Seas. East of Ianovo, a Russian rearguard offered battle, but was swept aside and Pinsk occupied in mid-September. Only one objective worth consideration now remained, the junction of the Pinsk railroad with the north/south line, some 50 kilometers (30mi) distant; the capture of which would deprive the enemy of lateral communications between Southwest and West Fronts. But a few miles east of Pinsk, the Russians dug in and blocked any forward movement beyond Gorodishche, on the Yaselda, a Pripet tributary. Linsingen's left tried to outflank this position; the terrain on the right was nearly impassable. The Oginski Canal was crossed on the 20th, but the Germans were ambushed near the town of Logishin and lost a thousand men in a confused battle in misty, smoke-choked woods. They retreated on the 23rd to beyond the Oginski Canal and dug in on the west side; the waterway thus becoming the front in that sector. Both sides then contented themselves with improving upon whatever defensive arrangements could be had in the difficult marsh country before the advent of winter.

In the only notable action at sea during September, a German submarine sank a British steamer in the service of Russia near the port of Odessa on the 15th. All was quiet in the Baltic where both sides were more interested in the fighting for Riga, possession of which would certainly affect the naval balance there.

The end of the month of September 1915 witnessed a stabilization of the front in the East, from the Gulf of Riga all along the line to the Romanian border. This new line extended for some 1,050 kilometers (650mi), as opposed to the 1750 kilometers (1,100mi) over which the hostile armies had faced each other in May. Moreover, it was, for the most part, covered by topographic features—rivers, lakes, and swamps—over much of that distance. Such a shortened, more easily defendable line had allowed the Russians to shift reserves in September and in doing so halt the German offensive. By the same token it had permitted the Germans to transfer forces elsewhere—Serbia and France—

without seriously endangering their own defenses. Seemingly, a shorter front would tend to favor the Austro-Germans, in as much as they were always heavily outnumbered and could benefit from a more concentrated position to defend; on the other hand it would be to their disadvantage to attempt to assault a similarly concentrated Russian defense. But Falkenhayn had always been opposed to the idea of attack in the East anyway, and Hötzendorf could hardly now entertain such schemes either, considering the state of his armies. So it was that the *Alliance* decided to merely defend the front in Russia for an indefinite period, and found themselves in reasonably good positions from which to do so.

From north to south, the new front line ran as follows: From the mouth of the Aa, at the extreme southern tip of the Gulf of Riga in a 32 kilometer (20mi) distant semicircle about the city of that name, to the great Dvina River; southeastward along the river to within 16 kilometers (10mi) of Dvinsk; then due south through forested country along a line of lakes—Sventen, Drisviaty, Obole, Narotch, Vishnevsky—to the open, but marshy area from the upper Niemen to Baranovichi; continuing south across the Pripet Marshes via the Oginski Canal to Pinsk, along the Styr; leaving the latter stream near Kolki and cutting across Volhynia between Lutsk and Dubno as far south as a point just east of Zlozow; thereafter following the course of the Strypa to the Dniester, and the latter to the Bessarabian frontier. This new line called for a new order of battle, and both sides regrouped as a result. For the Russians, the following deployment was used. North Front, commanded by Russki; stretched from Riga to Dristviaty and contained three armies: Sixth, (Churin), still guarding the Baltic Coast, Twelfth, (Gorbatovski), on the lower Dvina, and Fifth (Plehve) on the upper Dvina. West Front extended as far south as Kolki and in it Evert disposed of five armies: First (Litvinov). Second (Smirnov), Tenth (Radkevitch), Fourth (Ragoza), and Third (Lesh). South of the Pripet lay Southwest Front under Ivanov, who led three more armies: Eighth, (Brusilov) in Volhynia, Eleventh, (Shcherbachev), in eastern Galicia, and Ninth (Lechitski), straddling the Dniester.

On the German side, where large-scale transfer of troops to other theaters had taken place, the line-up was somewhat less formidable. The "Niemen Army" had been rechristened Eighth Army but was still under Below, while Scholtz's old Eighth Army had been reduced to the so-called "Scholtz Group" by some of the transfers. Tenth Army (Eichhorn), and Ninth Army (Prince

Leopold) had been left pretty much alone, but Twelfth Army was now commanded by General Fabeck. Linsingen's Army remained in the Pripet region; the remainder of the line was held by the Austrian Fourth (Archduke Joseph Ferdinand) and Second (Boehm-Ermolli) Armies, Bothmer's "South Army[102]," and Austrian Seventh Army (Pflanzer-Baltin).

Ludendorff was not slow to recognize the fact that on the northern end of the front, his armies had been stopped short of capturing positions which they might have transformed into favorable winter quarters. The great cities of Riga and Dvinsk still lay in Russian hands, which meant that the enemy possessed excellent transportation and communications centers, as well as major sheltering facilities, just behind the front line, and at critical points along its length. This, of course, spelt a tremendous advantage for Russki; Ludendorff determined to rectify the situation before the campaigning season ended altogether. He well remembered the bitter winter of 1914-15 and the effects it had had on his troops on the Polish Plains, and now, with the front many miles farther east in even more inhospitable surroundings, such effects were bound to be magnified. So it was that Below's Eighth Army was directed to attack and occupy Riga and Dvinsk before the onset of winter. The attacks were to commence on October 3rd, while the enemy was still somewhat off balance as a result of the retreats, and before he was able to consolidate his defenses. As a diversion, Molodechno and several surrounding small towns were to be bombed the same day. Both cities were tough places to assault from the southwest, as they were covered by marshy areas dissected by numerous lakes and streams within the forest. Unfavorable topographical features as such hampered the Germans in the movement and placement of their artillery, always a most valuable asset for them. Heavy guns in particular were generally kept out of range; Below's most distinct material advantage was thus denied him. Despite a respectable bombardment by the lighter artillery, and an air demonstration supposed to replace the destructiveness of the heavy guns, the attacks soon ran into trouble. As they advanced slowly down the Dvina toward Riga, the Germans had to fight for every yard. A battle at the village of Borkowitz on the 19th was followed by an attempt to seize a possible river crossing point at Uxküll two kilometers beyond. Here, an artillery barrage included the first use of 'Green Cross', as the Germans called it, gas. The new substance (phosgene) was much more effective than the tear gasses they had been using, but the result on the Dvina was as disappointing as had been the results on the Rawka, and the Russian line was unbroken. By the 24th an action at Kekken marked the limit of the advance, still over a dozen kilometers from Riga. Another effort from Mitau reached Olai at the edge of the Tirul Marsh and was similarly stopped, so tantalizingly close to the goal. The drive on Dvinsk fared no better. Russki, who possessed some fresh troops, countered as early as the 6th and repulsed the Germans at Lake Sventen. Shifting his weight to the north of the city, Below captured a few towns in battles lasting several days; the village of Garbunovka was put on the map by virtue of its changing hands several times, and Illukst finally fell to the Germans on the 23rd, after a particularly intense bombardment. Undaunted, Russki tried again near Postavy. Attacks there between the 6th and the 9th were broken up in a hail of machine gun fire. A third blow fell along the line of lakes Sventen, Demmen, Dristviaty and Obole, and action which soon degenerated into an artillery exchange in which Below gave as good as he got. But as at Riga, the German objective remained ever elusive.

Ludendorff, after three weeks of furious fighting in which he had lost 40,000 men, still refused to quit for the winter. After consulting with Hindenburg, he decided upon one final push. *Ober-Ost* headquarters had been moved to the recently conquered city of Kovno on October 20th. It was here, three days later that Hindenburg received the depressing news that the recently repaired heavy cruiser Prince *Adalbert* was lost in the Baltic, torpedoed and quickly sunk, with only three survivors amongst the crew. What the Germans could not know was that the deed had been performed by a British submarine.[103]

Nor was the news from Galicia encouraging. We have seen how the line south of the Pripet had been more or less stabilized by the third week of September. Certain points, however, continued to be hotly contested. The Olyka sector between Lutsk and Rovno was one such locality; battle here began on September 27th and lasted until the end of October, the action being characterized by a seemingly unending series of attacks and counters, none of which accomplished much save a lengthening of the casualty lists. Heavy autumn rains eventually made operations difficult enough that they were terminated, by both sides. In Galicia, the Russians had in their September offensive succeeded in pushing the Austrians back to the line of the Strypa, though the latter had stubbornly clung to the east bank of the river in several places, in order that they might themselves advance again, with less effort, to the Sereth. October 30th witnessed just such an attempt, but it was defeated by the Russians, whose counter in turn was stopped; a confused battle in mist then ensued in which the Austrians were expelled from the eastern bank of the Strypa and even lost some ground on the western bank. During subsequent days they again attacked and re-took the lost ground to the west of the river, but suffered terribly in futile attempts to regain a bridgehead on the eastern side. In one skillfully conducted counterattack, the Russians were able to cut off some retreating units and force them back upon the stream at a location where it was very awkward to effect a crossing. Following a heavy battle to disengage, the Austrians were frustrated, and large numbers of troops took to the water to avoid capture. Most were either drowned or killed by Russian fire.[104] South Army also attacked near Komorov on the 25th to little avail. The fighting raged on until November 16th, when both sides, prompted by a change in the weather for the worse, finally quit.

As for the area of the Pripet itself, Linsingen had been prudent enough to not take further offensive measures here following the defeats of Logishin and the Goryn, but it represented a menace to the whole line of the Eastern Front in that the only north-south railroad across the region remained in Russian hands. That meant that for the *Alliance*, the front was effectively cut in half by the Marshes; north-south traffic had to be diverted as far west as Brest-Litovsk. Considering Austria-Hungary's past record of having constantly to be bailed out by her German ally, this fact spelt trouble, in that future troop movements to the south would take unnecessarily long. Russian reserves, meanwhile, could flow unimpeded along the single railway. True, the Germans had captured the northern junction of this line when they took Baranovichi, but this point was north of the marshes and the Russians soon had constructed a lateral railway east of the town and therefore were not adversely affected. Linsingen could do little on his own, meanwhile, and the attention of the high command had shifted to other theaters. Save for a Cossack raid on the town of Nevel[105], southwest of Pinsk, on 25th-28th November, no further acts of war disturbed the Pripet that autumn.

As for Ludendorff's final effort, he might have spared his men. The final drive for Riga was begun at the end of October and consisted of a three-prong movement from the west, southwest and southeast. The western group attacking along a 4 or 5 kilometer wide corridor between the lower Aa and the Gulf of Riga was easily beaten off; both other groups faced similar problems of a narrow passage through difficult terrain, woods for one and marshes for the other. By November 6th the Germans had withdrawn behind the Aa. The Russians attacked two days later and advanced to Kemmern, about 8 kilometers into enemy-held ground; the Germans tried vainly to win ground for two weeks more, but when the action mercifully ended on the 22nd, they were farther than ever from Riga, perhaps 30 kilometers or so.

The final attack on Dvinsk went much the same way; the Germans trying to advance against enemy fire, natural obstacles, and poor weather, beginning on November 2nd. Gains were nil. A Russian counterattack began on the 11th. Then as the snows fell, both sides had finally had enough: the armies would have to winter where they stood.

Reluctantly, Ludendorff admitted his failure and ordered his armies to entrench all along the line. The new dugouts were to be permanent structures and constructed as such, the first such fortifications the Germans had inhabited since the Rawka lines of July, or the Angerapp positions of February. Nevertheless, a quadruple trench line was built, with all its innumerable communications and supply connecting-trenches and series of barbed-wire entanglements. To the rear, German engineers improved and enlarged the railroad and telegraph network between the front and their native soil, so as not to lose their advantages of more efficient transportation and supply. Every effort was made to ensure that the troops at the front were provided with all the necessary material to survive the expected harsh winter in at least reasonable comfort. All in all, the German preparations had been completed by early December. Falkenhayn was relieved that the campaign was over at last—though two months or more later than he had desired—for he had decided he disliked cooperating with the Austrians fully as much as he disliked Ludendorff. All German troops on the Austrian section of front were now withdrawn for service elsewhere.

The Russians, for their part, were exhausted and still quite disorganized from the long months of retreat and counterattack, and at any rate preferred to remain inactive for the time being, until the huge manpower and material reserves the high command had assured them were being built up in the rear, reached the front lines. They would have felt infinitely less confident had they known that the Supreme Commander, the *Czar* himself, had allowed the Empress to invoke the aid of Rasputin to secure divine assistance for weather changes at the front. It seems that when Nicholas complained that heavy and persistent fogs were hampering troop movements that autumn, Alexandra had appealed to her "Friend," who in turn announced that the fogs would no longer disturb the military operations.[106]

As somewhat of a postscript to the Dvinsk area fighting, the Russians claimed a Zeppelin, shot down with the aid of searchlights by anti-aircraft fire, was destroyed in the southern outskirts of the city, on December 5th.[107]

In September, Bulgaria had seen fit to declare herself for the *Alliance*, which as a result became the *Quadruple Alliance*. Although traditional friends of the Russians and enemies of the Turks, the Bulgar's loathing of the Serbs and desire to annex Serbian Macedonia weighed most heavily in their decision to intervene at this crucial point in the war. Confronted with stalemate on the Western, Eastern, and Italian Fronts, the Austro-Germans had already decided to eliminate Serbia in August, when talks had been held with Bulgarian military representatives. Early in October the Austrian Third and German Eleventh Armies struck at the Serbians, who reeled back and were taken in flank by two Bulgarian Armies. The resulting catastrophe destroyed Serbian military power for a long time to come; the remnants of the proud army fled across Albania to the Adriatic, where they found refuge on the island of Corfu. Frantic, the Western allies prodded Greece and Romania to enter the war against the Central Powers, promising them almost unlimited aggrandizement upon victory if they did. But the balance of power in the Balkans, so easily upset by Bulgaria, would not be restored that year. Romania would not budge, Greece wavered, but nearly declared against the *Entente* itself when, anxious and frustrated, they occupied the Greek port of Salonica in hopes of somehow aiding the Serbs.

For awhile, the Western Powers consoled themselves by verbally abusing the Russians, claiming that they had done nothing to help Serbia. *Czar* Nicholas's Chief of Staff, Alexiev, denied the allegations and pointed to the minor offensives of October to support his position. Unimpressed, the Allies demanded more, and this pressure led Alexiev to assemble a new army, the Seventh, on the Black Sea near the Romanian border to intimidate both Romania and Bulgaria. The former may have been somewhat moved; the latter certainly was not; at any rate Seventh Army could do nothing to help matters in the Balkans, where the fortunes of war favored the *Alliance* that autumn. Russia was never forgiven for her poor military performances of the year 1915, and thereafter the allies always threatened to withdraw their material support whenever they believed she was not making her best effort to win the war. Nervous, Alexiev grumbled about having been abandoned by supposed allies during the trying summer months; he then shook up the army commands somewhat, replacing Plehve with Gourko and Shcherbachev with Sakarov, while putting Shcherbachev in charge of Seventh Army.

With the *Entente* nations beginning to quarrel among themselves, an inter-allied Conference was clearly needed, and was called for. It convened in December at Chantilly, France. Belgian, British, French, Italian, and Russian points of view and proposals were all spoken, and received, here in an effort to coordinate *Entente* strategy and translate it into victory. All sorts of facts came to light in the debates; the French astonished the Russians with their detailed knowledge of Russian manpower strength, compared it to their own, and demanded to know why a nation with a population four times as great could not field a far more formidable force. Beyond this, they insisted that Russian troops in large numbers be sent for service on the Western Front and stated that further deliveries of war-goods to Russia were dependant on the Russian response. Furthermore, France, they said, was tired of fighting the war "on her own"; the British and Russians must assume a greater role. When their turn came, the Russians replied calmly that they would be glad to call up more men for service if they could provide them with arms; the immediate dispatch of more material aid was essential. As for fighting the war "alone," it was Russia which had done just that during the summer while the Western Front remained passive. Measures would have to be taken to see this situation did not arise again. Sending troops to the west was another matter. It was viewed as an attempt to place Russian forces under French command, and did not set well with Alexiev, who though in the event, had to yield.[108]

Despite such arguments, all the parties at Chantilly were aware of the fact that something had to be tried, lest the *Alliance* win the war. Bulgaria's entry into the war had added several hundred thousand soldiers to the ranks of the enemy, while a similar number were subtracted from their own by the subsequent collapse of Serbia. Worse still, the Austro-Germans now had uninterrupted land access to their ally Turkey, enabling them to supply her by rail, while at the same time isolating Romania from all the world save Russia. If that nation, ever wavering, followed Bulgaria's example, Russia might very well be forced to sue for peace, an event which would then be followed by a near doubling of the pressure on the Western and Italian Fronts and a practical nullification of the *Entente* naval blockade. All the Powers at least agreed on one point: the geographic position of the *Alliance*, coupled with their superior railway and communications networks, enabled them to quickly transfer forces from a quiet sector of front or fronts to a sector threatened by allied offensive action, thereby speedily creating a reserve with which to defeat the attack. In this way they had been able to cope with all allied strategy thus far, and had dealt remarkably well with the much-hailed Italian entry against them, as well as having found the necessary reserves somewhere to launch a few major offensives of their own. And all this was achieved while being rather badly outnumbered and outgunned. It was therefore proposed that in order to wrest this advantage from the enemy, all the *Entente* nations should synchronize their attacks for the coming year. Simultaneous offensives would render the *Alliance* helpless to transfer troops between fronts and would, once local reserves had been expended, be bound to succeed eventually, or so the argument went. All the Powers agreed to this plan, which was to be initiated in April 1916. The Russians were especially well pleased, as they believed that a situation such as had developed during their isolation of the past summer would not now be able to recur. They could not now be subjected to the punishment brought about by a major enemy effort as had been the case in 1915.

Erich von Falkenhayn had no way of knowing what was transpiring at Chantilly; unwilling to wait and play the enemy's game, he had ideas of his own. Ever opposed to strategies which did not revolve upon the Western Front, he had only grudgingly made his main effort for 1915 in the East, and agreed to the Serbian Campaign as the lesser of two evils as he saw it; either Serbia on the Italian front needed to be hit hard in order to once again bolster the fortunes of his disliked Austro-Hungarian allies. Once Serbia's fate had become apparent, in November, Falkenhayn began to plan German strategy for 1916; enough of the "sideshows," a supreme effort was needed in the West. Having long since correctly assessed Britain as Germany's most powerful enemy, he sought ways to defeat her, but alas, Britannia still ruled the waves and the German fleet, while powerful, could not directly challenge the Royal Navy. How then to defeat England? Her army in France was comparatively small yet very effective; even its defeat would be extremely costly but would not ensure her greater defeat; to the contrary it might strengthen her resolve. In grappling with the difficult problem for some time, Falkenhayn finally came up with a plan. If England could not be directly defeated, she would have to be indirectly defeated: The defeat of France would, by eliminating Britain's most powerful ally and best foothold on the continent, bring about her own suit for peace. Without France, he reasoned, England would not stay in the war alone.

Of course, the problem of defeating France was not an easy one to resolve. The Schlieffen Plan had already failed, and now Germany faced a seemingly unbreakable line of trenches, dugouts, and fortifications known as the Western Front. All efforts to break through it had failed. But Falkenhayn was no Ludendorff; his strategies, unlike those of the latter, always involved limited objectives to be obtained with limited forces. Realizing that the *Alliance* was the underdog in the war, he was unwilling to trade man-for-man or gun-for-gun with the *Entente*, whom he knew were potentially much stronger numerically and materially. "Limited" war therefore became his theme; defeat the enemy tactically, wear him down, hurt his morale, these were the only logical ingredients for victory. On the Western Front, this meant that France would have to be drawn into a battle which she could not win, yet could not afford to lose. As she threw more and more troops in the battle, she would be "bled white" by a far smaller German force. Sooner or later her army would be exhausted, decimated, ineffective. Only then would she talk peace.

After studying the line of the Western Front for some time, the German Chief of Staff concluded that the fortress of Verdun met all his requirements. Historically sacred to the average French mind, it moreover lay within an inviting salient which protruded well into the German line, making it assailable from three sides. As French reinforcements were brought up, they could be churned up from the fire of heavy artillery expertly placed to reach all corners of the salient. It would not be necessary for Germany to actually capture Verdun, only to threaten its capture, thereby assuring a determined French effort to hold it. Falkenhayn believed that nine divisions were sufficient reserves for the attack, and during the winter of 1915-16 drew these from the Eastern Front. The offensive against Verdun was scheduled for mid-February. No aggressive action was to be taken in the East for the foreseeable future, and none was expected of the Russians, who were thought to be still smarting from their recent defeats.

With the front mostly passive from mid November to late December, both sides could reflect upon their losses for the period of the "Great Retreat," that is, from about May 1st. The *Alliance* had suffered three-quarters of a million casualties, split fairly evenly between Germans and Austro-Hungarians, a telltale statistic, since the former had done most of the fighting, had gained most of the ground and taken most of the prisoners. But Austria's weakness was by now a mystery to no one. It had prompted Italian intervention in May; this act was somewhat balanced by Bulgarian intervention in October. As of December the *Alliance* order of battle on the Eastern Front had diminished to 49 Austro-Hungarian divisions—down from a high of 59 in March—and 56 German, also down from a peak of 74 in August/September. Opposed to these, Russia boasted an all-time high of 157 divisions in December, up from the 148 on the line in May. Many of these, of course, were battered and seriously under strength, and morale was poor in all but a few. Russia had taken grievous losses since May; over 900,000 had become prisoners of the *Alliance* and the killed, wounded, and missing (mostly deserted) reached totals nearly as, perhaps just as, high. Ironically, no one, friend or foe doubted the Empire's ability to make good human losses; her teeming masses represented a classic case of "cannon fodder" if ever there was one. But the tales of the millions of refugees, displaced persons, and wounded soldiers and deserters were having a profound impact upon the Russian citizens—and there were millions—who heard them. The cannon fodder had begun to question the necessity of self-sacrifice.

If the *Alliance* was content to allow quiet to prevail on the Eastern Front, at least for the foreseeable future, the *Entente* was not. Alexiev at *Stavka* was constantly being bombarded with exhortations to do something to relieve the pressure on Serbia, and he was already planning a new drive against the Austro-Hungarians, who were still believed to be ripe for collapse. Orders to this end went out to Ivanov of Southwest Front as early as November 23rd; all the Russian armies south of the Pripet Marshes were reinforced. But Ivanov dragged his feet—perhaps he at least had learned something from the previous winter's fighting—and did not issue his own directives for another two weeks. The main objective was Czernowitz and the whole of Bukovina if possible, so as to pressure Romania once more. Seventh and Ninth Armies struck on December 24th on the Strypa and Dniester Rivers; by the 27th the Eighth and Eleventh were on the move to pin down the enemy to the north. These latter two gained the only ground worth the effort, by taking the towns of Kolki and

Chartorysk on the Styr and causing the Austrians some headaches from January 1st. When informed of the action in East Galicia, *Kaiser* Wilhelm decided to make a New Year's Day inspection of Austro-Hungarian troops of Count Bothmer's army. Whether His Imperial presence inspired the soldiers or not would be difficult to determine; at any rate the main enemy assault failed to carry the Austrian bridgehead at Buczacz and thereby failed to breach the Strypa line. Although the Russians kept their gun barrels warm for two weeks, heavy snows and unanticipated Austrian resistance prevented them from gaining more than a few blasted villages for something like 50,000 casualties. The last shots were fired on January 15, 1916, when Ivanov halted the madness. *Stavka's* "Christmas Offensive" was a remarkable failure.

If the failure of another winter offensive showed that Russian generals had still learned nothing of the war, other more ominous incidents were becoming ever more frequent. One historian related an incident that took place on the night of January 8-9, 1916. A troop train was moving westward from Moscow to Kiev with 220 reinforcements for the front aboard, representing the 53rd company of Infantry Regiment 204, which was led by an ensign named Dolgikh, and guarded by eight armed men. When the train reached a certain location from which many of the men originated, some began to jump off into the night. Dolgikh warned that any further attempts to desert would be answered with deadly force, but the men persisted and one, a private named Ovseyenko, was shot and killed. Foolishly, the ensign stopped the train to recover the dead soldier, and the opportunity to escape was taken by several more troops. Others descended on the officer's quarters and insisted that both the ensign and the shooter be turned over to them, that they might mete out a brutal justice to the perceived offenders. Only at the point of guns were the men persuaded to continue the journey, but by the time the train reached Kiev it was discovered that eighty men had somehow deserted. Such incidents, he wrote, were "by no means unusual."[109] Such examples point up the sinking morale and lack of discipline of many Russian troops at this time. And these examples were about to be sent to Southwest Front, which faced the Austrians, commonly believed to be far less formidable than the Germans. Later that same month an observer wrote of having noticed on numerous occasions that Russian troops never held Austrians to be on the same level of ability as Germans. They considered them to be more like gentlemen, lacking the "skill, cunning, and bloodthirsty" ways of their more northerly neighbors.[110]

While the men on both sides of the front struggled to keep warm and stay nourished through the bitter winter weather of Eastern Europe, the generals, for once, left them alone. Aside from the usual sniping and occasional shell fire, no hostile action disturbed the Eastern Front from mid January until early March 1916. The Germans were busy preparing for the Verdun operation which duly began on February 21st. Invoking the Chantilly agreements, the French immediately began to demand offensive action from *Stavka*; the Russians had agreed to attack by June, perhaps as early as April, but February was much too soon for most. Even so the *Czar* was determined to support the French as faithfully as possible. Russki, who had long advocated defense only, was replaced at Northwest Front by General Alexei Kuropatkin, an antique old-schooler who would obey his Emperor. Alexiev was told two days later on the 24th to prepare to take the offensive. And thus before the calendar could report the passing of winter, Russian troops would be on the move once more.

Chapter Nine
Russia Resumes the Offensive

At the Chantilly Conference of 1915, all the *Entente* powers had agreed that an attack by the *Alliance* against any one of them must be followed by actions by all the others against the common enemy, in order to relieve the one that had been attacked. It had been the Russians in particular who had insisted upon this arrangement; they wanted insurance against the perceived isolation they had been forced to endure during the Great Retreat. But when on February 21, 1916, the Germans began a major assault around the French fortress of Verdun, it was the French command that sent out immediate appeals—demands really—for Russian support on the Eastern Front. *Stavka* did not need to be reminded of the recent agreements, but it certainly was in an awkward position regarding new offensive campaigns; to a man the Russian army commanders were horrified at the prospect. Northwest and West Fronts had recently conducted long retreats during which enormous amounts of war material had been lost, and had been obliged to use up fresh reserves in a never-ending series of counterattacks. Southwest Front had only more recently been savaged in the disastrous "Christmas Offensive." Everyone on the Russian side, it seemed, was complaining about something, be it low morale, increasing rates of desertion, lack of discipline, and of course the inevitable rifle, artillery, and shell shortage. But the *Czar*, as usual, was determined to support his French ally, and Alexiev, against his better judgment, ordered all armies to prepare for attack by March 1st.

The Generals whose armies faced Germans on the northern half of the front were by now suffering from the same inferiority complex *vis-à-vis* the Germans as the soldiers were. They believed the enemy weapons were superior and were supplied with limitless quantities of ammunition. The enemy soldiers were well fed and clothed and appeared healthier, and his supply services more efficient. Certainly, enemy transportation and communication efforts were better, as was his intelligence network. He possessed more medium and heavy artillery and mortars, superior aircraft...they, the generals, could, and did, go on and on. In fact, the situation was hardly as desperate as Russia's most responsible military leaders were claiming; they enjoyed a two-to-one numerical superiority by now, and many of the crippling shortages of 1915 had been alleviated, if not eliminated. Most soldiers carried a rifle with ammunition, and shell reserves were at the highest level of the war thus far. Because of the retreat, lines of communication and supply were shorter, and the troops were fighting on their own soil.

Somewhat different was the situation at Southwest Front. Here the troops faced Austro-Hungarians instead of Germans, and despite the failure of the last offensive, which after all could have been blamed on weather, the average Russian still believed he could beat his opponent across the front line. He was also somewhat demoralized, but believed his defeats had been caused by treachery in either the government or in the command, or both, not by enemy superiority. Had the Russian leaders been perceptive enough, or interested enough, to understand the needs and concerns of the troops at the front, they might well have ordered renewed offensive action in the south. As it was, *Stavka* wanted a general attack, but it reinforced only the northern Fronts, especially Evert's West Front, already the strongest of the three.

Alexiev's hastily conceived plan called for a two-pronged blow by Northwest and West Fronts to link up at Poniebitz, deep within enemy-held territory. It was felt that such a drive might dislocate the German front so thoroughly that Falkenhayn would be compelled to transfer major strength to the area to prevent the loss of Vilna and possibly all of Courland. Surely this would indirectly help the French. Evert's Western Front, the strongest of the three Russian Fronts, was called upon to make the primary effort. General Smirnov's Second Army, holding the line from Lake Obole south to Lake Vishnevsky, was to break through to Sventsiany, and push on to Poniebitz. Evert strengthened Smirnov by awarding him two additional Corps for the attack, so that Second Army would dispose of 25 divisions—somewhat over 350,000 men—and 275 heavy and 800 light guns. Ammunition allotment was generous. Evert protested the timing of the offensive, though, complaining rather correctly of a shortage of rifles, poor morale, and bad weather, and rather habitually of "shell shortage." When the Northwest Front commander joined in the protest, Alexiev gave in and postponed the attack until March 18th, with the result that the French were infuriated and the Germans alerted. Ludendorff was informed of the Russian preparations in front of his Tenth Army during the subsequent days, and he began to transfer a few divisions to the threatened area from quiet sectors of the front.

For Kuropatkin and Northwest Front the assigned task was to drive southwest from the Jacobstadt bridgehead and join Smirnov at Poniebitz. His Fifth Army was allotted for this task, and he decided to carry out diversionary attacks with his other two armies, the Twelfth and the First, on either flank of Fifth. Eight divisions would advance from Jacobstadt itself, supported by 200 guns.[111] But Kuropatkin, like Evert, was pessimistic of success for generally the same reasons. The fact was, the Russians had never been so well off with respect to manpower and material in quantity. "Shell shortage" was by now more a figment of the imagination than reality; each gun now was backed up with 1,000 rounds of shell.[112] Of course, no amount of material could substitute for zeal and determination on the part of the troops, and in this respect Russia was now sadly deficient.

In the event it was Southwest Front which actually heralded the March offensives by attacking the bridgehead of Uscieszko on the Dniester, that pesky piece of real estate which had held fast in December and January, on the 4th. Again the defenders resisted well and successfully. Then the Russians began to dig tunnels under the Austrian positions and filled them with explosives. When the attacks were renewed following an intense artillery barrage and the explosion of the subterranean charges, the position was finally won; this action occurring March 17th-19th. Then on the 21st, all of Ivanov's artillery began using its newly accumulated shell reserve by firing simultaneously up and down the front, probably to distract the enemy from the events further north. On the 27th another mining operation exploded a section of line near Bojan, but the accompanying Russian attack was too weak to penetrate the front. As a further diversion Ivanov threw all of his aircraft into the melee; one of these became Lieutenant Jindra's fourth victory near Sokal on the 29th.

The Russian command even tried to distract the enemy from the sea. In early March, a battle group sailed for the Bulgarian Black Sea port of Varna, an important point of inter *Alliance* communication. The plan was to bomb the seaside facilities, but it had to be cancelled on the 10th when German planes struck first and spoiled the element of surprise. German submarines were known to be lurking in the area.

Evert and Kuropatkin reluctantly gave orders to begin the main attacks, rescheduled for March 18th. The men of the German Tenth Army were waiting grimly in their positions when on the morning of the 16th the earth began to shake under the fury of the Russian bombardment. They had been forewarned of the assault and had had ample time to prepare to meet it; the intensity of the artillery fire was unlike anything they had yet experienced from the Russians, and it seemed to last forever. Yet it was typically inaccurate and not evenly directed. It had caused comparatively few casualties when on the afternoon of the 18th Smirnov launched Second Army on a 50 km (30 mi) front between Postavy and Lake Vishnevsky. The northern wing was the first to attack, on both sides of the railroad through Postavy village. Here the brown waves of the attackers were neatly mown down by cleverly concealed Germans in the forests. The 19th brought rain and renewed attacks in waves, each of which were shattered by German artillery, which now had the range. Another effort was made on the 21st; another repulse was the result. That same day the southern wing of Second Army was sent into the gap between Lakes Narotch and Vishnevsky where it faced northwest directly toward the initial—but distant—objective of Sventsiany. Both lakes were large bodies of water, but were still frozen over, though the marshy area which surrounded them had thawed somewhat. It was decided to use the ice on Lake Narotch in the assault, the thinking being that the German defensive positions could be turned from the flank at the edge of the water. In the event, the attackers were helped by the presence of a thick fog on that morning and did manage to advance slightly, carving a 1½ by 3km (1 x 2 mi) slice out of the defender's territory. Several thousand prisoners were also taken. Then, the Russians ran into a hail of deadly machine gun fire from dozens of well-placed, mutually supporting positions and were stopped with heavy loss. Meanwhile the artillery was becoming tied up in a duel between the opposing contingents, and the numerically inferior Germans were able to nullify the Russian superiority.

To the north, Northwest Front was also engaged, its offensives having also begun on the 21st. Kuropatkin used both of his frontline armies in a desperate attempt to confuse the Germans. Twelfth Army demonstrated near Riga, while a portion of Fifth Army launched a diversionary attack at Dvinsk. Neither of these actions succeeded in diverting any German strength, though the Dvinsk affair did worry Ludendorff for awhile when the attackers succeeded in making some gains at Lake Sventen near Kolki and beat off a German counterattack. But a renewed effort a few days later failed, as did a feeble demonstration slightly to the south, by the neighboring First Army. Again the Germans countered, making very slight gains in foul weather, before both sides, rather hurt, settled back into passivity. Kuropatkin's main thrust was made at the Jacobstadt bridgehead, as planned, on March 21st. It succeeded in driving Below's Army from its first line of defense, and in advancing a kilometer at best as a result of a week-long battle. Kuropatkin would have continued the attack, but ran low on shell and was refused further reinforcements, as all reserve ammunition was by then being diverted to Lake Narotch, where prospects for victory seemed brightest. Northwest Front thus disengaged about March 27th having lost some 35,000 men in a week.

It is difficult to imagine what sort of reasoning was going through the minds of the men of Russian Command at that time. Having allowed the March offensive to proceed in weather conditions which could not have been less favorable had they been chosen by the enemy himself, they now, after terrible losses had been sustained, halted all other actions to reinforce at Narotch, that very sector of front which realistically offered the least chance of success. For had they breached the German lines here, the Russians would still have to advance through a large forest known as the Great Marsh, an area not ill-named which barred the way to Sventsiany. But it was at Lake Narotch that the largest parcel of ground had been won, and most prisoners taken, as a result of the attacks of the 21st, so it was here also that the High Command determined to push on with its "battering ram."

Meanwhile, a follow-up attack had been made at Narotch on March 22nd, and another on the 25th. Both were defeated mainly by German machine guns, since the opposing artillery forces were still trading blows and the Russian gunners were unable to support the infantry effectively. The infantry, in turn, used the situation to once again accuse the artillerists of deliberate betrayal. After a further attempt on the 27th which too failed, the Russians began to withdraw their artillery, particularly the guns of the larger calibers, fearing that a prolonged slugfest with the German cannons would only decimate what was left of the shell reserve, and at any rate was bound to fail, owing to the superior handling of the guns by the enemy.

Seemingly undaunted, the Russians tried yet again on the 31st, and again on April 7th, and made a final effort on April 14th. Each succeeding drive was weaker than the previous one had been; all failed miserably. The whole affair had by then long since settled down to more or less an artillery duel in which the Russians, weakened by the transfers of late March, were no longer superior to the Germans, and in fact were tactically inferior. Attacks by the infantry were doomed to failure, proceeding as they did over almost nonnegotiable ground and against complex barbed wire obstacles guarded by numerous machine guns at the hands of cool-headed, experienced, troops. If a Russian unit here or there did manage to capture a section of enemy defense, it usually abandoned it shortly thereafter, unless the units on its flanks were similarly successful. Since such was rarely the case, many potential breakthroughs were thus wasted instead of exploited, simply because of the basic Russian apprehension of being deserted by friendly forces, which stemmed from a deep mistrust in the chain of command. By now Tenth Army had been strengthened by the arrival of two fresh divisions, and Eichhorn decided to counterattack immediately. On the 28th, his guns heralded the thrust, which soon had chased the Russians back to the old line, two to three kilometers distant. But the battle continued until the Germans had penetrated another roughly two kilometers into Russian territory, where they were halted, then pushed back, by Russian reserves committed at the last minute. The remarkable German success had been largely due to the adoption of new tactics by the artillery, instituted by a then unknown reservist officer of that branch of service, Lieutenant-Colonel Bruchmüller. In time, the name would become very well known. Bruchmüller devised a system by which he laid down short but highly concentrated barrages on suspected enemy strong points and nerve centers, and any known supply or communication junctions. The effect was to confuse and demoralize the Russians, who were then pushed back behind a creeping barrage to their original positions prior to March 18th. In a few sectors the Germans even advanced somewhat beyond the old line and ended the battle with a net gain of ground.[113]

History records the above engagement as the Battle of Lake Narotch. Rarely is any mention ever made of the related actions at Riga, Jacobstadt, Dvinsk, Drisviaty, or Postavy. Yet together, the March offensives were a major effort by a badly weakened and demoralized Russia; the result was that she was further weakened and demoralized. Northwest Front had suffered 35,000 casualties, Western Front 80,000[114], the Germans perhaps 25,000 total. Although Russia could replace her losses more easily than could Germany, she had suffered one casualty from which recovery would certainly be a long and difficult task: morale. Demoralization in the two northern Army Groups had now reached such proportions that the average soldier no longer had the slightest faith in his commanders or in his nation's ability to defeat Germany. After all, every operation undertaken against the Germans since the beginning of the war had ended in failure, and as more time had passed each new effort seemed more futile than the last had been. As usual, the infantry still blamed the artillery for failing to provide proper support, while the gunners blamed the foot soldiers for the inability to benefit from the impressive barrages, etc., but almost universally, all now believed that the Germans were unbeatable anyway. The Russian commanders should have noticed the depths to which morale had eroded and should have realized that such a state of affairs could easily soon lead to outright disobedience and possibly mutiny. But they themselves, for the most part, were now of equally bad attitudes and could not be expected to set a proper example for their men. Most could think of no better excuse, so blamed their failures on shell shortage, pointing to the ineffectiveness of their field pieces and conveniently forgetting that they had held a considerable superiority over the enemy, whose cannon were always very effective. Evert himself, never an aggressive leader, had lost all faith in the prospects for successful offensive action and lapsed into a passive state of mind. Kuropatkin resigned in frustration and bewilderment, convinced that a breakthrough was impossible. In general, north of the Pripet Marshes, the Russian forces developed a definite inferiority complex; the seeds had been planted during the Great Retreat, and they now had reached maturity. Interestingly even the Russian press, well aware of the mood in the country, could occasionally deliver a jab or two, notwithstanding the fact that it had to be very careful not to offend the Imperial family. One example could be found in an April edition of *Novoe Vremia* in which the writer mentioned that the recent offensive at Lake Narotch had gotten mired in the *rasputitsa* (the season of bad roads). This sarcasm slipped by the censor, but "every other inhabitant of Petrograd understood what was meant."[115]

The implication, of course, was the treason of Rasputin, which by 1916 was almost universally believed in Russia.

While the soldiers of West Front floundered in the slush and struggled with the German barbed wire around Lake Narotch, both other Fronts continued to give the appearance of support. Artillery duels along the Dvina characterized the efforts of Northwest Front for the first five days of April. The Germans replied in kind, and the entire river line from Dvinsk to Uxküll trembled with the almost constant roar of big guns. Exchanges on the 9th were particularly severe, and the Germans probed at Uxküll on the 11th. As if to offset this, the Russians pushed forward near Garbunovka again on the 13th, inviting the inevitable counter which was forthcoming there five days later, which regained the small losses of the earlier action. On the 19th, a particularly heavy barrage blasted Russian targets around Uxküll again; the Germans seemed obsessed with the place. They also stepped up air activity late in the month, sending ten airplanes to attack the island of Oesel on the 22nd and Zeppelins to bomb Dünamünde at the mouth of the Dvina on the 26th. The latter raid was remarkably destructive among the railroads and warehouses of the Riga suburb. In more obvious diversions farther south, a weak gas attack was delivered west of Smorgon, (15th) and a probe across the Schara River south of Baranovichi was distinctive only in that it was ambushed and wiped out (22nd).

South of the Pripet, indecisive fighting continued in Volhynia and Galicia. The Austrians tried repeatedly to recapture Olyka, another location for which someone seems to have had a strange obsession; attempts from the 1st to the 3rd of April and another on the 11th were all beaten off. They also struck on the middle Strypa on the 7th, but the Russians hit back on the lower course of the stream two days later and in a week's constant combat managed to advance slightly. The focal pint then became the Ikva where more see-saw fighting occurred from April 28th to May 1st.

All these actions were minor enough, but some interesting developments were taking place in the air. On April 9th, Captain Otto Jindra became Austria-Hungary's first Eastern Front ace when he downed his fifth Russian plane near Kamenets-Podolsk just outside the eastern border of Galicia. But the best was to come three days later. The *Czar* had appointed General Alexei Brusilov of Eighth Army to replace Ivanov as Southwest Front commander, on April 4th. On the 12th both men were in the city of Khotin conducting a military review with all its parading, bands playing, and full ceremony. Suddenly out of the sky flew the redoubtable Jindra with a certain Sargent Brumowski as his observer/gunner. The airplane dropped bombs, scattering the participants of the review and causing utter chaos on the ground. Russian planes were ordered airborne to intercept the marauders, who promptly shot two of them out of the sky. They were the 6th and 7th victories for Jindra, the 1st and 2nd for Brumowski,[116] of whom we shall hear more. On April 14th Kurt Gruber, who would also go on to become an ace, earned his first kill when he shot down a Russian monoplane into the wasteland of no-man's-land in the vicinity of Bojan.[117] He would not have long to wait for his second. Flying with Brumowski as his observer/gunner on May 2nd, the two destroyed another enemy airplane near Czernowitz.

Both the *Czar* and Brusilov, apparently none the worse for the incident at Khotin (Brusilov downplays the matter in his memoirs), traveled to Mogilev to attend a *Stavka* conference called by Alexiev for the 14th of April. The latter had dismissed Ivanov less for incompetence than for pessimism; always nervous to the point of being overcautious, the Southwest Front commander had turned defeatist after the failure of the Christmas Offensive. Brusilov shared no such sentiments and at Mogilev was the only Front commander to advocate offensive action. Perhaps he realized that was what the men at *Stavka* wanted to hear; at any rate he was able to persuade them to allow his armies to participate in the next round of attacks designed to take pressure off the French. All the actions of the past month had failed to achieve this end, and the *Czar* was determined to raise his esteem in the eyes and minds of his allies. Recently, he had told a French emissary of his uncompromising support of French war aims, agreeing "in advance to anything your government wishes." The left bank of the Rhine, Mainz, Coblentz, all these were offered and even more "if you think it useful."[118] First, of course, the war had to be won, and with France in danger since the commencement of the great Verdun operation, Russia must respond, and with the utmost energy. According to Brusilov,[119] both Evert and Kuropatkin were most dubious of any offensive success, yet they were to deliver the main blows of the coming attack. It can only be deduced that they did not follow Ivanov in dismissal because both were favorites of the Emperor. Whatever the case, Brusilov's Front was to be allotted no reinforcement, and its role in the general offensive was to be diversionary; it would occupy enemy attention while West and Northwest Fronts, heavily reinforced, delivered the principal strikes.

Therefore, the division of opinion within the Russian command which had existed since the earliest days of the war continued to manifest itself nearly two years later. Most of the generals still believed in the "Germany first" strategy, that is, that Germany, as the cornerstone of the *Alliance*, must be engaged by the bulk of Russia's strength, and her subsequent defeat would bring about a collapse of the entire enemy war effort. Yet overruled were those who favored the Austrian solution to victory which went something like so: Austria-Hungary, as the weaker of the two enemy powers in the East, could more quickly and easily be defeated, and her defeat was bound to soon bring about that of her stronger partner, since there was no question that Germany could not stand alone in the war. Brusilov was pretty much a member of the latter group, but Alexiev was not, and in the end it was decided that Evert's West Front should deliver the main blow. Twenty-six of its fifty-eight divisions were to be hurled against a narrow strip of front line west of Molodechno, and in the general direction of Vilna. It was well understood that this meant engaging the more formidable Germans rather than the less potent Austrian forces south of the Marshes, but as Alexiev pointed out, the Russian numerical superiority to the north was more than two to one, whereas in the south it was a bare six to five.

Ironically, Russia in the spring of 1916 was in better military shape than she had been since the start of the war. Not only did she possess more front-line troops than ever before—nearly 2,000,000—but for the first time virtually all of these carried rifles, though the reserve of small arms was still dangerously low.[120] In addition, another million and a half men filled the ranks of the reserve and a further two and a half million were either undergoing training, about to be mobilized, or were being employed in the rear services. Also, a new Guard Army, under General Bezobrazov, had been created and was ready for battle. Deficiencies in artillery and machine guns had for the most part been made good and would complement these infantry forces. Although still tactically inferior to their German counterparts, the Russian gunners were now considerably more numerous, and, thanks to increased production and substantial importation, were now at last presented with adequate if not overwhelming quantities of ammunition. On paper, at least, the army seemed a formidable force; considering the morale problem it was somewhat less formidable, yet still a force to be reckoned with. Unfortunately, most Generals, haunted by past failures, were either unwilling or simply unable to use their new strength properly; most still grumbled about a lack of sufficient shell when asked to assess the situation or to plan an offensive. Of course, such complaints were in reality merely attempts to conceal their own lack of imagination for developing new tactical methods. All knew what they must not do lest they fail, yet none were quite sure of just exactly what should be attempted next.

Back at the front, sporadic fighting continued throughout the month of May, as it had in April. South of the marshes, the Russians made small gains around

Olyka on the 2nd, then again on the 4th. Chartoriysk was again the scene of a small battle on the 5th, and there was action on the lower Strypa the following day. In the center of the line, German aircraft attacked both Minsk and Luninets on the 3rd; these were followed up by ground attacks along the Viliya River on the 9th and along the Oginski Canal on the 11th. The Germans also began a two day assault on Jacobstadt on the 10th. All these were unsupported probing actions designed to test the Russian defenses. For the soldiers on both sides, May 1916 would be remembered as a month of incessant artillery fire, as Russian gunners put new-found stocks of shell to good use and the Germans and Austro-Hungarians replied in kind. Along the line of the Dvina, the shelling was particularly heavy.

At sea, Russian torpedo boats attacked two small towns on the west coast of the Gulf of Riga on May 6th, but without success. On the 17th, however, a submarine sank three German colliers, certainly one of the most memorable exploits for Russian submarines in a single day of the war.[121] Casualties for both sides during the month were high and comparable to the attrition of trench warfare in the West during similar times of "inactivity." Also during May, Hötzendorf launched his long desired offensive against Italy, from out of the Trentino and designed to cut off the enemy armies on the Isonzo. This was the blow he had been petitioning Falkenhayn for support in delivering, but having been repeatedly refused, he at last determined to go it alone. The effect was similar to that of the German moves at Verdun; the Italian government immediately appealed to *Stavka* for help. On the 24th Alexiev informed the Front commanders of the need for early action. One of them need no urging.

Brusilov had accepted his new role, however secondary it might be in the minds of *Stavka*, with enthusiasm. He was confident of his ability to do more than simply "pin down" the Austrian army. He smelled a victory. Austria-Hungary was, after all, nearing exhaustion. Her casualties thus far in the war were already more than she could afford, and these had mainly been suffered by troops of German or Magyar nationality—the only two politically reliable groups in the Empire—but who made up less than half its total population. The remainder of the Hapsburg army was, therefore, comprised of a large percentage of disaffected nationalities who were less efficient and less reliable soldiers. Moreover, their training, equipment, and leadership were still far below German par. Brusilov reckoned that a decisive victory over the Austrian forces opposing him might well mean that Austria-Hungary would have no choice but to sue for peace. Thereafter, Germany's own defeat would be inevitable.

If such grand ideas were to become realities, the Austrian front first needed, of course, to be broken. Thus far in the war, such tasks had been much easier said than done, and few men on either side of the battle line of the Eastern Front believed that circumstances had, or could be, changed at all in the spring of 1916; if anything had been proven in the failing winter offensives, it was that strongly fortified trench lines could not be overcome by conventional attack, unless the assault was backed by millions of artillery shells, or so the reasoning went. Brusilov, however, did not agree with this mode of thought. He insisted, to the amazement of his contemporaries, that the very tactics supposed to ensure the success of the recent attacks had in fact been the cause of the subsequent failures. By massing huge numbers of men and large quantities of material behind a narrow sector of front, he pointed out, the enemy had easily been able to detect the offensive preparations and had been able to more or less guess the Russian intentions and take measures to stiffen the defense. Moreover, even when breakthrough had been achieved, because of the narrow dimensions of the newly won salient, the defenders had been able to direct artillery and machine gun fire into these areas from the shoulders of the same, with deadly effect. In this way many a promising breakthrough had been smashed before it could be exploited, or even the salient consolidated. And then there was the problem of reserves, both enemy and friendly. Previous experience in the use of friendly reserves had for the most part been bad, since by cramming these troops into the limited confines of space behind a narrow-front attack had simply assured that they would be subjected to punishing enemy barrages and air bombardments.

On the other hand, the enemy's use of his reserves for defense was very effective: if the Russians managed to tear open a breach in the front line at any one point along it, he would quickly transfer local, and if necessary, strategic reserves to that point to contain any possible breakthrough. This was possible because of the superior use of rail communications by the Germans, even when on Russian soil. Therefore if a breakthrough occurred, the attackers could usually be assured that they would soon be forced to face fresh troops—no doubt better able to resist and of course, counterattack.

Added to all of these difficulties was the fact that the Austrian line which Southwest Front was soon to assault was a very well fortified one. It consisted of several defensive belts, each of which contained at least three lines of trenches, fifteen to twenty meters apart, and a thick, well-laid barbed wire barrier. Often this wire was electrified and the ground around it was usually mined. There were also numerous deep, well-built dugouts and countless machine gun emplacements protected by carefully placed heavy logs. Reserve positions were similarly prepared. The trenches themselves were extremely well constructed and though modest by Western Front standards, were probably the best system of earth-works yet built in the East. A good many support and communications trenches also existed, connecting the front lines with a great number of roads and rail spurs which led to the main arteries behind the front. Later, when the Russians occupied these positions, they were amazed to discover such elaborate, decorated, even somewhat comfortable works as they found, but the Austrians had expected to remain in them for a long time and had evidently intended to make their stay as comfortable as possible. They had, after all, been confined to these same locations since the previous autumn, following the stabilization of the front after the Great Retreat; Ludendorff, it will be remembered, had ordered his armies to dig in for an extended stay back in October when he realized that no better winter quarters could be won that year, and Hötzendorf had followed suit. Now, in the spring of 1916, the *Alliance* had had six months' time to improve upon the defensive qualities of the very same line, and had done so as neither Germany nor Austria-Hungary planned any offensive action against Russia that year.

In order to ensure the success of his attacks against this extremely strong front, Brusilov initiated a series of preparations more thoroughly undertaken than any other thus far in the war. Reconnaissance aircraft combed the skies, photographing the Austrian front and rearward positions while spies and agents on the ground provided similar information though in different perspective, to the Russian intelligence. Taken as a whole, the knowledge gained from these different sources enabled Southwest Front to produce detailed maps of the enemy positions, maps which in not a few cases were superior in accuracy to those in use by the Austrians themselves![122] Using such maps, the Russian commanders carefully studied the ground over which they would send their forces; while the artillery sighted in on what it believed to be the best targets, and built up its shell stocks accordingly. The infantry, meanwhile, dug models of the enemy front line trenches and earthworks and rehearsed assaulting them again and again. In addition, every effort was made to feel out the weakest sectors of enemy front that they might be pierced more easily; by this time it was well appreciated that Czech, Slovak and certain other Slavic elements within the Hapsburg army had no desire to fight for the *Alliance*, but would, often, join the Russian cause.

Of course, Brusilov was not without his own problems regarding morale. Though more seriously eroded in the two Fronts to the north, the decline in the soldier's will to fight, especially attack, was noticeable even in the Southwest Front by the late spring of 1916. The disasters before Czernowitz and at Lake Narotch during the past winter had helped see to this condition, but the worsening political and economic chaos on the Home Front was also a major factor concerning the dispositions of the troops. Brusilov himself was an ardent opponent of indiscipline and had been horrified by reports of an occurrence on April 10th, the Orthodox Easter, just after he had assumed command of the Front. Evidently the Austrians had used the occasion to encourage Russian soldiers to fraternize at a few locations along the line, and the Russians had responded, only to find themselves subsequently detained as prisoners of war and interrogated. A few Russian officers had been included in the lot, and Brusilov was not slow to grasp the implications of such examples of the lowering of the quality of leadership and the respect it must command, with his army. We have seen how *Czar* Nicholas had also recently been dismayed at other similar reports on the decay of the army structure. He soon issued a directive which authorized senior commanders to take "punitive measures" if necessary, to prevent premature surrender and undisciplined actions on the part of the common soldiers. By the time of the opening of the offensive, Brusilov thought he noticed an improvement in the general situation, though he knew it had not been cured.

Another matter of concern for Brusilov was his lack of decisive superiority over his opponents. Though the Russian Fronts north of the Pripet outnumbered their German foes by three-quarters of a million men, the Southwest Front could count only 600,000 of its own numbers versus 500,000 enemy. The order of battle for the line between the Pripet Marshes and the Romanian frontier in the spring of 1916 was as follows: Astride the Marshes, south to a point parallel with Sarny lay General Lesh's Third Army; this force was not within Brusilov's command; it was opposed to Linsingen's "Bug" Army. South from Sarny, then, where the major advances were to commence, sat Kaledin's Eighth Army with its 15 divisions; on the other side of the line was the Archduke Joseph Ferdinand's Fourth Austrian Army, composed of 11½ divisions. These armies held the front as far south as Kremenets and Dubno, respectively. Next for Russia to the south stood the Eleventh Army of General Sakarov, consisting of 9 divisions, to a point just beyond Tarnopol, though on the upper Strypa. The opposite number here was the Austrian Second Army, under Boehm-Ermolli, with 10 divisions. Shcherbachev's Seventh Army, of 10½ divisions was next in line, and extended nearly to the Dniester; holding a roughly parallel, though opposing, front was German General Graf von Bothmer, who commanded the 11 Austrian divisions and one German division which made up the so-called German "South Army." Last in line from a point slightly north of the Dniester to the Romanian border were Russia's Ninth Army (Lechitski) and Austria-Hungary's Seventh (Pflanzer-Baltin). The former held 14 divisions, the latter, 12½. In terms of divisions, then, the Russian superiority was very slight, 48½ to 46. And, since Brusilov had expressly forbidden the use of the cavalry divisions for major roles in the initial attacks fearing a repetition of past failures caused by the clumsiness of these units, the number was whittled to 36 Russian and 37 Austro-German, seemingly poor odds with which to initiate a strategic offensive. Artillery-wise, the situation was little better; the combined Russian strength was 1950 guns compared to 1850 for the *Alliance*

What the numbers failed to reveal, however, was the real relative strength of the combatants. Whenever Russians had met Austrians thus far in the war, the former had generally come out on top, other things being equal. It was only when Hötzendorf's troops had been supported by German units that they were able to achieve much success on the Eastern Front either in defense or in offense; the Carpathian campaign of 1914-15 and Gorlice-Tarnow affair are prime examples. But now, in the spring of 1916, there remained on the Austrian sector of front only a single German division, and that under the German von Bothmer. Falkenhayn, ever contemptuous of his Austrian allies, would no doubt have removed even this last division for use in the West had he not wanted to see German command retained over "South Army." As it was, he had ruthlessly stripped the East of German forces for use in the Verdun battle; even Linsingen's Army retained only 4 German divisions, while disposing of 5 Austrian ones. Thus, Austria-Hungary was to be deprived of vital German support during the coming attacks, support she desperately needed, perhaps even more so than ever. Yet neither Falkenhayn nor Hötzendorf were much concerned for the safety of the Austrian sector of front. They were aware of the lack of superiority held by Brusilov here, and could not believe the lines were in any danger; after all if 300,000 Russians had failed to defeat 50,000 Germans at Lake Narotch, surely the strong defenses of Volhynia and Galicia could withstand any pressure the enemy might apply to them. Hötzendorf had even been confident enough of his Eastern Front to withdraw elements of six divisions from it during the later winter for use in his attack on Italy.

On May 4th, Austro-Hungarian forces were unleashed against the Trentino sector of the Italian Front. Hötzendorf had high hopes for this offensive, which was his own brainchild; his participating divisions were composed of good troops, well equipped and well mentioned, and supported by multitudes of artillery pieces. Moreover, morale was surprisingly high within Austrian ranks, the reason undoubtedly being that most inhabitants of the Dual Monarchy considered Italy to be the main enemy in the war, and a treacherous, back-stabbing one at that; even Slav troops, and especially Slovenes, served well when opposing Italians. The net result was disaster for Italy. Within two weeks Hötzendorf had inflicted 50,000 casualties on his foes, and was on the verge of breaking from out of the mountains onto the Venetian Plains, a movement, which if carried out, threatened to cut off the bulk of the entire Italian army, which held the line of the Isonzo, some miles to the northeast. The only power in a position to relieve Italy by immediately diverting Austrian strength was of course Russia, so it was to Petrograd that Rome now appealed, in desperate, frantic tones.

In the meantime, Brusilov had completed his preparations for the offensive of Southwest Front. His men had completely reconnoitered the enemy lines and were well rehearsed in the plans of attack. The only problem now was the weather; May was a month of heavy rains in Polesie and Volhynia, making ground conditions too difficult for military operations. But in lieu of the Italian plight it was clear to Alexiev that some action had to be taken—soon. If Italy was forced to drop out of the war, it would mean that all the Austrian strength opposing her would be released for service elsewhere, undoubtedly much of it against Russia. Evert, whose West Front was to make the primary effort in attack for 1916, complained that he was not yet ready to strike. Alexiev then contacted Brusilov, who replied that his Army Group was indeed ready, and could be set into action within days, though it would also be necessary for Evert to attack simultaneously, in order to prevent the transfer of German reserves southward. This response was of course indicative of Brusilov's determination to adhere to the principles of his new methods—he was certain that if allowed to proceed as he wishes, success was at hand. But neither Alexiev nor any other senior Russian commander had much faith in Brusilov's new, unorthodox tactics; most, in fact, believed his offensive would easily be defeated, and many did not hesitate to say so, and frankly.

Nevertheless, the rapid pace of events necessitated quick action, and Southwest Front was given the green light for June 4th. Brusilov was told that Evert would launch his drive on the 14th, somewhat later than the former had hoped, but a date to which he agreed anyway, realizing that the alternatives were nil. General Kaledin's Eighth Army, the strongest of the group, would make the main effort, though the Eleventh, Seventh, and Ninth Armies would also all strike simultaneously. Nothing like this had ever before been tried, and Brusilov well knew that his reputation and command were at stake. Even so, he remained most optimistic.

Then, at the last minute, Alexiev again telephoned Brusilov, asking for a further delay in the start of the attack. Frustrated, the commander of Southwest Front flatly refused and threatened to resign if overruled, citing various reasons for his firm stance, which included a supposed inability at that late hour to call off the imminent bombardment, and a belief that another postponement would adversely affect the morale of the troops. At this, Alexiev relented, but once again warned of the *Stavka's* general misgivings concerning the whole concept of the offensive, and informed Brusilov that a subsequent failure would be purely his own responsibility, thus covering the *Czar's* headquarters from any association with defeat. The attack was to proceed as planned.

On Friday, June 2, 1916, the Austrian front in the East erupted under the explosions of thousands of Russian artillery shells. The shelling was not particularly intense in any one location, but it occurred along the entire front line, and when the Austrian commanders realized this, they became puzzled. Actually, despite appearances, it was a very effective bombardment; the Russian gunners had done their homework well. Aiming at the enemy barbed wire entanglements, they blasted dozens of holes in these, thereby opening up gaps through which their own infantry could storm. Forward Austrian trenches were obliterated, dugouts smashed in, and communications disrupted. The Austrian artillery, itself a target of its Russian counterpart, was badly mauled and proved unable to effectively reply to the fire. Those pieces which did try to reply with shell were soon silenced from lack of ammunition, since no fresh supplies could be brought forward from the rear positions. As for the Austrian infantry, those who survived the explosions and shrapnel were blinded by flying soil and debris, deafened by the awful noise, and choked by dust, smoke, and gases. Brusilov had achieved the surprise he knew he so badly needed and had immediately created confusion and havoc amongst the enemy. In some places, the barrage lifted after twelve hours, in others, it was staggered over two days. But all along the lines, the Russian infantry attack commenced at dawn on the 5th, with wave after wave of soldiers assaulting the devastated Austro-Hungarian positions. Everywhere the story was pretty much the same; the Austrians, huddled together in their remaining entrenchments and dug-outs, were overrun or outflanked before they could organize an effective defense; each remaining position therefore became a trap in which one might only surrender or be killed. While all this was taking place, the Russian artillery was firing another barrage between the first and second defensive belts, thereby preventing Austrian reserves from being brought forward to save their hapless comrades. Once the first belt had been conquered, the Russians repeated the performance against the second, with similar results. By the time the third, usually final, belt had been reached, the Austro-Hungarian infantry was surrendering in droves, often without further resistance. Within this bewildered, demoralized mass the old shortcomings of the Austro-Hungarian Army were once again becoming evident—the multi-lingual problems with command, the inferior training and discipline, etc. The Dual Monarchy lost many thousands of its troops as prisoners during the first few days of the Russian offensive.

General Kaledin's Eighth Army, the strongest of Brusilov's group, attacked in two places, on a narrow front near Kolki on the Styr, and on a 25 kilometer (16mi) front around the village of Olyka. At first little progress was made at Kolki, where the outer fringes of the Pripet Marshes made the going difficult. No such natural hindrances could bother the Russians at the latter place, though; here the land was a gently rolling plain. At once the Austrian line was smashed, and the drive on Lutsk, some 30 kilometers (19mi) distant, begun. Lutsk was a major fortress of Volhynia, and one of the proudest strong points of Archduke Joseph Ferdinand's Fourth Army, but by the night of June 5th/6th, Kaledin was threatening its capture. The city itself was a strong enough position with some topographic advantages presented by the valley of the Styr River, on which it lay, however one or two adjacent points needed to be held in order to ensure its safety. Fourth Army, shattered within two days of fighting, was unequal to the task; the result being that the Russians occupied these points, placed their artillery upon them, and proceeded to shell the fortress. Unable to control the subsequent panic, Austro-Hungarian officers themselves gave up and fled, their men behind them, over the Styr bridges and to the west. By the evening of June 6th, Lutsk was in Russian hands again, and with it many thousands of prisoners including several hospitals full of wounded, and dozens of guns.

Having taken the great prize in the center, Kaledin decided to push out the flanks in order to protect his gains from becoming a vulnerable salient. The Styr crossings at Rojitche and Torgovitsa, north and south of Lutsk respectively, therefore became the objectives for the next few days; following heavy fighting the former fell on the 9th, but the latter temporarily held. Instead, the fortress of Dubno, outflanked, was taken without much fuss, the same day. This town had already changed hands three times in the war, the last being the Austrian recapture of it following the defeat of the Russian counter-stroke during the previous autumn. Resting barely within Austrian control, since it lay practically right on the front line, and as such it was immediately exposed to attack once the front to the north had been broken through. Southwest of Dubno was an area of heavy woods, extending to and beyond the Galician frontier, and it was into this expanse that the Russians now pushed. Initially, they were opposed, but the resistance slackened in succeeding days; June 16th found them at the Austrian border only a few miles from Brody. Meanwhile, the northern wing was beginning to make some progress. Kolki was captured on the 13th, the Styr crossed, and the Stokhod reached. Svidniki, on the latter stream fell after heavy fighting on the 16th; the Russians were then halted in this sector, and a German counterattack regained Svidniki on the 19th. Weaker Russian drives from the upper Shara south to the Oginski Canal proceeded on the 13th, but in several days of fighting (June 15th-18th) Linsingen was able to stop all aggression aimed at Bug Army.

The advance west of Lutsk meanwhile continued; Torchin was taken on the 12th and Zatursky reached by the 16th. At this time Eighth army had advanced to the halfway point between Lutsk and Vladimir Volynski, and in twelve incredible days taken about 70,000 prisoners and 100 guns. The Austrian Fourth Army had, for all practical purposes, been destroyed.

On the left flank of Eighth Army stood Eleventh Army, under General Sakarov. It was opposed primarily by Boehm-Ermolli's Second Army, though its left faced the left of Bothmer's force on a short sector of front. About the only success Sakarov enjoyed from his initial attacks came on the extreme right, in the Sopanow-Kremenets area; this probably came about because of the near rout of the Austrians by Kaledin; at any rate a local breakthrough yielded 15,000 prisoners and forced the line back nearly to the Galician frontier. Elsewhere, Sakarov failed, and the front along his sector remained intact.

To the south, Shcherbachev and Seventh Army fared little better. Shcherbachev had no one but himself to blame, however. As he, disbelieving in Brusilov's methods, had ordered a much longer preparatory barrage than the other Russian armies had done with, and paid the price when, as Brusilov had feared, the long bombardment merely alerted the enemy as to the attacker's intentions. Bothmer's "South Army," holding the front, which ran roughly along the River Strypa, shattered the attacks, inflicting 25,000 casualties on Seventh Army. Only on Bothmer's extreme right, where an Austrian Corps composed almost entirely of Slav troops held the line, did the defenders give any ground. Here, at Jazlowiec, Shcherbachev succeeding in forcing the Strypa, while taking 16,000 prisoners. In fairness to the Seventh Army leader, it should be noted that the sector of front that he faced was no doubt the most difficult of all to assault. Whereas Kaledin operated on the rolling, often open, plan of Volhynia, and Sakarov on the featureless watershed between the Pripet and Dniester River drainage basins, Shcherbachev had to contend with some very difficult terrain. The Dniester is a large river which rises in the uplands of Galicia and flows eastward through that province into Russia, after which it gradually turns southward to eventually meet the waters of the Black Sea. In Eastern Galicia, this river is met by several tributary streams flowing in a north-to-south direction; the easternmost, which formed the Galician-Russian border, is the Zbruch. The Sereth flows some 32 kilometers (20 mi) farther west, but on a parallel course, then comes the Strypa, Zlota Lipa, and Gnila Lipa, separated by 24 to 32 km (15 to 20 mi) spaces, and all on parallel courses, with many minor streams in between. Over the centuries, each of these tributary rivers has carved a deep canyon out of the Galician upland, so that their courses resemble narrow, deep gullies eroded out of an otherwise gently sloping landscape extending to the less pronounced valley of the Dniester itself. In most cases, the western banks of the many valleys are steeper and higher than the eastern ones, a feature which makes each river line defensible from attack from the east. It is easy to understand why the Russian attacks in this area generally met with little success; the natural obstacles alone are difficult enough to traverse, and when guarded by a resolute force like Bothmer's army become all the harder to overcome. Nevertheless South Army was under tremendous pressure all along its front. Particularly fierce was the struggle for Buczacz, the largest town on the Strypa line. On Friday the 9th of June an eyewitness with the advancing Russians noted how badly battered were the Austrian front line trenches. She was surprised at how much more carefully constructed they were when compared to those of the Russians, including as they did several rows of wire entanglements, and in one section, twelve. No fewer than three trench lines were discovered, connected by communications trenches "more than three *arshins* deep."[123] For once the Russian artillery had been most effective, and huge shell craters were everywhere. The very next day they entered Buczacz at 6:00 p.m., where the savage fighting had literally blackened the earth and battered the nearby trees. She was surprised to find two huge fallen oak trees on one side of the road which appeared to have been "slashed off and their riven trunks splintered."[124] The Russians continued to bash and tear at the line, but South Army would not be put to flight.

It was on the extreme southern end of the Eastern Front that perhaps the greatest Russian success of Brusilov's offensive came. Straddling the Dniester from the mouth of the Strypa to the Romanian border was poised General Lechitski's Ninth Army, opposed by the Austrian Seventh Army of General von Pflanzer-Baltin, a man who had gained somewhat of a reputation for defensive skill. The latter, who had easily defeated Ivanov's winter offensive, possessed a good army, composed of loyal, veteran soldiers and supposed that his front was relatively safe. But Lechitski had found a weak point in the line—on a bend of the Dniester itself—and, following the bombardment of June 4th, broke through here, capturing 10,000 Austrians in the process. The defenders now threw every man into the battle, every plane into the air in an effort to forestall a Russian breakthrough; Kurt Gruber scored his third victory in these actions. It was no good. His front now divided into two distinct halves, Pflanzer-Baltin committed his reserves, hoping to restore the situation; south of the river he succeeded, north of it he did not. Retreating over the stream, the northern group was put to flight, and a general withdrawal was ordered for June 9th. Pflanzer then attempted to maintain contact with Bothmer, but the effort only further divided his army, some of which had been forced to retire in a southerly direction, into the Bukovina. Lechitski, flushed with victory, pressed ahead hard, reaching the Pruth River on the 10th. The provincial capital of Czernowitz became the object of battle for the next week; on the 17th it finally fell, with over 1,000 more prisoners and a few batteries of artillery. By the 19th, the Austrian line was back on the Siret, at the very base of the Carpathian Range. Two days later Radautz was lost and now nothing could prevent the Russians from occupying all of the Bukovina. Kimpolung was captured on June 23rd and the south end of the province reached a day later. His flank now secure, Lechitsky could now turn all his forces to the west. The Austrian Seventh Army had been badly beaten, existing by then only on paper. Even more importantly, Austrian morale was at an all-time low; when Hötzendorf realized this, he was compelled to appeal to Falkenhayn for help.

Evidently, Falkenhayn needed no prodding. He, too, was well aware of the implications of an Austro-Hungarian collapse, and had already begun to scrape up reserves with which to rebuild the shattered Austrian line. Ludendorff released several German divisions from the northern sectors; these went mostly to Linsingen, who now took over strategic command of Boehm-Ermolli's Army.[125] Falkenhayn also reluctantly sent a few divisions from France. There was no time to lose, but the German railroad system was so efficient that one Corps was moved from Verdun to Kovel in only six days.[126] In addition, Austrian forces were en route from Italy and the Balkans, and a Turkish Corps was being sent to re-enforce Bothmer. Kovel and Lemberg, both vitally important rail centers, were considered the main targets of the Russians, and it was before these cities that the bulk of the incoming strength was positioned.

At this point it is perhaps worthwhile to pause and take note of the seriousness of the Austrian defeat. Within two weeks of the opening of Brusilov's drive, Austro-Hungarian losses have been put as: nearly 200,000 men captured, as well as nearly 200 guns, 645 machine guns, almost 200 Minenwerfer, and vast stores of ammunition and other war material.[127] In other words, roughly two-fifths of all Austrian troop strength south of the Pripet had been made prisoners; probably another fifth was either killed or wounded. One-third of its artillery was captured alone. Clearly, the magnitude of such a defeat contained catastrophic implications. For the Russians, it seemed that the knockout blow could surely now be delivered, and had the Romanians intervened at this time, the implications can only be imagined.

Of course, the supposed main Russian drive for the year, to be carried out by Evert's West Front, had yet to come. Alexiev had assured Brusilov that this action would commence on June 14th, but when that date came Evert's main force still did not move. Instead, a minor, secondary attack proceeded in the Baranovichi area. Here, General Ragosa's Fourth Army faced the right wing of Prince Leopold's Army group—a less than army-sized detachment under Woyrsch. Ragosa assaulted the line where it more or less followed the course of the upper Shara River to a point south on the Oginski Canal. Woyrsch and Linsingen easily defeated this effort and another several days later which occurred north of Baranovichi, on the Servech. Aside from six such half-hearted gestures, Evert would not move his army group; procrastinating, complaining, stalling, he then announced that the site of the major drive—the Molodechno area—was unsuitable, and that he would shift his strength to strike instead at Baranovichi. The attack, he said, could not take place until early July. When Alexiev finally notified Brusilov of Evert's intentions, the Commander of Southwest front was aghast. Then his shock turned into anger; he protested bitterly about being left so obviously unsupported, and went on to say that by the time Evert reorganized a new effort, it would be much too late to exploit the recent successes in the south; mere tactical success would be the net gain instead of strategic victory, or even a possible opportunity to win the war by completing the ruin of Austria-Hungary. Alexiev attempted to placate Brusilov by insisting that Evert had been ordered to attack by July 2nd at the latest and by offering several divisions from Evert's command as a reinforcement for Southwest Front. Brusilov was unimpressed. Predicting failure for Evert at Baranovichi for lack of time for proper preparation, he also sneered at the idea of being sent reserves, claiming that the Germans were bound to notice the troop movements and would then likewise send forces south. Because of their more efficient organization of the railroad traffic, they would arrive first on the battlefield and nullify any possible Russian advantage. But Alexiev stood firm, and promised to send a couple of divisions from as far away as the North Front of Kuropatkin, a man who had proved to be equally as timid as Evert.

On the other side of the lines, meanwhile, Falkenhayn and Hötzendorf were frantically trying to scrape up reinforcement for the shattered Austrian front.

By June 20th, they had gathered ten divisions, mostly from Italy. Hötzendorf, naturally, had been forced to shelve his offensive in the Trentino as a result, though he was loath to do so. Eventually eight divisions in all would be sent from that battleground to the East; he had strengthened it in the spring with only parts of six from his Russian Front. Falkenhayn still refused to part with more than a few units from France, though he ordered Ludendorff to send considerable forces south. The latter had been busy since the early days of the Russian offensive in attempting to look well occupied, so as not to lose too many of his troops; he had ambitions of his own and was not particularly disposed to helping either Falkenhayn or Hötzendorf out of their problems. A series of attacks had been made in the North, from the Riga salient all along the line of the Dvina and as far south as the lake country of eastern Lithuania; for the most part, these were artillery actions, as Ludendorff had no desire to expend much man power; a group of airplanes were sent to bomb Dvinsk on the 27th. He had hoped to appear as though to be pinning down or diverting Russian attention from the South, but considering Kuropatkin's obvious reluctance to fight it is hardly surprising that Falkenhayn was not impressed. Considerable forces were dispatched for Volhynia and Galicia.

By mid June, Linsingen reckoned that he had accumulated sufficient reserves to begin a counter-stroke. This was begun on the 16th, east of Kovel, at three different points. A weak effort by the Austrians on the Vladimir-Volynsk/Lutsk axis was beaten off, but German troops recaptured Svidniki on the Stokhod and drove the Russians back from that river to the Styr while taking 3,000 prisoners. Near Kiselin another fierce fight developed, lapsed into hand-to-hand combat, then was discontinued by a German withdrawal. On the Styr, the battle became a seesaw one, with a few villages changing hands several times within a short period; eventually the Germans prevailed and took another 1,000 men as prisoners. Everywhere the fighting was heavy, and was furious. About the only Austrian success came at Lokatchi, where over 1,000 Russians were made captives. Kaledin drew back his left center a few miles and held the new line. The Styr line was also held despite the most energetic German assaults. June 20th and the days that followed witnessed an ebb in the German tide, though the counterattacks were resumed with renewed vigor before the month was over. Both sides claimed victory, but neither could gain a decided advantage, and the battle in Volhynia became a stalemate. As if in frustration for their failure to regain Lutsk, German aircraft bombed the city on the 29th.

At bottom, the *Alliance* lost 40,000 men in these battles—troops they could ill afford to lose—and even German morale, once considered unshakeable, was beginning to decline.

Adding to the Germans' headaches was the fact that Lechitski's advance in Galicia was continuing more or less unchecked. Austrian resistance simply melted away, with a small remnant of Seventh Army fleeing through the forests and gorges of the mountains. Pursuing the other fraction of enemy trying to escape westward in order to maintain contact with Bothmer, Lechitski's men burst into Galicia, taking Kuty (June 23rd) and Pistyn, and driving to the outskirts of the important town of Kolomea. Bothmer's strong position to the north allowed the Austrians to make a stand at that point, and Ninth Army, outrunning its supplies, was temporarily halted. Within a week, however, the offensive was renewed, and in fierce fighting Kolomea was captured on the 29th. Thereafter began a three-day battle for Tlumach, on the road to Stanislav. Thoroughly beaten, Pflanzer-Baltin lapsed into despair; the southern door to Galicia was wide open.

Yet on the Russian side, problems were steadily mounting. After the initial successes of the first two weeks of the general offensive the fighting became more of a slugging match, and morale declined noticeably. As more German troops began to arrive by late June the soldiers will to do combat, especially attack, was seriously eroded. There were pitiful tales from the home front, sad letters (for the literate, when the mails got through) of despair and privation. And there was the pathos of it all: a decree was issued to all Austrian citizens living in districts near the battlefront which ordered them to hurriedly abandon their residences and travel eastward to Trebunovski. Everyone, regardless of age or physical state, was required to comply. Loading what few staples they could in their carts and wagons, they sadly took to the unpaved tracks, driving what livestock as they were able. An English-born witness with the Russian army could scarcely contain her sympathy for these people, forced as she saw it, "into strange surroundings under a strange, hostile government."[128]

The average Russian soldier, a peasant himself, was not likely to be unmoved by such experiences, especially since he had been led to believe that the enemy Slavic population were Russian sympathizers waiting for deliverance from German oppression. Many expressed their dissatisfaction by deserting. It has been estimated that approximately 57,000 men—nearly one-tenth of Brusilov's force—deserted the four armies of Southwest Front between mid-May and July 1ˢᵗ. It was the beginning of a calamitous new trend. Russian troop strength on the Eastern Front would peak in July 1916; 158 divisions held the line (on paper at least) by mid month. Thereafter, their numbers were in constant decline except for a short period during the following summer. No one could see it in mid 1916, but the Russian Empire had nearly reached the limits of its military capabilities.

Following Brusilov's astounding initial victories, Alexiev at *Stavka* had begun to re-think his priorities. No fool, he could see where the only hope for strategic success was possible. Evert spent the whole month of June stalling, stockpiling, and complaining of bad weather; Brusilov, without proper support, continued to think in terms of further advances. Accordingly, the Chief of Staff transferred Lesh's Third Army, the southernmost of Evert's command, to Southwest Front, as well as several other divisions from both Evert and Kuropatkin. Brusilov, he knew, would employ these units immediately, and offensively. In the event, Southwest Front was ready to launch its second phase of attacks by the time Evert was ready for the "main" blow, and well before Kuropatkin stirred. A heavy enemy build-up east of Kovel had been identified by late June, and Brusilov deduced that these forces would be used against Kaledin's right flank. It was his intention to forestall the enemy strike and push on to Kovel itself, an act that would effectively cut lateral communications between the German and Austro-Hungarian sectors of front.

The attack began on the morning of July 4ᵗʰ, over a broad front as Brusilov, pointing to his recent successes, had demanded. Kaledin was a believer by now, and Lesh was soon to become one. An intense artillery demonstration pounded the Austro-German emplacements to dust, whereupon the Russian infantry stormed ahead and scored a breakthrough. Heavy fighting commenced all along the lower Styr, especially at Kolki where German defenders held up the advance for a day, but in general, the Austrians, after an initial stiff fight, were simply swept away. By the 6ᵗʰ, the attackers had won even the secondary positions of defense, several miles to the rear, and were streaming westward. June had been a month of brilliant weather, and most of the wetlands having dried up made the advance all the easier. Retreat became rout; Linsingen ordered a stand on the River Stokhod, and took every possible measure to fortify that line in great haste.

Running a course roughly parallel to that of the Styr, the Stokhod flows northerly out of Volhynia into the Pripet. It is a sluggish stream, though the channel itself is neither particularly wide nor deep. However, the west bank is slightly higher than the east, and both sides are lined by wide belts of reed-strewn marsh; the river line is therefore defensible against attack, especially from the east. Its lower course is marked by a landscape typical of the Pripet Marshes region, and is some 40 km (25 mi) west of the Styr. The terrain of the upper Stokhod is likewise flat, but is overgrown with forests of pine; here, the river takes a sharp bend to the east, and at one point flows within 8 km (5 mi) of the Styr. The important Kovel-Rovno railroad crosses at Svidniki and the Kovel-Sarny line at Gulivitchi, just south and just north of the bend, respectively. It was at these latter locations that Kaledin and Lesh made their primary efforts.

Within a week of their attack, the Russians had not only reached the Stokhod, but had forced the stream at several points by the 9th. Svidniki was regained on the 10th and the great eastward bend of the river occupied, as well as the surrounding woodland, so that Kaledin now owned a sizeable bridgehead, perhaps 8 km (5 mi) deep from the extremity of the bend west. Lesh, for his part, advanced to the line of the lower Stokhod as far north as the Pripet, and himself carved a couple of footholds out of the west bank of the former. But now Linsingen had accumulated sufficient reinforcements to make a serious stand, and this he did, battling desperately to hold the already threatened river line, the last natural barrier east of Kovel. Despite a few anxious days, he gradually brought the situation under control, and so halted the Russians by mid July. Between them, Kaledin and Lesh had captured nearly 30,000 Austro-Germans with almost 50 guns, and though their own losses had been substantial as well, they had caused great anxiety amongst the enemy command and were now only 40 km (25 mi) from Kovel.

Evert, who had been expected to attack even after all of his protestations by July 2nd at the latest, finally began his pulverizing artillery preparation on that very day. For two entire days his numerous field pieces expended lavish quantities of shell. The infantry went forward on the 4th, and were promptly cut down by accurate German artillery fire from weapons mostly untouched by the Russian bombardment. A minor success was achieved at Gorodishche, north of Baranovichi, where 3,000 prisoners were taken, but the German line remained unbroken. Ragosa and his Fourth Army tried again on the 7th, but the defense was again too strong. In disgust, one observer reported that on July the 9th two entire infantry companies of Siberian troops "perished in a bog."[129]

Woyrsch's Austro-German force delivered a counterattack on the 14th without success; thereafter the battle spent itself. Evert had sustained 75,000 casualties to 15,000 defenders, and he, as he had feared, had nothing to show for his efforts.

The story was pretty much the same in the north. Hoping to at least distract the Germans near Riga, Russian warships attacked the Courland coast at Ragatsiems, at the extreme northern end of the German lines, on July 2nd; then they steamed slowly along the shoreline, shelling targets real or imaginary until the 5th. Kuropatkin had chosen to strike from the Riga bridgehead as his contribution to the summer offensive, but by the time it proceeded on the 16th, it had surprised no one, and was easily stopped. Although he would persist in his semi-feeble operations for a fortnight, Kuropatkin failed to divert a single enemy soldier from the crises to the south. The only other remarkable action in the north during July occurred on the 29th when two sizeable groups of hostile airplanes engaged each other near Dvinsk. Twelve Russian and a roughly equal number of German planes[130] were present; the Russian ace Kazakov shot down one of the latter.

Two other Russian diversionary assaults accompanied the "main" offensives north of the Pripet. On the 4th of July came an advance south of Lake Narotch to near Smorgon, and on the 5th another push north of Postavy. Evert might have saved his strength, as neither of these jabs attracted any German reserves and therefore did not affect the issue at Baranovichi.

Other issues which might have affected the outcome of the war were, however, being dealt with at this time. On July 4th, such a memorable date in the war on the Eastern Front, a deal was finally reached between the *Entente* and the Romanian government. Spurred into resolute action by Brusilov's apparent success, the Romanians were ready at last to enter the war, and were no doubt uneasy about the swift Russian re-conquest of Bukovina and advance to the Tatars Pass. This latter event went almost unnoticed in the hectic days of mid July, but it ensured that Lechitsky could, if he saw fit, pour his troops into northern Hungary—and into other areas besides Bukovina coveted by the Romanians. Bucharest naturally feared that a victorious Russia in possession of these lands might be difficult to eject, and it had decided to occupy what territory it desired with its own soldiers. Terms of the agreement included 200,000 Russian troops on Romania's border with Bulgaria to safeguard the southern flank, and active participation by Romania to begin on August 27th.[131]

The final participant of the war in the east was about ready to fight, confident that after two years of desperate struggle, Austria-Hungary was about to collapse.

Further south, Eleventh Army had also resumed the offensive. Linsingen had planned a major counterattack against both flanks of Kaledin's Army, but the events on the Stokhod had preempted his strike from that area; he still expected to launch the southern group on July 18th. Sakarov noticed the concentration, however, and struck first, on the 16th. This clever blow caught the enemy completely by surprise, creating havoc and confusion behind the lines so paralyzing that the Russians were able to capture three ammunition dumps intended for use in Linsingen's counter-thrust. Most of the Austrian Second Army was put to flight, the troops surrendering in droves. Desperate, Boehm-Ermolli tried to regroup his forces in order to hold the pivotal town of Brody, which lay roughly at his center, just inside the Galician frontier. Between the 22nd and 27th of July a desperate battle was waged here, amongst the oak-wooded hills and swampy dales of the Galician-Volhynian border area. An all-too-typical scene in the summer heat was recorded on the 22nd, while the dead were being buried. A mass grave for all fatal casualties of whatever nationality was being prepared, as swarms of flies covered the corpses, giving the appearance of motion over the bodies. The observer was sickened.[132] Both sides fought well, but in the end the Russians prevailed. Brody fell on July 28th. In twelve days Sakarov had taken 40,000 prisoners and 50 guns, and yet another Austrian Army was badly mauled. Perhaps more importantly, he now stood well into the flank of Bothmer's "South Army" and was presented the option of either turning against the latter or pushing on toward Lemberg.

During the fourth week of July, heavy rains lasting several days drenched the battlefields of Volhynia and Galicia, giving the commanders of both hostile armies a brief respite during which they might pause and re-determine their respective strategies. Brusilov had help. The evident failure of Evert had prompted Alexiev to send an entire army south to assist in the drive on Kovel. This force—the pride of the Czarist military—was the newly created Guard Army, a well-trained, well-equipped formation of 134,000 of the finest soldiers Russia could field. It was to be placed in the line between Kaledin and Lesh; the latter's Third Army was soon to revert to the command of Evert. Brusilov ordered all his armies to renew the offensive on July 28th, hoping that a final blow would be sufficient to cause the collapse of Austria-Hungary, a nation he believed to be mortally wounded. For the Guard in particular he had very high hopes. No one seemed to notice that it had been inserted into a sector of front practically within the Pripet Marshes. Not surprisingly, no one much noticed two further half-hearted attacks by Evert either. At the prodding of Alexiev, they were undertaken on, and stopped by Woyrsch's men on, the 25th and the 27th.

Toward the end of July the *Alliance* was meanwhile busy regrouping. Hindenburg and Ludendorff, who controlled the relatively quiet northern half of the Eastern Front, had of course been obliged to send considerable forces south since the opening of the enemy drive on June 5th. As the situation demanded more and more reinforcement, the famous duo released additional strength only more and more grudgingly; as such they pressed ever harder for a unified, international command in the east which would control the entire Front from the Baltic to the Carpathians. Since Hindenberg was already the German Commander-in-Chief East, it was he who should logically assume the greater role, they argued, at a meeting with Falkenhayn and the *Kaiser* at Pless early in June. The *Kaiser* was still not totally convinced of Ludendorff's capabilities, and at any rate would have to remain on good terms with his Austrian allies, but he realized that his own prestige was scarcely greater than that which Hindenburg now enjoyed. Falkenhayn was in a most difficult position; he did not wish to see Hindenburg's authority strengthened in any way, but disliked the Austrians even more and had always wanted to see their armies subordinated to Germany—i.e. to himself. The latter was further hamstrung by his own Western strategy; the Verdun battle had gone sour and was by now costing the Germans heavily, and late in June the British launched a major offensive on the Somme; not a single German soldier could be spared from the West to prop up the Austrian lines in the East. Therefore, Falkenhayn, his hands tied, would be forced to support Hindenburg, as he knew this was the only way to save the situation south of the Pripet.

As soon as Hötzendorf got wind of the German intentions, he protested vigorously, realizing that his own power was about to be drastically reduced. Citing nationalistic considerations as his reasons for opposing Hindenburg, he suggested that the Austrian Archduke Friedrich be nominated instead, but no one from either nation took him very seriously. It is most likely that he was chiefly troubled by the thought of losing control of reserves which might be turned against the Italians—most Austrians still regarded Italy as the main enemy—not so much by forfeiting command of his always troublesome Russian front. Already the Austrian Fourth Army, or what was left of it, was included in Linsingen's command, while the "South Army" was led by the German Bothmer. That left only the Austrian Second and Seventh Armies under his guidance, and Seventh Army had been badly mauled by Lechitski. In the event, pressure from the German Chancellor and *Kaiser*, Falkenhayn, and Ludendorff as well as some of his own countrymen finally forced Hötzendorf to yield, and at a second Pless conference in late July, Hindenburg was made Commander-in-Chief of the Eastern Front. Austrian sentiments were placated only to the extent that Hötzendorf was allowed to remain the theoretical boss of the Austro-Hungarian forces in practice, he now controlled only the southernmost Army Group, which was now led by the heir to the Austro-Hungarian throne, the Archduke Karl. The imminent Romanian intervention was also discussed on the 28th, between representatives of all four *Alliance* powers. A strategy was worked out which involved the use of troops from each nation to help crush Romania as soon as it declared war; their estimates of the timing were uncannily accurate. On August 2nd, Hindenburg's appointment was made public.

Hindenburg's order of battle now ran as follows: Eichhorn commanded the northernmost Army Group, his own Tenth Army, the Eighth Army of von Below, and the Scholtz detachment; Prince Leopold led the central army group of Fabeck's Twelfth Army, and Woyrsch's Ninth Army; then came Linsingen's Group, consisting of his own (now) Army of Manoeuvre, the Austrian Fourth Army, under General Tersztyansky (who had replaced the Archduke Ferdinand), and Boehm-Ermolli's Second Austrian Army. Archduke Karl, independent of Hindenburg, commanded Bothmer's "South Army" and the Austrian Seventh Army, the leadership of which was passing from the defeated von Pflanzer-Baltin to Kirchbach. In addition, this latter group was to be strengthened by the arrival of a new army, the Austrian Third under General Kovess, as soon as possible. But Hindenburg and Ludendorff were not bothered by this theoretical limitation of their authority on the extreme southern end of the line; as Austrian strength waned they might tighten their grip on, or better yet infiltrate with German troops, the Austrian armies. To a certain extent this had already been taking place for some time. Now, it became blatant policy; though a definite snub to Austrian military capabilities, no one could say it was not effective. As we have seen, German and Austro-

Hungarian divisions had already been mixed on several occasions to form mixed armies—"South Army" being a case in point—but with the ascendancy of Hindenburg as Supreme Commander in the East, divisions themselves were mixed with German and Austrian regiments; even smaller units, such as battalions, were formed of mixed companies. This practice became very effective regarding the quality of Austrian units; even the Slav elements of the Hapsburg forces would fight well when under good leadership and when adequately supplied. German efficiency could be expected to surmount these problems.

But the most advantageous development for the *Alliance* resulting from the leadership changes of late July was one regarding the use of reserve troops. To a certain extent, Brusilov's successes during June and July had been possible because of the defender's misuse of his reserves. All too often, local reserves had been overrun before they could be properly organized into a coherent defense, or had simply been wasted in attempts to plug the many holes in the line which the Russians had punched. Strategic reserves were too few, and were often similarly dispersed, without effect. All this reflected the essence of Brusilov's methods, of course, practices which had they been employed by all the *Entente* nations simultaneously, would certainly have spelled the ruin of the *Alliance*. But the strategy born at Chantilly was never energetically implemented, and the Germans were given another opportunity to shift forces between different theaters, and so contain *Entente* aggression. On the Eastern Front, where the situation was indeed desperate by mid summer, the appointment of Hindenburg perhaps saved the day. No sooner had Ludendorff been formally vested with the authority he sought, than train loads of reinforcements began rolling south, from the northern end of the front. North of the Pripet, the Germans had already been outnumbered by nearly three to one (a fact that Ludendorff had pointed to when previously asked to release forces for the Austrian end of the line), and these new transferals would seemingly worsen the odds even more; however, Ludendorff was not really worried about the North. He knew the timid dispositions of the enemy commanders there and besides noticed that they, too, were sending help to Brusilov. As the latter had feared, the Germans using their superior communications were able to reinforce the contested sectors faster than were the Russians. Soon, all five Austro-German Armies from the Pripet south had been rebuilt and restructured, and a sixth was being moved into the

Carpathians. Despite the heavy pressure in the West, Falkenhayn was even persuaded to send a German mountain corps from France. This force was renamed the "Carpathian Corps" and was delivered to the Archduke Karl's sector—possibly in an effort to further water down the Austrian content of the armies not directly under Hindenburg. Whatever the case, by pooling his reserves, Ludendorff was able to erect a formidable barrier in Brusilov's path.

On July 28th began the second great phase of Brusilov's offensive. At the fringe of the marshes was made the primary effort once again, this time with the Guard as well as the Eighth Army. After a short, violent bombardment, these forces pushed ahead, at about midday. The Guard were held up more by the difficult terrain along the Stokhod than by the badly outnumbered defenders. Carefully, deliberately, the men of the elite formation filed through the few paths which led across the treacherous marshes and into the dense woods beyond the river. Here on higher, dryer ground, Linsingen's men made their stand, and heavy fighting developed, with the Russians taking village after village, though at great cost to themselves. Once the pivotal height at Tristen had been won, the upper Stokhod was forced at several points, and with this, Linsingen was compelled to retire from his positions within the great eastward bend of the river, as these were by then outflanked from either side. Even so, he managed to slow the Russian advance, after its initial leap forward, to a crawl. Meanwhile his aircraft buzzed overhead, above the open fields. One German aviator who participated in these battles was Manfred von Richthofen who later lamented that his many victories included not a single Russian. "His cockade would look very picturesque on the wall."[133] What Richthofen did accomplish was to bomb the railroad station at Manjewicz numerous times. He described the flight to the place as "beautiful...over gigantic complexes of forests" and without much interference from either enemy aircraft or anti-aircraft fire. He shot up cavalry formations and bombed all sorts of Russian ground activity. Then one day he prepared to attack Russian ground troops about to move over a single bridge spanning the Stokhod River. Fully munitioned, he and his flight swept down and began dropping bombs amongst cavalry that had begun to dash across the stream, causing "immediate confusion and disorder." Apparently the bridge survived the attack, but the Russian cavalry and infantry scattered in all directions and for a while the river-crossing remained quite deserted.[134] By August 2nd, Bezobrazov had incurred 30,000 casualties, for an Austro-German loss of perhaps one-third this number, most of these being prisoners. Fifty German guns had been taken. The line of the lower Stokhod still held, however, and despite the moderate advances along its upper reaches, no breakthrough towards Kovel had been achieved.

Eighth Army fared no better. Its objective was the town of Vladimir-Volynski, the only major settlement between Kovel to the north, and the Galician border. At first its advance was impressive; 12,000 Austrians were made prisoners. Then the defense hardened and a heavy battle developed around the village of Koshev, which stalled any further advance. As soon as the Germans regained their balance they vigorously counterattacked and nearly forced Kaledin to retreat. Here, as well as in front of the Guard Army, Linsingen's counters were marked by extreme violence and were contained only with much difficulty. Despite a considerable numerical superiority, Kaledin, like Bezobrazov, could not bulldoze his way forward. Ludendorff's "mixing" policies and control of reserves had definitely toughened his defenses. Further south, where the German system of command had not yet permeated, the Russians were able to repeat their earlier successes. Sakarov's Eleventh Army which had gotten off to such a slow start, had not really paused in mid July as had the other armies. When on July 28th Brody was captured, Boehm-Ermolli had fallen back on Krasne, which lay halfway to Lemberg. He expected Sakarov to continue on towards the Galician capital. But Sakarov pushed due south from Brody into rugged terrain, a move which was completely unexpected, and one which would place him well into the left flank of Bothmer's Army. The latter force was the least disturbed of all the enemy armies thus far in the campaign, but with the Eleventh Army driving in its left and Ninth Army its right, Bothmer would be forced to respond. In the tangled forests of the Galician uplands, the Russians found the going rather slow; there was not much to oppose them, however, and by August 4th they had reached the line of the upper Sereth. With the vital Tarnopol-Krasne rail line only a few miles distant, Sakarov pushed on, though he was encountering increasing resistance. On August 10th his drive had virtually run out of steam, but the railroad was reached, making Bothmer's position untenable. Eleventh Army took 8,500 prisoners on its way.

Shcherbachev's Seventh Army, all the while, was still trying to dislodge Bothmer. It had met with little success since early June, save the tactical victory in the Jaslowiec-Buczacz area on the lower Strypa. Now, it was once again locked in a heavy frontal struggle with South Army. At first, the Austro-

Germans resisted very well, and it seemed that Bothmer could not be budged. A second push on August 9th, however, coincided with Sakarov's appearance upon the Tarnopol railway, and finally, with no real choice, Bothmer retreated. Abandoning first the line of the Strypa, he then fell back over the Kuropiets and reached the Zlota Lipa by 11th-12th August. He anchored his center around the town of Brzezany and checked Sakarov's and Shcherbachev's advance among the rugged, wooded hills of the Koniuchy-Zborov area east of the river. The Galician village of Monastyriska was, like many others, the scene of heavy fighting. A day or two after its capture by the Russians an eyewitness saw bodies lying all around, both Russian and Austrian, some resting as if sleeping, others torn, punctured, or crushed. Patches of earth were stained dark by the release of human fluids. And there were the inevitable masses of flies sustaining themselves and on open wounds moved other "thread-like things.[135] A few days later she heard that a peasant woman who lived in a nearby village had been executed as a spy. Further inquiry revealed that the woman had been spotting for the enemy artillery, and her efforts had resulted in the destruction of an *"Bronirovanuy Avotomobil"* (armored car). But someone had noticed that she frequently came and went in and out of her abode, and when the structure was searched a telephone was discovered.[136] Apparently not all the residents of Galicia were anxious to see the Russians return. In the air over the same area the Russians sustained another, more difficult loss on August 4th, when ace Lieutenant Edward Pulpe was shot down and killed in a battle with five Fokker fighter planes. Pulpe had scored his fifth victory on July 1st.

The most significant gains by the Russians continued to come from General Lechitski's Ninth Army which had earlier shattered Pflanzer-Baltin and reconquered the Bukovina. Acting in close cooperation with Seventh Army from late July, it continued its drive up the Dniester valley and toward the heights of the Carpathians. In the river valley, Bothmer's right wing countered and retook the town of Tlumatch, stabilized the line, and forced the Russians to suspend further operations until after the heavy rains of late July. On August 7th began a new offensive by Ninth Army; Tlumatch was immediately recovered and Bothmer's southern flank turned; Nizniov, on the Dniester at the mouth of the Zlota Lipa, fell on August 10th, as did Stanislau, an important junction south of the river. At this, even Bothmer's new position on the Zlota Lipa was threatened from the south, and a few miles of the lower reaches of that stream did indeed fall into the hands of the Russians, but just then reinforcements arrived, and Lechitski's westward advance was halted. Still, he continued to make gains in the mountains, until the arrival of the German "Carpathian Corps"; Nadworna fell on the 12th, the Tatar's Pass was seized on the 15th, and three days later the Russians were 5 km (3 mi) into Hungary, battling for possession of the western end of the pass. Elsewhere, fighting raged among the mountains as far south as the Romanian border. In general the Austrians held the spine of the mountain range, though only with difficulty; they made some minor gains in the Cheremosh Valley on August 5th, but Lechitsky kept up the pressure and was over the Bistritza by the 11th. The Kirlibaba Pass was reached on the 17th; thereafter the advance slackened as all available reserves were diverted into the Dniester valley.

Back in Volhynia, fighting of a different sort was taking place. It can only be described as a bloodbath. For here, Brusilov had decided to renew his drive on Kovel despite the disappointing results of the Guard's efforts thus far. On 8th August he launched a powerful attack on the enemy lines directly east of Kovel, preceded by a massive artillery barrage. The Guard Cavalry Corps was even dismounted for this blow, since the soggy terrain was most unsuitable for horsemen. Despite a lavish expenditure of shell, the bombardment was ineffective, owing to the swampy ground, which tended to muffle the explosions. German mastery of the air had prevented extensive photographic efforts by Russian airmen from revealing much information regarding the German positions, so when the infantry attacked, they ran headlong into well-prepared enemy locations which were practically unscathed by the shelling. The German defenders were well concealed in the thick Kukhari Woods, from which came a withering fire of artillery, machine guns, and small arms. Bezobrazov's men were neatly mowed down as they came forward, struggling through the marshes, without opportunity to return the deadly hail of fire. Hundreds of wounded drowned in the wetlands as they fell, unable to help themselves. Within a day the attack was completely shattered; the Russians returned to their former positions leaving nearly 7,000 casualties behind. Even a gas attack during which 4000 cylinders containing 140 tons of chlorine and phosgene[137] were released did not dent the Austro-German line. The total loss of the Guard Army from July 28th to August 9th was 55,000 men, and Kovel still lay 32 km (20 mi) distant. A few further, but futile, attacks were made until the 17th, when the action died away.

Heads were bound to roll. Brusilov blamed Bezobrazov, a man he had never liked, for the failures, but had no power to dismiss him, as Imperial Guard commanders were appointed and replaced only by the *Czar* himself. Nevertheless, Brusilov let his feelings be known to Alexiev who was of course in frequent contact with the monarch. Evidently the Chief of Staff agreed that Bezobrazov was incompetent; the latter was replaced by General Gourko. At the same time, however, the Guard Army was renamed the Special Army (as if such an act could wipe clean its recent record of defeat) and was re-subordinated to Evert's West Front. At this, Brusilov's command was constricted to his original four armies of early June. Other August 1916 actions had been relatively minor, and of the diversionary nature. The Germans had launched three such assaults on the 1st, at Logishin, Lake Nobel, and with gas near Smorgon. The Russians answered at Lake Narotch and on the Dvina within a few days and the remainder of the month saw fighting usually minor, all along the line from the Pripet to the Baltic. Both sides employed the use of gas but its handling was often amateurish and it caused few casualties. Weak Russian naval moves off the coast of Courland were frustrated by German artillery fire.

In the air it was the Russians who excelled in August. Lieutenant-Commander Seversky, who a year earlier had been shot down into the Gulf of Riga, was one of two seaplane pilots ordered to bomb the enemy seaplane base at Lake Angern, on August 12th. Having done so, they were in turn attacked by seven German planes. Seversky shot down two of these after a lengthy dogfight, and both Russians lived to fly again. Farther south, over the town of Nesvizh east of Baranovichi, another Russian shot down two enemy aircraft within two days. He was Captain Kruten, another pilot destined to become an ace. His victories were recorded on August 25th and 27th and were his second and third.

The most spectacular phase of the Brusilov offensive was over. For a series of attacks which were supposed to be secondary to the "main" offensive for 1916 to the north, it was certainly a smashing success. From the beginning of the campaign on June 5th, to roughly the middle of August, Brusilov's armies had eliminated between 750 and 850,000 soldiers from the ranks of the *Alliance*, including probably 375,000 who were made prisoners of war. The majority of these casualties were Austro-Hungarians, especially the captives, but the dead and wounded included a fairly high percentage of Germans, which was some indication of the relative fighting value of the forces of the two Teutonic nations. In addition, the Russians captured more than 400 guns and over 1,300 machine guns besides destroying hundreds more. They also seized vast quantities of war material, so much ammunition, in fact, that Russian factories no longer needed to produce rounds to fit the many thousands of Austrian-made rifles that Russian troops carried. Besides the material gains, 40,000 sq km (over 15,000 sq mi) of territory had been conquered, land on which stood several important towns, such as Lutsk, Dubno, Stanislau, Kolomea, and Czernowitz. All in all it was a most impressive showing considering the fact that few high-ranking Russians had given Brusilov and his new tactics the slightest chance of success when he told them of his intentions.

In a larger sense, the Brusilov offensive was very important to the Allied cause. For it had caused the transfer of more than 30 *Alliance* divisions to the southern portion of the Eastern Front by late August, and more were to come. So disruptive had been the actions of Southwest Front that Hötzendorf had been forced to abandon his May offensive against Italy, an operation that had very real prospects for success. Eventually, seven divisions were shuttled back to Galicia from the Trentino and Isonzo sectors, and Austria was once more obliged to take up the defensive against the hated Italians. Falkenhayn, the ardent proponent of a Western strategy, was equally frustrated. He could only watch in horror as seven German divisions—troops vitally needed at Verdun and on the Somme—rolled east by the end of July; eight more had departed by mid-September. The Turks were even implored to send help. This came in the form of an Ottoman Corps of two divisions. By far the heaviest reinforcement for the shattered line came from Ludendorff, but he dispatched only two divisions during June-July. Only when he had been given full authority for the East (July 28th) did significant forces depart for the south—forces to the tune of 16 divisions—but by then the worst of Brusilov's damage had been done. Naturally, Russia also suffered from the summer campaign. Southwest Front incurred nearly 600,000 battle casualties by the middle of August, and gone were the days that Russia could afford such losses. Much more frightening to Russian leaders were the figures for desertion; between the middle of May (when preparations for the offensive were nearing completion) and the end of August, no fewer than 65,000 men simply disappeared from the roles of Brusilov's command. Brusilov himself was alarmed and ordered severe punishments, even the death penalty, for desertion. To a certain degree, this helped ease the problem of disappearances for the next couple of months, but nothing could at that stage restore morale, which had been crumbling for well nigh a year. The futility of the winter battles had left a lasting impression on the troops, and new slaughters, such as took place on the Stokhod and the Zlota Lipa, only served to reinforce the average Russian soldier's deep sense of inferiority and belief in the futility of his tasks. By late August, the troops were openly grumbling their resentments. Many considered themselves merely "cannon fodder" to their generals. Russia's worst enemies were fast becoming her own sons.

Mid August marked the end of the *Alliance* retreat before Brusilov. The massive attacks of the Guard and Eighth Armies on the Kovel front had been stopped, Eleventh Army was frustrated in the rugged uplands of Galicia, and Bothmer, so recently dislodged from the strong positions he had built on the line of the Strypa, was now back on the Zlota Lipa and beyond it, having been dangerously outflanked and compelled to withdraw. Even Lechitski's advance in the Carpathians finally stopped, though perhaps as much from his outrunning his supplies as from enemy defensive action. At any rate, by August 20th the fronts were relatively quiet at last. But this lull was not to last; already Brusilov was preparing to renew the offensive despite the dwindling prospects for success. Since the appointment of Hindenburg as Commander-in-Chief East, the German's increased efficiency in handling reserves was making progress more and more difficult. At this point in time, however, Brusilov himself seems to have changed his tactics. Just why he did this is neither entirely clear nor reasonable. Circumstances had changed, to be sure; none of the advantages of June 5th could be expected by mid August, when a desperate enemy was taking every possible measure to prevent further Russian gains. Therefore lost were all the important ingredients of success: prolonged and detailed preparation, surprise, the diversion of German forces to other fronts, disruption of enemy reserves. But now the leader of Southwest Front threw his erstwhile radical tactics to the wind as well: those of short, accurate preparatory barrage, attack on a broad front, attack by all the armies in unison. The old formula could not produce the great victories that had the new.

Brusilov was still preoccupied with the capture of Kovel and Lemberg, the two most vital of the enemy communications centers in Volhynia and Galicia respectively. He realized that the seizure of either of these objectives would so badly dislocate the enemy's coordination of defense that he would be forced to withdraw his entire line between the Pripet and the Carpathians. If this happened, Austria-Hungary would be wide open for a knockout blow, especially if Romania intervened on Russia's side, an event which now seemed likely. So it was that the major Russian drives were renewed in late August. Alexiev, sympathetic despite his transferal of the Guard Army to Evert, tried to lend some assistance, though he could not budge the latter with whatever persuasion. Russki, who had replaced the over-cautious Kuropatkin as commander of the Northwest Front, proved as expected, not so difficult to move. On August 21st, Russian troops attacked from the Riga bridgehead, took some minor parcels of ground, and kept up the pressure on Below for several days. It was an action merely intended as a diversion to the Germans, but as things turned out more—much more—than this would be needed.

At the moment of Romania's intervention, Russia had passed her peak strength and thereafter her numbers of troops declined; their effectiveness declined even more significantly. No one could know it at the time, but the Romanians had missed their best chance to share in the spoils of victory, if only by a few months. Had they declared war coincidentally with the opening of the summer offensive in early June, it is difficult to imagine how Austria-Hungary could have avoided definite defeat. But again, no one had predicted such success for Brusilov. When they regrouped in August 1916, the Russians could count only 36 fewer divisions than they controlled in early July; on the line there remained only 122. Romania possessed only 13; a number raised to 23 upon her declaration of war. Against these totals the *Alliance* fielded (by September) 77 German, 52 Austro-Hungarian, 4½ Bulgarian (against Romania), and 4 Turkish. Totals, then, were 137½ *Alliance* divisions versus 145 *Entente*, and those of the latter, while numerically larger, had been seriously reduced in effectiveness by problems of morale. The Romanians, so assured of, so confident of victory, were in reality plunging into an enterprise which can only be described as a gamble.

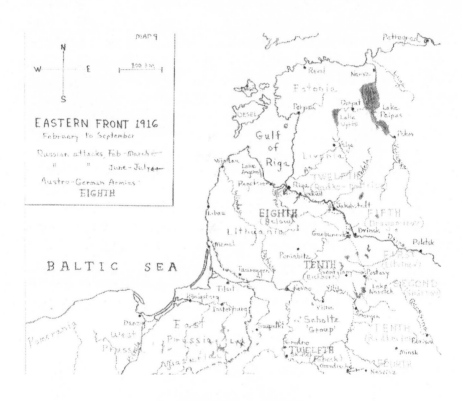

Eastern Front, 1916

Chapter Ten
Romania Joins the Fight

On August 27, 1916, the Kingdom of Romania declared war on Austria-Hungary. The next day Germany countered with a declaration against Romania, and Bulgaria followed suit on September 1st. Another small Balkan nation had become completely embroiled in the Great War—for better or for worse. The Allies were of course overjoyed, since Romanian participation meant the addition of over 500,000 men to the *Entente* cause. It also meant that the Austro-Germans would have to extend their Eastern Front considerably, and the Bulgarians would be forced to defend an entirely new front; such defensive measures would require a great deal of manpower from the *Alliance*, manpower which they might well be unable to account for at that decisive moment. To most even moderately optimistic minds that hoped for an *Entente* victory, the Romanian intervention seemed a dream come true—surely the scales of war had now, at last, been finally tipped in favor of their side, and the great struggle could now not last much longer. After all, they had for two years been trying to woo the uncommitted Balkan states into their camp. They had failed with Bulgaria and had watched in frustration that country go the other way, an act which only served to prolong the war, as they saw it. But now, with Greece tilting toward them, and Romania a full-fledged partner, their enemies were doomed. Surely Russia could take new heart in the war as she now was no longer isolated from all her allies. Expected to be equally significant was the effect upon morale within the ranks of the enemy coalition. Certainly, Romania's entry into hostilities did nothing to lift the spirits of the *Alliance*, but actually it did not come as a surprise. The Austro-Germans were convinced that it was an eventual certainty as early as June, when Brusilov's blows began to pulverize the Galician front; about August 20th they learned it was imminent, having been warned by spies and sympathizers in Bucharest, the Romanian capital. Nevertheless, the overall strategic situation was indeed desperate during that fateful summer of 1916. German resources were everywhere stretched to the maximum. In France the Verdun operation had cost heavily in every military sense; the subsequent Anglo-French initiative on the Somme meant that nothing more could be spared from the West, where the Kaiser's armies were always heavily outnumbered and outgunned. In June Brusilov had turned the Eastern Front aflame, threatening to drive Austria-Hungary from the war, an event which from German eyes could not of course be tolerated. Conrad von Hötzendorf's Italian venture had to be scrapped in order to produce reinforcements for the East. The Italians then countered; clearly Austria was strained to the limit. Turkey was defending two fronts against the British and one against Russia, and needless to relate, was completely engaged. Bulgaria was involved in the containment of the Allied beachhead at Salonika and the occupation of the Balkan conquests. How then could the *Alliance*, whose military and economic resources were fully committed by the summer of 1916 and were yet found to be somewhat lacking, possibly hope to meet the new crisis caused by a Romanian declaration of war against them? From where were a half million troops to be drawn to counterbalance the weight of the Romanian Army? How could the demise of Bulgaria or Hungary or both be averted? By the actual event of the declaration, on August 27th, the German High Command had no clear answers to such questions.

In fact, it was itself in transition. The Romanian action, though not unanticipated, was in the event the straw that broke the camel's back for the *Kaiser's* support of von Falkenhayn. Somehow, the effects of the shock to his beleaguered nation of the announcement of yet another new enemy had to be temporized. The Chief of the General Staff would have to go. His western strategy had been a disappointment, and his unshakeable belief in the overall policy of limited objectives required a patience to which few German citizens could relate by the late summer of 1916. As much as might be said in his defense, none could doubt that his prestige had been badly eroded by the costly, indecisive fighting of that bloody year. When Romania threw in her lot with the *Entente*, it was one more unwelcome example of Austria's liability to Germany, and it was well known that Falkenhayn held no patience for Austrian needs; indeed, he had little enough patience for an eastern or southeastern strategy at all. The *Kaiser's* choice for his replacement was almost a foregone conclusion, as the one man in all the Empire whose prestige and popularity equaled, or even exceeded, that of his own was Field Marshal von Hindenburg. His Majesty was well aware that to appoint Hindenburg meant in effect that the most powerful man in the *Alliance* would be Ludendorff, a personality for whom he had little liking. His only other possible choice might have been Mackensen, but there was just something about the idea of a non-Prussian (Mackensen was Saxon) at the head of German's mighty military machine that made such a move unthinkable. Besides, Mackensen had once quarreled with his eldest son, the Crown Prince. Falkenhayn was expected to resign, and did. On August 28th, Field Marshal Paul von Hindenburg und von Benckendorf was named Chief of the Great General Staff. General Erich Ludendorff insisted on, and was granted, the title of First Quartermaster General, an invention of his own designed to distinguish him from being just another number-two man. Prince Leopold of Bavaria took over the position of Commander in Chief East, or head of *Ober-Ost*. The fate and fortunes of the *Alliance* were now in the hands of two men whose careers had been virtually unknown two years earlier. And they had inherited a very dangerous military situation.

Germany's allies were pleased with the new command arrangements and agreed to consider the *Kaiser* as commander in chief of all *Alliance* forces. This acknowledgement was more symbolic than practical; thus far the Bulgarians had refused to participate in any except the Serbian campaign, from which they had won coveted territory. But they would need no urging from the German Monarch to help defeat Romania, whose "stab in the back" in the Second Balkan War of 1913 was still very much on their minds. As early as late July the Austro-Germans had secured Bulgarian consent for action against Romania and the frontier between the two Balkan countries soon hosted several Bulgarian divisions. Field Marshall Mackensen was sent to the region to take charge of all available *Alliance* strength; he was given command of the Danube Flotilla, an ex-Austrian collection of heavily armed river monitors now augmented with some German and Bulgarian vessels, on August 13th. The boats were shunted into a canal on the Bulgarian side of the river and prepared for offensive action. The Turks also promised support. When the declaration of war came, Mackensen was more or less prepared for action along Romania's southern border. His presence distracted one entire Romanian army—of four—from the front against Austria-Hungary. It was in fact the Russians who first made somewhat of a pre-emptive move when on August 25th a naval force steamed toward the Bulgarian port of Varna, which had become a base for German submarines in the Black Sea. This effort was thwarted by attacking German airplanes and the ships withdrew.

Before studying Romania's campaign it is necessary to understand her principle moves for acting as she did, and this requires that we should first briefly outline her then-recent history.[138] The Romanian language is included in the Romance or Romanic branch of the Indo-European family, which includes French, Spanish, Italian, etc. and the Romanians are quick to point out that they are akin to these Western peoples and are neither Magyars or Slavs. Indeed, even to this day, people from this group insist that they are Romanian, never Rumanian; they are quite proud of their heritage which began with the Roman conquest of the area then known as Dacia, about 107 A.D. Following the loss by Rome of Dacia in the third century, the province slipped into a turbulent and relatively obscure history for several centuries while scores of invaders and wandering barbaric tribes crossed its landscape, but the people never forgot their ties to the West. In 1462 the Turks completed their conquest of the lands south of the mountains by putting the famous (or infamous) Dracula to rout. The Turkish occupation was a long and difficult one, but in time, the three provinces populated by the Romanians—Wallachia, Moldavia, and Bessarabia—were drawn closer and closer together. Russia upset this trend by annexing the latter province at the close of the Napoleonic Wars; she occupied the other two during the Crimean War, but with the treaty of Paris in 1856 was obliged to withdraw in favor of the Ottomans once more. In 1861 this principality was the domain of a Hohenzollern Prince, and recognized by Turkey. This man, Prince Carol, was himself an ex-Prussian Guardsman and proved to be a most able leader. When war between Russia and Turkey came again in 1877, Carol allied himself with the former, hoping to win complete independence from Constantinople; this was accomplished the following year; however, the Romanians were not happy with the results of the war. Russia, to their frustration, would not yield them Bessarabia, instead they were awarded most of the province of Dobruja, a land populated mainly by Bulgars and Turkic peoples. Thereafter, many Romanians carried a grudge against Russia, who had seemingly exchanged them the semiarid steppes of Dobruja for the rich fields of Bessarabia, an area they did not want for one inhabited by their own kindred.

In 1881 the germanophile Carol became king. Two years later he had delivered his country into an alliance with the Germans and Austro-

Hungarians. Before long the Romanian economy was becoming ever more dependant on the members of the *Dual Alliance*, who accepted the bulk of her foreign trade and who supplied her with the technology and skilled labor necessary to build her industries and develop her resources. It was a classic case of industrialized countries needing the mineral and agricultural resources of the non-developed nation, which had no other natural customers: without a merchant fleet there could be no question of Romanian Sea-trade, and all her other land neighbors were themselves non-industrial countries. There were many good reasons for keeping on good terms with the *Kaisers*. The only stumbling block to Romania's Teutonic Alliance was the issue of Transylvania, a province of Austria-Hungary which bordered Carol's realm. This region was a part of the ancient Dacia and was populated by roughly four million persons who considered themselves Romanians, and were bound by religious and language ties to the latter. But since 1867, when Hungary had formally annexed Transylvania, Magyar politics were believed to be suppressing all other minorities across the mountains.[139] Although the disputed province contained large numbers of Germans and Magyars, most Romanians, sympathetic to their cousins there, believed it should be a part of their own nation. The Magyars claimed that most Romanian inhabitants of the region were settlers who had fled across the mountains during the centuries of Turkish-misrule to the south, and were therefore not in a position to complain about their adopted land. The Romanians, remembering the glorious days of Rome, disagreed; the issue remained a point of contention between the two countries.

As a result of the First Balkan War of 1912, the Turks were all but expelled from Europe by the combined efforts of Serbs, Bulgars, and Greeks. However, Bulgaria was dissatisfied with her share of the spoils and attacked her erstwhile allies, initiating the Second Balkan War in 1913. Romania joined in this fray; then the Bulgars, outflanked, were easily defeated and forced to yield to her the southern portion of the Dobruja. This area was home to few if any Romanians. But by annexing it, Bucharest had gained a vengeful enemy on her southern border. Now she needed her Teutonic Alliance more than ever.

When general war came to Europe in 1914, Romania was torn internally by rival political factions which pressed for intervention on behalf of one side or another or for strict neutrality; King Carol wished to support the *Alliance*, but the majority of the people sympathized with France, the leader of the Latin world, and were rather hostile in sentiment toward Austria-Hungary. Within a few days the government settled the issue by declaring that the alliance with the Austro-Germans need not be adhered to, as Austria was clearly the aggressor in the war.

This was a stance very similar to the one taken by the Italian government. Two months later Carol died, and with him any chance that Romania might join the *Alliance*. From then on, the only real question was whether she would remain neutral or join the *Entente*, though the pro-German parties refused to be silenced. Bulgaria's decision to participate in the enemy camp raised *Entente* hopes that Romania might be willing to come out of her neutrality, and they made generous promises to reward her with Austrian territory should they win the war. This was, naturally, what many Romanians wanted to hear. The country tilted toward the *Entente*, but the Serbian defeat and the many Russian setbacks kept her from taking the plunge. Then came Brusilov's magnificent offensive of summer 1916, which threatened to eliminate Austria-Hungary from the war. By the end of June the Bukovina had been cleared, and Russian soldiers were perched on the frontier of Transylvania. The hour for decision in Bucharest had been reached.

Still, the Romanians wavered. They wanted assurances of allied assistance in the form of munitions and supplies, as well as commitments to continue to pressure the *Alliance* on all fronts, so that little enemy strength could be mustered against them. It has often been concluded that had Romania intervened in June instead of August, the subsequent campaign would have turned out much more favorably. But Bucharest was, temporarily at least, acting sensibly; it was well aware of its own weaknesses. The nation was in a precarious geographical position, flanked as it was on three sides by enemy-held territory, and with longer boundaries in proportion to its relative strength than perhaps any other country in Europe. It was also totally isolated from outside help save through Russia, and only two main rail lines crossed the border of these two neighbors. Russia was, moreover, herself perpetually short of supplies; it seemed reasonable to assume that little aid could be expected to come from Petrograd. So it was that it took two months of bargaining to finally convince Bucharest to declare war, and the declaration, when it came, was directed only against Austria-Hungary. By allowing their greed for Transylvania to dictate their military strategy, the Romanians may have thrown away their best chance for success, an initial attack on Bulgaria (from which they coveted no further territory), coupled with an *Entente* offensive from Salonika, might have toppled the weakest of the enemy powers and led to an early peace. But Bucharest did not want the Russians to occupy Transylvania, and immediately following its declaration of war, sent its troops headlong into that province.

A study of the Romanian campaign of 1916 requires a basic awareness of the geography of that region. As stated earlier, the Romania of 1916 was comprised of three provinces—Wallachia, Moldavia, and the Dobruja. With few exceptions, the boundary of these was fixed on natural features. The spine of the Carpathian Mountains, which farther north formed the boundary between Galicia/Bukovina and Hungary continued southward to divide Moldavia from Transylvania, the latter being part of Hungary. The southernmost end of this range reaches to within 200 km (125mi) of the Black Sea, whereupon it swings around 100° and runs due east for very nearly 320 km (200mi) before being cut by the Danube at the famous Iron Gate. This latter end of the Carpathian Range is really only but an extension of the former chain; on its lower east-west course it is known as the Transylvanian Alps. The jutting provinces of Wallachia and Moldavia, then, lay at right angles to each other, and had as their Hungarian frontier the same mountains, though these might be known by different names in different regions. In all cases these mountains fell sharply on the Romanian side of the border and more gently towards the plateau on the Hungarian side. They are of medium height 1500 to 2500 meters (5,000 to 8,000ft) are rugged, and were heavily wooded. There are many passes, but most are rather steep and narrow; only three were good enough to permit railways. Since many of these passes were to play important roles in the subsequent campaign, they are worth considering. Four connected Moldavia with Transylvania: the Tolgys, Bekas, Gyimes, and Oitoz; of these only the Gyimes carried a railroad. Through the Transylvanian Alps ran seven major passes: The Buzeu, Bratocea, Predeal, Torzburg, Red Tower, Szurduk, and Vulkan; the Predeal and Red Tower were the most important, and had rail lines. An important military consideration regarding these passes is that all but two were within easy distance of a railhead on the Hungarian side, while only six of eleven were well served by rail from Romania. The lateral communications network was also far superior in the Hungarian realm. For example, the distance between the Predeal and Red Tower Passes, by rail, was in Austria 130 km (80mi) compared to the 435 km (270mi) needed to travel between the same two points using the Romanian system.[140]

Two thirds of the southern frontier of Wallachia, from the Iron Gate to near Turtukai, was formed by the great Danube River, which at that point along its lower course is a kilometer and a half wide and more. The river here is a very formidable natural obstacle and was quite likely to impede any attempted military operations not thoroughly planned well in advance. Moreover the northern bank, being somewhat lower than the southern, is constantly subjected to seasonal flooding, and is therefore a swampy line, broken by innumerable bogs and backwaters. Neither the Romanians nor the Bulgarians expected any major clash of arms along this giant stream. But the easternmost third or so of their common frontier, from Turtukai to the Black Sea was protected by no such obstacle. This was the Dobruja, a land sandwiched between the extreme lower Danube and the sea, linked therefore geographically more closely to Bulgaria. For that matter, the inhabitants included a large percentage of Bulgars and considerable numbers of Turkic-related peoples, but few Romanians. The seizure of the southern Dobruja by Bucharest in 1913 was of course still fresh on the minds of every Bulgar; few did not wish for its recovery. For the most part a treeless, arid, wind-swept plateau, the Dobruja invited invasion from the south. If this were carried out, Romania would be cut off from the sea, since the Danube delta formed the frontier with Bessarabia, a Russian land.

Only Moldavia was easily linked to Russia, in a geographic sense. This province was bounded on the west by the Carpathians, on the north by the Bukovina and on the east by the River Pruth, the common frontier with Bessarabia. To the south it was not hemmed in, but here, a mere 100 km (60mi) wide berth exists between the southeastern extent of the mountain range and the extreme lower Danube where that stream abruptly halts its brief northward course and turns sharply due east to meet the sea. This bottleneck is known as the "Galatz Gap," for that town located on the great river bend. About half the distance of the "gap" is covered by the marshy channel of the lower Seret River, the principle stream of the province, where it ends its generally southward flow and turns east to greet the Danube at Galatz. Moldavia, then, could best be defended from the east, or Russia. But because of Romania's pre-war ties with the Teutonic nations, communications between Bucharest and Russia had been deliberately neglected; only two main railroads crossed the Pruth.

All three Romanian provinces being thus relatively isolated from one another was a fact bound to produce problems regarding the national defense.

However, the allies had promised as the price of Romanian intervention to mount an offensive from Salonika in Greece to distract the Bulgarians and Russia had assured Bucharest of a force of 50,000 men to help defend the Dobruja. Furthermore, Lechitski was expected to force his way into Transylvania presently, a development which could inestimably aid in the Romanian conquest of that coveted land. Few persons in Bucharest expected serious danger to their country to come from the apparently near-exhausted *Alliance*; nearly all expected an offensive, not defensive, participation in the war.

Quite a few Russians were much less certain. Alexiev, for one, had serious misgivings about the wisdom of a Romanian alliance. He believed that Russia herself was much too weak and exhausted to contemplate sending considerable material and human resources to aid the Romanians. For one thing, the communications, as we have seen, were inadequate. For another, the Romanian Army was much weaker than its 23 divisions may have appeared on paper; there was not enough artillery, aircraft, communications equipment, transport, or even machine guns and small arms. Its level of training was low, its discipline sub-par, and its leadership sadly deficient in experience and efficiency. Alexiev saw all these problems and concluded that Bucharest's active participation alongside Russia would be more of a liability to her than an asset. Already, before the event, he was obliged to reinforce Lechitski for his push over the mountains, and to scrape up the three divisions which Russia had promised to send to the Dobruja. This latter force was formed of two Russian divisions and one division of Slavic former Austrian prisoners of war and called a "Serbian" division and was placed in the command of one of Brusilov's Generals, Zayonchkovski. Though this man was himself scornful of the whole idea of the "Dobruja Detachment," he was ordered to carry out his duties.

The twenty-three divisions possessed by Romania were organized into four armies, three of which were deployed along the Hungarian frontier. First Army, under General Culcer, with its six divisions held the line from the Iron Gate to the Red Tower Pass. Second Army, of five divisions, faced the mountains from east of the Red Tower to the Oituz Pass; it was led by General Averescu. From the Oituz north to the Bukovina lay General Presan's Fourth Army, with four divisions. The other army, the Third (Azlan), guarded the Bulgarian border with six divisions. In addition, two divisions were kept near Bucharest as a reserve. Third Army's role was to be a purely defensive one;

the other three were to invade and seize Transylvania before Lechitski's Russians burst into that province from the Bukovina. The allies would have preferred Romania to divert the bulk of her forces for a blow against Bulgaria; Alexiev in particular expounded this view, arguing that his forces alone were sufficient to wrest Transylvania from the enemy; if Romania helped knock out Bulgaria, the *Entente* cause would be better served. Bucharest did not see things this way. It was skeptical of a Russian occupation of its coveted province. Moreover, public opinion demanded a thrust against Austria-Hungary in hopes of "liberating" the millions of Romanian nationals living in Transylvania; besides, there was nothing further to be gained from Bulgaria. Bucharest even hoped to limit its war to a struggle against Austria-Hungary and did not expect Sofia to initiate hostilities. Of course, with the Germans now in supreme command of all Central Power's forces, such hopes were unrealistic. Before the Romanians knew it, all four *Alliance* nations were mustering strength to hurl against them.

Immediately following the Declaration of War, the three northern armies crossed the Transylvanian frontier. Their objective was the line of the Maros River, which if attained would have evened off the right angle formed by the provinces of Wallachia and Moldavia, and thus shortened the front line considerably. Initially, there was little to oppose them. The Austrian First Army which guarded the frontier posts was an army in name only; its five divisions— barely 35,000 men—were composed mainly of aged reserve troops and were hardly a match for 350,000 Romanians. The Austrian General von Arz von Strassenburg did not even attempt serious resistance. There was a short but stiff fight at Tomos Pass, a secondary pass north of the Predeal, as a result of a Szekler[141] holding action on the 28th, but the attackers pushed on and occupied Kronstadt on the 29th. Other Romanian troops took Petroseny, north of the Vulcan Pass at about the same time. Near the Iron Gate, the border town of Orsova was seized on September 1st; at the extreme other end of the line the Tolgyes Pass was forced and the town of Borsok taken on the 2nd. At the latter location, Fourth Army surged on, negotiating all the passes on its front and capturing the lateral railroad between them as well as the valley of the extreme upper Maros River at Toplitza. About a week later, the right wing of Presan's force made contact with advance units of Lechitski's Russians near Dorna Watra near the Borgo Pass, where Bukovina, Moldavia, and Transylvania join. The Eastern Front had been considerably lengthened.

Second Army was meanwhile clearing all of the upper Aluta Valley, and when it occupied Fogaras, on the 16th, no enemy force seemed to be in position to prevent a dash to Schassburg.

Only on the left did the Romanians have to struggle. After the quick capture of Petroseny, First Army had been anxious to march on to Hatszeg, a rail junction town more than halfway to the Maros. But here the Austrians dug in and could not be dislodged even after several days of battle. Culcer then hoped that his right, pushing on Hermannstadt, could at least produce success; the city was situated on a tributary of the Aluta, the one river that cut through the mountains—at Red Tower Pass—and only 25 km (15½ mi) from the border. After heavy fighting, the Austrians evacuated the place on September 10th. Tentatively, Culcer moved in, then halted all forward movement by the 15th. Reports of enemy troop movements were beginning to come in.

Mid-September marked the end of the Romanian advance into Transylvania. Nevertheless, it had produced substantial results. Generally, the worst of the mountains had been traversed, and though the line of the Maros had not been reached except on the far right, the front line had been shortened considerably. Another push, it seemed, and the Romanians would burst out of the difficult country and into the easier terrain of central Transylvania. Certainly the enemy seemed to think so—the German and Magyar inhabitants of the regions in the Romanians' path were fleeing their homes in large numbers. The roads and railways leading to the west were choked with thousands of these hapless people, with their horses and carts carrying what few possessions they had space to take with them. Some of these migrants reached locations as far distant as Budapest, spreading their tales of woe along the way as they went. However, the sands of good fortune for Bucharest were fast running out. Falkenhayn, the deposed Chief of the German General Staff, had been ordered by the *Kaiser* to take command of a new force assembling in the lower Maros valley. This was the new German Ninth Army, consisting of seven crack divisions, including an Alpine Corps. Hindenburg instructed Falkenhayn to hurl Ninth Army against the struggling Culcer, throw him back across the mountains, and into the Wallachian Plain. In the meantime, other blows were to rock the Romanians on their flanks; the new system of pooling reserves was being well put to the test.

While the drama in Transylvania was still unfolding, the Dobruja front was turned aflame as well. Field Marshall Mackensen had been in Bulgaria prior to the break with Bucharest, busily assembling an army with which to take the Romanians in flank should they intervene. During the four-day period between the Romanian declaration on Austria-Hungary and the Bulgarian response to it, Mackensen deployed this force—the "Danube Army"—with lightening speed along the border of the Dobruja. He had at his disposal the five divisions of the Bulgarian Third Army, a German Corps, and a Turkish Corps. Immediately following the breach between Bucharest and Sofia these crossed into enemy territory, (September 1st) catching the Romanians off balance; only scattered elements of Azlan's Third Army were in line to oppose them. As usual, the Romanians' lack of aircraft meant that they could only guess at the enemy intentions, and against the capable Mackensen, such methods of deduction were completely insufficient. Within a day, two Bulgarian divisions had reached the forts of the frontier town of Turtukai, on the Danube; three more days saw the place encircled. Then, German troops and heavy guns were moved up, and following an unsuccessful relief attempt from Silistria, the garrison—25,000 men with 100 guns—surrendered on the 6th. Silistria itself fell on the 9th, following its evacuation, without a fight. The right wing had in the meantime taken Dobritch on the 4th, and covered half the distance to Constanza within a week. German aircraft conducted a raid on Russian warships anchored at the latter city on two occasions, the 2nd, and the 10th of the month. As if to offset this, the Russians tried again on the 8th and 9th to destroy the submarine base at Varna. None of these actions achieved its purpose.

Mackensen hoped his momentum would carry him to the narrowest neck of the Dobruja; where the distance between the river and the sea is a mere 55 km (34mi). For across these narrows ran the only railroad connecting the interior of Romania with the sea; if this line could be cut, Bucharest would be practically isolated; even the bulk of Russian aid was directed along this route, since it was more practical than the badly developed, direct land contacts on the Pruth. The Black Sea port of Constanza, on the eastern end of the railroad, was a major facility, and Romania's only port for that matter, and its capture would have meant a serious blow to Russo-Romanian cooperation had it been accomplished. On the other hand, simply cutting the railroad to the west was for Mackensen just as effective, because no alternate lines could be constructed with the Danube an unavoidable barrier to Wallachia. Furthermore, the river end of the railway was rendered most vulnerable by the existence of a great bridge over that colossal waterway. Between the Serbian capital of Belgrade, hundreds of kilometers upriver, and the mouth of the Danube, there was in 1916 only this single bridge across what in those days was an extremely formidable natural obstacle. The massive structure connected the towns of Chernavoda and Feteshti, stations some 18 km (11mi) apart; most of this distance, on the wet, low western bank was carried by trestle and viaduct, but the main spans stretched for more than a kilometer over the larger arm of the stream and another kilometer over the small western arm. Such a bridge could of course easily be destroyed by artillery fire if Mackensen could get close enough, or it might be damaged by aircraft or gunboats. At any rate, the Romanians would somehow have to stop the advance of "Danube Army" lest they risk losing the vital railroad. Luckily for them, Zayonchkovski's three divisions arrived at Constanza even as Mackensen approached, and were immediately sent to help stop him.

Evidently the Russian Command had hoped that the Bulgarians, a Slavic nationality traditionally friendly towards Russia, would have no desire to fight Zayonchkovski's men. In this it may have been correct had all the troops been Russians, but the inclusion of the "Serbian" division in the Dobruja Detachment was a severe misjudgment. The Serbs and Bulgars had long despised each other; Bulgarian hostility towards these men as well as the Romanians was intense enough to be directed against any allies these groups might have, including the Russians. And so it was that Mackensen experienced no problems relating to any absence of will to fight from the Bulgarians during the subsequent campaign. On September 16th came the first major clash of arms, just as the "Danube Army" approached the ancient Roman Wall of Trajan, which lay just south of the Constanza railroad. Mackensen opened the action with a vigorous attack by his left along the Danube. Four days of heavy, indecisive battle followed after which the defense had not budged. Zayonchkovski then counterattacked, using three fresh divisions which had been hurried from the Transylvanian front in order to save Romania's seaport. In three days, "Danube Army" was forced back 16 km (10 mi); it dug in at that point and the battle stalemated for a time.

Back in Galicia, the combatants had by no means been idle. Upon hearing of Romania's entry into the war at least some Russians celebrated to the stirring strains of military bands, shouting cheers and dancing in the rear areas. One participant was encouraged by the news of the Romanian declaration upon Austria-Hungary, and the nearly simultaneous declaration of Italy against Germany. "Two new allies...in the last 24 hours," she beamed.[142] If morale in Southwest Front was thus temporarily boosted, its commander was determined to take full advantage of it.

Following the Russian seizure of the Stokhod bend early in August, Kovel, the great prize, lay only some 25 km (15mi) distant. Brusilov was convinced that this ground could be overrun and the town captured, and to this end launched another blow here during the opening days of September, but the effort was defeated by a reinforced Linsingen. Lemberg proved an equally tough nut to crack; Bothmer's "South Army," which lay before it, was the least ravaged of the *Alliance* armies opposing Southwest Front since June 5th, and it had retreated only when outflanked; it had yet to be decisively beaten. Nevertheless, at Brusilov's prodding, Shcherbachev attacked Bothmer on August 29th, hoping to unhinge his line. The initial blow was aimed at the line of the Zlota Lipa near Zavalov. The Russians scored an early success and pushed beyond the river, and next day the battle was extended to the south, to Mariampol on the Dniester. Four days of heavy fighting followed; Shcherbachev gradually gained the upper hand and captured Jezupol with its railway bridge intact on September 3rd. North of the Dniester, among the wooded hills west of the Zlota Lipa, savage fighting commenced, often becoming hand-to-hand struggles within the forests. Eventually the Russians prevailed, forcing Bothmer to retreat; as he went 4,000 Austro-Germans were made prisoners. On the 4th a Turkish division was routed on the Zlota Lipa, an act which effectively smashed that line and sent all but Bothmer's left reeling back towards the Gnila Lipa. Already Halicz, at the juncture of the latter stream and the Dniester, was being threatened. For the next few days, the fighting centered around this small but important Galician town with each side apparently determined to possess it. The Russians slowly bludgeoned their way forward to the very outskirts of Halicz; they even forced a tributary of the Gnila Lipa north of the town and extended their lines south of the Dniester to a point west of it, effectively surrounding that location on three sides. Bothmer ordered Halicz evacuated, its military installations removed or destroyed, and its railroad bridge demolished, deeds accomplished by the 9th, but he continued to hold off the heavy Russian attacks, and in the end the place still held fast. Fighting here was prolonged for well nigh another month before Shcherbachev admitted defeat. Finally, in early October, the attacks were suspended, and with this, Brusilov's advance up the Dniester was at last halted for good. Meanwhile, some 32 km (20 mi) farther east on the Zlota Lipa, Bothmer's left was locked in an equally desperate struggle around Brzezany. The German knew that the loss of the river line here meant that he would be forced back upon the Gnila Lipa, from which the enemy might well outflank his positions at Halicz.

Therefore he demanded that the Brzezany-Koniuchy sector be held at all costs; Shcherbachev had seen the possibilities here was well, and the battle commenced in earnest. The first week of September witnessed a seesaw engagement in the forested ridges just west of the Zlota Lipa. 3,000 prisoners were claimed by the Russians, who seemed to gain the upper hand, though only very slowly and at great cost, throughout the remainder of the month. By October 4th, Shcherbachev had battered his way to the very suburbs of Brzezany and initiated a fierce, three-day fight for the main portion of the town. When it was over, Seventh Army had crossed the river south of the center, and in so doing had partially invested Brzezany, but it had been repulsed from its main objective. Thereafter the battle petered out and the situation lapsed into a stalemate, the attackers having exhausted themselves.

If Brusilov's main thrusts at Kovel and Lemberg were being frustrated by late summer, his secondary attacks were yielding no better results. Sakarov's Eleventh Army had made little progress since its capture of Brody late in July. When Bothmer withdrew from the Strypa to the Zlota Lipa, it had attempted to push on to Zloczow, but the effort was contained. After the Germans made a definite stand at Koniuchy, the front more or less straightened itself out from that town north to the Volhynian frontier. Sakarov then shifted the bulk of his weight to his right and attacked in a westerly direction along the River Lipa, a tributary of the Styr, which flows just north of the border. The assault gained some ground on its first day, September 1st, but the terrain was marshy and proved difficult to negotiate. On the 20th a second major effort was made; the results were again less than spectacular. By this time it had become evident that his neighboring armies had similarly failed to advance much, so Sakarov ceased further offensive activities. Lechitski's Ninth Army, on the extreme southern end of the line, had paused following its capture of the Tatar's Pass in mid August. Political developments in Romania had necessitated that it should strike again before the month was out however; this renewed attack was carried out on the 28th. Progress was very slow. It was during this fighting that Otto Jindra scored his penultimate victory over Solka in Bukovina on the 26th.[143] The Austrians had reinforced their positions by inserting an entire new Army into the mountains (Third) and were moreover strengthened by the assistance of several German divisions—including the Carpathian Corps—which had been moved here by Ludendorff to help hold the line of the Carpathian Range. Lechitski did take 3,000 or so prisoners within two weeks, but gained little in the way of ground. His heaviest attacks were directed at the various mountain passes which led into Hungary, especially the Kirlibaba, but none were allotted sufficient weight to ensure their success; most Russian reserves were still being sent elsewhere. By mid September the first snows were falling amongst the high peaks of the Carpathians, an occurrence which though unusually early, severely handicapped the operations of Ninth Army and soon forced a suspension of Russian offensive action on the southern end of the front for that year.

All the while, the slaughter in Volhynia continued. The capture of Kovel had seemingly become an obsession with both Brusilov and Alexiev, a goal for which no price was too high to pay. By September 1916 the Stokhod front rather more closely resembled conditions in France than anything as yet experienced in the East. Gone were the days of the headlong advances by Southwest Front, and Brusilov's new bulldozer tactics could be expected to achieve no more than had those of Evert implemented at Lake Narotch or Baranovichi. Although Alexiev had constantly supplemented the strength of the Southwest Command to the degree at which it far overshadowed that of the *Alliance*—unlike the conditions of June 5th—he too had evidently failed to learn any important lessons from the war since being made Chief of Staff to the *Czar*. So it was that the push on Kovel was allowed to continue even after the drives against Lemberg and Hungary had either been called off or simply defeated by the Austro-Germans. Following the Russian seizure of the great Stokhod bend in August, Kovel lay only some 25 km (15mi) distant with no formidable natural obstacle before it. But Ludendorff had sent substantial reinforcements to Linsingen during August and early September; the Germans were equally determined to hold the town as the Russians were to take it, and the defenses would not be easy to penetrate. By mid September the front line in Volhynia lay gouged across the low-lying plain like an open wound on otherwise healthy skin. Here the pine woods were smashed, cut down by the fierce fighting. Artillery shells had shattered the trees and churned the already often-marshy ground into a pockmarked wasteland saturated with foul water that reeked of decay. Among the craters and quagmires of this horrible wasteland were strewn thousands of unburied corpses attracting insects and breeding disease. This whole tortured landscape might easily have been mistaken for the ground around Verdun or at the Somme, ground which at the very same time was being punished by the desperate fighting. Naturally enough, even the most steadfast soldiers hesitated to attack over this type of terrain, where water-filled craters, deep mud, and twisted debris made going extremely difficult. Facing enemy fire alone was bad enough; under conditions such as these it had become nearly impossible.

On September 21st the battle was renewed. Brusilov hurled Kaledin's Eighth Army against Kovel on a 20 kilometer (12mi) front. To the north Gourko's Guards joined in; neither force gained any ground, though both suffered heavily in the especially heavy fighting. Having halted their tormentors, the Germans counterattacked and prolonged the struggle for a few more days. Thereafter, Brusilov called off the main thrusts but kept up strong frontal pressure, a decision which ensured the continuation of sporadic, local actions along the entire line. German aircraft, which as usual held mastery of the skies, played an important role in these battles by spotting Russian positions for Linsingen's artillery, and by machine-gunning and bombing hapless Russian units caught in the open. Clearly, Kovel was not going to change hands again. For all of his earlier successes, Brusilov had, in the end, been frustrated in his attempts to capture his strategic objectives.

Mid September 1916 was a turning point in the fortunes of war, even if the fact was not immediately apparent. On the 15th, the Turkish Corps in Galicia stopped a Russian gas attack, an event seemingly less than significant, but for the effect it had on the morale of soldiers of the *Alliance*. If the Turks, already engaged on these other fronts, cared enough to support their allies in a theater of no special importance to them by sending some of their best divisions, which in turn proved their worth, then the *Alliance* must be for real. In both Transylvania and Dobruja where the multi-ethnic armies were employed to counter Romanian aspirations, such news was very well received by the troops. And on the same day in Bucharest, a hastily assembled Crown Council decided to water down the offensive into Hungary by recalling one-third of the troop strength there for employment against Mackensen's threat from the south. The reserve divisions, of course, were also diverted to the Danube. That left ten divisions for Transylvania, where the German Ninth Army was ready now for action. Falkenhayn arrived by the 16th and wasted no time on niceties; his Chief of Staff had already worked out a plan of offense. The Germans were already in fact moving forward in the Striu valley south of Hatseg when the new commander ordered a general attack for the 18th. One blow was delivered to First Army's left, north of the Vulcan Pass. Petroseny was recaptured on the 20th and the pass reached two days later. Although Culcer was able to restore this situation somewhat, and even achieved moderate success with a counterattack from the northern end of the Vulcan, his army was now in danger of becoming separated as it fell back into the rugged mountains.

On September 19th, Ninth Army's main thrust was begun against his isolated right wing in the Hermannstadt area; this force, outflanked, without support, and vulnerable in the valley of the Aluta, was easily put to flight and the city retaken. Falkenhayn's aim here was to cut off the entire right wing of First Army, and he very nearly succeeded. The German Alpine Corps, a specialist force in the art of mountain warfare, fought its way over the difficult ridge of the Transylvanian Alps and in a brief encounter captured the Red Tower Pass on the 26th. The southward leading road and railroad were thus cut, and the route of escape for the Romanian units retreating from Hermannstadt was blocked. At that point it seemed that the nearly encircled forces could only surrender, but their leaders displayed an admirable courage during those hours of desperation, and instead opted for a retreat in the only direction yet open to them—the mountains to the southeast—a roadless wilderness traversed only by footpaths and goat trails. The move was not without precedent, for every Romanian well knew the story of the similar flight by the hero Count Dracula, following his defeat at the hands of the Turks in 1462, over these same rugged highlands, with but a handful of followers. In 1916 the deed was repeated, though the flight was in the opposite direction; the defeated army lost heavily but refused to quit and eventually emerged from the ordeal somehow still intact. The Germans took only 3,000 prisoners though they captured great quantities of equipment and supplies.

Meanwhile, the Romanian Second and Fourth Armies were trying to help ease the pressure applied to the First Army. General Crainiceanu, who had replaced Averescu as Commander of Second Army, attacked in the valley of the Kokel River, towards Schassburg on September 29th, while at the same time, Presan's Fourth Army advanced on Maros Vasarhely, a rail town on the

Maros River. Both of these drives had nearly reached their objectives by October 4th, but on that date Falkenhayn struck at Second Army's left flank near Fogaras and scored a victory. The high tide of the Romanian invasion had been reached and would now begin to ebb. October 7th saw Kronstadt evacuated and reoccupied by the Germans. By the 10th, Crainiceanu, like Culcer, had been forced back upon the frontier, having suffered heavy loss. Fourth Army, opposed only by the weak Austrian First Army, was much less heavily engaged and in fact had not been defeated, but because of the retreat of its neighbor, it too was obliged to withdraw in order to protect its left flank. This retirement was undertaken much more slowly, however, and for a time some Hungarian territory on a line Toplitza-Czik Szereda was retained.

With the invasion of Transylvania now a disaster, the Romanian High Command could only hope that its scheme in the south would work out; it had, after all, practically sabotaged the former in favor of the latter. At least everyone agreed that Mackensen had to be defeated decisively. To this end a plan was conceived whereby the reinforced Third Army would cross the Danube near the Dobruja-Bulgarian frontier, then wheel around and attack the rear of Danube Army, which of course faced northward. If successful the move would have caught Mackensen between Third Army and Zayonchkovski's Russo-Romanian Army and crushed him. The place chosen for this maneuver was midway between Rustchuk and Turtukai and the date fixed was October 1st. Interestingly enough, the *Alliance* had also decided to try and cross the river; their attempt came a day earlier, on September 30th at Corabia, a railhead on the northern bank. This adventure was really only a rehearsal for bigger things to come and was therefore thwarted easily enough. However, the Romanian bid the next day was a serious one, though it fared no better. Several thousand men were shuttled over the stream, but these were largely unsupported by artillery, as the hastily constructed, temporary bridges over the lagoons and backwaters on the Romanian side proved too feeble to bear the weight of horses and guns. Moreover, high water caused by the autumn rains handicapped the whole effort, and Austro-Hungarian gunboats on the river shot up the ferries and docking points. German and Bulgarian frontier troops concentrated against the soldiers who had crossed, and attacked them on the 2nd, while river monitors shelled their pontoon bridges. Nearly all were killed or captured; on October 3rd, the entire affair was called off so that Romanian forces could be sent back to the northern front.

Mackensen had scarcely been made to glance over his shoulder at the attempted river crossing; his enemies had never possessed any real chance of success there. He had, however, been obliged to meet a violent frontal attack undertaken by Zayonchkovski as a sort of holding action, on the lines south of Constanza. The Russo-Romanians advanced slightly, and took a couple of thousand prisoners, before being stopped. For two weeks, thereafter, the Dobruja remained calm.

All eyes were now fixed on Falkenhayn's Ninth Army. King Ferdinand of Romania, desperate to restore the situation, personally assumed the position of Supreme Commander. He replaced Culcer with General Dragalina and recalled Averescu to once again lead the Second Army. Snow had already begun falling in the heights of the Carpathians, an occurrence which fostered new hopes that the Germans could be held off in the southern approaches to the mountains; the frontier ridge was not to be defended. Falkenhayn, however, held the trump card. Having pushed the Romanians back onto their own soil, his very presence had sabotaged the effort to cross the Danube and had drawn large enemy reserves to his front. He could now concentrate his forces and strike hard at any one of the many mountain passes, or could push on as deployed, or could simply go over to the defensive himself and perhaps send help to Mackensen. As it was, he had kept the enemy stretched very thin; events shaping up at the Torzburg Pass convinced him to continue his present policy.

The Torzburg Pass changed hands a few days after the fall of Kronstadt in a relatively effortless maneuver. Driving on, the Germans pushed many kilometers into Romanian territory, reaching the town of Rucar before being halted on October 14th. Falkenhayn had hoped that similar gains could be recorded all along the frontier, but such was not to be the case. A few miles to the east, at the Predeal Pass, General von Morgen's men became locked into a savage battle and were unable to break out with any haste. Ten days of bitter fighting, accompanied by very heavy shell fire, were needed to secure the Pass, which was finally cleared on October 25th. Morgen then attempted to advance further, but was stopped in his tracks only a very few kilometers inside the border. The story was similar south of the Red Tower Pass, where General von Kraft von Delmensingen's Bavarian Alpine Corps ran into trouble. It had begun an offensive on the 15th, which within a week had been defeated by both the defense and the weather. So, too, was the right of Ninth

Army bogged down south of the Vulcan Pass, where the advance proceeded at a snail's pace. Falkenhayn's efforts seemed to slacken from mid-month; he was learning that the rugged, heavily wooded valleys, ridges, gorges, and defiles of the terrain south of the main spine of the Transylvanian Alps were extremely difficult to assault, yet excellent for utilization by the defenders. And the weather was unusually cruel that autumn; snow lay several feet deep in many locations by the end of October. Further north, the Austrians also failed to break into Moldavia. Towards the end of the month the Gyimes Pass was captured (October 17th) and some progress down the Trotus River Valley made; suddenly the Fourth Army counterattacked and retook most of the lost ground. At the end of October, the Moldavian Front ran roughly along the border with Hungary. Both sides paused to reassess the overall situation in Romania during the third week of October. Falkenhayn reckoned that he could not break into the Wallachian Plain before the onset of an apparently early winter without moderate reinforcement. Since his army represented the German strategic reserve, there could be no question of receiving aid from other fronts. Mackensen's army could send help, but this would mean the Constanza railroad could not be captured, and this was a prize of extreme strategic significance too tempting to be forgotten. Therefore it was decided to first reinforce Mackensen, a Turkish Corps had been made available for this purpose; capture Constanza; and then deplete Danube Army in favor of the Wallachian campaign.

On the *Entente* side, the Romanians were already pleading with Alexiev for more assistance; the latter, who had all along been very skeptical of the whole Romanian participation in the war, would do little. Zayonchkovski's constant barrage of complaints, warnings, and requests for further aid for the Dobruja front also fell on deaf ears. In fairness to Alexiev it could be argued that he himself had little to spare until the offensive of Southwest Front to the north had definitely died away. Besides, no one in Russia felt any too much sympathy for the Romanians, who had not been an historically friendly people, nor did many have much faith in their ability to fight a modern war, especially after some initial reports from the front reached Russian ears. Even Colonel Knox observed in an October 25th note that the Romanians, despite having attached observers to the armies of the *Alliance*, seemed not to have grasped the precepts of modern warfare. He scoffed that their habits were reminiscent of the Russo-Turkish War of the late 1870s and that they possessed only one telephone for every six batteries of artillery and were totally without telegraph machines. Their Russian allies were scornful, but lent them 150 field telephones and a thousand versts of wire.[144] About the only help for Bucharest came from the French, who in late October dispatched a military mission under the experienced General Berthelot to assist in the reorganization of the Romanian Army and to lend its advice as to how best to counter the German methods and tactics of war. Also sent were several dozen badly needed reconnaissance aircraft. But no extra troops were at hand to help Romania during her hour of crisis.

Mackensen's guns opened up on the 19th of October, turning the wind-swept sands of the Dobruja into great clouds of smoke and dust. The infantry attack commenced next day, and soon the Romanian left crumbled. Two days later Zayonchkovski was badly beaten, had lost Tuzla, and began the evacuation of Constanza. There was little time for such an undertaking. Bulgarian cavalry appeared on the 23rd, whereupon the remaining Russians and Romanians fled, having failed to burn the vast stores of war material present there because of the rainy weather. Russian warships in the Black Sea attempted to bombard the city, but then turned and sailed off, leaving the place in full *Alliance* control by nightfall. Large stocks of oil and wheat, the two principal Romanian exports, were captured intact; the foodstuffs especially were a most welcome prize for the always-needy peoples of the *Quadruple Alliance*. More importantly, Romania had now been virtually cut off from the sea. Even then Mackensen did not rest. Pressing on, he took Cernavoda on the 25th and tried to seize the great bridge. The retreating Romanians demolished one of the spans, however, so as to deny him easy passage over the Danube, but the Field Marshall's business was east of the river. By the end of the month three-fourths of the Dobruja was conquered. Alexeiv replaced Zayonchkovski with Sakarov, the former Eleventh Army commander, hoping to restore the situation. Mackensen, though, had reached all of his objectives and by early November began releasing troops to Falkenhayn as well as moving other parts of his army southward again to participate in a new, more serious effort to cross the Danube and outflank the enemy in Wallachia. Prince Boris of Bulgaria, with the remainder of Danube Army, was left behind to guard the Dobruja. On November 6th, Sakarov counterattacked and drove Boris some miles to the south, but failed to reach the railroad. Another attack from the west end of the Cernavoda bridge likewise gained some ground, but was defeated in its purpose. Soon the Bulgarians had improved their positions to a considerable degree; Sakarov, noting this, decided against further offensives, and the Dobruja front was still once more.

The Russians did not take kindly to the loss of Constanza. Already angered by the loss of the Black Sea Fleet flagship the battleship *Empress Maria* on October 20th at Sebastopol to a freak accident,[145] they determined to destroy the petroleum storage tanks at the recently surrendered Romanian port with naval shellfire. After a few failed efforts in the early days of November, a cruiser finally wrecked 15 of 37 tanks on the 4th.[146] Ships then returned on the 9th to shell the port further, but increasing numbers of German aircraft tended to discourage additional raids as such.

During the early days of October there was still heavy fighting in Galicia, from Brody to the Dniester, as Brusilov continued to urge his commanders on. But trouble was simmering just beneath the surface, and on the 2nd, mutineers were reported in Seventh Army. Then, the staff of Eighth Army was moved south for the purpose of creating a new army between the Seventh and the Ninth, in order to counterbalance the enemy insertion of the Austrian Third Army in that area. Eighth Army's troops were absorbed by Gourko's Special Army and augmented that force considerably; Gourko then planned to use his reinforced command for a new offensive. When the troops of the old Eighth Army got wind of this, they too mutinied on the 9th. Next, the *Czar* ordered Brusilov to suspend all offensive activity; his Southwest Front Offensive should finally be considered over. Special Army, subordinate now to West Front, was of course not affected by this command; the prestige of further advance would go to Evert and Gourko.

The plan, if in fact such repetitive futility could be called one, was for a massive, all-out final drive to secure the towns of Kovel and Vladimir-Volynski before the weather broke. It was to go forward despite all protests by local commanders, and was justified as necessary to divert the *Alliance* from Romania; 15 divisions were assembled for the operation. The attacks came on October 16th in the Kisielin/Witonitz area of the upper Stokhod. Despite lavish use of shell, including poison gas, the Russians could gain no ground. German artillery, firing an even mixture of high explosives, shrapnel, and chemical, leveled the waves of brown as they tried to advance for two days, until the slaughter became too great even for Special Army brass. Thereafter quiet returned to the bloodstained battlefields and Galicia and Volhynia for the first time since June. The only other notable action on this section of front for the remainder of the year came on November 9th when the Germans, as if to mock their enemies, delivered a very violent assault on the Russian positions at Witonitz behind a thick cloud of poison gas. The German artillery specialist Colonel Bruchmüller masterminded the attack and used it as a sort of trial test for some new tactics with the use of gas that he was working on. Following some hard fighting during which the Russians were pushed back slightly, Bruchmüller, apparently satisfied with the results, called off the battle and began planning bigger things.

Events in Romania were now unfolding rapidly; Falkenhayn was anxious to break out of the mountains before the onset of winter made such a task an impossible one. Having been checked in his advance of mid-October, towards the end of the month he began another. The Romanians had been reinforced by the arrival of units that had participated in the abortive Danube crossing, and at first offered stout resistance. They were soon aided by an unlikely ally—Alexiev—who, under pressure from above, agreed to extend the front of Lechitski's Ninth Russian Army southward from the Bukovina for another 80 km (50 mi), thus releasing part of the Romanian Fourth Army for service in Wallachia. Furthermore, the Russian had been convinced to send an entire army—the Fourth—south to be taken over by Sakarov with the object of defending what was left of the Dobruja and the Danube Delta area. When this force arrived, the Romanians could expect to transfer more of their units from the Danube to the west, but for the moment, they were happy to be able to just shift part of Presan's troops. Thus encouraged, they launched violent counterattacks at various points along the line, and in several instances were able to gain ground. South of the Vulcan Pass, the Germans were stopped, then defeated and put to flight (October 27-31); however, for Romania this turned out to be an expensive victory, as General Dragalina was mortally wounded and died a week later. He was replaced by General Pitale. In the Aluta valley, Kraft's men progressed, but only very slowly and at great cost in lives. Falkenhayn, frustrated and growing impatient, devised a new plan whereby he shifted the bulk of his weight to his extreme right, where the Romanian lines of communication were overextended and weak. In doing so, he abandoned his earlier grandiose plans of an encirclement of most of Wallachia from out of the eastern passes, but he also gained his victory, however reduced it might seem. On November 10th this new effort was set in motion south of the Vulcan near the headwaters of the Jiu River, while farther east von Kraft and von Morgen launched pinning attacks to confuse the defense. German superiority in artillery proved decisive. Targel Jiu, the northernmost railhead on the river, fell on the 15th; thereafter the Romanian position deteriorated. Hoping to yet save the day, Petale rushed troops from the Aluta to the Jui, but on the 17th a decisive battle was fought in which First Army was thoroughly beaten. Now, the way was clear for Falkenhayn's Ninth Army to flood out into the Wallachian plain.

As if Bucharest needed another problem to contend with during those fatal days, Mackensen was now ready to cross the Danube from Bulgaria. He had had ample time to pick his spot and prepare the operation, and was in position by the time of Falkenhayn's breakout. Two crossing places were chosen—at Sistova and at Somovit, both having the advantages of being ferry crossings with islands in mid-stream which would help facilitate bridging. Mackensen's guns shelled the north shore from November 19th to the 22nd when the first boats filled with troops disembarked from the Bulgarian side. With little or no opposition, a bridgehead was consolidated by the 23rd; three days later it extended some 32 kilometers (20 mi) north. Meanwhile the Bulgarians also forced the river at two points on the flanks, Corabia on the left and Rustchuk to the right. By November 25th a bridge over the Danube at Sistova was opened. Clearly, Wallachia was outflanked and would have to be abandoned.

Wallachian towns began to fall one by one in rapid succession. Falkenhayn seized Filiasa on the 19th, a capture that threatened to cut off the Romanian division at Orsova, beyond the Iron Gate. Crajova fell on the 21st; the Germans then swung east and reached the Aluta on the 23rd. After a couple of days of battle on this river line the Romanians retreated, and von Kraft's men, who had hitherto been stalled in the northern valley, joined in the pursuit. Only on the 25th did the commander of the Orsova division order a retreat, not knowing, evidently, that his force was already 160 kilometers (100 miles) behind the front, so fast had been the Romanian collapse. On the 26th. elements of Mackensen's army and others of Falkenhayn's command joined hands near the Alt, and the front thereby shortened considerably. Von Morgen joined the action on the 29th, by finally capturing Campolung. Next day his men linked up with those of von Kraft in the Piteshti area. Bucharest itself was now in grave danger. Averescu, now in supreme command of all Romanian armies, was persuaded by Berthelot to attempt one last maneuver before the enemy reached the capital. The plan called for the remnants of the First and Second Armies to hold off Falkenhayn while the remains of Third and Fourth Armies, reinforced by two Russian divisions, struck at Mackensen's left and drove in a wedge between it and the rapidly converging Ninth Army of Falkenhayn. Presan, who would lead the counterblow, agreed and attacked on December 1st. Catching Mackensen somewhat off balance, he advanced slightly, taking perhaps 1,000 prisoners, but failed to seriously upset either German commander. Ninth Army countered two days later, and the troops which were to block it could not hold; Presan's Army was smashed and put to rout and with it any hopes of holding Bucharest. Meanwhile Titu fell to von Kraft, and Targoviste, the medieval capital of the legendary Dracula, was taken by von Morgen. It was for Mackensen to occupy the premier city of Romania.

Actually, the Romanian government had begun its evacuation of Bucharest as early as 25th November, when it became clear that Mackensen was across the Danube to stay. During the succeeding days, the general population learned of the strategic situation, and the city soon became gripped with panic. Thousands of frantic civilians tried to escape using every conceivable means of transportation. By December 1st, the sounds of battle to the south could easily be detected. To add to the misery and confusion, squadrons of German airplanes prowled over the roads and railways, machine-gunning people, horses, and vehicles. Zeppelins dropped bombs. Hundreds of persons, mostly civilians, were killed and wounded. On December 4th, the last remaining military installations were destroyed, and the arsenal blown up. Two days later Field Marshall Mackensen entered Bucharest in triumph. By far the most important single location in all Romania was now in the hand of the *Alliance*; the political implications, and effects on *Entente* morale, were bound to be far reaching. The Romanians, down but not out, moved their capital to Jassy, a town some 320 kilometers (200 mi) to the northeast, near the Russian border.

Simultaneous with the capture of Bucharest was the fall of Ploesti, a city at the center of the oil-producing region; however not before the wells, refineries, and storage tanks of the area had been put to the torch. As Falkenhayn's army advanced, it witnessed a sight not seen since the Russians had fired the Galician oil fields in the spring of 1915—huge columns of black smoke rising from incredible flames fed by the burning petroleum. So awesome was the destruction that the air in Bucharest, some 48 kilometers (30 mi) distant, was fouled for several days. At the same time, the end for the Orsova division came at Carocalu, in the lower Aluta valley, now some 120 kilometers (75 mi) behind the front, on December 7th. This remarkable group of men had wandered for twelve days behind enemy lines since they had left Orsova and only surrendered when all of its paths of escape had been blocked. But now the remnant of the Romanian Army was no longer even attempting to stand and fight; even with the appearance of the first Russian units—finally—in mid December, it had no heart for battle. Amidst hordes of fleeing refugees on congested roads and lanes it plodded to the northeast, towards Moldavia. The Predeal Pass was abandoned. Falkenhayn reached Buzeu on the 14th, and forced the river of that name two days later. No natural obstacle now confronted him before the waters of the Seret, at the "Galatz Gap."

Even so, the Germans' pursuit soon slackened, as the *Alliance* offensive began to run out of steam, for the same reasons all successful military advances eventually wind down. The outpacing of supply functions, lack of time to establish necessary communications networks, troop exhaustion, and other factors all served to shackle the invaders from about mid December. The weather was no help for either side; that winter of 1916-17 would prove to be the coldest in many years. Of paramount importance, however, was the increasing Russian commitment to the Romanian Front. Alexiev, it will be remembered, had always resisted pressures to help with the defense of Wallachia, in as much as his own belief was that owing to geographical considerations, Moldavia was the only portion of Romania worth defending in earnest. That Russian troops should only begin arriving in significant numbers when Wallachia was all but lost and Moldavia about to be threatened, seemed to many Romanians a disgustingly convenient coincidence, but in fact it was not due to any special planning on Alexiev's part, rather to general Russian inefficiency; Fourth Army, which had been ordered to the south back in early November, had only arrived in full by mid December, and because of supply problems, was not in a good state for battle for another two weeks. There was a battle which lasted several days between these troops and the men of Falkenhayn at the important town of Rimnic Sarat, one of the last outposts of Wallachia. This struggle was finally won by the Germans who entered the town having taken many prisoners, on the 27th, and celebrated the Christmas holiday a little late. Meanwhile in the Dobruja, the Bulgarians had resumed the offensive on the 26th of November and had cleared the remainder of the province by the end of December, and turned to meet their German allies at its northwestern tip. Here, at Bralia, the two armies met on January 5th. Galatz, at the mouth of the Seret, lay only 16 kilometers (10 mi) north. Next day the river was reached; since it was to be heavily defended, the *Alliance* did not try to cross. Sakarov, who had been forced to escape over the lower Danube into southern Bessarabia, had completed the maneuver by January 5th, and was reinforced and was expected to hold the river line from Galatz to the sea. If Mackensen (who now exercised overall command in Romania) was going to break into Moldavia, it seemed he would have to do it from the flank west of the Seret, or from the mountains to the north. Therefore, Falkenhayn and von Arz von Strassenberg were urged on, for a final push.

An event almost unnoticed during the drama of the Romanian campaign was the death of the old Austro-Hungarian Emperor, Franz Joseph, on November 21st. He had been born in 1830 and had been Emperor since 1848, the year of widespread revolution in Europe. His nation had been involved in many wars during his reign, and had been generally unsuccessful in these, but somehow he had managed to hold the empire together, despite the anti-imperial forces of nationalism and socialism which had constantly gained momentum. It is probably fitting that he was spared the outcome of the Great War; his contribution to its coming was limited to his desire to punish terrorist elements in Serbia, and thereby hold his realm together. He was succeeded by his nephew Karl, a much younger man married to an Italian princess suspected of pro-*Entente* sympathies. What Karl had really inherited was a crown almost completely dependant on its more powerful German neighbors.

In other actions, the Gulf of Finland was the scene of naval action on November 10th, when the Germans sent a fleet of about a dozen destroyers along with a number of torpedo boats to attack the Estonian coastal town of Baltic Port. Unbeknown to the ships, the whole area had been heavily mined. They did succeed in shelling their targets, but the cost was terrible; seven vessels were lost to the mines. The stunned Germans tried no further enterprises in the Baltic that year.

December also hosted some minor fighting other than that in Romania. There was combat around Dorna Watra in southern Bukovina during the first week of the month, battles in the Jezupol area from the 16th to the 18th, and a severe bombardment of the front lines in the Brody/Zlozow sector by the *Alliance* on the 25th. On the 20th, the Russian ace Kazakov downed another Austrian plane, which was attacking the city of Lutsk.

By New Year's Day 1917, the German and Austrian Armies were once more arranged at right angles to each other as they had been at the time of Falkenhayn's arrival. Only this time, the angle opened to the northeast instead of the northwest; the Austrians had hardly moved while Ninth Army had pivoted a full 180° and now faced north, from the Wallachia/Moldavia border area. If Falkenhayn were to try to advance north out of the "Galatz Gap"— a bare 100 kilometers (60 mi) passage—he would logically shift his greatest weight to his left, since the eastern half or so of the gap was protected by the waters of the sizeable Seret River. But if the lower reaches of this stream could be by-passed to the west, the river channel could be assaulted further north, where it is a less formidable natural obstacle, as its flow is generally north to south for all of its course excluding the final 32 or so marsh-ridden kilometers above Galatz. To this end Falkenhayn pressed hard on Focsani, a rather large town on the only main railway line leading into Moldavia. It fell on January 8th. In the meantime, Ninth Army's left was cooperating with the right of the Austrian First army in the mountains, where the two Teutonic forces jointly cleared the Romanians from the area of the Oituz Pass and drove into the eastern Carpathian foothills. This was the high-water mark of the *Alliance* offensive for the campaign; fighting continued for another two weeks among the wooded hills from the Oituz to the Seret, but the defenders could not be dislodged. An attempt to cross the river was frustrated on about the 20th, and thereafter Mackensen decided to suspend operations. Strassenberg had similarly gained nothing. His army in the mountains was totally paralyzed by the unusually bitter weather and moreover faced mostly more formidable Russian troops. The last offensive effort of the campaign came on January 23rd, when the Bulgarians in the Dobruja, attempting to use the extreme cold weather to their advantage, threw a cavalry detachment over the frozen Danube delta in hopes of turning Sakarov's left flank. Somewhat blinded by a thick fog, the Russo-Romanians were initially confused, but then they reacted well and dealt the invader a severe defeat. The line had stabilized once again.

While the battle for the gates of Moldavia was still in doubt, Alexiev decided to try and divert German attention away from Romania if possible, by mounting an attack at some other point along the Eastern Front. It is interesting to note that despite the almost complete failure of purpose of these diversionary attacks for the Russians since the end of the Great Retreat of 1915, they were still, early in 1917, being put into practice. Noticing a minor withdrawal of enemy troops from Eichhorn's group, Alexiev finally decided to instruct Russki undertake the operation. The latter did so on January 5th. He hurled his North Front westward out of the Riga bridgehead over great expanses of frozen marsh, in a surprise attack; there was no artillery preparation or other measures taken which would serve to alert the Germans, and as a result, Eichhorn was caught napping. Russki pushed as far as the Aa River, taking several thousand captives and a few dozen guns. Four days later a second blow was delivered many miles upriver, near Dvinsk, though its success was less spectacular. Taking unusually long to react to these actions, Eichhorn finally counterattacked vigorously, during the last week of the month. Some of the lost ground was subsequently retaken and perhaps 1,000 Russians as prisoners. Satisfaction having thus evidently been achieved by both sides, the battle subsided and the sector returned to calm. Of course, neither German military strength nor strategic attention had been "diverted" from Romania; Russki's move was far too feeble and came much too late to alter events there.

So it was that by January 1917, Romania's initial campaign was over. Seemingly, her decision to enter the war on the side of the *Entente* had been an ill-fated one. In four months' time she had been badly defeated and had lost two-thirds of her land area—all of Wallachia and Dobruja—including her capital, had been cut off from the sea, and had been forced to watch the fate of her national existence be passed into the relatively unwilling hands of her Russian protectors. Additionally, her armed forces had been decimated; of the more than 500,000 troops she could count in August, fewer than half remained to her by January, the rest being casualties. Entire divisions had been destroyed or captured. What little equipment as had been available was almost totally lost, and Russia, in a bad way herself, could not be expected to make good the difference. Worse still, the capture of a good portion of her harvest by the *Alliance* meant that the Romanian population living in the occupied areas would be subjected to hunger as well as the trying conditions imposed by an enemy military presence. Meanwhile, this enemy was free to requisition the agricultural and mineral wealth of the country for his own use. But the Romanian government had made a serious miscalculation in its decision to enter the war, and now the nation would have to pay the price for failure. By selfishly concerning itself more with the desire to annex Transylvania at an opportune moment than with the military realities of the war, it had left itself exposed to attack by the forces of all four *Alliance* powers along borders far too lengthy to be effectively guarded. In fairness to the Romanians, it might be argued that the decision to declare war had been made at a time when the enemy seemed on the verge of collapse, and before the advent of Hindenburg/ Ludendorff perfected his system of pooling reserves. And the *Entente* promises to Bucharest had never been made good; Russia provided only minimal aid, and that grudgingly, while the army which was to advance north from Salonika in the fall made only a half-hearted and ultimately unsuccessful attempt.

From the point of view of the *Alliance*, the Romanian Campaign had come to a very beneficial conclusion. Although their Eastern Front had been lengthened by some 320 kilometers (200 mi) from the Bukovina to the Black Sea, this distance was less than half that which they would have been forced to defend as a result of the Romanian intervention in the war, had they not conquered Wallachia and Dobruja. For casualties totaling certainly well less than 100,000, they had all but driven Romania from the war and had compelled Russia to spread her own resources much more thinly.

Of greatest significance, however, were the new resources suddenly made available by the recent conquests. Just when the *Entente* naval blockade was beginning to ruin the economies and demoralize the civilian populations of the member nations of the *Quadruple Alliance*, the vast captures in Romania helped ease the situation somewhat, thus forestalling the hour when Germany and her allies would exhaust themselves. The amount of material forcibly exported from the rich Romanian lands for the next year and a half has been put at: 1,000,000 tons of oil, 2,000,000 tons of grain, 300,000 farm animals, and 200,000 tons of timber[147]; not bad booty from such a relatively small area. Extremely well received, of course, were the foodstuffs, for the Teutonic peoples were growing hungry. Perhaps more important militarily was the increased distance put between the Salonika Front and the next nearest *Entente* Army, or perhaps the psychological effects upon both sides that the campaign had produced. At any rate, it is not unfair to state that the Romanian intervention produced a negative effect for the *Entente* cause in the war, and a positive one for that of the *Alliance*. In other words, the Great War was indefinitely prolonged, and the scales of war seemed to tip back away from the *Entente* side and once again strike an uneasy balance.

Romania 1913-1918

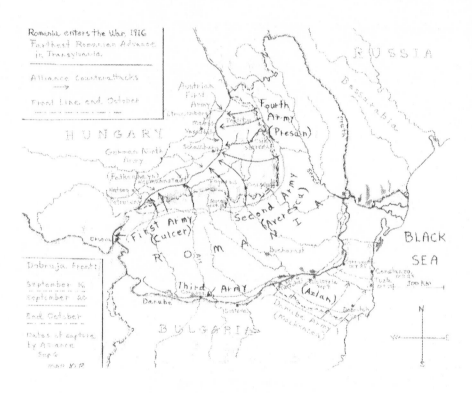

Romania Enters the war, 1916

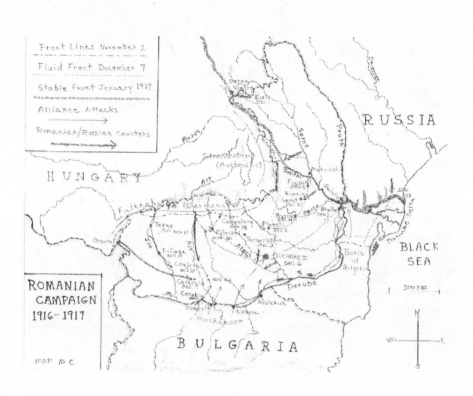

Romanian Campaign 1916-1917

Chapter Eleven
Behind the Lines

It is often stated that the First World War was the first of the modern wars. Acceptance of this statement by the individual would of course depend on one's awareness of a universally agreed upon definition of the word "modern" as well as a general understanding of at what point in history the "modern" era is supposed to have begun, and though for some the American Civil War might well lay claim to the title, certainly it can be said that World War I was the first great international conflict since the early years of the Industrial Revolution. As such it was the first total war, that is, the first war in which the total nations of the conflicting governments became involved. Previously, wars had generally been fought by relatively small, professional armies financed by a royal treasury for special, rather than national, interests. Battles had often been decided by superior generalship, training, or morale. Engagements, as costly ventures, were usually few and far between, enabling the "war" to sometimes continue for decades. These early wars rarely affected the average peasants of the day, unless one or another hostile army happened to pass over the land on which they lived. Their interest in the military campaigns was apt to be slight; they frequently cared very little which side won a war, since their life remained pretty much the same regardless of which authority to which they paid tribute governed the area in which they lived.

The above is of course an oversimplified example, the point being that prior to the 19th century, national populations were neither much involved in, nor affected by, war. The 1800s themselves were something of a transition period from Napoleon on. But by 1914 the world had changed; war had become everyone's business, from the highest royalty to the most obscure inhabitants of remote districts. Entire populations were now conscripted to fill the ranks of huge armies which formed continuous lines of battle from sea to sea, or at least from neutral (Switzerland) to sea. The national economies of the combatants were mobilized to the utmost so that maximum weight could be thrown into the war effort. No sacrifice was too great to help ensure victory. And at bottom, the people were led to believe, or perhaps feared anyway, that their national existence was at stake should the war be lost.

War had become a struggle between opposing blocs of human and economic resources, though it took some time for all the Powers to realize this fact. In August 1914, it will be remembered, the populations of the various countries had gone almost cheerily to war, confident of swift, decisive victory. The grim realities of the front lines had soon dashed these early hopes, however, and as the Great War dragged on and on the world came to realize that the inherent strengths of a nation went deeper than simply the size of its pre-war military establishment. Population, industrial base, overseas commerce, quantity of certain vital raw materials, amount of fertile, arable land, development of transportation and communications networks, faith in leadership; all these things had become indispensable for a nation involved in a prolonged conflict; they were the preconditions for an economically strong nation, and now in the 20th century, it had become essential for any great military power to also be a great economic power.

Modern economic strength, however, is usually linked to a nation's involvement in international trade and commerce, as no great industrial power has ever been totally self-sufficient. For this reason, possession of a powerful navy is essential for the maintenance of overseas supply to any modern warring state. During the First World War, before the days of significant air transport, this was a doubly important fact. For the combatants on the Eastern Front, it translated into disaster: the foreign trade of each was brought practically to a halt by the opening of hostilities, and was, for the most part, held there throughout the war. Geographical realities were, as usual, the deciding factors.

Before the war, Germany had possessed an extremely strong navy, second only to Britain's though a poor second to Britain's and France's combined. Those of Austria-Hungary and Russia were far less formidable. The British merchant fleet, however, composed of some eleven and a half million tons of steam vessels to the German three million, French one million and Austrian and Russian half million. On the other hand, the value of British foreign trade only slightly exceeded that of the German, while being two and one-half times that of the French and six times that of the Austrian and Russian figures. In this way it is easy to see that an extremely valuable German international trade was being carried on by a relatively small commercial fleet, protected by a strong though still inferior navy. Disruption of this commerce was bound to cripple Germany economically, and as she was the mainstay of the *Alliance*, it was sure to affect her allies as well.

But Germany was never truly defeated at sea during the Great War, that is, her High Seas Fleet was never overwhelmed and sunk in battle. Rather, it was condemned to uselessness by the very geography of Europe. By no means a landlocked nation, Imperial Germany in 1914 possessed many miles of seacoast, but most of it was along the Baltic, that inland Sea effectively choked off from the vastness of the Atlantic by the narrow passages of the Kattegat and Skaggerak. In the northwest corner of the country, there was a strip of coast directly on the North Sea, but even that great body of water could be effectively blockaded by the huge British navy at the Straits of Dover and the corridor between the Scottish islands and the Scandinavian mainland. As long as Britain remained in the ranks of her enemies, Germany would be isolated from the outside world save the small neutral states she bordered— Switzerland, Holland, and Denmark, Sweden, across the Baltic, and of course her ally Austria-Hungary.

The Austro-Hungarian Empire was in no better a position, actually a worse one. Her only outlet to the sea was a few ports along the Adriatic, another inland Sea which was an arm of the Mediterranean; the latter being easy to blockade by the British at the Strait of Gibraltar. The Adriatic itself was even restricted by straits between Italy and Greece, two nations which were both to ultimately join the *Entente*. Thus was Austria blockaded from all the world save Switzerland and Romania, and the latter was in time to become an enemy. At least the Austrian economy was not nearly as dependant on seagoing trade as was Germany's, but then, it was also much shallower and less stable.

After the defeat of Serbia, in late 1915, the Austro-Germans were able to make direct land contact with their allies to the southeast, the Bulgarians and Turks. This development greatly aided the workings of communications among the four Powers and assisted in the movement of troops, especially strategic reserves which could then be rapidly shifted from one front to another. The Bulgars and Turks were also able to receive fairly large quantities of German military aid via rail. Other than the satisfaction of knowing that their allies would not collapse, the Germans got nothing in return, for these countries were far too impoverished to offer anything of much economic value, so the effects of the sea blockade could not be eased in this direction. Bulgaria bordered only the Black Sea, another offshoot of the Mediterranean, and Turkey bounded the Black, Mediterranean, and Red Seas, and the Persian Gulf. The Red Sea and Persian Gulf were, incidentally, both hemmed in by the narrow straits—of Babel Mandeb and Hormuz—and quite easy for the British to close to hostile shipping.

If the *Alliance* was forced to feel its isolation, so incredibly, were the Russians. As the largest political entity in the world, the Russian Empire certainly had no shortage of seacoast, but of the thousands of kilometers which it did possess, few were useable for trade, the bulk of the frontage lying on the icy Arctic Ocean. There were numerous ports on the Baltic, rendered useless by the German control of that sea's outlet to the North, and some excellent facilities on the Black Sea, an expanse easily contained by the Turks at the Bosporos and Dardanelles, that area long coveted by the *Czars*. On the Pacific was but one decent port—Vladivostock—but this was 11,300 kilometers (7,000 mi) from the front and accessible only by the Trans-Siberian Railroad, a line broken by topographical difficulties at Lake Baikal, and therefore subjected to a ferry-crossing of that feature by barges, and extremely slow and arduous task. There was one major port on the White Sea, a southerly inlet of the Arctic Ocean, at Archangel, but this was ice-bound for half the year and was connected to the interior of the country by a single, narrow-gauge railroad.

Despite the shortcomings of the facility of Archangel, its importance to the Russian war effort swelled shortly after the outbreak of hostilities, as it was the nation's only European window on the world. Great efforts were made to improve the wharves and supplement the warehouse space there during the enforced lull in ship traffic in the winter of 1914-15. It should have become readily apparent that a bare six months' activity at such an inadequate harbor was hardly enough to alleviate the crippling material shortages that Russia had begun to suffer. Nevertheless a frantic effort commenced throughout 1915 to improve communications to Archangel. First, the narrow gauge railroad was broadened to the standard gauge, later, the whole line was double-tracked. Meanwhile the port itself was renovated and enhanced in usefulness by the introduction, for example, of floating docks and icebreakers for the White Sea Channel. By early 1916, the war material was pouring into the country along the railroad, but the supply still fell short of the demand.

At the extreme eastern tip of Siberia, the Pacific port of Vladivostok was at the same time strained to the maximum; huge quantities of supplies constantly poured in there year round, especially from Russia's Japanese ally. Somehow, the trains to this far flung location kept running despite the enormous distances involved. The main problem from this end was that the Trans-Siberian Railway was broken at one point. Evidently the builders of that lengthy line could not survey a suitable course for it around great Lake Baikal, one of the largest and deepest bodies of fresh water in the world, and the ridges of mountains which surround it, so they decided the lake would have to be traversed by barge. Of course, the speed of train traffic therefore became totally dependant on the speed of transferal of freight to barge, the actual ride across the water, and the reloading of the material to railcars. Not surprisingly, it was all a very slow procedure and in time great stockpiles of goods built up at the eastern end of the lake. In wintertime, the rails were extended across the ice for a seasonal link up, which helped matters somewhat, but all in all Vladivostok, like Archangel, could hardly be expected to handle but a fraction of the trade necessary for a major power to carry on a war with.

St. Petersburg was forced by the crippling shortages and severe defeats of 1915 to look elsewhere for a solution to the problems of blockade. Owing to Russian control of Finland it in time found one. In extreme northern Lapland, at the far end of the Scandinavian Peninsula lies the Murman Coast, a shoreline the western end of which remains free of ice even during the most severe winters. The reason for this is the existence of that remarkable feature of nature, the Gulf Stream. This warm ocean current is responsible for a much milder climate in northwestern Europe than the latitudes there would suggest, and the last faint traces of the stream reach just far enough to the northeast to keep the western end of the Kola peninsula free of ice. Here, not far from the Norwegian border, existed the small village of Novo-Alexandrovsk, a place which would witness a most spectacular boom and growth in subsequent years. In 1915 it was but an obscure fishing settlement; by the year 1917 it was Russia's busiest port. But the task of connecting Novo-Alexandrovsk with the interior of Russia was even more formidable than had been that of connecting Archangel, for it lay well north of the Arctic Circle, and over 485 kilometers (300 mi) farther north than the port on the White Sea. Moreover there was not even a decent road leading to it from the south. Though feverish work to construct a railroad to Petersburg went on from late 1915, problems caused by the severe climate and manpower shortages proved difficult to surmount, and the distance to cover exceeded 1,000 kilometers (650 mi). By July 1916 a third of the workers employed on the project were Austro-Hungarian prisoners of war. Many of these men perished to exposure, exhaustion and the unfamiliar temperatures and there is some truth to the claim that the railroad is "built on the bones of Austrians." Nevertheless, the line was theoretically opened on November 28, 1916, though from a practical standpoint the date should have been March 1917. It was one of the most constructive projects undertaken by the Russian government throughout the war, and would have gone a long way toward alleviating Russia's supply problems had it been given a chance to function. But by March 1917 little in Russia was given a chance to function.

All three belligerent Powers on the Eastern Front, then, suffered heavily from the effects of naval blockades. At the same time, they suffered in different ways. The war material used by the *Alliance* was created entirely from their own industries and upon their own technological skill. After an initial, temporary shortage of munitions in the early days of the war, Germany had converted her advanced chemical industry and her highly inventive engineering industries to the production of weaponry and ammunition. Her modern machine-tool industry had little difficulty in equipping new munitions plants and factories. In fact, Germany was the only nation in the world—except the U.S.A.—which possessed a solid enough machine tool industry to be self-sufficient in this area, as machine-tools, the tools from which to construct machinery, are a basic prerequisite of modern technological development. The Austro-Germans would have little trouble producing the weapons with which to continue the struggle.

They would, however, have considerable trouble producing the food with which to feed their populations. Though Germany had efficiently used her advanced technology to help develop her agricultural resources in the years before the war, in 1914 she was still importing one-third of all her food. Using her scientific inventiveness and substitute materials she was able to overcome many immediate shortages, but clearly, the longer the blockade was enforced, the more desperate her situation would become. Austria-Hungary could offer no help; in an exceptionally good harvest year, she might just produce enough food for herself. Most of this food came from the fertile plains of Hungary, yet was demanded more in the densely populated, industrialized, Austrian half of the Monarchy. Friction between the two halves of the Empire was thus generated; the net result being that the war effort was further eroded by the use of over half a million Austro-Hungarian troops throughout the summer of 1915 to help with the harvest.[148] At any rate the 1916 harvest was for much of Europe a disappointing one, and the *Alliance* powers were the hardest hit. They in fact never recovered from the shortages which followed. Berlin and Vienna had both hoped that their 1915 conquest of Russian Poland and other areas to the east might in time, by augmenting the amount of arable land they controlled, help ease the food problem, but the effects were not noticed.

Deaths in Germany directly attributable to the Allied blockade have been estimated at 88,000 in 1915, 121,000 in 1916, 260,000 in 1917, and 294,000 in 1918, a good illustration of the grim effects of this weapon of war. Naturally the German home front wearied as time passed and the war seemed no nearer a conclusion. All sorts of revolutionary left-wing activity flared up sporadically in various locations across the land. The year 1916 alone witnessed the outbreak of food riots in 32 cities. Such subversive activity gradually produced a counter-movement by a hardened, embattled right-wing which drew considerable support from the populace. It demanded the establishment of a military dictatorship with full powers to mobilize the entire nation for a total war, the use of any weapons technology could produce regardless of how barbaric they might be considered by outside observers, and a supreme effort to bring about a crushing, decisive victory. Of the few national heroes to have emerged from the war thus far, Hindenburg, the father figure, was overwhelmingly looked to as the one man who could deliver such a victory.

In August 1916, Hindenburg became Chief of the General Staff. Immediately, he and Ludendorff began to tackle the main problem as they saw it—manpower. A recent census had revealed that in mid-1916 there were three and a half million fewer persons in Germany engaged in productive employment as there had been before the war. The "Hindenburg Program" of December 3rd was supposed to reverse this trend, as its terms stated that every able bodied male citizen between the ages of seventeen and sixty not already serving was to be drafted into "Patriotic Auxiliary Service." In the event, this measure had only limited success, and actually fell considerably short of expectations. Meanwhile, the labors of the weary, underfed German people became less and less efficient. Transport, never before a problem under Teutonic organization, began to slowly break down. This was due in part to the actions of local authorities across the country who, acting independently, sometimes stopped trains and pillaged their cargoes of foodstuffs, clothing, or other essential commodities. In part it was due to a decrease in coal production in turn caused by a manpower shortage and less efficient labor.

Food, however, remained the principal concern of the average German throughout the war. Rationing had first been imposed in 1915 on bread, butter, milk, and meats. As time passed, other items were added to the list and the ration for each category was reduced further and further. By 1917 the average daily calorie intake was scarcely more than a quarter of what it had been in pre-war years despite an honest effort by the government to make available substitute foods. A healthy black market sprang up. Profiteering became commonplace. Companies and municipalities alike attempted to use their economic and financial strength to corner eatables for their own workers and families. Soon it became questionable as to whether or not the average citizen would in fact be able to obtain the ration to which he was entitled, as whatever food was available was very inequitably distributed. Not helping the national situation at all was the presence of large numbers of enemy prisoners, especially Russians, held by Germany. At the end of 1915 the figure was roughly 975,000; a year later it was 1,230,000; and by the end of 1917 it had risen to 1,400,000, all mouths which had to be fed. In Austria-Hungary the numbers were 725,000, 845,000, and 915,000 respectively.[149] These men, combined with those prisoners from other hostile countries, imposed a further serious strain on what was already a desperate state of affairs regarding food within the *Alliance* nations.

Not surprisingly, the hardships suffered by the people eventually boiled over into extreme social discontent. When in April 1917 the German government announced a further reduction in the meager bread ration, it was met by a wave of strikes which was in turn followed by another wave in June. German soldiers from the idle navy bottled up in its own ports joined this second wave. Frustrated, hungry, and despairing, they helped spread a fever of protest which swept the land and inestimably damaged the already sagging war effort. The worst was yet to come; in January of 1918 the *Alliance* powers were struck by an extremely disruptive wave of strikes. Clearly, the people could not be expected to bear the burdens on war much longer; their message could not be ignored indefinitely. Yet discontent within Germany and Austria, though very real and becoming ever more dangerous, was actually quite subdued compared to that which had come to express itself in some *Entente* nations, especially Russia.

By no means did the *Alliance* have a monopoly on problems caused by the wartime naval blockades; as we have seen, Russia too suffered to nearly as great a degree as did her enemies. Her grief did not result from being cut off from vital supplies of foodstuffs or raw materials, for within her vast expanse, she had adequate potential to produce far more than her own society could utilize. Rather, Russia's new isolation itself became a source of weakness and speeded the process of decay with which the Imperial government had already been afflicted for several decades. Historically a curious blend of both East and West, the Empire had in recent centuries turned ever more towards establishing closer ties with the nations of Western Europe in an effort to pull itself out of a state of true feudalism and introduce modern Western ideas and culture to its semi-primitive peoples. During the latter half of the 19th century great progress had been made toward achieving these ends. But in the Japanese War of 1904-05 Russia had found herself isolated, and her subsequent defeat had revealed the truly wretched state of her army and her society as a whole; the only positive development resulting from that conflict had been the formation of the Duma, and this resulted only after a tide of revolution had swept the land. The Duma, the first parliamentary body ever to come into existence in the *Czar's* realm, was in reality not particularly powerful nor effective, though it did serve to mollify the people until the coming of the new, great crisis. Meanwhile, Western influence was again at work in St. Petersburg, and for a while the universal peasant's dream of true social reform seemed a very real possibility.

But the Petersburg government, particularly the *Czar* himself, was unable or unwilling to read the handwriting on the wall. Had he been able to, he would certainly have realized that the Great War with Germany was bound to produce a repetition of the 1905 social disorders, or worse. The situation of 1914 was further complicated by the fact that a large number of government and military leaders bore German surnames. As far back as the reign of Peter the Great, *Czars* had traditionally imported large numbers of Germans to work in the state service, chiefly because of their organizational and improvisational abilities. Many of these Germans had remained in Russia over the decades or centuries, their hard work and value to the state having often advanced them to fairly high positions in the armed forces or civil service. Usually German in name only, they had by 1914 been completely Russianized and were as loyal subjects of the *Czar* as was anyone in the country. Just the sound of their names, however, aroused suspicion that they were in league with the *Kaiser*, especially after their names came to be associated with military disasters for Russia—Rennenkampf, Sievers, and Evert just to name a few. St. Petersburg was in fact infested with German spies, the Teutonic influence having always been strong there. Unofficial reports that the *Czarina*, herself a German princess, was a traitor turned out to be false, yet served only to intensify the popular mistrust. Before the war was old the capital itself was renamed Petrograd in an effort to disassociate the government from the German connection. Much more dangerous to the war effort and far less conspicuous were the multitudes of corrupt and incompetent bureaucrats, typifying a Czarist regime, who sometimes selfishly, often ineptly, misdirected and misused the nation's resources. After the army had met with a string of disasters, many of these men were arrested or dismissed, but their replacements were not persons likely to restore the faith in leadership to the people, which was never very great anyway, nor were they going to repair the damage to morale simply by their presence. Though the nation had apparently cheered the declaration of war in August 1914, its enthusiasm had very quickly subsided. Determination soon gave way to impatience.

The beginnings of the first truly anti-government resentment on a large scale began, however, when the *Czar* himself replaced the Grand Duke Nicholas as Commander-in-Chief of the armed forces in September of 1915. Only a month previously, on August 1st, the Duma met and in a notable session had resolved to change the spirit of government. The war, it had declared, would henceforth be a "people's war," waged no longer solely in the interests of the autocracy. The *Czar's* subsequent usurpation of authority with which to change the supreme direction of the war therefore came as a double shock to those who hoped his power might be somewhat limited, rather than enhanced. Later in the same month, when the next class of youthful recruits was called up one year early, the flames of discontent regarding unfair conscription were further fanned. As usual, the Monarch's answer to the problems of social unrest was simply that discipline should be strengthened, but inflation and hardships on the home front would make such solutions impractical, if not counter-productive.

Initially, the underlying problem concerning Russian morale was of course the fact that on the battlefield, Russian armies were being beaten and forced to retreat. General Sukhomlinov, the corrupt head of the War Ministry, was the most obvious scapegoat for Russia's unpreparedness for war, and as we have seen, came under attack from Duma politicians and Supreme Command leaders alike, and was finally dismissed in June 1915 and arrested shortly thereafter. But blaming scapegoats does not solve problems, and actually, Sukhomlinov had not done too bad a job considering the relatively scanty resources he was given to work with. Earlier belief in a short war had led to a stockpiling of ammunition instead of a program to construct new factories, or perhaps the lack of funds for such projects had by necessity led to the "short war" philosophy as a sort of wishful-thinking expediency. At any rate, huge material losses were incurred as a result of the enemy capture of fortresses such as Novogeorgievsk and Kovno, and though Ivangorod and Osowiec had served Russia rather well, they too in the end were lost. This coupled with the staggering losses in manpower during 1914-15, meant that Russia would, for all practical purposes, have to reequip her entire Army. Russian industry, relatively underdeveloped before 1914, was simply unable to do so as quickly as the military situation demanded. True, the potential for great expansion did exist, but such a transition would take time, even under extremely efficient organization; a blessing which Russia had never enjoyed. For the meantime, the country would have to look to foreign sources for her material needs. It is interesting to note that at first, very little or no effort was made to mobilize and expand the existing Russian industries. Indeed, many small firms sat idle, facing bankruptcy while the government sought contracts with English, French, or American firms. Domestic organizers complained of machinery and labor shortages and faulty transport. The former had before the war largely been German exports, even the technical skilled labor, the latter suffered from manpower shortages and an overstraining imposed by the demands of the military. On the other hand, foreign imports were subject to the problems caused by the blockade, problems which were not alleviated until well into 1916. It was a vicious circle.

Shell and small arms and ammunition were the areas in which developed the most acute shortages, and it was for these items that Russia most earnestly looked abroad. Sukhomlinov had at first dragged his feet, worrying (correctly as it turned out) about problems which were bound to arise from differences in caliber in foreign and domestic arms and ammunition. As a result, by the time the Russians went to put orders to overseas suppliers, the latter were already months behind on urgent orders from other belligerents. America offered some hope, but was so distant that doing business with her was bound to be slow and risky. England seemed the best bet, and by the autumn of 1915 the first large-scale British loans were arranged. In time, these became more and more generous as Russia declined, and the possibility of a separate peace between Petrograd and Berlin seemed to London to become a more and more distinct possibility. Delivery on the orders placed in Britain was another matter, however, and generally this was a much slower process than even the most pessimistic Russians had imagined. Soon, resentment toward Vickers and other firms flared, and there began the popular myth that Russia was being "left in the lurch" by her allies. The fall of such universally detested figures such as Sukhomlinov and the Minister of the Interior, Malakov, might take some of the sting out of the public frustration, but could hardly help to improve the plight in which Russia now found herself.

Eventually, foreign shipments did of course arrive. Following repeated requests and appeals for a reliable, scheduled delivery of goods by the Russian government to the British, England did promise 15 million Japanese rounds for May 1916, 25 million in June, and 45 million in July and later months, and 100 deliveries per month as well.[150] We have noted the problems often caused by the supplying of these Japanese rounds (and rifles) to the armies on the field, but early in 1916 the Russian position was desperate, and even captured Austrian weapons were now commonplace within the ranks. Russia had become a beggar and could not be a chooser. Although her own industry had by then upped its monthly production of rifles to over 100,000 a month, a new all-time high, the estimated requirement for normal battle actions was twice that figure.[151] The story was much the same regarding other munitionment; foreign assistance, though it left much to be desired, was still vital. As for non-delivery, in fairness it must be said that the contracted firms usually did as best they could, all things considered, and they did so without a great deal of faith in the Russian government's ability to repay its debts. Throughout the war, Russia ran up 757 million pounds in debts to Britain[152], 760 million dollars to France, 280 million to the U.S.A., and 100 million each to Italy and Japan.[153]

Because so few large industries existed in Russia, building the nation's industrial base would necessarily involve much of the small business community. Most of these firms, however, could not afford to convert their operations to war production without the aid of government loans. The government, in turn, hesitated to issue such loans, claiming that foreign production was less expensive and more reliable. This option for a short-term solution to material shortages as opposed to a long-term one may have been attractive, but was less practical, and in the event, many Russians in responsible positions tried to take steps to redirect official policy. Duma politicians and representatives from business and industry began to organize in hopes of finding ways to boost the nation's war effort. In June 1915, so-called "Special Councils" were set up to oversee the production of armaments, fuel, and food, and others to help streamline the transport and defense systems. These councils were further broken down into subdivisions, sections, committees, conferences, etc., the end result being that too much bureaucracy was created and private enterprise was thus kept from working properly. Meanwhile, a struggle for allocation of raw materials between large and small businesses was waged; competition for available manpower was similarly intense. Then the government, breaking from its traditional gold standard, began to spend freely, unleashing a wave of inflation. Prices and wages skyrocketed. Under such difficult conditions it is surprising that the economy did not break down altogether, but in fact it was greatly stimulated and eventually, as government, large and small business began to cooperate, it grew enormously in strength. Production of fuels, munitions, chemicals, and machinery slowly but steadily rose. The banking industry underwent a boom. It seemed that Russia might yet pull herself up, provided the front lines held a while longer. But beneath the surface of economic prosperity lurked dangers which threatened to undermine the very fabric of society.

The great rise of industry in Russia during 1915-16 was not paralleled by an equal expansion of agriculture. While industries reaped great profits, farms stagnated. This was in part due to a manpower shortage, but every segment of society was functioning with a similar handicap, so logically this one problem should not have proven to be a crippling one. Yet production of foodstuffs did decline in Russia throughout the war. Grain and potato harvests had peaked in 1914, then fell off in succeeding years. For cereals, the year 1915 yielded the largest harvest; later years witnessed a decrease in volume.[154] Perhaps the overall causes of the decrease are obvious: lack of manpower and fertilizer, loss of territory to the *Alliance*, less incentive to produce due to inflation; perhaps they are less conspicuous: 1916 was in all Europe a bad year for the harvest, and 1917 was a year in which everything was upset by the Revolution, therefore the apparent decline after 1915 was misleading. At any rate, less and less food found its way into the cities and towns as time passed, and the situation was worsened by the fact that the majority of refugees from the Great Retreat of 1915 had flocked into the towns for security. Many of these localities were already overcrowded due to the recent boom in business and industry, and when the food shortage came, it caused widespread suffering.

Nevertheless, the agricultural capacity of Russia should have been sufficient to feed her population notwithstanding. The real problem was that the food distribution system had broken down. In February of 1916 a Special Council for Supply was set up, its functions being to regulate transport, control prices, and oversee a rationing program if necessary. Already bread, flour, meat and sugar were extremely scarce in the cities and their prices, as well as those of fuel and clothing, had gone sky high. Wages had also gone up, but had been nullified by the increasing rate of inflation. Members of the Duma, united in their dissatisfaction with the Monarchy, had banded together in a "Progressive Bloc" which included all but the extreme parties. In an unprecedented show of defiance, over two-thirds of that body endorsed a resolution which called for a transition to representative government. Their frustration was increased when it was realized that the Special Council for Supply would not exercise control of the army's needs—these were placed under a separate set of commissioners from the civilians. The net result was that in the confusion and competition between "Councils" which followed, prices simply rose even higher and the existing supplies of food became the targets of corrupt profiteers and those involved in the Black Market. Farmers became reluctant to release their harvests into this whirlpool of disarray, believing that by holding back for a time, they might realize larger profits later. Many used their grain to feed an increasing quantity of livestock[155] especially after the price of meat jumped so enormously. All the while, the shortages in the urban areas became more and more acute.

Underlying the problems of food distribution were the awful difficulties regarding transportation in Russia during the war. The Czarist state had never laid enough mileage of railroad track, possessing as it did in 1914 only slightly more mileage than Germany for an empire forty times as large. With the coming of hostilities and mobilization, a large percentage of the nation's available rolling stock had been requisitioned for troop movements to the front, and thereafter for supply of the armies facing the enemy. Through increased production and foreign purchases, Petrograd was able to increase the number of its locomotives and freight-cars during the 1914-17 period, but this increase was overmatched by the increased demand for transport. For example, the double-tracking of the rail line to Archangel meant that the quantity of supplies sent inland from that port could theoretically be doubled—provided the available rolling stock was doubled. Similarly, the construction of the line to Novo-Alexandrovsk was vital to Russia's war effort—but its very existence necessitated the availability of rolling stock if it were to be a worthwhile venture. True, the war's stoppage of Russia's grain exports had freed a lot of trains for service elsewhere, but events proved that the new availability of these could not offset the increased demands of 1915-16. Despite a gradual improvement in the efficiency[156] of the railroads, the quantity of both freights and foodstuffs moved by rail declined from 1913 on.[157] One notable observer noticed several causes for the strain on Russian railways. The fact that the capital, Petrograd, was built in an extremely northern latitude ensured that nearly all of the food consumed there would have to be sent from areas far to the south, since the surrounding countryside contains little acreage suitable for agriculture and the growing season is so short. And Petrograd had recently experienced a considerable increase in population as thousands of refugees streamed into the city, and additional industrial labor was summoned to work in the rapidly ballooning munitions factories. In addition, the capital's pre-war fuel supply had come mostly from British and German shipping in the Baltic, an avenue now closed by the enemy. As the small Arctic ports were inadequate to handle the new demands, more coal and oil had to be railed from points far to the south, 3,200 kilometers (200mi) from the Donets Basin or 4,800 kilometers (3000mi) from Siberia. Longer journeys, of course, tied up rolling stock for longer periods, decreasing the actual number of freight trains which could be sent. Lastly, thousands of kilometers of track were constantly tied up for army use, transporting thousands of horses, millions of men, and all the necessary supplies involved.[158]

Another factor which figured in the disruption of Russian transport was one purely of geography. The bulk of the military traffic ran, of course, east to west, but trains carrying food products more often took a south to north route, simply because the greater percentage of Russian farmland lay generally in the south, while more of a consumption demand existed in the population centers of the north. As might be expected, these perpendicular movements tended to conflict with one another; at first, orders were issued that the army trains be given the right-of-way at all times, later, as the civilian populace became increasingly restive over the food shortages, these directives were cancelled. In fairness to the Russian administration, it should be stated that the authorities at least tried, and often succeeded in, numerous measures to streamline the confusing system. In fact, every source of information seems to show that the amount of work performed by the railroads during the war was somehow increased considerably. After the initial disruption of service following the opening of hostilities, the situation was being improved constantly until the disastrous Great Retreat of summer 1915, when the military withdrawals were complicated by hordes of refugees attempting to flee eastwards with their soldiers. These vast migrations almost completely ruined the transport services for a time; then matters improved again, slowly, until late 1916 when discipline began to become a problem, and the whole structure collapsed with the Czarist government which had spawned it, in 1917. From that time on, the efficiency of the railways began to nosedive, as less productive labor on the part of the workmen meant that fewer man-hours were being devoted to the job, and the rolling stock and rail lines fell gradually into disrepair.

Urban Russia began to suffer when the war was about a year old. While the army was still being well supplied, people in the larger cities such as Petrograd and Moscow found themselves face to face with hunger. By October 1915, provisions for these had fallen to 60 percent of the pre-war quantities, and certain foods became almost impossible to obtain. Grain, for example, which had decreased in delivery more rapidly than almost any other commodity, was extremely scarce, yet this was not due to lack of supply, but rather a failure of transport. As one account states, grain for shipment gradually accumulated at railway stations, choking the facilities. By 1915 these accumulations had reached levels two-and-one-half times greater than in 1913, and by 1916, three-and-one-half times. Special efforts were indeed made to disentangle the knots, but the situation was never completely relieved.[159] Similar examples might be cited for a score of other foods as well. It was not so much that foodstuffs were unavailable altogether; rather, they were often simply unavailable to the city dweller, especially those in the north; people who were physically separated from the producing areas were deprived of the products those areas offered because of a very basic inadequacy of the transport system. Far away in Siberia, food, mineral and fuel supplies were plentiful and inexpensive, but there was no way of sending these supplies to the very needy northwest, except for the trickle that rolled over the Urals by wagon. The Trans-Siberian Railway could certainly offer no assistance, jammed up as it already was with foreign shipments of warm material imported via Vladivostock.

In the long run, neither heavier loads nor longer hauls were measures sufficient to overcome the obstacles which the railways faced during the war. As a result, many of the necessities of life became scarcer and scarcer in certain areas of the nation, and the population became more and more discontent with the government, which they believed was remaining callous to their deprivation. All the while, the law of supply and demand had pushed the price of food, clothing, and fuel to a new high in the areas suffering from shortage, and these rises coupled with the runaway inflation which was sweeping the entire land meant that the day was nearing when the people would demand a change in government, perhaps even a change in direction of the war. The *Czar*, as usual, dismissed such possibilities when warned by his subordinates, and in so doing sealed his own fate. It is generally believed that the endless string of disasters for Russia on the battlefields of the Great War were the primary reason for the Revolution of 1917; the people were just fed up with defeats caused by the bungling Autocratic regime, or so goes the argument. A closer examination of the facts however, will reveal that most Russians were willing to carry on the war to a victorious conclusion right up until, and even somewhat after, the *Czar's* downfall. Most antiwar agitation, at least until the rise of the Bolsheviks, stemmed from sufferings on the home front. If history has taught any lesson over its long tumultuous course, it is that hungry people are easily driven to desperate measures; nothing can breed discontent faster than lack of enough food to eat.

More than any other country, Russia was bedeviled by an anti-war movement from the earliest days of the conflict. In large part, this was due to the efforts of a single, then-obscure figure: Vladimir Illich Ulyanov. An unknown socialist revolutionary at the outbreak of war in 1914, this man (who subsequently proclaimed himself Nicholai Lenin) was to prove himself one of the ablest political organizers of the 20th century. Having already been banished to Siberia and later exiled from Russia altogether for subversive activities, Lenin was in Galicia in August 1914 where he was immediately arrested and imprisoned by Austrian authorities upon the outbreak of war. He was soon released, though, and made his way to neutral Switzerland, from where he was to plot the overthrow of the Imperial Russian government.

By 1914, every European nation had its share of socialists, many of whom actively participated in their respective governments. With the coming of the war, and the nearly universal demonstrations in every country in patriotic support of it, most of these men had supported the call to arms; for example, the German socialist view was that Germany, threatened with encirclement by powerful adversaries, was only properly defending herself. In Russia, most of the liberals believed that the alliance with the democratic states of Britain and France was likely to lead to the democratization of the Romanov regime, probably once victory had been achieved. But a small minority of radicals, led by Lenin, held to the view that the war was an evil struggle between greedy capitalistic systems, fought at the expense of the common people, and that therefore the war should not be supported; to the contrary, the governments which were waging it should be toppled. This extreme view was at first overshadowed by the fervent nationalism of 1914, but Lenin was not discouraged. He kept in constant touch with his followers in Russia—the Bolsheviks, a few of whom held Duma seats—and directed their efforts towards the ultimate goal of Revolution.

Soon, Lenin had conceived a propaganda program designed to undermine the will of the soldiers to fight. He advocated fraternization with the enemy, believing that if the troops could make contact with their counterparts in the German and Austrian armies, they would easily see that their supposed enemies were really just common people like themselves with whom they had no quarrel. Only then, he reasoned, would Russian, German, and Austrian alike realize that the real enemy was the "capitalist oppressors." Using his own small but well organized party as a model, Lenin went on to call for the formation of units within the armed forces from which his propaganda might be distributed, units with unswerving loyalty to the party which could always be looked to by the troops as an alternative to their officers as a guiding force. By November of 1914 these units were coming into existence, though all in all the initial Bolshevik efforts were mostly unsuccessful in winning much popular support in the army. However, the December call-up of the first students for military duty had provided Lenin's followers with a large group of recruits who were quite susceptible to the anti-war, anti-regime rhetoric. The extremists also concentrated on the troops who were responsible for the operation and maintenance of the railways, realizing that these men controlled a vital link in the chain of army organizations. Surprisingly, these railway battalions were found to be rather willing listeners—they could see firsthand the intense corruption within the system—and before long were influencing many of the army units which rode the rails with their radical beliefs. In January and February of 1915, troops trains carrying reinforcements to the front consisting of the erstwhile students as well as nationalities from the far-flung points within the Russian Empire began "losing" many of the new recruits en route. On certain trains, as many as 50-65% of the men who had boarded had disappeared by the end of the journey. The *Czar's* reaction was to strengthen discipline; Lenin's was to redouble his efforts.

During that same month of January 1915, the Bolsheviks began distributing printed leaflets which called upon the peasants as well as the soldiers to refuse to go to war. The have-not groups were all appealed to; peasants should receive all the land, industrial workers an eight-hour day, and soldiers an end to the fighting. This joining of anti-war sentiment to anti-establishment sentiment was bound to be effective, since the latter had long existed in Russia anyway, and for a time the Bolsheviks mobilized an ever-increasing number of adherents to their cause. Then, in April the government cracked down on dissidents, arresting many and sentencing them to terms of banishment in Siberia. Still, Lenin and his creed were undeterred and as a counter move determined that henceforth their political agitators must simply become more inconspicuous, that is, they should infiltrate the very core of the army itself. Thus was born a campaign which was to erode the very essence of the strength of Imperial Russia—that of the army, over which Nicholas himself had taken supreme leadership in September.

For the moment, however, the problems caused by revolutionary advocates were still insignificant compared to those which came with popular waves of anger such as the unrest of September 1915. As mentioned earlier, the dismissal of the popular Grand Duke and the calling-up of the next class of youth one year early had unleashed a series of anti-government demonstrations in many localities in which many persons demanded representative government in the form of a Duma independent of the *Czar*, and a reduced role with less supreme authority for the latter. Nicholas, angered, responded in his predictably short-sighted, narrow-minded fashion by dissolving the Duma altogether and announcing new measures to be taken to suppress dissidents. Order was once more restored, though often only at gunpoint. The apparent willingness of the regime to instruct its troops to shoot down civilians, even disorderly ones, only served to fan the flames of revolt. Yet still, the majority of Russians entertained no such thoughts.

Lenin, meanwhile, decided to try another psychological tactic. Once the front had stabilized following the Great Retreat of the Russians, Germany had seen fit to transfer her main attention to other theaters, first Serbia, later France in the Verdun operation.

Therefore, the Germans had remained passive on the Eastern Front during the winter of 1915-16, when the only actions fought were incited by the Russian armies. All this was of course due to purely military reasons, but Lenin tried to distort the facts by insisting that the German idleness at the front was due to an unmistakable unwillingness on the part of the *Kaiser's* troops to fight. They had come to understand, he claimed, the nature of the class struggle which had begun to be waged, and as such had refused to do battle with the Russian soldiers, whom they regarded as brothers in the larger conflict against the criminal capitalistic governments currently in power. There can be little doubt as to whether or not Lenin actually believed what he was saying. His outlook was, however, always international in scope, and he did unquestionably hold the conviction that a pacifist revolutionary seizure of power in Russia would soon be followed by similar occurrences within all the warring nations, until the worldwide demise of capitalism, monarchism, and Imperialism had been achieved. Having emerged from two International Socialist Conferences held in Switzerland during 1915-16 as the undeniable champion spokesman of the extreme left, Lenin finally called for the ultimate in radical acts to be committed—the weapons of all the mobilized soldiers of all the world's armies should be turned against the common enemy: the existing capitalist order.

Such extreme views had little chance of attracting much support from any social groups of any nation of the time, even the "proletariat" of Russia, for whom they were supposed to be especially drafted. In general, the subversive efforts of the Bolsheviks were little more than a nuisance to the Russian government for the first two years of war, though little by little, Lenin's ideas were at least being given an audience. What made the anti-war movement such a potent force from late 1916 was the fact that it was the only well-organized and familiar alternative to the status quo, which had become unacceptable. The seeds of revolution were sown in the disastrous military ventures of 1914-15, the social injustices on the home front, the corrupt and inefficient monarchist regime, the inadequacy of transport and supply, the food, clothing, and fuel shortages, the uncontrolled inflation, the lack of faith in both civil and military leadership, the endless casualty lists, and a score of other reasons. Lenin and his Bolsheviks, never a particularly popular bunch, simply moved into the vacuum created by all the Imperial government's failings. Like all great political achievements, it was more or less a matter of being at the right place at precisely the right time. By late 1916, the crisis entered its most decisive phase.

Despite all her internal problems, Russia was somehow about to increase her strength during the winter of 1915-16. In part, this was due to the very capable efforts of the Minister of War Polivanov, who had replaced Sukhomlinov. He has been referred to as the ablest military organizer in Russia at the time, and a look at the state of Russia's armies in the spring of 1916 would seem to bear out this claim. By closing many of the loopholes in the inequitable system of deferment from conscription, and by reforming the policies of the training of new recruits, he had raised the number of men within the armed forces to a new high, about 6 million[160], and had accomplished all this, the terrible losses of 1914-15 notwithstanding. And for the first time in the war, practically all of the front line troops were armed with rifles, thanks to his efficient distribution of the growing number of foreign imports and those domestically produced, as well as captures, these mostly Austrian in origin. The artillery were provided with a fair number of new field pieces, and were so lavishly supplied with shell that there could not be no further talk of "shell shortage." Transport facilities were temporarily improved as was, therefore, the supply of the field armies. And to his lasting credit, Polivanov had furthermore reorganized and revitalized a traditional yet lapsing elite of the Russian army—the Imperial Guard—and had welded it into a confident, formidable force, the new Guards Army.

Unfortunately for the Russian war effort, Polivanov, who had never been well liked by the *Czar*, was dismissed as Minister of War in March 1916, before he had held that post for even a full year. Yet he departed leaving the Russian forces in a better state than they had hitherto enjoyed thus far in the war, and certainly capable of carrying out the role expected of them in 1916. Many senior Russian commanders, however, had little faith in the forces with which they were entrusted; Lake Narotch and the winter battles had seen to that. On the other hand, for some the advent of the new campaigning season meant an opportunity to lead their armies to final victory was at hand, provided the high command could be persuaded to unleash them before the growing political and economic chaos on the home front served to seriously undermine morale and sapped the common soldier of his will to fight.

Brusilov's stunning victories of early summer seemed to confirm that the army could still defeat the Austrians, but as more and more German troops arrived by mid summer, progress slowed and Russian enthusiasm waned. As we have seen it had all but evaporated even before Romania's disastrous campaign; following the enemy occupation of two-thirds of that country, no Russian soldier cared to be sent to the "Romanian Front" and in those units that were, discipline soon became a real problem. Russo-Romanian relations, never good, can be considered as rather poor in general by the end of 1916.

At the end of December, the Empress's most trusted advisor, Rasputin, was murdered by angry and disgusted members of the Royal Family. This act terribly upset Nicholas and Alexandra, especially the latter, who sank into a state of despair and paralysis from which she never really recovered. The government, which by then was pretty much in the hands of ministers appointed at the behest of the murder victim, found itself unable to function without an autocrat to attend to all the formalities that accompany such a position of power. The ministers, mostly inept and insecure, were unable to cope with the discontent which was surfacing everywhere. One— Protopopov—so desperate for advice from his former benefactor, went so far as to try to contact the spirit of the deceased Rasputin in order to ask advice of the ghost.[161] Ironically, even the weather seemed to go against the Russians that winter. The 1916-17 season was the harshest anyone could remember, with extremely low temperatures and record amounts of snow. And it was heavy snowstorms in January which blocked roads and retarded shipments of products, especially food, into the northern cities, which caused some severe shortages, which in turn led to more unrest. On January 9th, the 12th anniversary of the "Bloody Sunday" massacre—an event few Russians had forgiven or forgotten—was observed by the walkout of more than 150,000 workers from more than 100 factories in Russia. The crisis only worsened. One historian claims that during the final third of the month of January, the city of Petrograd received only one-sixth of its minimum requirements of grains and flour, a fraction that dropped to one-twelfth by February. Then came a wave of biting cold, "fifty degrees below freezing."[162] He goes on to quote Protopopov as having reported the immobilization of 60,000 rail cars loaded with necessities such as food and fuel, by heavy snows. About that time the wife of Rodzianko, the Duma president, advised a friend that the mood of the populace had become so ugly that even a minor incident might "start a conflagration."[163] Other accounts from less prominent individuals are similar. A nurse wrote of the growing discontent of the Russian masses. Everywhere she heard the government being denounced, at first somewhat timidly, but as time went by the disparagement became more and more bold. Upset at what she believed was deliberate sabotage of railroads, industries, factories, mills, workshops and laboratories, she felt sympathy for the *Czar* and his family, who were also the objects of insult. Anti-war demagoguery constantly increased in volume and in pitch, and before long "riots and insurrections" were commonplace, the crowds shouting for "Peace and Bread." Unconvinced of the mob's sincerity, she added that as the "erstwhile docile rabble" became hungrier and hungrier, they dropped the "Peace" and screamed only for "Bread, give us Bread."[164] By early 1917 it had become obvious that major political change was on the horizon for Russia.

During November, a second gathering of *Entente* nations' representatives in Paris had concluded that Russia would need additional material support from the West, but that the only persons capable of authoritative decisions for the Empire were Alexiev and the *Czar* himself, and owing to their unique positions within the command structure were unable to attend meetings outside Russia. Therefore a conference on Russian soil must be undertaken. The importance of the Russian commitment on the Eastern Front was universally recognized and increased military aid for it was pledged. As had been the case at Chantilly a year earlier, the need for combined and simultaneous actions on all fronts was resolved as essential. Military decisions were deferred to the anticipated later meeting with *Stavka*. In late January 1917 this gathering finally sat down in Petrograd. The western delegates as usual pressed the Russians for immediate action, and by so doing betrayed their complete misunderstanding of the true situation in Russia that winter. The Russian position was that absolutely no aggressive moves could be expected before late spring, and what they expected to accomplish even by then can scarcely be imagined. At any rate, they never got the chance.

Naturally, the *Alliance* also had its problems. Despite the smashing success in Romania and subsequent seizure of some of the 1916 harvest there, the food supply in Germany and Austria had gone from bad to worse. The Hungarian harvest for the year was disappointing; the German potato crop had failed. The terrible "turnip winter" followed, during which the population was forced to live on roughly one-half of the caloric intake considered necessary for good health. Thus weakened, industrial workers became less efficient and more susceptible to disease. All the ingredients for social unrest were thus present, but such tendencies were somewhat offset by the knowledge that the government had tried to make peace and had been rebuffed. The average German could believe, as he was told, that the enemy was waging a war of annihilation against him.

The peace move was a German initiative in December timed to take advantage of the recent success in Romania, that Germany could negotiate from a position of relative strength. It asked the *Entente* for "propositions" which might lead to the "restoration of a lasting peace." But because it was not worded in submissive terms, the *Entente* rejected it as "vague and insincere." The Russian Duma and Foreign Minister Pokrovsky agreed that Russia would fight on until victory had been achieved. They were loathe to contemplate the heavy losses the country had suffered, which they declared would have been in vain if Germany was left undefeated.[165] Other *Entente* replies were equally uncompromising. Despite disappointment not only in the *Alliance* nations, but virtually all neutrals as well, the war would continue.

Austro-German hopes were shattered in another arena as well, and at about the same time. In one of his last official acts before his death *Kaiser* Franz Joseph had affixed his signature, alongside that the *Kaiser* Wilhelm, to a manifesto which called for the restoration of a Kingdom of Poland. No doubt the timing was significant; as long as the possibility of a separate peace with Russia lingered such declarations would have been impossible, because Russia, as we have seen, controlled the lion's share of pre-partition Poland, and before its loss in 1915, all of Congress Poland. Evidently the *Alliance* had given up all hope of a separate peace, and such a realization may well have prompted the December offer of general peace. At any rate, the manifesto was read publicly on November 5th. The Germans soon agreed to the formation of a Provisional Council of State, which would oversee the judiciary and educational functions of an independent state. One member of the Council was General Pilsudski, who commanded a Polish brigade recruited from Austrian

Poland, and who had been serving in the Austro-Hungarian army since the beginning of the war. Before long, Pilsudski was calling for an independent Polish army and insisting that Polish soldiers not take an oath of allegiance to any *Alliance* power. When his boldness led to conflicts with the Germans, he resigned from the Council; most of his men followed his lead and were disarmed by the Germans and sent to internment camps. The rest were merged into the Austrian army. Eventually (July 22nd), Pilsudski was arrested and imprisoned, though he was well treated. The *Alliance* Powers then created their own puppet Polish Government, but by then no Pole was taking them very seriously. Most were quick to remember a report of the message of American President to the U.S. Congress on January 22, 1917. It stated that a united, independent, and free Poland should be established. Thereafter, few Poles would settle for anything less.

Chapter Twelve
The Russian Breakdown

However disappointing the results of the Russo-Romanian campaign of latter 1916 may have seemed to the nations of the *Entente*, none could claim that it had failed to attract a significant military response from the *Alliance*. In August, when the Romanians had finally declared war, Germany could account for 70 divisions on the Eastern Front; Austria-Hungary counted 50, Turkey 2 and Bulgaria 4½ (watching the common frontier with Romania). At the height of the fighting in November, the totals had reached 88, 52, 5, and 5½ respectively. As against this, the Russians fielded 141 divisions on the same front and, as we have seen, the Romanians were soon to commit 23 of their own. These latter numbers were to be reduced drastically as a result of the horrible losses suffered in Volhynia, Galicia, and Romania; by the time of the winter lull from mid January, the Russian total had fallen to 116 divisions; and the Romanian 13. Across the lines, the *Alliance* possessed on February 1, 1917, 80 German and 49 Austro-Hungarian divisions; added to the 10 Turkish and Bulgarian units a total of 139. For the first time in the war, the numbers on the orders of battle had swung away from the *Entente*, at least in Eastern Europe. And although a Russian division had always been numerically larger than its enemy counterpart, the wretched state of the Russian army at this point in the war probably ensured that the imbalance was worse, rather than better, than it seemed on paper.

No one could have known it at the time, but in fact the Russian Empire had ceased to be a first-rate power, if in fact it ever had been. The "steamroller" had definitely broken down and could not be fixed. It would have to be scrapped, and a new one built. But again, this fact was not much evident at the time; the *Alliance* for example maintained fairly consistent levels of troop strength in the East throughout the year. The Germans even increased their presence significantly from spring until autumn. Had they only known what was really going on in Russia they would not have bothered. Temporarily maintaining a façade of normalcy, *Stavka* added 25 new divisions during March, then was forced to strike 53 off its roles in April, and another 17 in May, before adding 47 in June! This was magician's work at its very best, but it could not help the Russian army. From mid-summer on, trying to establish numbers (of anything) in the Russian military establishment becomes practically impossible, so great had become the chaos and turmoil.

In February, a report listing all losses of merchant ships up to that point in the war was published in the New York Journal of Commerce.[166] Germany was 5th on the list with 83 vessels of 195,887 tons lost. Russia was tenth at 59 of 69,399; Turkey was eleventh at 101 of 55,282; Austria-Hungary fifteenth at 11 of 22,439; and Romania made the list (18th) having lost one ship of 3,688 tons. The United States was 14th on the list (seventh among neutrals), having lost 10 ships totaling 24,559 tons. Compare these numbers to the nation first in losses, Britain, which lost 1,153 vessels weighing 2,568,317 tons. Despite being far less injured than six other neutral nations, the U.S.A. decided to break off diplomatic relations with Germany that very month. Hindenburg and Ludendorff had agreed to the German Admiralty's request to renew its all-out submarine campaign that winter. Their reasoning was that the *Alliance* was running out of time to win the war. Anything and everything must be tried in an attempt to achieve victory, American belligerency notwithstanding. The war was 2½ years old now and Germany's allies were beginning to waver, and no end was in sight. Had they only known how desperate was the situation in Russia, they almost certainly would have made other arrangements.

As it was, neither Ludendorff nor Hötzendorf had any plans for the East in 1917. Both their nations were war-weary and neither considered the Russian Front to be the main theater of war. Turkey was engaged on three other fronts and could not be expected to be overly concerned with Eastern Europe. Bulgaria had already achieved her goals against Serbia and Romania and was anxious to turn her full attention to Greece. Other than the re-conquest of eastern Galicia and perhaps the capture of Riga, there seemed nothing worth much sacrifice to achieve against the Russians. Both *OHL* and Hötzendorf decided to remain on the defensive for the time being and await further developments from the submarine campaign.

There was very little ground action at the front during February 1917; the skies over the front were another matter. Despite the bitter cold, the Russian command ordered its airpower into action for an unusually busy month. The 13th of the month was noted by the enemy to be especially heavy in attacks, which came all along the line both north and south of the Pripet and targeted mostly railroad facilities. On the 19th, Russian ace Ensign Thomson shot down a German over Smorgon, then repeated the act a day later. Thomson was himself shot down before the year was out, by which time he had achieved eleven victories, which tied him for 5th most among Russian pilots in the war.[167]

Then on February 27th, the Duma reopened after a two-month recess. This event was the occasion for revolutionary groups who had been planning demonstrations to act. In Petrograd perhaps 85,000 workers from dozens of the city's factories struck, demanding higher wages, better working conditions, and a responsible government. At first they shouted simple slogans, but later the tone changed to revolutionary in nature, and Cossack cavalry had to be called in to disperse the mob. But within a few days the strikes had spread to several cities and involved at least a quarter-million workers, who began carrying banners which read "Down with the war," "Down with the Government" or "Bread." Although such demonstrations usually broke up of their own accord, often before sundown, the writing was on the wall. Major change could not be long delayed.

For several days social unrest simmered both beneath and above the surface of calm. March 8th arrived. It was, for the working class, International Women's Day, an occasion which in the recent past had been used by Russian socialists to disseminate propaganda of anti-Monarchist or pacifist nature. But on this occasion it indeed became a woman's day, as thousands of weary Petrograd working women, fed up with hunger, cold, and privation and tired of being deprived by the war of their husbands, brothers, and sons, took to the streets demanding "Bread!" Later that day they were joined by thousands more men and women strikers. There was very little violence that day; a few bakeries and places suspected of containing food were broken into, and by dusk the disorders seemed to have ended. But the real internal enemies of the Russian state, their ranks swollen in recent months by opponents of the war and victims of the increasingly difficult living conditions in the Empire, were not about to let the tense atmosphere be defused. In the words of one historian, organizers had been hard at work throughout the night, "like an army of industrious termites slowly undermining the bulwarks of the old order of the Russian Empire."[168] Over the next few days, the unrest not only continued, it began to turn violent against the police. It also began to turn revolutionary in character. When the *Czar*, who was at *Stavka* in Mogilev, was informed, he ordered the rioting put down. March 11th was a turning point; on that day the first widespread use of firearms against crowds was undertaken, and in response the first military personnel were killed by civilians. On the same day the Duma unanimously decided to ignore an order to dissolve, and determined to henceforth become a truly representative body of Russian democracy. Rodzianko, the Duma president, sent a series of frantic telegrams to the Emperor, begging him to allow the formation of a new government and warning him of the consequences if he did not, but Nicholas would only listen to Protopopov, the Rasputin protégé who tended to downplay the significance of the events then shaking the capital. Demonstration had become rebellion and now threatened to become revolution. On March 12th the commander of the Petrograd garrison reported to *Stavka* that he could not restore order in the city; more and more military units were going over to the revolutionaries. The *Czar* ordered General Ivanov to crush the revolt and Alexiev promised various infantry, cavalry and artillery units, which had they been combined, would have constituted at least a Brigade-sized force, for the task. In the event, neither Ivanov nor the troops he had promised ever reached the capital. As revolution spread from Petrograd into other towns and cities, it paralyzed what little remained of Russia's transportation and communications networks that had not already fallen into the semi-paralysis resulting from war or weather. With the Emperor's authority thus neutralized, his ministers began to flee Petrograd, fearful for their lives. The last vestiges of the old regime were swept away. On the 13th, the workers and soldiers of the city organized a council (soviet) of workers' deputies which first convened that evening. Now the Duma was in a difficult position; spurned by the Emperor in its requests to form a responsible ministry, it had no real power to control events, and it was unwilling to leave the country without a government, or to leave the creation of a government to the revolutionary masses. When Moscow flew the flag of revolution on March 14th it was painfully clear to all that a new government must be formed—immediately.

Nicholas, meanwhile, had left Mogilev to join his family outside the capital; his family inclinations now outweighing his *Stavka* duties, despite the pleadings of Alexiev not to put himself at such risk. The Imperial Train got only as far as Pskov, where further progress was impossible due to revolutionaries holding the tracks. There he was met by General Russki who desperately tried to persuade him to grant the Duma's wishes in order to save the Monarchy. Finally, after a telegram from Alexiev urging the same course had arrived, the *Czar* gave way; he authorized Russki to telegraph Rodzianko with the news that the Duma was to form a government no longer under his Imperial control. Typically, Nicholas missed the boat. By the time Rodzianko was able to reply, he insisted it was too late; the *Czar* must abdicate. Nicholas was stunned, then his mood turned angry, and finally he was able to calm himself. Alexiev, when informed of the new developments, began to collect opinions from all Russia's leading military men; he knew the Emperor's mind well by now. The replies were all similar. Nicholas must abdicate (most assumed his son would become Emperor). Alexiev passed the responses on to Russki, who confronted the Monarch with them. By then, Nicholas had had time to think over the matter, and he agreed to renounce the throne without further ado. Shortly thereafter, word came that the Duma was sending two representatives to witness the act of abdication. By the time they had arrived, Nicholas had changed his mind again; he would abdicate for both himself and his unhealthy son, and hand the throne to his brother, the Grand Duke Michael. Following some wrangling concerning the legality of the proposed changes, the representatives accepted the last act of the *Czar*. But back in Petrograd, Michael, upon receiving news of his sudden and unsolicited promotion, also renounced the throne, worried as he was about the consequences of trying to right the sinking ship of Monarchy. Duma members there present approved the decision and with a stroke of a pen Russia's 304-year-old Romanov dynasty was at an end. Alexiev was now supreme commander of the army, or rather what was left of it.

The ex-*Czar* left Pskov the next day, with no other desire than to be reunited with his family. As he traveled he wrote that: "All around me, there is nothing but treason, cowardice, and deceit."[169] Only recently millions of Russians had practically worshiped him, hundreds of thousands of soldiers had died for him, and millions more had suffered indescribable hardships and pain. Apparently he still could not understand that he himself may have had something to do with the reasons for fomenting such treasonous, cowardly, or deceitful behavior. At any rate, he finally arrived at the palace where his wife and children awaited him, on March 22nd, the very day the new "Provisional Government" was eagerly recognized by the British, French, Italians, and Americans. The ex-Royal Family were basically under house arrest, and would never regain their freedom of movement.

From the first, the Provisional Government was a government in name only; in reality it shared power with the soviets, of which the Petrograd Soviet of Workers and Soldiers Deputies was the most notorious. Fearful lest "privileged elements" gain control of the new regime, these groups of soldiers and workers refused to be disarmed, and therefore there was never any question of their being disbanded. And as long as they existed there was no chance that any conservative, perhaps not even any centrist government could evolve, as their leanings bent ever to the left. They would not allow the old "bourgeois" members of the Duma to appoint new ministers of whom they did not approve; Kerensky was accepted as the new Minister of Justice only because his reputation held him to be a socialist. Essentially, Russia had become a nation without laws, without authority.

Not slow to recognize the almost total lack of discipline in the new revolutionary state, ambassadors and diplomats from the *Entente* nations were properly concerned about Russian resolve to continue the war, and they began pressing for answers to questions regarding Russia's continued willingness to fight. Despite positive assurances (they generally inquired of only those who were likely to respond favorably), they remained skeptical, and balked at sending the Russians further material aid, half convinced it would never be put to good use. For their part the Russians now demanded thousands of artillery pieces and machine guns, millions of shells and rifles, and hundreds of millions of small-arms cartridges before they would agree to any new offensive moves. At bottom, the Provisional Government was ready to continue the war effort, but the Soviet was most certainly not. Since neither group could initially out-leverage the other, no one, civilian or soldier, knew exactly what the new Russia stood for. Most agreed that the Monarchy was gone for good and that they enjoyed an unprecedented amount of newfound "freedom," but freedom from what or to do what had yet to be defined.

At the front all the news was generally well-received, but it did nothing to help the war effort; to the contrary, many of the troops now assumed the war would soon be over and that there was little need for further sacrifice. Others translated "freedom" to mean they were no longer obliged to obey orders or to at least not subordinate themselves to officers that they disliked. Discipline suffered further deterioration and desertion increased. The army was beginning to disintegrate.

Fortunately for the Provisional Government, the *Alliance* was in no mood to attack that spring. There were minor German probes made north of the

Pripet on the 21st and 26th of March, and others south of the Marshes from the 12th to the 14th, and on the 27th. An Austro-German move in the Carpathians at the border of Bukovina and Moldavia gained some ground on the 23rd, then beat off the Russian attempt to regain it. A somewhat more serious effort was made on April 3rd where the German artillery specialist Colonel Bruchmüller was directed to secure capture of the Russian bridgehead at Toboly on the Stochod River, which was known to contain munitions depots. Bruchmüller directed a concentrated fire of "Green Cross" gas shells upon the enemy artillery positions and apparently effectively neutralized them, as the German infantry attack was a smashing success. The munitions depots were taken and the Russian defenders driven across the river with heavy losses. Ludendorff later wrote that he was "astonished" at the number of prisoners taken in this attack, and claimed that the Imperial Chancellor personally requested that he not play up the recent success,[170] which he took to mean that negotiations for peace must have been underway. In fact, the German government had adopted a wait-and-see attitude, and preferred to allow the Russian army to continue to disintegrate, with minimal cost to its own. Later revelations showed the battle at Toboly had cost the Russians 10,000 men in prisoners alone. Two days later, a similar gas attack was launched on a section of line in the much larger Russian bridgehead south of Riga; this time after an initial success, the Germans were beaten back. From April 6th to the 8th, the *Alliance* also made several minor assaults in Galicia and in the Carpathians, but the Russians easily held their positions. The only other combat of any consequence in April took place on the 16th and 17th of the month. On the latter occasion, the Germans probed near Zborov in Galicia; on the former it was the Russians who attempted an advance behind a cloud of poison gas near Konkary, but were stopped by enemy machine gun fire.

For the most part, the Russians were incapable of serious campaigning at that time. Of his command, General Anton Denikin observed trenches in terribly poor condition, with crumbling sidewalls. The troops could not be induced to make the necessary repairs; they were simply not inclined to do such things. He further complained that more than fifty men had been allowed to desert, while others were given leave by the soldier-elected Soviet. Others were relieved of duty to enable them to attend committee meetings at various levels, whether as delegates, or simply as observers. Often, delegations were dispatched to high-ranking officers, even to Kerensky himself, to confirm the orders they had been given. Still other soldiers terrorized physicians into granting them certificates of ill health so that they might avoid service. Thoroughly disgusted, Deniken declared that "matters were hopeless."[171] Another witness at about the same time was given a copy of printed replies by the German and Austro-Hungarian governments to the Proclamation of the Provisional Government of April 10th. The statements were conciliatory and expressed a willingness to "live in peaceful harmony and in friendship with the Russian people." She wrote of her belief that the statements were a ruse, designed to further undermine Russian army morale, already seriously eroded since the abolition of the Monarchy. It was a good thing, she recorded, "that so few (soldiers) were *gramotnie* (literate)."[172]

The Germans were indeed anxious to untie their hands in Russia at this time; the United States of America had declared war on Germany on April 6th. Yet the mood was not all bad; if the Eastern Front could be eliminated, Austria could divert all her forces to Italy, and Germany all hers to the Western Front, and *OHL* believed that victory could still be attained before the Americans could intervene effectively. They accordingly began to play every card at their disposal. German agents had maintained contact with a Russian revolutionary exile group in Switzerland, and they now informed these radicals that they would be allowed to cross German territory in order to reach Sweden, from which they might cross into Finland, an autonomous land of Russia. Terms for the transportation were secretly worked out; neither the German authorities nor the exiles could afford to allow information to be made public that they were in contact with the other. On April 9th, a special train left Swiss territory for the three-day passage across Germany during which no one aboard it was allowed any contact with anyone outside it, and vice versa. Among the thirty-two passengers was a man who had taken the name of Nicholai Lenin. By April 16th, Lenin was in Petrograd where he immediately began to confront his first task: to take control of the Soviets. A tireless, focused, and uncompromising individual who cared little for his own comfort, he could be expected to work with unequaled determination and ruthlessness to achieve his ends. And he had no use for the Provisional Government, which he immediately branded "bourgeois" and "counterrevolutionary." The Germans were content to sit back and watch the brewing pot of Russian politics, confident that it was about to boil over.

For the time being, it was Alexander Kerensky whose fortunes were rising. He was a very gifted orator who possessed the ability to win support for his ideas. But his main asset in the early days of the new government was that he was the only man in a visible position who was more or less acceptable to the Soviets, the moderates, and what few conservatives as still lingered in government. He could be most anything to anyone politically, but Russia had reached a crossroads, and would soon have to take one path or the other. The *Entente* nations continued to bombard the capital with inquiries as to whether Russia was going to continue the war or not, and if so, when she could be expected to retake the offensive. The foreigners reminded the Russians of their *Entente* obligations, they pleaded, and they threatened to discontinue all material aid, and to demand payment for that which they had already sent. Russian replies were still generally positive and reassuring, but never quite satisfactory in the minds of their inquisitors.

As the *Entente* increased the diplomatic pressure, the Russians turned to Kerensky, who was made Minister of War on May 16th. Three days later the government declared publicly that the war would continue, that it would not sign a separate peace with the *Alliance*. The Soviet did not object, but it issued its own statement in which it urged the troops to continue the struggle against "Emperors and Capitalists" and to be wary of enemy offers to fraternize. The thankless job of trying to re-inspire the soldiers at the front was left to Kerensky, with his eloquent, charismatic style. He thus embarked on several tours of the front at various points behind the lines and put his skills to the test. On the 24th, Florence Farmborough observed that she believed that the reforms instituted by Kerensky had been unsuccessful and in fact had only caused a bad situation to become even worse. Most troops were by that time completely without manners and disrespectful to everyone including, perhaps especially to, their officers. They believed, she related, that they were free to do most anything they chose to, without consequences. Kerensky, aware of the widening gap between officers and men, resolved that he could yet repair the army by appealing directly to the troops; thus began his "oratorical campaign" of influence. She goes on to write of the wild enthusiasm which greeted Kerensky wherever he went, and refers to him as a "born orator" who was trusted by the troops, who were "willing to listen to him." Only two days after this entry she was all exclamation points upon learning that Kerensky was coming to Podgaytsy, where she was temporarily stationed. The scene was described as a wide arena with soldiers closely packed onto the hillsides and personnel everywhere. Then Kerensky came into her view. Apparently he seemed unimpressive in stature, but as soon as he began speaking she "realized immediately" the reason for his prominence. "His eloquence literally hypnotized us," she remembered, when he could actually be heard above the enthusiastic cheers and applause. When he asked that they continue the war until victory, they shouted approval. When he insisted they drive the enemy from Russian soil, they heartily agreed. And when he inspired them to attack, they were frantic to begin at that very moment.[173] This spectacle was witnessed by about 12,000 troops, and it was repeated many times over the next several weeks along the front. Unfortunately for those Russians who wanted to get on with the war, the wild enthusiasm of the soldiers quickly waned once Kerensky had departed his stops, and it was soon replaced once again with apathy. General Brusilov observed that despite the obvious enthusiasm of the men in his presence, they broke every one of their promises to him once he had departed.[174]

In fact, Brusilov had already noticed that by May soldiers on all sections of the front line were beginning to definitely disobey orders, and lamented that no measures could retrieve the situation.[175] He offers no adequate explanation in his memoirs as to why he at that time and under such circumstances, accepted his appointment to replace Alexiev at *Stavka*. At the end of May 1917, he wrote, "I was appointed Supreme Commander in Chief. I accepted the post, although I realized that the war was over as far as we were concerned, for we had no means of getting the troops to fight."[176] Indeed. On the other hand, he makes no mention of the entire episode of the offensive of the Southwest Front that summer—a venture often called the Second Brusilov Offensive—and it is likely that his and all Russian officers' hands were almost completely tied by then. At any rate, General Gutor was to replace Brusilov at Southwest Front; in the event he was declared unacceptable by the Soviets and was succeeded by General Kornilov, who was better liked by the troops. The men might have had second thoughts about the newer choice however, as Kornilov was an old-school, hard-nosed disciplinarian who attempted to have the death penalty restored along Imperial lines.

At the front, most of June remained fairly quiet. Russian pilot Captain Kruten shot down an enemy airplane on the 1st, west of Tarnopol, then another on the 6th, also over Galicia. However, about a week later he himself was killed when he crashed while trying to land. Kruten was credited with seven victories, and claimed eight more unconfirmed kills.[177] On the 22nd, it was the

Alliance which drew blood in the air when two Russian balloons were destroyed near Loschina, their observers killed in the flames.[178]

At sea, the Turkish/German light cruiser *Breslau* attacked a small island in the Black Sea opposite the mouth of the Danube, and destroyed its lighthouse and communications facilities. It then laid a belt of mines, one of which sank a Russian destroyer before the month was out.

With three months now past since the Revolution in Russia, the *Entente* nations were becoming increasingly anxious for renewed military action on the Eastern Front. The United States government accordingly dispatched an eight man "Advisory Commission" headed by Senator Elihu Root and an "American Railroad Commission" under John Stevens to Petrograd, at which they arrived on June 13th. The latter was designed to lend technical assistance for the failing transportation system in Russia; the former was invested with considerable political authority to do whatever it took to keep Russia in the war. There followed a good deal of speechmaking and all the usual diplomatic niceties, but Root was no true diplomat, and had soon adopted a simple formula—"No war, no loan"[179]—for dealing with Russian duplicity. It is surely no coincidence that on June 21st the "Congress of Workmen's and Soldiers' Delegates" from the whole of the country voted confidence in the Provisional Government and *unanimously* passed a resolution calling for an early resumption of the offensive and a complete reorganization of the army. The Commission met with Brusilov at *Stavka* on the 26th, by which time Russian troops miraculously began a series of probes south of the Pripet Marshes. The long-awaited offensive was launched a few days later, but the Commission loitered around Russia for another two weeks, then departed for home; Root's last statement betrayed a certain amount of self-satisfaction when it began: "The Commission has accomplished what it came here to do."[180]

Brusilov was well aware that he was expected to attack; he had already inspected all three Fronts in the west and decided (or convinced himself) that Southwest Front—his old command—was best able to attack. This feeling may have been due to the fact that while Northwest and West Fronts faced only Germans, there were still a number of Austro-Hungarians facing Southwest Front. Then, there were two worthwhile objectives tantalizingly close to the front lines—Kovel and Lemberg. To take either of these, a feat his troops had almost performed last year, meant to disrupt terribly the enemy communications. And there was the fact that advances tended to raise army morale, while long periods of inactivity, as was at that time the case, had the opposite effect. At the very least, *Entente* anxieties might be diminished.

Accordingly, every army unit still considered reliable was to be sent into attack. There was little to work with. On June 21st Kerensky had reviewed a newly formed "Women's Battalion" consisting of all-female soldiers who, it was alleged, had taken up arms in disgust of the fact that Russia's men no longer had any will to fight. Several of these formations would eventually be raised, but few if any ever reached true battalion-level numbers. If the idea was to shame Russian men into adopting a more belligerent attitude, it can only be referred to as a bad one. Few of the female troops made effective soldiers and at any rate they were far too few and inadequately trained for their task. By July 1917, the last point in the war for which adequate records are available for the Russian army, the number of divisions at the front had fallen to 117. Romania was desperately trying to maintain 15.

The *Alliance*, on the other hand, was now using the Eastern Front as a resting place of sorts for exhausted, decimated or otherwise battered formations, as well as *Landwehr* and other second-rate troops. It could count a total of 146 divisions, of which 89 were German and 49 Austro-Hungarian, in July. Many if not most of these were of course under strength, but still far more formidable than their average Russian counterpart. And every day brought new intelligence of enemy intentions due to the increasing number of deserters who now crossed the lines unimpeded, since few Russian soldiers were willing, and few officers dared, for fear of their own lives, to fire at them.

On June 29, 1917, the soil of the province of Galicia began to tremble violently once again under the explosions of thousands of Russian artillery shells. The furious bombardment tortured the earth from the upper Strypa west of Tarnopol southward past Koniuchi and Brzezany and as far as the Narayuvka River. This latter stream rises in the hills between the Zlota Lipa and Gnila Lipa and flows north to south roughly halfway between the two until it gently bends slightly southwest and joins the Gnila Lipa a few kilometers north of Halicz, on the Dniester. The rugged, wooded hills surrounding the valley of this rather inconspicuous stream had been the scene of bitter fighting in September/October for several weeks, then again later in October for another week. It was here that Bothmer's South Army had prevented Russian breakthroughs, which had they succeeded, would have flanked the strong

Alliance defensive positions before Brzezany and Halicz. To lose those two towns was to subject Lemberg to attack, or so the Austro-Germans believed; they had placed their best units on the line here, including a Turkish Corps which enjoyed a distinguished record; Colonel Knox was aware of their worth and once wrote that they "fought with even greater ferocity than the Germans."[181]

Although conscious of the fact that they had received bloody repulses in this area before, the Russian command still considered its capture as the chance to obtain the ultimate objective of the Galician capital. The Eleventh and Seventh armies joined in the vicinity and the plan was to push forward with the best units of both, and attain a breakthrough. Following two days of lavish expenditure of shell, the Seventh struck on July 1st. An eyewitness, watching from a hilltop, described the action which began at 6:00 am with a barrage from Russian artillerymen. "Our men were advancing!" she remembered, while artillery and small-arms fire replaced the quiet of dawn. The noise, smoke, and dust, and the flashing, flaming explosions reminded her of a magnificent fireworks display. "Our offensive had begun!"[182] On a thirty kilometer (18½mi) front southeast of Brzezany, the Russian infantry stormed forward from out of their trenches. The Austro-German artillery until this time had made little reply to the enemy bombardment; now its full fury was unleashed against the attacking waves, and shattered them. Once again the waters of the Narayuvka ran red. Most Russian troops who were able to do so returned to their trenches.

Somewhat farther north, the offensive was more successful. In heavy fighting the town of Koniuchy was taken, and the stricken defenders fled to the line of the Zlota Lipa, but this too was forced in places on the following day. West of Zborov and in the vicinity of Zloczow some ground was gained and 6300 prisoners taken. Czech and Slovak troops were responsible for one-half of these. They were former Austro-Hungarian soldiers who had surrendered to the Russians and later had volunteered to fight against their former masters. Now they were some of the most reliable men in the Russian ranks. With the Zlota Lipa river line now broken both north and south of its main town, Bothmer reluctantly ordered the evacuation of Brzezany on the 3rd; new positions were taken up along the upper Narayuvka. From July 4th, the Eleventh Army began to attack in a series of uncoordinated assaults over the next several days. Its artillery had been very busy along the Stochod, and it delivered a diversionary attack on the railroad to Kovel. But the main blow was to come between Zloczow and Brody, that is, to the immediate right of Seventh Army; unfortunately the state of the chain of command, or rather lack of it, ensured that the half-hearted thrusts, lacking lateral support, never had a chance to succeed. By the 8th Eleventh Army's "attack" had turned sour. Troops ran away or hid in woods. Officers, frustrated beyond belief and hoarse from shouting orders which were routinely ignored, threw away their caps and revolvers and threw up their hands in disgust. Knox noted that the Russians were "done"; other observers were less sparing in their criticism.

Eighth Army began its drive south of the Dniester on July 6th following a heavy barrage on the lower Bistrzyca extending to beyond Stanislau to the southwest. For a few days, the attackers were successful; Jezupol was captured on the 8th, and Halicz approached. This latter town on the railroad to Lemberg had been the center of heavy fighting during the prior summer, when all efforts to wrest it from Bothmer's army had eventually ended in failure. Now, however, as the Russians closed up to the lower Lomnica, the place was seriously outflanked. As it sits on the south bank of the Dniester opposite the mouth of the Gnila Lipa, and could easily be isolated from points farther west. South Army, therefore withdrew on the 9th, the same day the Russians crossed the Lomnica and set their sights on Kalusz, a sizeable town near the edge of the Galician oilfields. Further advances claimed some villages in the Carpathian foothills, extending the fighting as far south as Zolotvin. At least the Russians were well equipped for the campaign. One writer tells us of the great abundance of machine guns, mortars, and field guns, all of which were very well munitioned. Armored car detachments were also assigned at Corps level, these consisting of British and Belgian, as well as Russian contingents.[183] Brusilov tried to provide Southwest Front with every sort of support and urged diversionary actions farther to the north, but deterioration of the army precluded any worthwhile efforts. Artillery exchanges were about all that resulted; the most energetic of these shook the front along the Stochod and around Pinsk beginning on the 7th, and there was a probe towards Vilna on the 12th, but nothing which might have occupied *Alliance* reserves ever resulted.

The last significant forward movement of the Russian army occurred on the 11th and 12th of July when Kalusz and several other villages west of the Lomnica were taken. Then the rains came, heavy, drenching downpours which soaked Volhynia on the 13th and 14th, and the area south of the Dniester for three days beginning on the 15th. Water and mud seemed to dampen whatever remained of offensive spirit amongst the soldiers of Southwest Front. But neither weather nor military fortunes—good or bad—could explain Russian behavior in the unfortunate town of Kalusz. Colonel Knox bitterly recorded that the troops who liked to consider themselves as the "freest army in the world" committed crimes that "surpassed in sheer brutality every horror of the Great War."[184] Clearly, by mid July the Russian Army was a spent force (It could be argued that it had long since been spent), and had degenerated into a condition somewhat similar to that of an armed mob.

More than a few of Russia's radicals believed that the Provisional Government had become a spent force as well. In response to the worsening conditions in old Russia, and perhaps eager to take advantage of the chaos, the National Assembly of the Ukraine (Rada) in a surprise move proclaimed an independent Republic of Ukraine in Kiev. While this crisis attracted the attention of the Petrograd government, thousands of demonstrators and strikers returned to the streets, demanding the immediate removal of all "capitalist" ministers and shouting radical slogans. Lenin, who had been working tirelessly against the Provisional Government, now urged restraint— he felt the time was not yet ripe for its overthrow. The Soviet wavered, then stopped short of advocating a new Revolution. After four days of confusion (16th-19th) the "July Days" insurrection was put down in the name of the Revolution, and with Soviet assistance. Conservative elements insisted some radical heads must roll, and Lenin wisely departed for Finland before he could be arrested. The effect of the July Days at the front was a further decline in morale and increased desertion; the effect in Petrograd was to sweep Kerensky to the head of the government as premier. Not surprisingly, two days later the All Russian Council of Workmen and Peasants Organizations addressed the nation, denouncing the mutinous spirit of the army. Such ramblings were, of course, exercises in futility, since the army now existed only in the minds of the misinformed, the naïve, or the overoptimistic.

If the Russians had become their own worst enemies, the *Alliance* was still running a close second. Well before the heavy rains, *Ober Ost* had begun to reinforce the threatened sectors in Galicia; neither the oilfields nor the capital would be lost without an all-out struggle. Kalusz was recaptured without a battle, the mere appearance of fresh forces had induced an evacuation by the Russians on the 16th. But the main counterattack was to proceed along the

Lemberg-Tarnopol railroad, which generally followed the height of land between the Dniester and Bug/Pripet watersheds. Colonel Bruchmüller was once again entrusted to provide an effective artillery preparation. All was ready by the 18th. Early the following day the guns roared on a 20 kilometer (12½mi) front. The German breakthrough was swift and deep, scattering the enemy resistance and penetrating to a depth of 15 kilometers (9½mi) on the first day. Thereafter the battle became somewhat of a rout; many Russians threw away or abandoned their weapons and ran for their lives, and for most the war was over.

There were, of course, exceptions to the rampant cowardice and desertion. Russian aviator Ensign Pisanov shot down three enemy aircraft between the 17th and the 24th, and Vasili Yanchenko, another ace, survived an encounter with eight German planes on the 20th.[185] An Englishman with Locker-Lampson's armored car contingent reported that the roads were blocked with every sort of impediment, including all sorts of military vehicles and equipment, and droves of deserters. Nevertheless, he claimed, his unit was able to force its way through the melee, amidst the billowing dust and under a scorching summer sun, to the head of the rout. Once there they blocked the road with their machines, threatened away all menacing deserters, and "dammed the tide of panic."[186]

Too late and too distant to affect events in Galicia, the other Russian Fronts launched diversionary attacks beginning on the 21st. West Front drove in a *Landwehr* division at Krevo, south of Smorgon, but the advance was short lived. Northwest Front allocated six divisions for a similar push, but only two took part, one of which "had to be forced into the line at gunpoint." The other advanced somewhat, captured two lines of German trenches, but then willingly withdrew to its original position.[187] Romanian Front was last off the mark on the 23rd and assaulted the lines between Focsani and the Hungarian frontier. Some ground was gained when the Austrians were forced back to the Putna River, but the Russian command stopped the action after a few days fighting, citing lack of reserves with which to exploit a breakthrough. Some Romanian units, bitterly disappointed with Russian half-heartedness when they had a chance to reconquer lost soil, fought on. Even unsupported, they were able to advance against the Austrians, whose fighting power according to Ludendorff "showed a dimunition which was in the highest degree alarming."[188]

All the while, the German offensive in Galicia continued to roll. Over the Strypa by the 21st, they began to anticipate the capture of Tarnopol, which had been under uninterrupted Russian occupation since the 1914 campaign. The city came under shellfire a day later by heavy guns, and when resistance seemed to harden along the line of the Seret River, on which the Tarnopol sits, Colonel Bruchmüller was at hand to prepare another gas attack with which he had broken so many defensive positions. Heavy fighting raged for three days, with the German *Kaiser* present as an eager witness. The Russians fought well for this stage of the war, rallying around armored-car detachments, and for once making good use of the respirators against the German "Green Cross" agents; in the end they slowly gave way, abandoning the Seret line. Tarnopol was evacuated on the 24th and reoccupied by the *Alliance* the next day. Without hardly a pause, the soldiers moved on to the east towards the river Zbruch on the Galician frontier.

Farther south, the Russian left had begun a steady, if slow, retreat. The positions around Halicz and on the Narayuvka River, for which so much blood had been shed over the last eleven months, were abandoned on July 22nd. Stanislau changed hands by the 24th, as did Nadworna. A day later it was Buczacz and Delatyn. At Tlumach on the 25th Nurse Farmborough recorded one scene within the massive retreat. She described a hectic determination on the part of the Russians to retire eastwards under whatever circumstances, "no matter what the injury to man, horse, or cart." Deserters passing by made derogatory remarks intended for female ears, and she was distressed that for the first time in three years of war, matters had come to such humiliation.[189] Such scenes were commonplace, and the pace of the frantic retreat was dictated by the speed at which the *Alliance* was able to advance. No serious effort was made to defend Bukovina; Kolomea was lost on the 26th, and Austrian troops forced the Cheremosh River both north and south of Kuty, prompting its abandonment on the 28th. In the Carpathian foothills, the upper reaches of the Seret, Suczawa, and Moldova were overrun and only the presence of Romanian troops in the mountains to the south prevented the entire line in Moldavia from becoming completely unhinged and the whole province lost. Nothing, of course, could now forestall an Austro-German capture of Czernowitz, far and away the most important prize of Bukovina or east Galicia. Once it had changed hands again, during the night of August 2nd/3rd, the attackers stopped the pursuit of the fleeing Russians. The capture of Kimpolung on the 3rd pretty much completed the reconquest of Bukovina, and eastward advance was halted in favor of a push into Romania.

Following the entry into Tarnopol, German troops had driven on to the Zbruch. This border stream was crossed in several places during the last several days of July, but no further advance into Podolia was ordered. It is likely that the men at *Ober-Ost* were satisfied with having cleared all of Austrian territory, and desired no new drive into Russian lands with all the transportation problems involved; at any rate their offensive had run out of momentum, and would require new reinforcement to get it going again. This was about the last thing *OHL* was likely to sanction, but Ludendorff did inquire of Hoffmann the feasibility of taking Riga before cold weather, and Bruchmüller was accordingly sent north to plan to work his magic in that sector.

On the Russian side, heads were bound to roll, despite the fact that the advanced degeneration of the army meant that few, if any, commanders possessed any real control of their troops, and therefore could hardly be blamed for the catastrophic events of the latter half of July. Although some 38,000 enemy troops had been made prisoner, over 200 artillery pieces captured, and perhaps 60,000 casualties inflicted on the enemy during the summer offensive, its subsequent collapse and the general rout which followed dictated new command changes, as if, at that stage of the war, it really mattered who held this or that title. Kerensky called a conference at *Stavka* on July 29th ostensibly to discuss how discipline in the army might be restored. Armed with alarming reports such as a communiqué from the 25th which read "On the Dvinsk front whole divisions, without attack by the enemy, left their trenches and some sections refused to obey commands,"[190] he had probably already made up his mind to promote Kornilov, who was the foremost proponent of cracking down on indiscipline of anyone in advanced command. And this at a time when Colonel Knox was writing about the simultaneous military and economic crisis. All semblance of order and restraint had vanished, and the mobs, both military and civilian, were beginning to demand conditions or wages which were absolutely unrealistic and impossible to secure. Anyone in a position of authority who showed the slightest resistance to this anarchy was in danger of being murdered. Farmers refused to sell their produce, claiming, quite correctly, that all paper currency had lost any value. The larger estates had ceased to be productive, as the aristocrats who had run them had been driven off, forced to flee for their lives. And the railroads were barely functioning. By August of 1917, he wrote, more than one-fourth of all engines and about one-twelfth of the rail cars were broken down, as compared with figures of about one-sixth and one-thirty third, respectively, from August of the previous year. He made it clear that despite the shortcomings of the Imperial government, he had nothing but contempt for that which replaced it.[191] Kornilov was appointed Commander in Chief two days later (July 31st); there was a host of other changes as well, none of which could possibly alter the state of affairs on the Eastern Front or on the home front.

With summer waning and the Provisional Government apparently unwilling to seek a negotiated peace, the possibility of having to face another winter in the East began to nag at the minds of the commanders of the *Alliance* forces. It was believed that at two areas along the front, positions could be considerably improved before the onset of cold weather, or before the demands of other theaters reduced troop levels deployed against the ineffective Russians. In the north, Riga and Dvinsk remained unconquered, as had been the case a year previously. And one mountainous sector of line remained, in western Moldavia. Ludendorff directed a diversion of troop strength from the area of the recently successful counteroffensive in Galicia to the Riga bridgehead vicinity. Since no fresh reserves were available for the mountains, he decided to send Mackensen's group—which had been spared the worst of the summer fighting—into an attack designed to shove the Romanians and Russians out of the Carpathians and into the less difficult plains beyond.

The Moldavian operation kicked off on August 6th in the valley of the Susitza River north of Focsani, while the Austrians pushed eastward in the dale of the Trotus. Both forces made some initial progress; the rail towns of Marasesti and Okna were pressed upon, the Germans coming to within 3 kilometers of the former. Then, Russo-Romanian resistance hardened to a level greater than what the soldiers of the *Alliance* had become accustomed to, and the advance slowed, and faltered. Energetic counterattacks began on the 12th, and the combat shifted to and fro with both sides acquitting themselves well. Mackensen threw considerable reserves into the fray and the Romanians of First and Second Armies fought desperately to hold the line; the town of Marasesti became something of a Romanian Verdun and is remembered as such. In the end, after a final push on the 19th, the Germans were denied victory, but the cost was too high for the defenders; they now could only draw replacements from one-third of their original base, and it was insufficient. Despite a local success in the Trotus valley, where some 10 kilometers were recovered in mid-month, the army began to decline in numbers. On the right of Second Army, the Russian Fourth began to disintegrate as soldiers deserted in droves. It was just as well for both sides that after August 20th, the fighting began to die away. Thereafter, the "Romanian Front" became a backwater of the war.

At the other end of the front, the Germans were far more serious about a local offensive. Of the two potential targets, Riga and Dvinsk, the former was selected without much debate. It was the larger of the two cities, and was an important port at a strategic location at the mouth of the Dvina on the southernmost tip of the Gulf, and had a substantial German population. Its capture would unhinge the northern section of the Eastern Front, provide a good base for German naval activity in the Baltic, and ensure decent winter quarters for General Oskar von Hutier's Eighth Army, as well as depriving the Russians of such benefits; beyond the city there was no natural defensive position south of Lakes Peipus and Vyrts. *Ober Ost* provided the reinforcement, and Hutier and Bruchmüller began to plan the operation, fully mindful of the many prior unsuccessful bids for the city. Both came up with plans calling for new tactics, and the coming battle would put these new ideas to the test.

Probing began as early as August 22nd, and initiated a series of minor actions which lasted for eight days, after which the Germans reported to have pushed forward to points along the Gulf and the river Aa. In the tense atmosphere of the city, which had often been attacked, bombed, and shelled, the revolutionary attitude of the defending troops was fertile grounds for an undercurrent of rumors which swirled about, frightening and demoralizing soldier and civilian alike. Then on the 31st, German warships steamed into the Gulf while aircraft bombed Russian naval and air facilities on the islands therein. Thousands of mutinous men and deserters who lurked in Riga became extremely agitated; the populace braced for trouble and feared for the morrow.

Early on the morning of September 1, 1917, as though the ripping of a calendar page could cause an atmospheric disturbance, Hutier unleashed Eighth Army. Bruchmüller had concealed 750 medium and heavy artillery pieces and 550 *Minenwerfer* on the wooded, south bank of the Dvina, and these began a drum roll of fire at 4:00am. His plans called for 75% gas and 25% high explosive[192] shells—some 116,400 and 38,800 respectively—to rain down upon Russian infantry, artillery, and command and communications posts, shifting about from sector to sector, mixing the shells and varying the trajectories. After over five hours of this pulverizing hail of intense bombardment, Hutier's infantry moved forward using new tactics of infiltration. Rather than attacking strong defenses with waves of flesh and blood, small groups of men would carefully probe the enemy line, slipping through the weak spots and subsequently taking the strongholds from the rear.[193] Against the bridgehead, these tactics were immediately successful, but crossing the near-kilometer-wide Dvina was another matter. Boats were used on both sides of Uxküll; these made the seizure of the mid-stream islands possible by 9:30am. Engineers began to throw pontoon bridges to these, and despite some losses to Russian small arms fire, they had several usable bridges in place by the day's end. Next day was spent mopping up the bridgehead west and south of the city, and in building up the Uxküll force for a drive along the north bank of the river. Submarines in the Gulf surfaced and shelled the coast road. The Russian Twelfth Army hastily prepared to evacuate the city; what troops as were still behaving like soldiers destroyed the railway stations and arsenals, and finally on the morning of the 3rd, the Dvina bridges. There followed an inevitable period of several hours characterized by looting and anarchy before German troops arrived in the evening. Riga, which had been owned by Poland, Sweden and Russia since its loss by the Teutonic Knights in 1561, had after three days of fighting, become German again.

As Russian resistance melted away, Hutier decided to pursue the fleeing enemy, who crossed the Livonian Aa[194] on the 4th, and marched up the coast road towards Estonia. German warships in the Gulf shelled coastal towns and upset this exodus. Dünamünde, the actual port facility, was captured with all of its heavy coastal artillery the same day, and an advance along the railroad to Pskov was begun. By September 8th Eighth Army vanguards had reached Sigulda and were well over the lower Aa, but it was the extent of the attackers' momentum. Some loyal Russian units, including a woman's "Death Battalion" counterattacked on the 9th, and for the next several days the Germans were stopped and the Russians regained slight amounts of real estate. As if to herald the end of the offensive, Berlin announced the captures of the whole affair: 9,000 prisoners, 325 guns, and "several" trains loaded with foodstuffs and military equipment. Also taken were a number of armored cars. The relatively small number of prisoners, it claimed, was due to the fact that most enemy troops had simply run away.

Embarrassed by the loss of Riga, and completely fed up with the indiscipline of Russian troops who in some cases were now beginning to murder their officers, Commander-in-Chief Kornilov, who had long been advocating a restoration of the death penalty, and who had several times been officially denied the wish, had reached the end of his tether. Perhaps he sensed that he was about to be dismissed, or that the hour for action was now or never. At any rate, he had been gathering what he considered to be absolutely reliable units and forming a special army outside the capital of Petrograd. When questioned about this force, he claimed it was to defend the city against a German attack, but Kerensky was unconvinced, then became alarmed when he was informed that Kornilov was tired of his (Kerensky's) catering to the extreme leftist revolutionaries, who had become known as the Bolsheviks. Kerensky was, of course, walking somewhat of a tightrope between the conservative elements (such as Kornilov) and the Bolsheviks, who were gradually taking control of the Soviets. To appease one meant to offend the other. But Kornilov had had enough of such duplicity, and determined to smash the Bolsheviks, while there was still time. On the 7th of September, he waved his Petrograd force towards the city. Kerensky believed, with some good reason, that the move was directed against him, that is, the weak Provisional Government which had no choice but to tolerate the leftists. With no real forces of his own, Kerensky was forced to appeal to the Soviets to stop Kornilov whom he now branded as a traitor, and whom he ordered to surrender the post of Supreme Commander. But Kerensky need not have worried; the "Kornilov rebellion" never came to pass. The "reliable" troops who were to sweep away the revolutionaries were themselves swept away by them; most willingly switched sides without any semblance of violence. The net result of the whole affair, which occupied the interest of most Russians for a few days, was that the Soviets became bolder and more militant, denouncing anyone who disagreed with them as a "counterrevolutionary." Kornilov himself surrendered in the suburbs of Petrograd on the 14th. Thereafter, Kerensky assumed the position of Commander-in-Chief, with Alexiev as his Chief of Staff. He now disposed of near-dictatorial power, yet he had done nothing to raise his esteem in the eyes and minds of the Bolsheviks. To the contrary, the latter, who had obtained arms when the Soviets had been issued weapons from the Petrograd arsenals with which to stop Kornilov, now considered themselves the real power in the country. Lenin, who still dared not return from

Finland, offered a new slogan which easily gained popularity: "All power to the Soviets!" Kerensky, desperate to be taken seriously, declared Russia a republic on September 14th. The truth was that Russia had succumbed to anarchy.

Nevertheless, the war continued, at least officially. On the 10th there was action of a minor sort at Husiatyn, on the Zbruch, which continued sporadically for several days. Russian ace Kazakov shot down an Austrian during these encounters. On the 11th, a local Russian attack gained some Austrian trenches near Solka in Bukovina; on the same day ace Jindra was shot down for the third time. Fortunately for the Austrian captain he was able to land, near Kimpolung, and would live to fly again. Jindra survived the war. September 21st witnessed another German bombardment around Jacobstadt, halfway between Riga and Dvinsk. Following a morning-long barrage, German infantry attacked in earnest and effected a capture of the town, an outcome which had eluded them for two years. Fifty-five guns and considerable foodstuffs were taken, but few prisoners, as was becoming the norm. Two days later a renewed Russian effort north of Riga pushed the Germans back slightly, to about 11 kilometers south of Sigulda. In the Gulf, a Russian destroyer was mined and sunk off Oesel Island. The mine had been laid by aircraft; one historian considers the event as probably the first instance of successful aerial mining in warfare.[195]

As September turned to October, Russia's Provisional Government was practically paralyzed. All infrastructure in the nation had broken down and there seemed neither the ability nor the will to effect repairs. All levels of authority had vanished, and events were dictated by the whims of mobs, who in turn were swayed by agitators and rabble-rousers. If the army still existed it was due to the desires of the soldiers to remain where food, clothing, and shelter could be attained without effort, an existence not available elsewhere, especially in Russia's cities, where anarchy reigned. Most soldiers would fight the enemy now only if attacked, so as not to be dislodged from their accommodations; they might be willing to listen to an officer's "suggestions," but they more often than not had no intention of following orders that they disliked. Soldiers' committees were the real decision-makers now, but they often lacked the will to enforce their decisions, if challenged. Army Intelligence reports for October revealed the awful reality of it all. Northwest Front reported the alarming increase in the influence of Bolshevik ideas; many soldiers believed that all behavior was now beyond punishment. Peace at any price is now desired. From West Front: Defeatism, insubordination, and fraternization are widespread. Southwest Front: The army is disintegrating. Peace at any price the dominant theme. Every order is met with hostility.[196] The Romanian and Caucasus (against Turkey) Fronts described similar conditions.

Behind Russian lines the situation was even worse. On October 1st, at Gomel, 8,000 troops bound for the front as replacements, refused to proceed and demanded to be sent home. On the 3rd, a mob of soldiers destroyed the courthouse of Dubno, and roughed up members of the jury and court when one of their own had been condemned for disorderly behavior.[197] A week later another group of soldiers arrested several generals at Berdichev and sent them to the rear as prisoners. Because no passenger car was at hand, they were thrown into a freight car. Podolia province reported widespread theft by soldiers of food, horses, and oxen. Prolonged drunken and disorderly conduct by soldiers and sailors in Feodosia, a naval base in the Crimea, led to a state of siege being declared in the unhappy city on the 26th. Meanwhile, beginning in mid September, food riots had broken out in a dozen or more major cities. At the same time, peasants attacked estates of the larger landowners, intending to divide up the land among themselves. They also robbed and pillaged across the countryside; dozens of such incidents were reported by November 1st. Burning of estate homes was widespread, forests were often set on fire, and even food, in this time of famine in the cities, was not immune from destruction. At Voronezh, more than 60,000 puds of wheat and grain were sent up in flames.[198] Although moderate socialists had gained a majority in Kerensky's newest coalition government on October 8th, the constant debating and resolution passing could effect no noticeable change for the average Russian. The country was unwilling and unable to continue the war, yet only the Bolsheviks were demanding immediate peace. By refusing to admit that Russia could not go on, the Provisional Government ensured its own downfall. Clearly, major change was on the horizon.

Although the German command had planned no new offensive action in the East for 1917, it did not fail to notice what was occurring across the front lines. The counteroffensive in Galicia and the attack on Riga had gone well enough, but the continuing refusal of the Russians to sign a separate peace troubled all of the *Alliance* nations; they were certainly not immune from internal disorders themselves, and with the war now in its fourth year, it could only be a question of time before they too would be unable to control the growing unrest brought about by the war. The conflict would have to be won soon, or it probably could not be won at all. Accordingly, one more blow was to be directed against the enemy in the east before the onset of winter. Ludendorff is notoriously silent about the reasoning for this operation, which he only stated was aimed at Petrograd, and implied that morale would be raised in the ever-restless navy by employing at least part of it as well. But the navy would necessarily have had to have been used in any Petrograd operation anyway, since the main naval base for the Russian Baltic Fleet was at nearby Kronstadt, and a drive through Livonia, Estonia, and Ingermanland would seem to have been much more direct than that which was eventually launched. Most likely it was probably the best Ludendorff could manage, given the scarcity of resources. In the event, he withdrew only one division plus one brigade from the West for the new assault.

The idea was to take control of the large islands off the Estonian coast thus securing the Gulf of Riga for German shipping and bottling up the Russian Baltic Fleet in the Gulf of Finland. Vital iron ore shipments from Sweden would be thus secured, and the whole scheme of things in the Baltic would be heavily weighted in favor of Germany. Code named *Albion*, the operation was ordered on September 18th, once the capture of Riga had improved the military situation at the southern end of the Gulf. Major naval forces were made available from the High Seas Fleet, including about ten battleships and several cruisers; also sent were all the destroyers, submarines, torpedo boats, minesweeps and other assorted support vessels that could be spared from other theaters. All told, the massive effort floated more than 300 ships of all types and disposed of well over 100 aircraft.[199] General Hutier was in overall command, while General von Kathen exercised direct control of the one and one-half division strong landing forces. This mixed group was to be put ashore on the northwest coast of Oesel, the largest and most populous island of the target area.

Extending southward from Oesel is a 30-kilometer-long peninsula, which blocks half of the channel between the northern tip of Courland and the main mass of island. At the southern tip of this neck of land the Russians had placed powerful naval guns capable of defending the narrow Irben Strait, the main access to the gulf. These weapons, mounted near the only town in the area—Zerel—became the targets of the first actions of the campaign when German aircraft attacked on September 30th and caused considerable damage. Air activity was continued until the campaign concluded with certain days, such as October 10th, noteworthy for the large number of sorties flown. The German fleet steamed from Libau on the 11th, and on the following morning German troops put ashore at Tagga Bay and Pamerort on Oesel. These landings were successful, though local Russian naval forces acquitted themselves well against the far superior attackers. By the evening of the 13th, Arensburg, the principal town on the island, had been captured. The Sworbe Peninsula was cut off the following day, while many of the island's defenders began to surrender. Zerel itself hung on for another day, then was evacuated by sea after its garrison had destroyed the gun batteries. Now all but the northeast corner of the island was in German hands; what was left of the defenders began to flee over the narrow causeway connecting to Moon Island. But Moon too was soon under direct attack and its land defense was half-hearted at best. By the 19th it too had been occupied by the Germans, who claimed 5000 prisoners for both Oesel and Moon. The last remaining island of importance, Dagö, was assaulted by a landing on the 17th; that same day the German navy scored the biggest victory of the campaign when the Russian battleship *Slava* was sunk. Following the loss of this warship, the Russian navy began to withdraw into the Gulf of Finland, as the stronger German fleet closed in for the kill. Then, on the 19th, the German Admiralty ordered operations among the islands to cease and the battleships to return to Germany. The naval score: A Russian battleship, a destroyer, and a submarine lost and several ships damaged; for the Germans: twelve vessels, the largest of which was a destroyer, and many ships damaged.

Operation *Albion* came to an end on October 20th, when Dagö island was declared secured. The affair had been a complete German success, the naval imbalance notwithstanding. Its effect on the Russians was that which had been desired, somewhat of a panic in Petrograd, a city that needed no additional worries. Fearing a German approach, the Government was transferred to Moscow on the 19th and Kerensky left for the front at the same time. He might have saved himself the trouble. Despite a German raid on the mainland coast of Estonia and a German naval bombardment of the same over the next few days, *Alliance* offensive moves against Russia were all but over for a time. Russia's capacity to resist was, however, gone for good, at least as would concern Kerensky. Hammered by defeat after defeat, the record of the

Provisional Government in the war was considerably worse than that of the old Imperial government, and like its predecessor it could not long survive with such a record.

Russian Final Offensives, Summer 1917

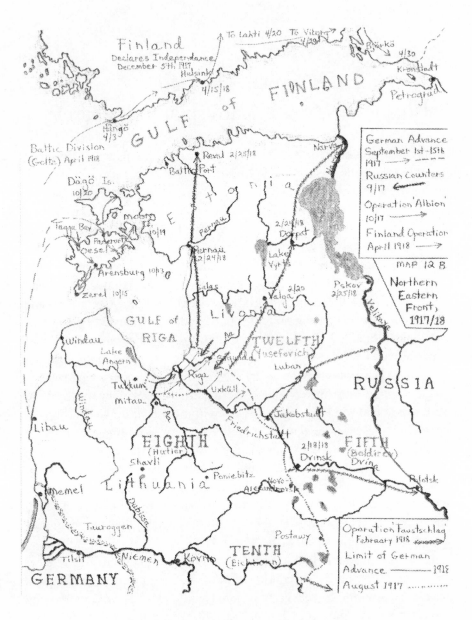

Northern Eastern Front, 1917-1918

Chapter Thirteen
Bolsheviks, Brest-Litovsk and Bucharest

The last two months of the year 1917 were marked by a conspicuous absence of combat along the Eastern Front. Russian troops, though no one could say how many, were still encamped in the trenches and dugouts. Everyone now knew, or should have known, that they would no longer attack and would probably run away if attacked, that is, that their fighting power was nil. The Romanian army had declined to 13 divisions as a result of the summer battles and subsequent regrouping; without a population base of much depth, it could not hope to expand. For the *Alliance* victory seemed achievable, indeed already won if only the enemy would acknowledge his defeat. But on the home front, it too was wavering, and all four members, exhausted by years of incredible military effort, needed desperately to conclude peace, lest they be overwhelmed by the resource-rich *Entente*. Germany still maintained 83 divisions in December, but 13 were to be transferred by year's end. Austria-Hungary's commitment had fallen to 42, the lowest level of the war, and one more would leave in December. Turkey withdrew its last two divisions in November; these were urgently required elsewhere, as Ottoman Army roles had shrunken to alarming new lows. Bulgaria still fielded three divisions on the lower Danube, no doubt in order to enjoy a louder voice at the final allocation of the spoils of war. Therefore 128 *Alliance* divisions now faced an unknown, but certainly smaller, number of *Entente* divisions, the fighting value of which was suspect, to put it mildly. If there was to be any negotiating, the position of strength would certainly go to the *Alliance*.

Kerensky, of course, had staked his entire political position on a policy of not negotiating, that is, of continuation of the war at any price. He was therefore becoming increasingly isolated as the months wore on, and by November he retained very few political allies, yet faced a growing and strengthening anti-war movement. On November 1st, an enemy naval move in the Black Sea led to action by the Russian Fleet to forestall it, but before the warships could fire a shot, Russian sailors flatly refused to go into combat. The fleet was obliged to return to port. The army too, as we have seen, was all but paralyzed; even non-combatants were routinely insisting that the war be brought to an end. For example, the staff of a mobile medical unit informed its doctors on November 9th that all it wanted for the present was peace. "We must have peace quickly," they claimed. "Perhaps the English and French can continue for another 15 years, but we Russians cannot." "Russia must have peace," they parroted, "Peace, Peace above all else. Peace now."[200] This obscure conversation, which took place in Moldavia, was one of thousands, probably millions, which were audible all along the line at that time. Soviets had been set up in every major population center—and many minor ones—by now, as well as in virtually every army unit. More and more of these groups were voting to transfer "All power to the Soviets" and were willing to resort to violence to see the deed accomplished. Members of the provisional government, aware that what little authority they possessed was rapidly evaporating, decided that they had no choice but to confront the Bolsheviks, who now controlled many of the Soviets, or at least the more powerful ones. Kerensky himself ordered the Bolshevik press suppressed and some key militant individuals arrested, and this act was really the spark which ignited the flames of Revolution.

In the early days of November, a Russian infantry division on the Northwest Front was ordered to relieve another. Its troops refused, whereupon the men of the tired division simply left their trenches for the rear. Neither pleas nor threats could alter the behavior of the soldiers of either unit; most "front line" troops were in fact far behind the lines by now, scouring the countryside for whatever loot was to be had. The local population naturally suffered as a result of the inevitable excesses; on November 6th a delegation of Baltic people petitioned Hindenburg to bring the remainder of Livonia and Estonia under German occupation so as to suppress the anarchic conditions there.

Behind the West Front, soldiers marauded at will and there was no authority willing or able to stop them. As early as the previous summer the Provisional Government had, according to Bolshevik accounts, detained hundreds of revolutionary agitators at the front and sent them to Minsk, where apparently the prison was so overcrowded that "guardrooms, several army barracks, and even the Girl's High School"[201] of the Bylorussian capital were filled with troops. When the city came under the control of the Minsk Soviet in late October, these and large numbers of other "political prisoners" were amnestied, and their effect upon the already chaotic conditions prevailing in area directly behind the battle line can only be imagined.

At Southwest Front, the commander of the Eleventh Army reported on November 2nd that his 5th Army Corps was restive and becoming increasingly prone to Bolshevik ideas. One unit of the 32nd Corps supported a Bolshevik resolution condemning the use of front-line troops to restore order in the cities. "Bolshevik temper among units of the Corps is growing."[202] Even the more remote Romanian Front had not escaped this infection of indiscipline. Near Jassy, the following scene was recorded. A young Russian soldier asked an older Romanian why he had not gone home; when the answer came that he had not received permission to do so, the Russian retorted that "Permission" was no longer necessary. Declaring that all soldiers were now free men, he went on to say that since the soldiers had not begun the war, they should not have to fight it.[203] It was just one example of the attitude which prevailed among the Russian troops at this stage of the war.

Despite the fact that the vast majority of Russian troops were no longer willing to risk their lives in combat, there were still some who had not lost the will to fight. Airmen, for instance, less vulnerable to the pressures of mob rule, continued to serve, as long as peace had not been declared. Ace Captain Smirnov, with ten victories to his credit, shot down yet another enemy airplane near Husyatin on the Zbruch on November 23rd. A few days later, he was forced to leave his unit, having been forewarned that all officers were about to be shot.[204] Another pilot and ace, Grigori Suk, made his last flight on the 28th; he was killed in combat over Moldavia. On November 11th, the elements of the Russian Second Army repulsed a local German gas attack supported by an estimated 150 guns at Nesvizh, east of Baranovichi. About 1,500 casualties[205] were incurred, but the successful defense was pointed to by the Bolsheviks to attempt to disprove the increasing number of accusations against them regarding wholesale desertion from the front lines. Both they and their political opponents were constantly claiming that the other was in league with the enemy. Since most Russian troops were by now refusing to fight even if attacked, the Nesvizh case would seem to be somewhat of an analogy; in fact it was not. Revolutionaries had convinced the soldiers that the Germans had attacked in an attempt to break up a divisional "Congress" taking place at that time, and most troops would defend their Revolution. At any rate it was certainly not in the best interests of the German cause for *Alliance* attacks to provoke vigorous resistance at this stage of the war. Ludendorff's policy of allowing political discord to weaken his eastern opponent was beginning to pay off and his decision to enable Lenin to return to Russia was about to yield a substantial dividend.

Most of the news in the East for November concerned the fall of the Provisional Government and the advent of the Bolshevik regime. It is not our purpose here to follow the course of the second Russian Revolution within the year, but a brief chronology of events is useful for the narrative. Kerensky, as we have seen, walked a precarious political tightrope, especially since the "July Days" disturbances. He was mistrusted by Left and Right alike and never possessed any real authority which might be enforced with any armed strength beyond city police. His determination to keep Russia in the war had not much helped the *Entente*, but it did cause his increasing unpopularity as time went on. His position had eroded so badly by November that the Bolshevik leaders became convinced that their time to strike had come. The trouble began when the Soviets, almost completely now under the influence of the Bolsheviks, called for a "Petrograd Soviet Day" to serve as a review of the growing strength of striking workers and mutinous soldiers. Huge mass meetings were held in factories and military facilities. A good portion of the sailors of the Baltic Fleet were also involved, and soon the mass strike turned into a mass movement designed to seize control of the city. On the third day of the mass unrest, the government began to take measures to prevent an all-out Revolution; Cadets, Cossacks, Death Battalions and Police were all employed in a desperate attempt to stem the rising tide. A few available armored car units were even brought into the city to defend key points. Then the garrison of the fortress of the Saints Peter and Paul went over to the insurgents at the same time Red Guards—fanatic Bolshevik soldiers—beat back an armored car unit and captured some of the vehicles. That evening, November 6th, Lenin returned; he had sent word to begin armed rebellion earlier that day.

The critical day of the whole affair was the 7th, which began with a brazen declaration by the Petrograd Military Revolutionary Committee—written by Lenin—announcing the overthrow of the Provisional Government. It was intended to be a *fait accompli*, and in the event, it was effective. One by one, elements of the government infrastructure were occupied by Red Guards; the

Post Office, Telegraph and Telephone Offices and State Bank were all in Bolshevik hands by late afternoon. Overnight, revolutionary soldiers and sailors and other Red Guard units, assisted by the heavy guns of the cruiser *Aurora*, attacked the old Imperial Winter Palace, which was being used for the offices of the dying government. Following a brief, feeble resistance made mostly by adolescents and women, the huge structure was captured and ministers of the Provisional Government arrested. Kerensky, who had fled the capital earlier that day, was meanwhile trying desperately to employ any available anti-Bolshevik military unit to suppress the revolutionists while there was still time, but precious hours, even days were lost as he waited for replies to his dispatches which came back, for the most part, with unsatisfactory responses. Most units were unwilling, some unable, to move toward Petrograd. Those that did begin to move usually dispersed, deserted, or simply refused to proceed, after a few hours had elapsed. Every Front along the battle line was appealed to; only the remote Caucasus Front indicated that it controlled troops willing to restore the situation in the capital. Considering its distance from Petrograd this information was useless. With time running out for his political fortunes, Kerensky finally managed to collect a small force of mostly Cossacks and a few armored cars at Gatchina, a rail junction not far south of the capital and ordered its commander, General Krasnov, to fight his way into the city. The actual size of this force cannot be exactly determined, though it cannot have been very large; Bolshevik accounts first claimed it was only a few hundred strong, then later stated it was 5,000 or so. At any rate, it swept aside a few ill-disciplined units of revolutionary workers, mixed with a few soldiers, and advanced nearly halfway to the city before Red Guard units, reinforced with armored cars and armored trains stopped it on November 11th. On the same day the last of the anti-Bolshevik resistance in Petrograd was suppressed. Then the "loyal" troops began to desert to the side of the revolutionaries. A last, listless engagement was "fought" on the 13th in the hills around Pulkovo, after which Krasnov's men had either switched sides or begun a headlong flight to parts unknown. Soviet troops recaptured Gatchina the following day and arrested Krasnov and Kerensky's staff. The last hopes of anti-Bolshevik politicians were dashed. Kerensky, once again, managed to disappear, but his power and influence were gone for good.

Once the Red Revolution had triumphed in Petrograd, other Russian cities began to embrace a Soviet government and over the next several weeks all the major population centers of the old Russian Empire thus came under control of the new regime. Moscow was a tough nut for the Bolsheviks to crack and only submitted after a good deal of fighting and the capture of the Kremlin on the 16th, three days after representatives of seven field armies[206] had notified the new government of their full support. Although much of the country, along with the armed forces, was easy enough for Lenin and his followers to secure, there were exceptions and some of these would prove difficult to deal with for some time to come. The best example is the Ukraine which declared its independence on November 20th, less than two weeks after the fall of the old government, and long before the new one could consolidate its hold on the far-flung lands of the old Empire.

For Lenin, the number one priority was to remove Russia from the war. As early as the 9th he had authorized radio messages to be transmitted to all of the belligerent powers, proposing a three-month armistice to be arranged as soon as possible. He also contacted General Dukhonin, now the senior officer at *Stavka*, ordering him to initiate contact with the commanders of the enemy armies, for the purpose of finding a way to open peace negotiations. Dukhonin did not reply; three days later telephone contact was restored and Lenin inquired of the general whether or not he intended to obey instructions. Dukhonin's reply was unsatisfactory for the new head of government, and he was accordingly dismissed and replaced by the Bolshevik "Commissary of War," Ensign Krylenko. The Russian armed forces were now under the command of an erstwhile junior officer. But Dukhonin stubbornly refused to accept the new arrangements and remained at Mogilev, surrounding himself with loyal troops. He arranged for the "release" of General Kornilov and a 20-man entourage from Bykhov Prison, some 20 kilometers distant, an action which infuriated the Bolsheviks, who were now determined to arrest him. Dukhonin chose not to flee with Kornilov and the others; it was a decision he would soon regret when on December 3rd, Bolshevik troops entered Mogilev and his "loyal" soldiers disappeared. Despite protests from the cooler heads among them, the disorderly revolutionaries dragged Dukhonin from his quarters and murdered him. Kornilov, ever the survivor, escaped into the countryside on horseback.

General Headquarters was dissolved; its remaining personnel had either fled with Kornilov or stayed and embraced the new Revolution. As for the new Commander-in-Chief, one of his first official acts was to authorize fraternization with the enemy (he believed he could help bring about peace in this manner). Two days later, on November 23rd, he announced that a gradual demobilization of the army would henceforth proceed. It was for Trotsky, however, the new "Peoples Commissar for Foreign Affairs," to dictate policy towards the men of the foreign armies on the Eastern Front, and on the 26th, he formally called for an armistice with the *Alliance*. For German Colonel Hoffmann, Chief of Staff at *Ober-Ost*, the appeal was the godsend he had been waiting for. He quickly obtained Ludendorff's permission to proceed; on November 28th a Russian delegation crossed German lines under a flag of truce. Subsequent discussion fixed peace negotiations to begin on December 2nd at Brest-Litovsk, behind German lines. All hostilities were to cease at that time.

Representatives of all four *Alliance* powers were duly sent to meet the Russian delegation. Hoffman later recalled that Prince Leopold (C. in C. *Ober-Ost*) had "entrusted" him with the direction of the negotiations. The tall, stiff, cool-headed Prussian, who spoke perfect Russian, was an excellent choice for the one side; Joffe dominated the personalities on the other, who included Trotsky's relative Kamenev, an industrial worker, an agricultural worker, a sailor and an army N.C.O., and a certain Madam Byzenko, whose claim to fame was the alleged murder of a government Minister.[207]

Considering the Russian military position at this time, its delegation made some heavy demands upon the *Alliance*, insisting that the Germans withdraw from the Baltic Islands so recently conquered, that no *Alliance* troops currently on the Eastern Front be sent elsewhere, that Bolshevik propaganda be allowed free admission into Germany, and that all the nations at war join the armistice and sit down to work out a general peace. Hoffmann politely refused these demands; he knew he spoke from a stronger position, and he realized early on that what the Russians were attempting to achieve was universal revolution. With no diplomatic training, Hoffmann played his part well, but he hardly needed consummate skills considering the plight of his opposite numbers. Finland, following the example of the Ukraine, declared its independence on December 5th. The Baltic Germans made another desperate appeal to Berlin for German protection at about the same time, and a Romanian delegation joined the Russians at Brest before the talks were a week old. With the Ukrainians claiming independence, Russian troops of the Southwest Front had been cut off from those of the two more northerly Fronts. And with the

Romanians talking peace, the troops of Romanian Front faced the possibility of being interned on foreign soil. Eventually the patient and confident manner of Hoffmann enabled a temporary agreement to be arrived at. On the 15th, a 28-day Armistice was signed, effective for the 17th, and extending until January 14th. During the ensuing period, both sides were to prepare proposals for a permanent peace, and both were to invite all other warring nations to join the peace talks.

Once the Armistice agreement had been signed, Lenin and his advisors turned their attention to the Ukrainian problem. As early as the 16th Rada representatives were at Brest-Litovsk seeking recognition by the *Alliance* as an independent entity wishing to participate in the proceedings. But the Bolsheviks made no attempt to conceal their contempt for the "bourgeois nationalist" fledgling regime in Kiev, and with their hands untied by the Armistice, issued the Rada an ultimatum on the 17th, demanding it get in step with Petrograd. The Ukrainian Rada rejected it on the 20th, inciting a declaration that a state of war would exist between the two governments "within 24 hours." This "war" would amount to an ever-increasing effort on the part of Bolshevik sympathizers to undermine the shaky authority of the Rada; neither Petrograd nor Kiev was capable of a real military campaign at that time. Both parties, in fact, faced serious problems *vis-à-vis* the other. For the Soviets, the loss of the Ukraine would not only be economically devastating, it would also strand the countless Russian soldiers still at Southwest Front and Romanian Front and all their equipment and supplies would likely be forfeited to Kiev. The principal Ukrainian concern, on the other hand, was that these very soldiers were already in good geographic positions from which the occupation of their lands would be rendered relatively easy; then there was the problem of the presence of large, undisciplined bands of soldiers, or ex-soldiers, roaming and marauding the countryside. In one of her last diary entries before leaving the war zone, Florence Farmborough recalled a fearful December night through which none of her unit slept, fearful as they were of the intoxicated and uncontrollable gangs of ex-soldiers who "shouting, singing, and swearing" slowly made their way past the shivering, frightened nurse's "hiding place." Sadly she recalled that matters had come to extremes. "We were afraid of our own soldiers."[208] The incident took place at Botushany, Moldavia. It is perhaps needless to relate that the Romanians, as well as the Ukrainians, wanted desperately for Russian troops to leave their soil, and to be done with the whole messy business of the war. Nor were they alone in their desires; on December 24th, the Baltic Germans sent a third desperate appeal to the German government for protection from similar unbearable conditions in the unoccupied areas in Estonia and Livonia. It was the third, that is, since the Bolshevik Revolution, but earlier requests dated back to the March Revolution. On the 24th, the Ukrainians asked the representatives of the *Alliance* to be "officially" included in the talks at Brest-Litovsk. Two days later they were informed that their request had been granted.

Actual peace negotiations commenced on December 22, 1917. Heading up the German delegation was Secretary of State von Kühlmann, with Hoffmann again representing the military. According to the latter, the Russians arrived with about four hundred people all told, but Joffe was still the leading personality. They immediately proposed a general peace without territorial or monetary aggrandizement for any belligerent. Of course it was convenient for them to make such suggestions, since the armies of the *Alliance* were deep inside Russian and Romanian territory along the Eastern Front. Elsewhere, German armies were also within enemy ground in the West, Austrian troops were on Italian soil and the Bulgarians had occupied all they desired in land from Serbia and Romania. Of the four *Alliance* nations, only Turkey stood at a net loss of ground at that time. Understandably the Germans and Bulgarians, especially the latter, rejected the idea; the Turks did likewise. Only the Austrian delegation, led by Count Czernin, a man convinced that the Empire needed immediate peace lest it disintegrate, was amenable to the formula. In the end the *Alliance* agreed to a general peace "without annexations or indemnities" in the firm belief that the western *Entente* powers would never agree to it. Moreover, they had decided (with good reason, as we have seen) that the western Russian border areas now under their control would never consent to being handed back to Russia, especially a Bolshevik Russia, and that therefore these areas should be allowed the right to "self-determination," a phrase the Russians had long been using with regards to the Polish and Ukrainian inhabitants of Germany and Austria-Hungary. The Germans were certain that any "self-determined" areas could easily be brought into their economic, perhaps eventually political, control. But when the Russian delegates were apprised of the German intentions, Hoffmann noted that Joffe looked as though he had been the recipient of a punch to his head.[209] Czernin, too, was upset; he earnestly desired immediate peace, at any price. He even threatened his allies with the possibility of a separate peace between Austria and Russia. For their part, the Russians, stunned, or at least pretending to be, (they after all possessed nothing to bargain with) broke off the talks, and Joffe and some others returned to Petrograd.

When informed, Trotsky was not upset by the flow of events at Brest. Convinced that it was the Soviets who now held the trump cards because all the "capitalist" nations now feared Revolutions of their own, he spoke of the "great success" of the talks with the Germans, and believed that the other *Entente* powers had no longer any choice but to join in a general peace. Accordingly, he once again invited all the warring nations to negotiations "in a neutral country" for the purpose of ending the war. He gave them ten days to respond, assured them that this was the last such offer, and warned that if they did not respond "the working class of every country will rise against the imperialists of their own nations."[210] That was on the 29th.

Thus passed 1917, another terrible year of all-out war in Europe. The German command was already preparing for a massive offensive on the Western Front for the new year, before the Americans could tip the scales in favor of the *Entente*. Despite its agreement not to move forces from the East while the negotiations at Brest were ongoing, it began to furtively do so. The entire order of battle at *Ober Ost* would have to be reshuffled; the first move came on the last day of the old year when General Remus von Woyrsch's command north of the Pripet was disbanded. Its section of line was taken over by Tenth Army.[211]

New Years Day 1918 dawned with high hopes for peace among the nations that had been parties to war on the Eastern Front. Though the fighting was over, at least temporarily, no peace agreement had been reached, despite the fact that every one of them desperately needed it. The Ukrainian Rada had sent a delegation to Brest-Litovsk which arrived that very day, hoping for an acknowledgement of legitimacy from the *Alliance*, and frantic to forestall a Bolshevik takeover in Kiev. In Berlin, the *Kaiser* had summoned a Crown Council for the following day during which he pressed Ludendorff to accept smaller annexations in Poland and a veneer of "self-determination" for the Baltic States. It was roughly the view espoused by Hoffmann, who was present, but it did not satisfy the men at *OHL*. Hoffmann returned to Brest certain that he could not yield very much to the Russians. The latter spent several days debating whether to recognize Finnish independence; in the end they did so, mindful of securing the good graces of Sweden, a key neutral link to the West, but one which clearly favored the *Alliance* in the war. When the Soviet delegation finally returned to Brest on January 7th, a new, key spokesman was with it: Trotsky. Hoffmann, in his memoirs, claimed that with the arrival of Trotsky, the whole atmosphere of negotiation was radically altered; the Bolshevik leader was more interested in speechmaking and propagandizing than with making peace. There can be little doubt that the real purpose for the presence of the Foreign Secretary was to stall for time, and at this, Trotsky proved to be a master. All of the senior Bolshevik leaders were still completely convinced that Revolution was imminent in the cities of all the nations at war, and that their strategy must be to confidently await such developments while they consolidated their hold on power in Russia and smashed all the opposition, including such separatist tendencies as the Ukrainians were exhibiting. Certainly, encountering delegates like the nervous, impatient Czernin did nothing to dispel these notions. Yet their position remained weak; at times it seemed precarious. Already, behind the scenes ex-Czarist officers such as Kornilov and Alexiev were conferring, and outlining plans for resisting both the Reds and the *Alliance*. It was the beginning of the "White" movement which one day would begin civil war in all parts of the old Empire. Another deed that made the Bolsheviks evil incarnate in the eyes of many foreigners, occurred on the 8th, when the government announced it was repudiating all of the debt piled up by the old Imperial government. At the stroke of a pen, billions of rubles owed to *Entente* and other countries was waved off, an action that incensed the creditors perhaps even more than the act of dropping out of the war. Then there was the problem of the lack of an army; having destroyed the old one the Bolsheviks now found themselves without that which they needed to leverage concessions at the bargaining table.

Undaunted, Trotsky grudgingly agreed, finally, to accept the Ukrainian delegation as legitimate, on the 10th. He then advanced his own proposals by the 12th, but they were speedily rejected within two days by Kühlmann, who icily declared that not an acre of ground would be abandoned until peace had been concluded. On the 15th an ultimatum was dispatched to both Kiev and Jassy, demanding both governments stop harboring "bourgeois" elements and allow the passage of Red troops. Both capitals declined. Quietly, the Ukrainians began to negotiate separately with the *Alliance* on the 16th, and Trotsky, at a loss for the moment, decided to go home still sputtering and protesting over the German terms.

At the same time the long-awaited Constituent Assembly was opened in Petrograd. The Bolsheviks had no intention of allowing any sort of democratic institution to function, and it was soon forcibly dissolved, while a wave of terror, punctuated by murder, swept over Russia. Whatever utopian sentiments among foreigners as existed prior to these events were certainly swept away within two days of mayhem in January (18th-19th). No one could longer doubt the real nature of the Red regime. The lesson was not lost on the leaders of the *Alliance*; even Lenin began to call for moderation. He also began to call for immediate peace, at any price. In prolonged debates over the next several days, he advocated accepting the German terms. Trotsky took the other side, and eventually won over most of his colleagues. His stall tactics would continue.

During a Reichstag speech on January 25th, Kühlmann announced that an agreement with the Ukrainians had been reached. When the news was relayed to Trotsky, his response was a definite break with the Rada and to initiate prosecution of the "war" that had been declared some weeks ago. Red troops under Muraviev were to advance on Kiev; Bolshevik elements in Odessa took control of the city that very day. Matters also came to a head with the Romanians, whose troops had exhibited considerable hostility towards Russians in recent weeks. Fighting between the two groups flared up at Galatz on the 20th and at Kishinev on the 26th. The latter city was secured for the Romanians the next day, and Trotsky soon declared that the two governments had broken ties to each other. He also announced that a battle for Kiev had begun.

Such was the tense atmosphere when the Brest-Litovsk Conference resumed on the 30th. All the *Alliance* nations were more than eager for a peace settlement and were losing patience with Trotsky, who was correctly identified as the main obstacle to peace. More and more army divisions were being withdrawn to satisfy the demands of other theaters of war. On February 3rd, the Austro-Hungarians disbanded General Böhm-Ermolli's army group which had consisted of the First, Second, Third and Seventh Armies and the "German" South Army. All German forces were withdrawn and the front south of the Pripet was entrusted to only Second Army, subsequently to be known as "Eastern Army."[212] Austria-Hungary's commitment to the East had slipped to 37 divisions by February, and six more would depart that month. Germany still retained 65 divisions at the beginning of the month, but she would also send six away by March 1st.

Early in February it became obvious to all interested parties that a Ukrainian-*Alliance* treaty was soon to be completed. It would certainly be advantageous for both sides, leaving the Russians as the odd men out, a situation desired by all but the Bolsheviks. Once a settlement was near, the Germans sent what amounted to an ultimatum to the Romanians, demanding that they too begin to talk peace. Only the day before, (5th) the Baltic Germans had sent yet another—their fourth and last—plea for a German occupation of all the former lands of the Teutonic Knights. From the Ukrainian point of view, matters were also coming to a head; Bolshevik forces now controlled much of eastern and northern Ukraine and were fast approaching Kiev, the capital. The Rada prudently decided to relocate to Zhitomir.

The ninth of February can be considered the apex of the Brest-Litovsk negotiations; the Ukrainian Treaty was signed to the relief of the Rada as well as the *Alliance* delegates. It was not a moment too soon for either, and later that day news arrived of the Bolshevik occupation of Kiev. Trotsky could certainly read the handwriting on the wall and it was no coincidence that on the following day he stunned all the *Alliance* representatives by announcing that for his government, the war was over. He would not agree to the terms of peace presented to him, so the Russian delegation was going home without having obtained an acceptable peace. The Russian army (or what was left of it) would be demobilized. The issue had passed. Almost simultaneously, Lenin authorized the announcement from Petrograd that the new government was now renouncing all loans and debts incurred during the period of the Provisional Government. The slate had been wiped clean, diplomatically and economically.

These moves were intended to come as a terrible shock to all the nations still at war, but in fact most *Alliance* delegates did not receive them as such and were willing to accept this sort of pseudo-peace. Hoffmann and *OHL*, however, would have none of it, and after some hesitation, Kühlmann agreed. Pressure would have to be applied to Petrograd.

Outwardly, the week following Trotsky's abrupt departure from Brest may have appeared quiet and calm, at least in the eyes of the soldiers still holding the front. Behind the scenes, however, the wheels of political activity were turning rapidly. Trotsky himself began a new project—to create a Red Army out of Red Guard units and volunteers—and February 14th is often cited as the date of its birth. The Russians also at this time agreed to allow the numerous

Czech formations, who were now stranded behind Russian lines and who wanted nothing to do with the Bolsheviks, free passage along the Trans-Siberian Railroad and out of the country via Japan and the Pacific. The French had declared the Czechs to be part of the French army, and the Red leaders were only too pleased to be rid of these "counterrevolutionary" (i.e. non Bolshevik) troops in their midst. The Germans also had plenty to do. Faced with the loss of a new satellite state in the East if the Bolshevik forces were to overrun Ukraine, they decided to lend armed assistance to the Rada. On the 16th, Ludendorff dispatched a detachment of nearly one thousand Ukrainian former prisoners of war, all properly uniformed and led by German and Ukrainian officers to Kovel in Volhynia to join Rada forces awaiting it.[213] Concerned with the legality of such moves Kühlmann suggested that the Rada make a formal appeal to Germany for protection; it was forthcoming the following day. Thereafter Berlin proceeded to authorize the creation of two entire Ukrainian divisions from the pool of Russian prisoners of war, and later the Austrians followed the lead.

Ober Ost was also ordered to prepare to resume the offensive. Since the Bolsheviks would not sign the peace treaty, they would have war again. On the 17th, Petrograd was reminded of the expiration of armistice conditions on the following day. German aircraft in large numbers buzzed the skies over the long front, reconnoitering Russians positions in an undisguised attempt to intimidate the few stalwart soldiers still braving the winter weather in the trenches and dugouts. Berlin also allowed representatives of a new "Kingdom of Lithuania" to declare the complete independence of the area from Russia, as if to reinforce the German position at Brest that the conquered lands had no wish to reunite with a Russian state. The Baltic Germans were also informed that their year-long requests for German help, which had assumed desperate tones since November, were about to be answered in the affirmative. The new drive was code named operation *Faustschlag*.

At noon on the 18th the armistice officially expired. A few hours grace were allowed, but before darkness fell in the late afternoon, German commanders waved their units forward, all along the line. Even the Ukraine, with which Germany was now at peace, was invaded, despite a lack of sufficient strength to cover such a huge area, and despite the Austrians' refusal to participate in the offensive. Nothing quite like this had been experienced in the East thus far; even Brusilov's 1916 offensive had not covered so vast an expanse of front.

Very little resistance was encountered, it being chiefly small arms fire which was scattered whenever the Germans paused to bring up artillery. Other than the cavalry divisions, the actual movement was made by automobiles and especially by railcars, and because most of the objectives lay on the railroads anyway, the overall strategy was to advance along these arteries; speed and the ease of supply were the primary considerations. Within a day after the advance had begun, the Bolshevik government communicated to the Germans its willingness to sign the proposed peace treaty, but this time the latter were in no hurry, and stalled by demanding the Russians repeat their compliance in writing. Dvinsk, the prize that had so long eluded the Germans as a winter quarters, was captured that first day, and with it much unused war material, including artillery pieces. Minsk was taken on the 20th.

The German advance provoked something of a panic all across Russia among Bolsheviks and their sympathizers and even more moderate revolutionaries; there was a widespread belief that foreign monarchists and imperialists had sent their armies to crush the revolution, enslave the populace economically, and perhaps even restore the Romanov dynasty. A terrible backlash against persons who supposedly represented the old regime was begun; the Bolshevik leaders in Petrograd did little to suppress it. One account of those bloody days relates occurrences in the Crimea, where at Simferopol on February 23, 1918, 170 officers and civilians were shot without trial. Officers of the Black Sea Fleet were cruelly murdered by slowly incinerating them in the ships' furnaces and by weighing down their persons and tossing them into the harbor. Apparently these bodies were visible for some time afterward, moving eerily about beneath the waves, propelled by the tides and currents.[214]

New and more unfavorable terms were forwarded by the Germans to Petrograd on the 21st. Lenin, who had favored signing the original ones but was prevented from doing so by his colleagues who wanted to give Trotsky's strategy a chance, now used every tactic he could summon to convince the others that even a harsh peace was preferable to no peace. Insisting that the government would be toppled within a few weeks if the Germans were not conciliated, he even went so far as to threaten to resign and retire if his wisdom was again ignored. In the end, and with the belated support of Trotsky, he finally won his point; peace must be secured immediately, at however steep a price. On the 24th, the Germans were informed; on that very day they occupied both Pernau and Dorpat in Estonia. The next day the invaders reached Reval and Pskov. They were getting dangerously close to Petrograd.

Meanwhile, the *Alliance* was also applying great pressure on the Romanians. Isolated now even from the Russians by the formation of the Ukrainian state, the fugitive government at Jassy had no choice but to parley; with German forces sweeping across the Ukrainian Plains, it would soon be surrounded and crushed. Bucharest was selected as the site for the negotiations, and German delegates arrived there on the 23rd, carrying a harsh set of terms. The Romanians, with few cards to play, nevertheless proved to be tough bargainers; no doubt they realized their predicament was precarious, given that all four *Alliance* powers had demands upon them. Austria-Hungary wanted Wallachia, or at least frontier rectifications which would push her borders beyond the mountains; both Bulgaria and Turkey wanted Dobruja. Germany insisted on control of the railroads, the port of Constanza for a German naval base, control of the oil fields, and other economic concessions. When the proceedings stalled, Berlin issued an ultimatum to the Romanians on the 27th, and followed it up with another two days later. *Kaiser* Karl sent a telegram to Wilhelm asking that the German demands be eased. Later he wrote a personal letter to the same effect, but Wilhelm was unmoved, and at any rate was overshadowed at this stage of the war by OHL, the prestige of which had risen as the result of Germany's apparently favorable military fortunes, and the demands of which were getting greedier with every success. Karl, thus rebuffed, refused to reopen hostilities with Romania for the sake of "excessive" German demands, much as he had also passed on restarting the war against Russia for the sake of what he saw as German ambitions in the Baltic region. Fortunately for all parties, events to the north overtook the impasse in the south.

Finally, during the first week of March came a series of events which had for so long been anticipated by so many, and which would permanently alter the map of Eastern Europe. Despite all the hysteria in Petrograd, *Ober* Ost had never intended to occupy the city, fearing the effects would be more harmful than helpful to the German cause. Once the line Narva River-Lake Peipus-Velikaya River had been reached, the advance in the extreme north was stopped; Berlin never intended to extend its direct control over areas east of those of the old Teutonic Order. A final act of terror was done on March 2nd, when German aircraft bombed Petrograd,[215] sending the Bolshevik government scurrying off to the relative safety of Moscow. The big news came on the 3rd: the Bolshevik delegation at Brest-Litovsk, no longer headed by Trotsky, who now admitted his very presence would continue to be a stumbling-block to peace, signed the revised terms of the Germans, and the war was officially over at last.

But peace with Russia did not mean general peace in the East; there were still Bolshevik forces in Ukraine to deal with, and of course the Romanians. After a rapid advance, German troops entered Kiev March 1st, strengthening the Rada's position and weakening that of Jassy. There was nothing left for the Romanians to do but sign the peace they so dreaded. Due to a shakeup at that time in the Jassy government, some questions were raised as to whether anyone in Bucharest possessed the legal authority necessary for a formal peace signing, so in the event a "preliminary peace," thereafter known as the Peace of Buftea was inked on March 5th. On the same day an agreement between Russia and Romania was reached, through which the latter agreed to evacuate all military units from the province of Bessarabia, which it had designs upon. This was a curious arrangement, given the fact that Bessarabia was geographically separated from Russia by the large mass of the Ukraine. Nevertheless, the agreement was ratified by the Russians in the (Ukrainian) city of Odessa on the 9th. It was obvious that the Bolsheviks had no intention of allowing the resource-rich Ukraine to slip from their grip without further conflict.

The *Kaiser's* government was entertaining no illusions as to the trustworthiness of the Bolsheviks, peace or no peace. It concluded a treaty of friendship with the new Finnish state on March 7th, to create a sort of bulwark against the spread of Bolshevism in the far north. Lenin and his group, whose interest in Finland was minimal anyway, recognized Finnish independence (and thus the German treaty) on the 10th; they were ensconced in their new capital, Moscow, the next day. It was not until the 16th that news of the worst sort reached the Western capitals; Russia had ratified the Treaty of Brest-Litovsk.

It must be borne in mind that at the moment of Russia's formal withdrawal from the war, the Germans were poised to strike hard on the Western Front. The strategy had been conceived months earlier and every sort of preparation had been made for an all-out bid for victory in the spring, before the Americans could intervene in great numbers. Everyone on both sides of the line knew the blow was coming; no one knew exactly when or where. To receive the news from Russia at a time when every French, British, Belgian and even Italian soldier was bracing for the coming storm, was indeed difficult. For the *Entente* press, no amount of demonization of the Bolsheviks could be adequate, no adjectives too strong to describe such vile human beings who would leave their ex-allies in the lurch during their hours of greatest need. Surely the Bolsheviks were in league with the Germans, were receiving German gold. As for the Germans, now the *Kaiser* and his kin had at last thrown off the masks; the utter brutality of a German victory was now apparent to all. The terms of the Brest-Litovsk Treaty were denounced as the ultimate example of German military ambition, of boundless greed, and a perfect showcase of the might-makes-right mentality of cruel "Prussian militarists." Years later, many historians were still espousing this line, the product of wartime hysteria, still using Brest-Litovsk as an illustration of the triumph of a ruthless, uncompromising bully imposing his will on an exhausted, helpless foe.

Hopefully, enough time has passed for such fictions to no longer be necessary. But truth has nothing to do with calendar dates; it is absolute, that is, timeless and inviolate. One of the finest experts on Russia and the Soviet Union of the 20th century, writing in the late 1950s, was unimpressed about all the hype over the Brest-Litovsk Treaty. He believed that the document was a perfect example of how the *Entente* portrayed the German actions of the war as brutal uses of a "mailed fist." Instead, he wrote, it was the *Entente* nations themselves, who after insisting on the unconditional surrender of their enemies after two world wars, imposed settlements on the vanquished nations the realities of which were far more brutal than anything the Germans ever imposed at Brest, the terms of which were "not inordinately severe." No monetary reparations were originally demanded, and the lands of which the Bolsheviks were to be deprived were populated by ethnic groups who had no wish to be governed from Moscow, especially a Communist Moscow. The eventual settlement imposed by the *Entente* that lasted from 1920 to 1938 was much less favorable to Russia than that agreed upon with the Germans in 1918. He then pointed out, quite correctly, that Russia had gone to war and had been defeated, and usually, he reminds us, there is a "price to be paid for that."[216]

And what were these terms that have been the object of so much controversy? There were ten of them. Since no one complained about the legal and diplomatic ones, let us consider only the ones involving geographic changes. Russia was obliged to recognize the independence of Finland and Ukraine, the boundaries of which had already been established. Russia had to give back to Turkey the lands she had annexed in 1878. Finally, Russia was required to evacuate and renounce all claims to Congress Poland and the Baltic lands (which subsequently became known as Estonia, Latvia, and Lithuania). Neither side took this arrangement to be final; elsewhere the war continued and no one could predict the final outcome. What both wanted from the Treaty signed at Brest was a respite; Germany to win victory in the West, Austria to finish with Italy and the Russians to consolidate their power in Moscow and to smash all the noisy opposition to their rule. The peace achieved exactly what it was designed to achieve in that all parties got more or less what they had bargained for. And the loss of the non-Russian lands was probably a godsend for the Bolsheviks in the long run; they had difficulty enough in controlling what was left to them. If the Germans can legitimately be accused of any shenanigans regarding the deal struck at Brest it would be in the manner in which they handled the lands which, according to the treaty, they were supposed to evacuate. In Bylorussia, they had advanced as far as the upper Dnieper in the Mogilev area, and were in no hurry to withdraw. They went so far as to allow a collection of anti-Bolshevik elements in Minsk to proclaim a "Bylorussian National Republic" on March 25th, knowing full well that it had no forces of its own for self-defense and would therefore be totally dependant on the presence of the German army for its salvation. They also encouraged a pro-German group in Courland to offer the crown of a new "Duchy of Courland" to the Hohenzollern dynasty.

Such slaps in the face no doubt annoyed the Bolsheviks, but they had far more serious problems to address. As far as the terms of the Treaty were concerned, they were equally if not more cynical about the immediate or short-term effects. Trotsky predicted that Soviet Russia would one day soon wage a "holy war" against the Germans in order to settle scores; Lenin openly boasted that his government had no qualms about ignoring or breaking the terms of the Treaty, and added that only "fools" entertained no such thoughts. The Red leaders were well aware of just how unpopular the settlement lingered in the minds of many Russians, and closely associated with it was, for most, the Bolshevik leadership. Very soon, they had changed the name of the party to the Communist Party.

All the while, the German advance into the Ukraine continued. Odessa, a major hotseat of anti-Rada activity, was occupied on March 13th, Nikolaiev on the 17th, Kherson on the 21st. As many Romanians had feared, they were now surrounded by *Alliance* forces with no hope of relief. Permanent peace negotiations commenced on the 21st and within five days basic agreement had been reached. Even so, the new Romanian government managed to stall the actual signing of a peace treaty for some time, hoping for a miracle to deliver it from the nightmarish terms. The Germans, their attention diverted to the Western Front where the first phase of their great offensive campaign had also begun on the 21st, were for once in no rush to insist on a speedy closure of such formalities, so for the time being, further proceedings were halted.

March ended with a further restructuring of the German command in the East. As of the 28th Eichhorn's group of three armies was disbanded, an army removed, and a few days later renamed Army Group Riga. General Graf von Kirchbach was placed in command. Gronau's army, situated slightly to the south, was also dispersed. And Linsingen's command, formerly astride the Pripet, was redesignated Army Group Eichhorn-Kiev to accommodate its new positions, on March 31st. At roughly the same time, the Austro-Hungarians, amazed at the ease with which the Germans had advanced, agreed to assist in the occupation of the vast Ukraine. They were motivated by the desire to share the rich resources of the area, especially the foodstuffs, and in the end had taken on an area amounting to approximately 40% of the new nation.

Another area had been opened to the Germans once the Brest-Litovsk proceedings came to an end. By the terms of the peace, Finland had been recognized by the Russians as independent; they could hardly object to foreign intervention there. Since late January the Finnish capital of Helsinki had been in the hands of Red Guards, and by March conservative elements were pleading with Germany for assistance to "restore order." The *Kaiser* was sympathetic, and by the time the ice began to melt in the northern Baltic, *Ober Ost* had allocated a division and a half—15 to 16,000 men—for a landing on the north coast of the Gulf of Finland. Commanded by General Rüdiger von der Goltz, the force was referred to as the "Baltic Division" and its mission was to cooperate with "White" Finnish troops led by ex-Russian cavalry general Karl von Mannerheim. It landed at Hängö on April 3rd, secured the port and began to move on Helsinki a few days later. The moves intimidated the captains of several British submarines which were based on the Finnish coast to assist the Russians in the Baltic naval struggle, and they ordered their vessels scuttled. Another landing party of Germans put ashore at Helsinki on the 13th in synchronization with the troops moving overland from the west. By April 15th the capital had been cleared of all revolutionaries; most of the Reds withdrew to Viborg, near the Russian frontier, while Mannerheim pushed from the north to secure the bulk of the country. Cooperation between Finns and Germans led to an important victory at Lahti after three days of fighting. When the city was captured on the 20th, Red forces were split in two. Mannerheim advanced on Tampere and reached it by the 25th; a smaller group moved into Viborg from the surrounding forests and held it until the arrival of the Germans on the 29th. By month's end the coast road along the Gulf had been cleared of all Red troops right up to the Russian border. Only some mopping up remained to be done, and by May 7th, Berlin was announcing a big victory in Finland. As many as 80,000 prisoners[217] may have been taken by the Finnish and German troops, and a northern bulwark erected against the spread of revolution. For the remainder of the war, Finland was a virtual satellite of Germany.

The drama in Ukraine was also approaching its final act. A major old Bolshevik stronghold, the city of Kharkov, was entered by the Germans by rail on April 8th. A week later they were poised to strike into the Crimea; the *Alliance* grip on the country was tightening, while that of the Russians had all but been severed. "White" Russian forces were also interested in the general area, but these received a setback on the 13th, when General Kornilov was killed in an encounter with Reds. Another old Czarist general was gone. He was succeeded by General Deniken as commander of the "White Volunteer Army," but this force was too weak to much affect the events of 1918.

By contrast, it was the *Alliance* that now controlled events in the southeast. As of mid April, most Austro-Hungarian troops had been sent away, leaving only Second Army, which was renamed East Army for the occupation of Ukraine. Only 19 divisions remained in the East by May 1st. Germany retained 43, a considerable number for a theater supposedly at peace, but chaotic conditions from Finland to Romania dictated their presence. It is left to the imaginative to consider what 43 additional divisions might have accomplished in the West at this time, and this is the main reason that the Eastern Front, even in spring 1918, figured so critically in the mathematics of the war.

Austrian and German alike had long been dissatisfied with the Rada government and had long plotted its overthrow by a group more amenable to *Alliance* schemes.[218] Following the notorious "cultivation decree" issued by Eichhorn on April 6th, an order designed to ease the food supply problem then at a critical stage within both of the *Kaisers'* realms, the attitude of the fledgling Ukrainian government was considered inappropriate and preparations for its removal accelerated. On April 26th the relatively few Ukrainian troops were disarmed, and two days later the Rada ministers were arrested while in their chamber. By the 29th a former Czarist Cossack commander, General Pavlo

Skoropadsky had been proclaimed *Hetman* (essentially a dictator) of his native Ukraine, naturally with full backing and approval of the Austro-Germans. The *Coup* was bloodless; the vast majority of the population wanted only a return of peace and order under a non-Communist regime. Apparently the *Alliance* feared some sort of backlash against Skoropadsky, for they certainly did not move quickly to recognize his government, and over a month had passed before they took this diplomatic step, on June 2nd.

With the advent of May, German troops reached Rostov on the Don, just beyond the eastern boundary of the new Ukrainian state, and finally stopped their advance. They did, however, begin a drive into the Crimean peninsula, home of the bases of the Russian Black Sea Fleet, and there began a heated debate among personnel of the Fleet as to what action, if any, should be taken. Questions surrounding the future of the peninsula and the Fleet were quite complex. Some German circles wanted the peninsula for German colonization and the fleet for Germany. Others insisted both should go to Ukraine, others said both to Russia, and still others thought it was a problem to be left for Moscow and Kiev to work out. Turkey also wanted both the land (it had once been a part of the Ottoman Empire) and the ships. In the event, the peninsula was occupied by German troops by mid May; part of the fleet steamed away to Novorossisk at the last minute, and the other part stayed and was captured. The German booty: Seven battleships, two cruisers, ten destroyers, ten submarines, and a "large fleet" of minelayers, minesweepers, and torpedo boats.[219]

The official end of the war in the East came on May 7th, when the Treaty of Bucharest was finally signed. Its provisions included the transfer of a narrow strip of territory in the mountains, including the approaches to all of the passes from both Wallachia and Moldavia, to Hungary. Bulgaria received the southern Dobruja; the northern half was to be held in condominium by all four *Alliance* powers. The mouth of the Danube was to come under joint Romanian-*Alliance* control. Germany was granted a host of economic privileges, including practical control of the oil wells and the transportation networks. The Romanian Army was reduced to four divisions (it could only field nine by May), and the nation was to maintain at its own expense six Austro-German Divisions. Roughly 9450 square kilometers (3650sq.mi.) of real estate were lost. As against all the losses, the *Alliance* was to allow Romania to annex Bessarabia, a border province with a slight Romanian majority, containing 35,00 square kilometers (13,500sq.mi.), Bucharest would seem to have enlarged its nation considerably, despite the condominium, for having lost the war, but it had been crippled economically and reduced, like so many other areas, to a status akin to that of a satellite of the *Alliance*. With the signing of the Treaty, the remaining German (nine) and Bulgarian (three) divisions in the area were grouped and re-designated the "Mackensen Army."

Peace or no peace, the Germans would be allowed little respite in regions formerly part of the Russian Empire. On May 11th, a "Republic of the North Caucasus" of mostly Moslem tendencies, was declared as an independent state. Three days later, Berlin recognized Lithuanian self-sovereignty. Then on the 23rd, an independent Georgia was proclaimed; it immediately appealed for German protection, fearing Turkish ambitions toward a Christian populace in a region dominated by Moslems. The Germans too were suspicious (or jealous) of Turkish designs in the entire area of the Black Sea, and the significant oil reserves of Trans-Caucasia no doubt influenced the subsequent decision to send troops. A force somewhat larger than a brigade, but smaller than a division was hastily scraped up and transported across the sea to the coastal town of Poti in Georgia. It departed Turkish territory on May 25th, but for reasons unclear took two weeks to reach its destination. It had seized the Georgian capital Tibilisi by June 11th, and remained in the country to maintain order, despite protests from Moscow, which still claimed all formerly Russian lands not signed away at Brest. At about the same time, small numbers of German troops crossed the Kerch Strait from the Crimea to the Taman Peninsula, threatening the last stretch of Black Sea coastline not already in *Alliance* hands, around the port of Novorossisk. This move obliged the men controlling what was left of the Black Sea Fleet to make a final decision regarding the fate of the ships, which included the newest and best of the entire group. In the end seven ships, including one battleship, returned to Sebastopol to be interned by the Germans with the others that had remained in May. The other dozen or so vessels, also including one battleship, were scuttled by their crews on June 19th.[220] The end had come for the Black Sea Fleet, and all that remained for the *Alliance* was to decide what to do with what was left floating.

Eastern Front 1918

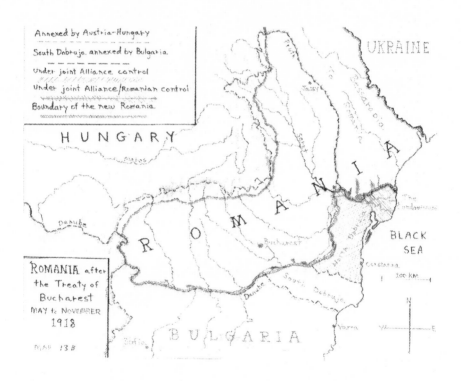

Romania After the Treaty of Bucharest

Chapter Fourteen
Post Treaty

For both Russians and Germans, the formal end of the war on the Eastern Front, accomplished with the signings and subsequent ratifications of the Treaties of Brest-Litovsk and Bucharest in March and May 1918, did not mean the end of the fighting and dying in eastern Europe. Germany, ever fearful of a Russian revival, conscious of Bolshevik bad faith, and desperate to secure economic hegemony in the sprawling lands she had occupied, felt compelled to maintain substantial military force in the area; the forty-two divisions still present in June had slipped to forty-one by August, 39 for October, and 36 remained at the time of the Western Armistice in November. These numbers, when contrasted to those of Austria-Hungary, clearly indicate the dominant role Germany had assumed in this theater (Austrian numbers for June, August, October and November were 19,14, 9, and 8 divisions respectively). The *Kaiser's* forces became bogged down in a guerilla war with Ukrainian nationalists and Russian elements, mostly pro-Bolshevik, who battled to expel the invaders from lands not German in character or sympathy. A campaign of terror was begun by both sides; its net result was unfavorable to the cause of the *Alliance*, as an anti-occupation movement slowly gained momentum. The new German ambassador to Russia, Count Mirbach, was assassinated in Moscow on July 6th, and no connection of the act to the Lenin government could be ascertained. In Kiev, Eichhorn, who had recently been promoted to Field Marshall, but who had come to be hated by many Ukrainians for German policy regarding the forcible acquisition of foodstuffs, was also murdered, on July 30th. All told, the Ukrainian campaign is reported to have caused the Germans nearly nineteen thousand casualties.[221] It certainly caused a good deal of consternation at *Ober-Ost* and constant regrouping of the ground forces. On July 18th, Mackensen's army was renamed "Romanian Occupation Army," and General Hugo von Kathen replaced General von Kirchbach at

"Riga" Army Group. Ironically, it was Kirchbach who soon replaced Eichhorn. His new command was redesignated "Kiev" Army Group. Meanwhile, Mirbach's successor, Dr. Karl Helfferich, was nearly killed as well. Following two unsuccessful attempts on his life, he was excused of his duties in Moscow by the Soviet government, and took up residence in Pskov on August 13th; both the Russian and German governments, wanting to maintain normal diplomatic relations, would overlook such abnormalities.

For the Soviet government, the summer of 1918 was a time of constant crisis and great uncertainty. It had the Germans and their new satellite states to deal with. It had the Western *Entente* nations, who were making no attempt to conceal their contempt for the new regime, and in fact were sending military forces to the White Sea and to Siberia in an unabashed attempt to influence events in Russia, to deal with. It had the "Whites," that loose collection of any and all anti-Soviet Russians determined to overthrow the Reds, to deal with, and this meant civil war. Then there were other internal groups such as the Czechs and Slovaks, stranded in Russia by the Revolution and strongly anti-Bolshevik in sentiment. Initially offered free passage across the Trans-Siberian Railroad to the Pacific where they were to be transferred by sea to the Western Front, these Slavic troops soon came into conflict with Red Guards and other revolutionary soldiers and were declared enemies by the Moscow government before they ever had half a chance to leave the country. Perceiving enemies wherever it turned, the young Russian government began to lash out, like an individual gripped by paranoiac fears.

The most noticeable victims of the Red terror were members of the ex-ruling class. They began to fall as early as June 12th, when the Grand Duke Michael and his secretary were shot at Ekaterinburg in the Urals. Within a fortnight, Nicholas and his family were also transferred to this city where they, together with several close aides, were all shot in the basement of a small house on July 16th. The immediate excuse for the murders was the Czech troops were about to capture the area and would no doubt have freed the ex *Czar*, where after the Whites could have used him as a figurehead to rally all anti-revolutionary forces under one banner. A day later, it was the turn of Grand Duke Sergius and his wife; in the six days from July 13th to 18th, at least 14 Romanovs were killed. Nor was Soviet vengeance limited to members of the family that had ruled Russia for 300 years; many, many former Imperial ministers were dispatched and other figures associated with the Monarchy or the "counterrevolution." Old General Russki and General Radko-Dmitriev, ill and unable to flee, also died in front of firing squads. Ironically, those Romanovs who escaped Russia often did so with the cooperation of the Germans, who, it will be remembered, had assisted in the return of Lenin. When German troops overran the Crimea in May, they took several prominent Royals into their custody, insuring their survival. The Dowager Empress (the ex *Czar's* mother) Maria Fedorovna and the Grand Duke Nicholas were two of the more prominent members of this group. Germany's *Kaiser* wanted no royal blood on his conscience, though the fortunate ones who lived their last years abroad never uttered a kind word about him, in keeping with family tradition, after July 1914.

With regard to the other enemies of the Soviet state, its leaders tended to lump them into a vast pool of antagonists branded as "bourgeois," "capitalist," or "counterrevolutionary" to which similar, if not identical connotations were attached. *Entente* nations sent military expeditions to the Murman Coast, Archangel on the White Sea, and Vladivostok, the Pacific terminus of the Trans-Siberian Railway to protect their investments there, that is, to prevent the enormous accumulations of war material stockpiled there and awaiting shipment to the now defunct front, from falling into the hands of the Germans. Since the Bolshevik Revolution, the Western press had been consistent in its accusations of a Red/German secret arrangement directed against the *Entente*. Now, Red and *Entente* troops engaged on the periphery of Eurasia, as if somehow such efforts could restore the Eastern Front. To their lasting credit, the *Entente* nations withdrew their forces once they realized the error of their beliefs. Czech and Slovak troops proved to be a problem for both the Reds and the *Alliance*. *Kaiser* Karl had sent a special envoy promising amnesty for all these former Austro-Hungarian soldiers, and offering autonomy for a Czecho-Slovak homeland within his Empire, if they would only disarm and return home. They answered by initially opposing the German occupying forces in the Ukraine with force of arms, and in a battle at Bachmut inflicting several thousand casualties.[222] As they withdrew to the east, they also fought with Red Guards, bands of newly armed Austro-German ex-prisoners of war, and anyone else who tried to prevent their planned exodus to the Western Front. But like the crisis with the *Entente* detachments, this period of Czech troubles passed without serious injury to the Soviet cause. By the time the former had taken Ekaterinburg, for example, Nicholas and his entourage had been dead ten days.

It was the so-called "White" Russians that would give the Red government far and away the most trouble. Both *Entente* and *Alliance* nations alike were sympathetic to the White cause, but the latter were very careful not to give the Reds the slightest cause to complain of aid to, or interference on behalf of, any groups fighting against the government with which they had so recently signed a favorable treaty. The story of Red versus White is a story of long, bloody, ruthless Civil War, but it has no place in our narrative here. In the end it was the Reds who prevailed; the *Alliance* was doing business with the people that it wanted to do business with, the people who were, for better or for worse, at the helm of the Russian ship of State. It is useless here to speculate on what might have been, had the Whites prevailed over the Reds in the summer of 1918. What did happen then was that the war on the Western Front turned decisively against Germany, and any German defeat necessarily meant an *Alliance* defeat. By late summer this coalition no longer believed in outright victory, especially in the West (including Italy), but it did still hope to salvage a decent settlement in Eastern Europe. For the Soviets the war was no longer an issue; their preoccupation had become survival as a State, on which all long-term goals were dependent.

A turning point in the evolution of the young Russian socialist state was reached on August 30th, when the head of Petrograd's secret police was killed by an assassin. Only hours later, Lenin himself was shot twice by a woman with a handgun when he emerged from a facility at which he had given a speech. The Red leader was seriously injured, and though he survived, his health was never really the same again. The immediate result of these almost simultaneous attacks was that the government, fearing a widespread conspiracy, began to crack down hard on all forms of opposition. Thus was begun the period known as the Red Terror during which tens of thousands of human beings would be destroyed in order to satisfy the impulses of vengeance and paranoia that gripped the party leaders in Moscow.

While the Soviet government consolidated its hold on the territories within the grip of the infant Red Army, it also moved closer to developing a lasting understanding with the Germans. As we have seen, neither party held a very high opinion of the Treaty of Brest-Litovsk, yet both desperately needed peace in Eastern Europe, in order to concentrate their energies elsewhere. No one aside from the Western Powers wanted a return to hostilities along the old Eastern Front, however scaled-down or relatively minor these might actually have become. Accordingly, negotiations continued for the best interests of both sides; the Germans needed a semblance of normal relations with their neighbors to the east as a way to escape the stranglehold of the British blockade, while the Russians needed the *Alliance* nations to recognize their regime as legitimate. By August 27th, a deal had been cut and what would become known as the German-Russian Supplementary Treaty to the Brest-Litovsk Treaty was signed. The most important provisions were as follows: Russia promised to make determined efforts to expel *Entente* forces then on Russian soil; Germany guarantees no further attacks on Russian territory. Russia renounced all claims to the Baltic lands of Estonia, Livonia, Courland, and Lithuania; Germany allowed Russian trade to be conducted through three "free" ports at Reval, Riga, and Windau. Russia recognized the independence of Georgia; Germany would evacuate all Russian lands on the Black Sea. Russia agreed to allow 25% of the Baku oil field production to go to Germany; the latter was to return the warships of the Black Sea Fleet to Russia. A second agreement was made public during the first week of September. It was financial in nature and amounted to an indemnity for Germany, to the tune of six billion marks, to be paid by Russia in a series of installments. No advantage for Moscow was gained by this announcement, leaving interested parties to wonder what the Reds were up to, until on the 15th of the month, the third and final accord was revealed. By the terms of this final deal, the Germans were to evacuate Bylorussia in five stages, as each of the Russian indemnity payments were made. Outwardly, these "Supplementary Treaties" seemed to carry tremendous advantage for Germany, since all that she agreed to do in them should have been done as a result of the original Brest-Litovsk peace of March 3rd, with some minor exceptions, such as the "free" ports on the Baltic. It seemed that having given almost nothing, Germany had gained a great deal. But appearances are often deceiving, and Lenin and his clique were certainly no fools.

By September 1918, the *Alliance* powers were staggering and wavering like an overburdened individual who has carried a much too heavy load for too much distance. Clearly, the burden could not be borne much longer. Centrifugal forces within the Austro-Hungarian Empire were flinging that nation apart, as its various subject nationalities began to consider themselves as independent nations and began building political institutions as such. The Ottoman Empire had been at war almost continuously since 1911, and could not carry on; it had lost all of its Arab provinces by now and *Entente* soldiers were closing in on Anatolia itself. Bulgaria, having conquered practically all she wanted within her first year of war, had grimly held on for two more without gain, and did not want to go on. And Germany, the cornerstone of the *Alliance*, was facing increasing political unrest at home, and like the others, was exhausted and hungry, almost starved. There can be little doubt that the Russian leaders understood the problems these countries faced by late summer and were thus hardly reluctant to sign any agreement with them, in the smug knowledge that no such deals could longer be considered as final. In the event, the Russians made the first two payments of the proposed installments, then suspended further transactions, without consequence.

Despite a growing, almost universal belief that the end of the war was near, the German government tried to maintain an appearance of normality. *Hetman* Skoropadsky was received in Berlin on September 4th to consult with key figures, including the *Kaiser*, of the state which was basically sponsoring him. On the 10th, Germany announced plans for the future administration of the Baltic lands, without much consideration for the peoples who lived there. By the 15th, the German force that had been sent to Trans-Caucasia reached Baku, the center of the oil industry of the region on the Caspian Sea, and by its very presence established a firm basis for the German claim to the rich resources coveted by a half-dozen nations located there. It was the last of the good news for the *Alliance*.

Then the bad news began to come in. Towards the end of September, Bulgaria signed an armistice with the *Entente* and dropped out of the war; an enemy army, operating from Salonika, was threatening the Bulgarian capital. This act caused Ludendorff to lose his nerve, and he never fully recovered. In mid-October the Lithuanians sent a note to the new German Chancellor Prince Maximillian of Baden, demanding the evacuation of all Lithuanian territory by German military forces. Before the month was out the Turks became the second domino of the row to fall, capitulating in the face of internal collapse and an irresistible British advance. With her southern allies gone, Austria-Hungary could not hope to forestall an invasion from the Balkans. Already both her northern and southern Slavic groups had declared themselves as independent; she had come apart at the seams of nationality and sought an armistice which was instituted on November 4th. At about the same time, both Estonia and Lithuania declared complete independence. All alone and abandoned by allies and satellites alike and rocked by internal revolution, Germany could not continue the war. With a new Polish state sure to emerge from the ruins of old Europe, General Pilsudski was released from Magdeburg Prison on November 8th. The next day the *Kaiser* took refuge from the revolution in Holland, and on the 11th an armistice took effect on the Western Front. The Great War was over.

With his sponsor in defeat *Hetman* Skoropadsky wasted no time in dealing with the new set of circumstances prevailing in the East. Polish nationhood on his western border was now a certainty, as was renewed Russian interest in the desirable grain-lands of his young and feeble regime, and on November 14th, he declared a reunion of the Ukraine with Russia. The move satisfied no one but the Red sympathizers within his realm—though their number was considerable—but Skoropadsky's options were limited. An *Entente* naval force was soon steaming through the Dardanelles and into the Black Sea; it landed troops at Odessa on the 26th to help secure the area for "White" armies forming in south Russia. The *Hetman* would have none it of; perhaps he sensed the inevitability of a Red victory. At any rate he remained in Kiev as long as the Germans did so, and when they began to withdraw their forces in early December, he decided to go with them. Lacking any effective military establishment of his own, he could hardly have done otherwise; waiting for an uncertain fate at the hands of the Reds was not, in his mind, an option. On December 14th he resigned, and the *Hetmanate* passed into history. Skoropadsky never renounced his German inclinations, in fact he left Ukraine for good with the retreating German troops and later took up permanent residence in Germany, where he lived for the rest of his life.

Two days before the resignation of the *Hetman*, the German-placed King of Finland had abdicated. On December 16th all remaining German forces in the country were evacuated and the last German satellite had broken out of its orbit. Now, only the fate of Poland remained to be decided; the Poles themselves were determined to count most among those who would decide it. Relations with Germany were severed on December 15th, and the first shots between the two peoples were exchanged later in the month in what had been the German province of Posen.

Thus did the year 1919 dawn with continued fighting in Eastern Europe. While British, French, Italians and Americans celebrated the end of the war and its accompanying victory in the West, Red Russians fought White

Russians and Germans battled Poles, and the combat was about to escalate when both Russian and Pole began to claim the same ground. Disputes over Polish boundaries had caused the rift between Pilsudski and Berlin, and the ongoing feud over a Polish-Ukrainian frontier was inherited by the Russians, once Ukraine had rejoined the Russian state. Matters were further complicated by the unwillingness of many German commanders to retire from the eastern lands in a timely manner. By the terms of the Western Armistice, Germany was to evacuate all occupied territory in the East, but no one was present to enforce such terms, no actual Treaty had been signed, and no one knew exactly what land was to go to what country. What all knew was that possessing this or that province as certain to enhance one's claim to it, and it would be infinitely preferable to enter a Peace Conference in a strong position rather than to go begging for something already held by someone else.

Many Germans were loathe to surrender the provinces in eastern Germany, even ones in which Poles enjoyed a clear majority, without a fight. Posen, West and East Prussia, and upper Silesia were all coveted by the latter, who began a campaign to secure them in January; the Germans countered by raising "Defense of Border" formations and recapturing several cities and towns in February, until they were ordered to desist by the government at Berlin, which in turn was under pressure from the dictates of the Western Powers, who intended to turn over much of the area to Poland.

The Romanians were certainly not about to wait for events to overtake their ambitions. On November 10th, one day before the German armistice in the West, the Jassey Government re-entered the war, in violation of the Treaty of Bucharest, in order of course, to absolve itself of defeat and to occupy what territories it desired, before the spoils could be allotted to someone else. On the 9th of November, Mackensen and his army was ordered to leave Romanian soil within 24 hours. Bucharest itself was re-occupied by *Entente* troops advancing from Salonika, in conjunction with the Romanians, on December 1st. Two days later the last of the Bulgarians had evacuated Dobruja. Mackensen's force was able to withdraw nearly as far as Budapest before it was forced to surrender on December 16th; thereafter nothing could oppose the forces of the South Slavs, Slovaks, and Romanians as they began to seize whatever lands their hearts desired.

By late March 1919, the Russians had been defeated by a Romanian army on the Dniester, and the latter had secured the border province of Bessarabia.

Now, Bucharest could concentrate on Hungary; it had already occupied Transylvania that winter. On April 21st an advance into the Hungarian Plains brought the Romanians as far as the River Tisza by the 26th, and it was to be on this river line that the invaders staked the limit of their claims. Budapest was presented with the new terms on May 5th, and when no favorable response was forthcoming, the military advance was ordered to continue. This action brought a speedy reaction from the Western Powers, who ordered the Romanians to stop, on the 8th, and for a while the latter complied. But relations between the two camps continued to deteriorate and by July 1st had erupted into war when fighting broke out along the Tisza. The Hungarians, whose shrunken state had few forces with which to defend itself, attempted to counterattack their tormentors on the 20th, but were beaten after several days of combat. Then on the 29th, Bucharest waved its soldiers to advance on the Hungarian capital, which was entered on August 3rd; the occupation would last until the 14th of November. During those three months the Hungarians would experience behavior from the Romanians that they would never forget; their constant appeals to the West for deliverance would prompt many protests, threats, and pleas, but all these were consistently ignored by Bucharest, which denied all the charges but allowed, if not encouraged, the abuses. Hungary was thus systematically looted of everything that was not nailed down, and much of what was. Former Austro-Hungarian officers were all arrested. Supply lines to Budapest were deliberately cut so that the population could be made to endure privation. Romanian vengeance seemed to have no limits. A British member of the Inter-Allied Military Mission in Hungary was shocked at the behavior of troops who were associated with the *Entente*. He witnessed individuals beaten, food and agricultural animals and equipment stolen, and railways disrupted by removal of rolling stock, erection of barricades, and outright destruction; the Budapest-Vienna line was demolished in one section.[223] The Hungarians, powerless to resist the systematic plunder of their country, would soon begin to bitterly resent the inaction of the Western Powers, from whom they had hoped to receive a just settlement. Finally, when the *Entente* declared its intention of severing all ties to Romania if the latter did not withdraw its troops from all territory allotted by the peacemakers to Hungary, the Romanians decided they could live without further plunder, and complied. It was not until February 1920, however, that the last Romanian troops left the new limits of Hungarian soil.

A much freer rein was allowed the Germans in the Baltic States, where Red troops were already overrunning the three new and weak national governments that had temporarily arisen in the vacuum left by the German defeat. A commander familiar with the region, General von der Goltz, was selected to lead a division- (later Corps-) sized force to restore order within the remnants of the Eighth Army still posted in the area, and expel the Reds. Goltz and his men landed at Libau on Feburary 1ˢᵗ, and remained mostly passive for a month while they tried to determine friend from foe, and set about to re-discipline the lackadaisical soldiers of the old wartime Eighth Army.

Farther south, at Bialystok, Germans and Poles were cooperating instead of fighting in early February. The idea was to allow the Poles to pass through the lines that the Germans were still holding at that point, while the latter's army units withdrew from deep inside Russia. If this could be arranged, Polish troops could hold back the Reds at a point much farther east. The Germans had nothing to gain, but nothing to lose by the arrangement, and the deal was done on the 5ᵗʰ; no doubt most German military men preferred the idea of "White" Poles as neighbors to the thought of Red Russians at the borders of Germany.

Von der Goltz, who definitely preferred a German presence in the Baltic, began to advance on March 3ʳᵈ. His first objective was to occupy Courland and seize Riga, but after some initial success his force was soon stopped by Latvian troops, many of whom were pro-Communist. Much time was then wasted on political wrangling and eventually Goltz lost his patience and arrested the Latvian government, its premier only escaping in a ship of the Royal Navy's Baltic Squadron.[224]

By the time Goltz was ready to strike again, an order from Berlin had arrived, demanding he reduce his forces by at least half and insisting he stop enlisting new recruits. The German General suspected that the Western Powers were behind the dispatch, so he pretended to comply while pushing on to Riga, which once again fell, on May 25ᵗʰ. Waving his soldiers farther on, he then invaded Livonia and Estonia, determined to conquer all of the territory once held by the Teutonic Knights of the Middle Ages. The high water mark of this invasion was reached in mid-June; thereafter, Estonian and Latvian troops began to push the Germans back toward Courland. Before long, Goltz was told by his government that the Western Powers demanded the withdrawal of all German forces from the Baltic States, so he disengaged and began to contemplate his next move. For awhile, the fighting in the Baltic region died away.

If the fires of war were squelched in one place, they seemed to flare up in another. In August 1919 it was upper Silesia, a land of mixed German and Polish population, that became a scene of battle. *Freikorps* activity here had been stopped by a government order in February, as had been the case in Posen. But by midsummer the Poles felt strong enough to take the whole area by force, and duly attacked on August 16th. They advanced for two days, then were countered on the 18th by strong German units who drove them back to their start line within a week. Both groups knew the issue had by no means been settled; they warily held their positions and braced for the next round.

In defiance of his government, Goltz and the bulk of his command decided to continue campaigning. By late summer, he had attached his force to the "White" Russian movement in the Baltic, a group determined to destroy the infant Baltic Republics, and the Riga area once again became the arena for a battle in early October. This time, however, ships of the British navy joined the fray, bombarding German positions and helping the Latvians to repel the invaders. The Germans, isolated in an increasingly hostile environment, were too few to prevail and were finally driven from Latvia in November. They made no attempt to subdue Lithuania as they retreated across its territory to arrive back in East Prussia in December. The Baltic would not be host to a 20th century version of the domain of the old Teutonic Order.

While Germans battled Poles and Baltic peoples for more favorable frontiers in post-war Europe, the Russians had been busy consolidating their "Proletarian Dictatorship" and fighting to ward off encroachments by foreign and "White" military units. During 1919 a new headache for them was forming to their immediate west. On April 21st, Polish troops under Pilsudski, who had become a commander-in-chief of all Polish forces and virtual dictator of the emerging Polish state, captured Vilna after two days of combat with Red soldiers. It was a wake-up call of sorts for Lenin, who had not expected the Poles, who seemed to be distracted by events in Posen and Silesia, to begin to move east at such an early date. Although the young Soviet state was gaining strength as Red Armies were beginning to multiply, most of these forces needed to engage the Whites, who were very active in the south and east. Poland, by contrast, was receiving aid from the Western Powers, as all self-proclaimed anti-Bolshevik groups were.

Moscow responded with peaceful gestures towards Finland and the Baltic States in order to secure the northwest flank, and by allocating new and fresh resources to build a new Front in Bylorussia and perhaps western Ukraine. Peace talks between the two sides dragged on throughout the autumn, but it became clear that neither would trust the other and no real accord was reached. In fact, Soviets and Poles alike desperately needed time to create a viable military machine with which to confront the other. In the end, both would fight with weapons and equipment largely Western in origin. The French led all the Western Powers in the actual amount of aid sent to Poland and large quantities of German and Austrian war material would also end up in the hands of Polish soldiers. Russian troops also used a variety of ordnance, from Imperial issue to British-, French-, American-, and Japanese-made material captured from "White" forces or at the stockpiled depots at Russia's few ports. Pilsudski had one important advantage in staking claim to the eastern borderlands: the railroads. The West European gauge, used by the *Alliance*, now extended as far as the old Eastern Front which had remained fairly static from autumn 1915 to early 1918, and therefore was ready-made for Polish use into lands beyond the farthest eastern use of the Polish language. For the Russians to re-conquer all the areas of Bylorussian and Ukrainian habitation, the difficulty was thus increased.

Pilsudski's dreams of restoring Poland to something of a pre-partition behemoth extending far into Russia and including Lithuania were easily a match for those of the most extreme German proponents of the *Drang nach Osten*,[225] sentiments that would take another quarter-century to smother. He was soon to understand that the Lithuanians had other ideas, preferring complete independence in 1919. Thus snubbed, he determined to invade the Ukraine, the aversion of which to Russian dominance had so recently been demonstrated. Convinced that such a campaign could easily succeed, Pilsudski hurled his armies against the Reds on April 25, 1920. The Poles advanced swiftly and without serious opposition, taking Zhitomir on the 26th and pushing all the way to Kiev by May 7th. Two days later they were sixteen kilometers (10mi) beyond the capital, and had yet to fight a difficult battle.

That the Poles had a tiger by the tail they could not have known in the early days of this new Russo-Polish War. But the Soviets were about to respond with new armies trained by veteran ex-Czarist officers and hardened by constant propaganda into dedicated Communist crusaders. A Red cavalry army approached from the southeast, taking Uman on the 13th and offering battle before the month was over. Following heavy fighting during the first week of

June, the Soviets recaptured Zhitomir and Berdichev on June 7th. The Poles fell back and for most of the summer the story was one of Russian advance, and by mid July they were approaching the old Austrian capital of Galicia, now renamed Lwow.

Impressive as the Russian re-conquest of western Ukraine had been, it was overshadowed by events farther north, where the Russians had gathered a powerful force under General Tukhachevsky for an offensive north of the Pripet Marshes. Careful to confirm the independence of Lithuania before the summer attack, Moscow also offered it the city of Vilna, then under Polish occupation, in order to ensure it would make no effort to help Poland. The bribe worked, and the Russians could count on a secure right flank when they delivered the blow on July 4th, supported by 600 artillery pieces. For several weeks, the Russians advanced westward, sometimes easily, sometimes in the face of heavy resistance, but by early August, were in sight of their goal, the Polish capital of Warsaw.

The complete story of the Russo-Polish War is beyond our scope here, but much of the fighting took place on earlier battlefields of the recent Great War. The Germans, alarmed by the close proximity of Red divisions to the East Prussian frontier, rushed much of their small army of 100,000 men (stipulated as a maximum figure by the Treaty of Versailles) to the province to "enforce neutrality." In the event it was a wise move. After a savage battle at the gates of Warsaw, the Russians were defeated and scattered, and considerable elements of two Red armies escaped annihilation by the Poles only by crossing the border into East Prussia, where they were interned by the Germans. Polish troops pursued the remnant of Tukhachevsky's force to the east and northeast. A final action occurred on the Niemen River where the retreat was turned around for a week of combat, but in the end the Russians withdrew.

Pilsudski, who no longer trusted the Lithuanians, felt it important to advance far enough to establish a common frontier with Latvia, and for this reason the Poles advanced beyond a line that seemed prudent, to many observers, for Poland's new eastern boundary. By the time of the signing of an armistice that effectively ended the fighting, the Poles had taken all they wanted, Pilsudski's dreams aside.

While Poles and Russians fought the last great cavalry battles in history,[226] more trouble was brewing in Silesia, where British, French, and Italian troops had arrived to maintain order. At Kattowitz, a skirmish between French troops and German nationalists began the fighting, on August 17th. Soon the whole area of upper Silesia experienced a staccato of small arms fire. Angry Germans destroyed the French and Polish Consulates in Breslau on the 26th, and escalating violence led the German government to offer a bounty on firearms that autumn. Meanwhile, a plebiscite in the southern half of East Prussia—the area known as Masuria, where large numbers of Poles resided—was won easily by the Germans, further frustrating the Poles. The districts of East Prussia returned a 97.9% preference for Germany, while an adjacent 4 districts in West Prussia voted the same by a 92.4% margin.[227] It would have been interesting to see how the remainder of West Prussia and Posen would have voted had the people been given the opportunity.

Western troops eventually were able to maintain a semblance of peace until the long-anticipated plebiscite for upper Silesia actually took place in March of 1921. About 15,000 French, British, and Italians policed the exercise of the 20th; the atmosphere was tense, as both Poles and Germans were ready to do battle for the rich, industrial region. When the votes were counted, the tally favored Germany by a margin of roughly 3 to 2; the Poles immediately cried foul and prepared to take the area by force if necessary. Convinced that the West would not oppose them, the Poles struck on May 2nd, and the Silesian "Plebiscite War" had begun. The French did not engage the Poles—they were certainly more sympathetic to their cause than that of the Germans—but the British and Italians both suffered casualties trying to enforce the results of the voting. *Freikorps* units fought back for the German cause. Within three days Polish troops had pushed as far west as the upper Oder River, but began to encounter increasing numbers of German troops, rolling in voluntarily, from all over the country. Soon, the latter were strong enough to assume the offensive, and on May 21st did so, despite receiving absolutely no support from the regular army or even the government. A three-day battle for Annaberg mountain, the highest point of land in the district, commenced, and was won by the Germans. Emboldened, they advanced to the east, and by the 28th a second skirmish with the French at Kattowitz took place. Thereafter, as the *Freikorps* units morale improved, they began to get the upper hand; another victory was won on June 4th at Gross Strehlitz, and in the north German units reached the frontier east of Kreuzburg.

Throwing off the mask of impartiality, the Western Powers suddenly reacted strongly, once it appeared that the "wrong" side was winning, and ordered the German government to stop and withdraw all troops from Silesia, though they knew it had never sanctioned the deeds of these soldiers. Eventually, both Germans and Poles were persuaded to remove all military forces from the area of the plebiscite, and despite some last-minute clashes, peace was pretty much established by mid-July. That October the Silesian problem was settled with a partition of the area along lines about as close to being fair as anyone could have devised at the time, and for Germany the fighting on the eastern frontiers was finally over.

By 1921 peace had also come to the Russians at long last. Having dealt the Whites a series of severe defeats towards the end of 1920, the anti-Communist cause finally collapsed through lack of proper coordination of effort, difficulty of supply, and above all insufficient numbers to match the growing roles of the Red armies. The last bastion to fall to the Soviets was the Crimean Peninsula, which was evacuated by the remnants of the White army which defended it in November of 1920. Thereafter, all that remained for the Moscow government was mopping up operations around the periphery of the defunct Russian Empire. Georgia was the final region to be re-conquered, an effort completed by February of 1921. Although the new regime would—as had the old—have to deal with occasional uprisings within its far-flung borders, it never again was in danger of losing its grip on the land. There remained only to sign some sort of peace with Poland.

Negotiations with Warsaw proved difficult for the Lenin government; following the rout of the Red Armies before the capital, Pilsudski began to demand an eastern border consistent with that of pre-partition Poland. By contrast, the Russians insisted upon the boundary recommended by the Commission headed by the British Lord Curzon defined on December 8th, 1919, which called for the Bug River and the limits of the Prussian partition share of 1795 as the most equitable frontier on the basis of ethnicity. This "Curzon Line" would form the basis for dispute for another quarter-century. But the Poles were in the stronger position for bargaining; they had advanced deep into Bylorussia by the time the Russo-Polish armistice had been signed. As both parties earnestly desired an end to war, a deal was eventually cut, albeit one more favorable to the Poles than the Russians. On March 21, 1921, the Treaty of Riga was signed; it would soon be ratified by both nations, and the fighting in eastern Europe came to an end. Not since July of 1914 had such conditions prevailed.

Once the nature of peace in the East had been determined, it was at last feasible for all interested parties to settle back and count the dead and contemplate the losses or gains to the nations involved, or the residents in the zones of, the Great War and the parochial wars which raged in its wake. The three great empires that had partitioned old Poland and by so doing had created for themselves common frontiers, and thus set the stage for the future clash, had all been swept away, consumed in the awful inferno of war. The German Empire, so young, dynamic, and proud had died at the age of 47 years, 10 months, having been forced out of existence by a vengeful *Entente*, determined to attach the onus of the conflict to the Berlin government, citing its "militaristic" nature and its perceived "lust for world conquest." How it was anymore "militaristic" than any of the other Great Powers, or how it was expected to conquer the world with 65 million people, no one was prepared to debate. It had to go, and when it did the world would be "safe for democracy" and free of future wars. Just how this was to be achieved or indeed whether it was truly desirable, no one (or at least no one in a prominent position) was allowed to question. *Kaiser* Wilhelm was branded a "war criminal" and demands were forwarded to the Dutch government calling for his extradition. To its lasting credit, the latter consistently refused, and the ex-Emperor would remain in Holland until his death in 1941, politely refusing even an offer from the Nazi regime to return to his homeland. Wilhelm did, however, write a congratulatory letter to the *Führer* when France was defeated in 1940. It is altogether fitting that he was spared the final destruction of his beloved Prussia a few years later. Just what "war crimes" the *Entente* would actually have prosecuted him for is difficult to imagine; if it was for violating the neutrality of Belgium or some such nonsense, it would have been interesting to learn what his defense might have done with it, considering later *Entente* behavior in Greece. His real crime, of course, was loyalty to his ally Austria-Hungary; had he only behaved like so many other predators of the time, he would simply have ordered an invasion of the Dual Monarchy in 1914, in conjunction with Russia, Serbia, Italy and Romania and taken the German-speaking provinces for his Empire, while the French and British stood helplessly by, mouths open in shock. The outcome: everyone (but Hungary) wins and no World War. But such a scenario could never have been with an honest, conscientious (if annoying) man like Wilhelm at the head of the army.

By the Versailles Treaty, Germany lost territory to six nations, only two of which had she been at war with. In the East, Poland took the lion's share of

German losses: nearly all of the province of Posen, much of West Prussia, and the small, if important, piece of Silesia following the 1921 plebiscite. Southern East Prussia, which was ethnically Polish voted to remain German, probably because the mostly Protestant Masurians had no desire to be joined to a 30 million strong Catholic Poland. A very small area including the town of Hultschin went to the new state of Czechoslovakia. In addition, two major seaports, with the surrounding hinterlands, were put under League of Nations control; one was Danzig, at the head of the new "Polish Corridor" and therefore claimed by the Poles. It disposed of 2056 square kilometers (794sq.mi.) and was to be within the Polish Customs Union. The other was Memel, consisting of all the ground of East Prussia north of the Niemen River but only slightly larger than Danzig. This "Memelland" was home to a mixture of Germans and Lithuanians and was claimed by the latter; a few years later the Lithuanians, complaining of a lack of a good seaport, annexed it without incident. Years later Hitler's government took it back, but the Soviets awarded it to Lithuania again after the Second World War, and the German population was driven out. All told Germany lost 13% of its land area—from 540,800 sq. km. (208,800sq.mi) to 470,600 sq. km. (181,700sq.mi.)—and nearly 12% of its population—66 million to 57 million—as a result of the war, and East Prussia was geographically separated from the rest of the country. She also lost 2,937,00 sq. km. (1,134,000 sq. mi.) of colonies, with a population of about 13,000,000 and all of her navy and air force. Her army was limited to 100,000 men, or that of a minor power.

Kaiser Karl also lost his Empire and his throne. Having reigned less than two years, he had had nothing to do with the events leading up to the war, though it is difficult to imagine how he might have been more successful in preventing its coming than had Franz Joseph. His property was all confiscated by the post-war Austrian government and he was expelled and went to live in Switzerland, without formally abandoning his royal titles. Later he returned to Hungary to try to claim his vacant throne, whereupon he was exiled from that country as well. The island of Madeira became his last residence, and he died there in April 1922. The Habsburg dynasty passed into history; as for the Empire, it too was destroyed as a result of the war, broken up as it was into seven different parcels.

Austria, before the war, had encompassed 300,400 sq. km. (116,000 sq. mi.) with a population of 28,500,000; post war it had been compressed to 83,800 sq. km. (32,360 sq. mi.) with 6.5 million people, 28% and 23% respectively of its former self. Hungary had gone from 325,000 sq. km. (125,500 sq. mi.) to 92,900 sq. km. (35,875 sq. mi.) and 21,000,000 people to 8,400,000, 29% and 40% respectively of its former glory. Bosnia-Herzigovina, along with Croatia, Slavonia, Slovenia, Dalmatia and part of Hungary proper had accepted the House of Karageorgevich, in essence had agreed to incorporation into the Kingdom of Serbia (as had Montenegro) though the new state would be known as the Kingdom of the Serbs, Croats, and Slovenes. Serbia and Montenegro had enlarged from 87,300 sq. km. (33,700 sq. mi.) and 14,180 sq. km. (5475 sq. mi.) with a combined 5,060,000 people to a state of 247,345 sq. km. (95,500 sq. mi.) and a population of 13.9 million. Another Slavic nation, Czechoslovakia, was entirely carved out of old Austria-Hungary, taking parts of both for an area of 140,400 sq. km. (54,200 sq. mi.) and 14 million residents. Like the Serbian experiment, this Czech state was an exercise in futility; its very geography was not conducive to a sound infrastructure and it needed four official languages (Czech, Slovak, German and Ukrainian) just to conduct the business of governing. For all their talk about the "ramshackle" Austro-Hungarian Empire, the *Entente* had sanctioned the formation of two ramshackle states out of its ruins.

They also allowed Romania to take much of what it desired for territory. Naturally the Romanians took Dobruja back from Bulgaria, though it was home to very few Romanians. They also took Transylvania and a wide swath of Hungarian soil, with large numbers of Germans and Magyars included, as well as Bukovina and Bessarabia, home to many Ukrainians and a mixture of other minorities. Romania thus incurred the wrath of all of her neighbors save the new Slavic states, with whom she could celebrate over the spoils. Hungary in particular had become a bitter rival, and an ongoing dispute over the two nations' mutual frontier would boil over again before two decades had passed. Italy took all the ex-Austrian ground which was inhabited by Italians, and a good deal that was not, absorbing Germans and Slovenes in the process, and still complaining of lack of sufficient "compensation" for her treachery against a former ally. The last piece of Austrian real estate to be grabbed was Galicia, which was taken by the Poles, who now had re-established their pre-partition frontiers with Prussia and Austria.

The third Empire conspicuous by its absence after the war was Russia, which, as we have seen, fell into a state of civil war, and was pressed by

Alliance expansionism and *Entente* intervention. Once all of these pressures had been relaxed, Lenin and his henchmen could, and did, claim enormous success. They had lost a major war, but had been saved from the worst consequences of the loss by the subsequent defeat of their former enemies. They had incurred the wrath of the *Entente*, but beaten off its half-hearted probes. And they had defeated all internal challenges to their rule and consolidated their hold on the vast lands of the huge nation. Russia emerged from the years of conflict with 21,346,800 sq. km. (8,242,000 sq. mi.) of soil, down only 5% from that which the *Czar* had ruled. The population loss was more serious; war losses and territorial losses had reduced the number of Russian citizens by some thirty million between 1914 and 1920, an 18% reduction. Four new republics had been created out of the old Empire: Finland, 388m,500 sq. km. (150,000 sq. mi.), 3.3 million people; Estonia, 47,526 sq. km. (18,350 sq. mi.), one million people; Latvia, 65,786 sq. km. (25,400 sq. mi.), 1.75 million; Lithuania, 58,275 sq. km. (22,500 sq. mi.), two million. In addition, much of the new state of Poland was from Imperial Russian territory and its eastern frontier was pushed, thanks to the Polish victory of 1920, to beyond Russia's 1795 partition share and into the 1793 share; it was less than what Pilsudski had originally hoped for but it did, not coincidentally, include all of the static front line from 1915 to 1917, that is, the main line of fortifications in the East. The Poles could therefore feel fairly secure in their new borders. The only other ground lost was that which had been ceded back to Turkey at Brest-Litovsk, and even some of this, the port of Batum, was recovered when Georgia was re-conquered at the end of the Civil War.

As for the other two *Alliance* powers, both were obliged to surrender ground. Bulgaria came out of the war more or less intact, having lost less than 10% of both its territory and population to Serbia and Greece, but still unsatisfied, as she had been after the Balkan Wars, that three neighbors held large amounts of land that she claimed. Turkey was much more roughly handled, in fact the Ottoman Empire would become the fourth Empire in the East to disappear as a result of the war when it finally collapsed a few years later. By then it had gone from a land of 1,768,971 sq. km.(683,000 sq. mi.) to 762,755 sp. Km. (294,500 sq. mi.) and 19,850,000 people to 13,200,000. Its sole net gain was the small parcel from Russia in Armenia, around the city of Kars.

Losses incurred by the various combatants on the Eastern Front have never been exactly known, nor ever will they be. Records when kept were too often lost or destroyed in the chaos that plagued the remnants of the three great Empires immediately following the official end of the conflict; other information would be destroyed in a second round of warfare a generation later. Russian records, in particular, are wholly incomplete, as they were bound to be, considering that most everything associated with the Imperial regime was often wantonly obliterated by angry mobs that ransacked government facilities during the frantic days of Revolution and Civil War. Similar, if less thorough, conditions prevailed for a short time in both of the Central European Empires. Nevertheless, we can still arrive at a fairly good estimate of the human loss caused by the war. The estimates vary widely and should be remembered for what they in fact are—estimates.

Beginning with Germany, we find estimates of the number of men mobilized at between 12 and 13.4 million. Using a figure of 65 million total residents in 1914, we find that the German Empire managed to call between 18 and 20% of its people to war. The percentage is high, but not unattainable, and we do know that its leaders made a maximum effort to win the war, so it is not unreasonable to suspect these numbers may be correct. The number of killed is put at between 1.7 and 2 million, an annoying spread of 300,000 lives, but some sources listed "missing" men as dead, while others did not. A century later, we now know that most of the "missing" of the First World War were probably killed—their remains shredded to bits by artillery fire or buried by such and never rediscovered—as very few of these ever returned to their homes. Using the high figure, then, we can more or less apportion the dead to the different fronts on which Germans fought. A total of 257 infantry and cavalry divisions had taken the field. The average number of divisions on the Eastern Front for the entire 52 months of war was 62, or roughly 24% of the total. A reasonable number of lives lost in the East then, for the sake of our own estimate, would be about half a million, and this number is consistent with those of sources which do list figures. Using the same formula we see that of the 5.4 to 5.7 million wounded the Germans suffered, probably 1.35 to 1.425 million were injured on the Eastern Front. An exception to this formula would certainly be allowed for numbers of prisoners of war. Germany lost nearly one million men to her enemies as prisoners, but the vast majority were taken on the Western Front, especially in the last three months of the fighting. The number lost in the East Probably did not reach 200,000. Total casualties in the East then were probably 2.05 to 2.15 million men. An estimated 650-750,000 civilians also died as a direct result of the war as a whole.

Austria-Hungary mobilized something like 7.8 million men for her armed forces, or approximately 15 to 16% of her population, not bad for a nation historians have generally been so contemptuous of. Of her 90 divisions an average of just over 44 were to be found in the East, or nearly half (49%) of her total commitment to the war. This is all the more remarkable when one considers that she had gone to war to punish the terrorist-sponsoring regime in Serbia in 1914, and after May 1915 considered her main front to be against Italy. Estimates of Austro-Hungarian war dead for 1914-1918 range from 540,000 to 1.540 million; the latter figure is almost certainly too high and probably includes "missing" men, of whom there were many for the Dual Monarchy, and we have seen how many of these soldiers simply deserted to the Russians, or never returned from captivity and were listed as "missing." Somewhere between 1.94 and 3.20 million more men were wounded, and between 1.23 and 2.12 million were taken prisoner. Nearly one-half million of these died in captivity, mostly in the frozen wastes of Siberia or working on the railroad to the Arctic. As mentioned above, about half of Austro-Hungarian total losses can reasonably be attributed to the Eastern Front.

Bulgaria raised and committed 14 divisions to the *Alliance* cause, and averaged 4.75 divisions on the Eastern Front over 18 months. About one-third of her 75-80 thousand dead and 150-155 thousand wounded were doubtless casualties of the East, but certainly fewer than that fraction of her 150,000 men lost as prisoners. Another at least 25,000 Bulgarian troops died of disease while at the front lines, and 275,000 civilians are believed to have lost their lives as well.

The Ottoman Empire was able to field 72 divisions in all for the war, but averaged just over four for 16 months of service on the Eastern Front. Turkish losses there, then, would be less than 6% of the totals. The Empire mobilized nearly one million men, or 20% of its citizenry for the struggle, and suffered between 235 and 435 thousand dead and between 405 and 510 thousand wounded. Another 100 to 145 thousand Turks were captured. Even if the lesser figures are to be believed, they show that most Turkish soldiers of WWI became casualties. Many writers believed 2 million civilians also perished; most of these were Armenian victims of genocide. Perhaps 16 to 18 thousand

Turks were losses on the Eastern Front, and without proper medical attention, as many as 10,000 may have died.

Moving to the *Entente* side of the coin, we find that Romania was able to mobilize 500-600,000 men for the war, of whom between 220 and 240,000 were listed as killed and roughly 60,000 taken prisoner. If, as was the case with most armies, about three times as many soldiers were wounded as killed, the numbers do not add up; it is logical to conclude, then, that the available figures are inaccurate. We do know, however, that at least half, perhaps as much as two-thirds, of the Romanian army was destroyed in the field, making the nations' losses quite high based on percentage. Romanian civilians who died as a direct result of the war are believed to have exceeded 265,000 in number.

Estimates of the losses of Russia in the Great War have long been widely at variance, but to arrive at reasonable figures is by no means impossible, as some have suggested. By comparing population totals for before and after the war and subtracting the 28.1 or so million people residing in states newly carved out of the old Empire, we find that some 1.9 million people are missing. This figure is in conformity with the most frequently encountered numbers of Russian dead for 1914-1918, usually listed as 1.7 to 1.8 million. It is, of course, dependent on the accuracy of the census figures, which in the case of Russia, were notoriously inaccurate. At any rate, the same sources give 4.8 to 5 million men as wounded, and 3.4 to 3.9 million taken prisoner. The East Prussian campaign of 1914 had cost 265,000 casualties; the Galician of the same year perhaps 10,000 fewer. By year's end another 125,000 had been sustained. The year 1915 was disastrous, and crippled the armed forces with another 2 million men lost; 1916 was almost as terrible, Russia suffering another 1.6 or 1.7 million human losses. The only major Russian offensive of 1917, by contrast, caused fewer than 50,000 casualties, and thereafter most soldiers more often fled then fought, as the army began to disintegrate. No estimates for Russian civilian dead are available, though the number must have been high; in all likelihood most of these people lived in the areas invaded and therefore were mostly Poles, Lithuanians, and Ukrainians.

Whereas it is understandable that Romania was able to average only 53% of its total initial strength over its 28 months of combat in the war—two thirds of the country came under occupation after 3½ months of fighting—the statistics for Russia are very eye-opening. For the 37 or so months of war for which records are available, the Russian Empire was only able to average

47.6% of its total 294 divisions raised, for service on the Eastern Front. It did, of course, have to defend a second front in Trans-Caucasia, but this theater was never host to more than a half-million troops or so (20-25 divisions) a fraction of the 12 million men mobilized. Russia was notorious for having inordinately large numbers of soldiers tied up as "support troops," but to field an average of less than half of its strength on its main front was inexcusable and doubtless did much to nullify the numerical advantage it should always have enjoyed over the *Alliance* nations, each of which considered its main front to be elsewhere.

Herein lies the problem of why the Eastern Front has never been given the respect it deserves, by the vast majority of historians of the war. For the Western Powers—Britain, France, Belgium, Germany and later the United States—the Western Front was the only theater which really mattered, all others were annoying distractions from the "real" war. The Italian Front was of secondary importance to all but the Italians and the Austrians, who both were junior partners in their respective coalitions, and not likely to persuade the senior allies to make much of an effort there. The Balkan and Middle Eastern Fronts were treated with even greater disdain, and because the Russians were less effective in the East than the Westerners would have preferred, and eventually dropped out of the war, the Eastern Front was subsequently treated as if it had never mattered. For a while in Germany, it seemed as though the Easterners might prevail when Hindenburg and Ludendorff were elevated to the top posts at *OHL*, but they, like their predecessors, soon adopted the Western mode of thought. It is left to the imagination to consider how differently the war may have ended if *OHL* had made its major effort for 1918 in the Balkans and in Italy, while standing on the defensive in the West. With all of Europe east of France in *Alliance* hands, how were the Western Powers to win the war? If the dominoes in the East had not been the first to fall, how was Germany to be defeated? Would her morale have cracked if her allies had remained in the conflict? It seems unlikely; by being lured into the maelstrom of the Western Front, Ludendorff may have forfeited a very good chance to avoid defeat. As it was, he struck West while ignoring the danger in Italy and the Balkans, and still maintained considerable forces in the East. In the end the Germans were defeated in the West, the Austro-Hungarians were defeated in Italy, and Bulgaria was defeated in the Balkans. With Russia and Romania already defeated at the hands of the *Alliance*, we have the unfortunate conclusion of every nation that fought on the Eastern Front having been defeated convincingly, by the time of the signing of the Armistice in the West. Hence the conclusion that only the Western Front mattered for the final verdict of the war. The myth of the "sideshows" was thus born and has persisted to this day, and modern historians still feel the need to reinforce it, so sure they are that only ground west of the Rhine is worth the effort of a Great War. A quarter of a century later a new Eastern Front would be the decisive theater for an entire world at war, and again, it would receive scant coverage compared to that attributed to the fighting in Western Europe.

The men and women who fought and died or suffered agonizing wounds or were deprived of their freedom of action as prisoners of war, were raped, burned out of their homes and villages, or lost all of their earthly possessions or perhaps were weakened by disease spread by passing armies or fouled food and water were victims of war. Thousands upon thousands lie beneath the earth in unmarked graves without so much as a headstone to commemorate their very existence. All too often, their lives were far too short, and filled with hardship and violence. All the efforts they made, however dedicated, selfless, or well directed, have been largely forgotten, eclipsed by the eventual outcome of the war, and by other conflicts of more recent memory. No eternal flames burn in the pine woods east of Kovel or in the environs of Lake Narotch. The names of the rivers Biala or Narayuvka have no meaning for most who remember the Somme or the Marne. There are no walking tours available for those wishing to visit the fields outside of Halicz, or the ridges among the Carpathian Passes. Yet it is here, just as surely as at Ypres or the Argonne or at Jutland, that the Great War was decided, here where occurred events that changed the course of history. The Eastern Front deserves a more prominent place in its story. May the memory of its participants be preserved forever.

Unfortunately "their" number will never be known, but for our purpose of showing just how enormous was the scale of the combat in the East, we have a minimum casualty (killed, wounded, and prisoners of war) list of some 14,471,000 human beings, and a maximum tally of 17,476,000 people whose lives were either erased or would never be the same.

For anyone interested in the First World War, such awesome totals cannot have been sustained in a "sideshow." Let us hope that future historians do not treat the Eastern Front as such. It was an integral part of a larger movement which would never have been the same, from beginning to end, without its appendage in the East. So let us treat it for what it meant for the other theaters in which fighting occurred; it did, in fact, determine the nature of the beginning, the course, and the outcome of the Great War, a war which made the world what it is today.

Post-War Romania

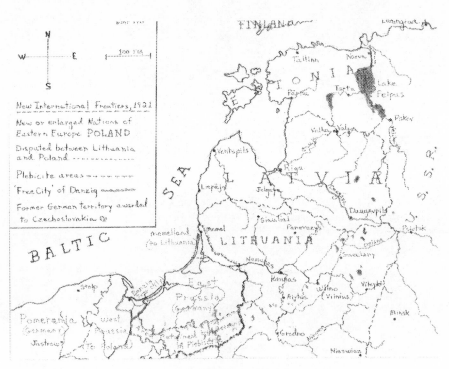

Post-War Eastern Europe

Consequences

There are few instances in history where one encounters such a strange end to a war as that which occurred as a result of the war on the Eastern Front from 1914-1918. Strictly speaking, the *Alliance* had won the war in the East, but could not long take advantage of victory there, owing to its subsequent defeat in other theaters, and its own loss of the general war. All of its gains were nullified as a result; the greater result was that no one who had begun the fighting in 1914 was to emerge as a victor. The three great Empires, which had at one time long been allies, had come to blows and all had disintegrated in the end; all lost considerable territories, and their successor governments found themselves as outcasts on the world scene. Germany had been forced to change its government and declare itself the aggressor, solely responsible for the war and willing to pay for all damages it had caused to all the remaining *Entente* powers. Austria-Hungary had been undermined by Pan-Slavic nationalism and forced to yield all lands not inhabited by Germans and Hungarians (and many that were) to new states and expansionist neighbors. Turkey or the Ottoman Empire was likewise broken up and slated for partition amongst the victors. Bulgaria was further penalized for having joined the "wrong" side and shrunken even further by neighbors who had already robbed her in 1913.

In some respects, the losers became the winners. Romania, having been badly beaten and occupied, emerged from the war over twice as large as she had been upon her entry into it, by which time it was already half over. Not content with taking virtually all the Hungarian and Bulgarian—and even some Austrian—territory that they wanted, the Romanians also found it necessary to grab a slice of ground from ex-ally Russia. And the Russians, despite having lost Finland and the Baltic States, were able to regain the rich lands of Ukraine and much of Bylorussia, and establish a fairly reasonable western frontier with Poland. Moreover, they retained all the other vast expanses of the former

Empire, except a very small piece of ground in Armenia. Having outlasted all its political and military enemies, the new regime in Moscow now found itself master of one of the largest, most resource rich areas of the globe. Lenin had been right all along in insisting that his war-torn land needed peace, in order to consolidate government control over a core area from which the political experiment that was the new Russia could have an opportunity to function, and create the promised utopia. For a small group of hard-core Communists, it was a dream come true.

An examination of a pre-war European map compared to a post-war one would have been enough to convince most individuals that the real beneficiary of the war in the East had been Poland, a state which had disappeared in 1795 and suddenly reappeared, with frontiers which would have been recognizable to persons of the earlier period. The new nation had regained all of the ground—save a few insignificant corners—lost to Prussia and Austria during the three partitions, as well as most of the 1795 Russian share and a few nibbles of the 1793 Russian piece. To have gone even further east was contemplated, but contrary to geographic (and ethnic, if there were any) considerations, and too far distant from the line of fortifications of the 1915-1917 period which were important to the military-minded Pilsudski and his lieutenants. These latter mostly earthen structures would continue to affect military thinking as late as July 1944, when after a massive Russian offensive in eastern Bylorussia had torn a huge and unplugable hole in the German lines, some *Wehrmacht* officers wondered whether they might be able to make a stand in the fortifications of the earlier war.

But Poland, like the other Slavic states of Eastern Europe created from the ashes of the war, was not without its problems, especially regarding minorities. As a nation composed of people who had hitherto been minorities within three empires, it might have been more careful about becoming itself a dominant nation within a state encompassing several important minorities. There were Germans and Czechs in the west and Ukrainians, Bylorussians and Lithuanians in the eastern portions of the new country, and mostly all would have preferred reunion with their brethren across the young frontiers. It would take another World War, a compulsory and drastic change in the borderlines and the forcible expulsion of millions of Germans from their homes to finally settle the issue of Polish frontiers. And the Russian leader at that time—a man named Stalin—would refer to the recommendations made by British Lord Curzon in 1920, to define Poland's final eastern border.

Following the collapse of Communism in the late 20th century, the other Pan-Slavic states created from the ruins of old Austria-Hungary would also unravel. In spite of ridding itself of a large German minority by expelling the entire population after the Second World War and of having its Ukrainian province lopped off by the Russians and joined to Ukraine, even the remaining Czechs and Slovaks found that they could not live together politically, and Czechoslovakia ceased to exist by the mid 1990s. Similarly, Yugoslavia broke up into its component parts, but not without experiencing the horrors of civil war and genocide. Eventually, even little Montenegro decided to divorce Serbia, so for the latter, the wheel has come full circle; a century after sponsoring the terrorist act that precipitated the Great War from which it expected such vast territorial gain, Serbia has been reduced to a state no larger than it was in 1914, and even so includes many unwilling Albanian and Hungarian residents. It is tempting, but probably useless, to wonder whether anyone believes that the past century of violence has been worthwhile for Serbia.

Of course, the Soviet Union also broke up into its component "republics," they being 15 in number, and ironically including the Baltic States, Bylorussia, and Ukraine, all of which we have seen created as a result of the war on the Eastern Front, then subsequently destroyed (The Soviet Union re-annexed the Baltics and Bessarabia in 1940) when Russian strength was restored. From a century distant, perhaps the peace of Brest-Litovsk seems less shocking than it did to the *Entente* at the time.

Probably the most serious consequence of the war on the Eastern Front of the First World War was one among the many myths that grew out of it: the myth of German superiority over the peoples of the East. The Germans had been the best trained, best equipped, best supplied and best led military force to fight here, and when they possessed anything like equal numbers to the enemy, they often prevailed. They were able to prop up their stumbling Austro-Hungarian allies and still seize huge swaths of real estate from their enemies, whenever they determined to make a serious effort to do so. We have seen how they came to be feared by their opponents who themselves began to develop inferiority complexes when placed in the lines opposite them. German artillery pieces and machine guns were initially more numerous than those of the Russians, but, more importantly, they were handled more skillfully. German innovations such as poison gasses and flamethrowers and steel helmets were only slowly matched by their Russian opponents who felt that they were constantly having to play catch-up to the new technologies. Serious small-arms and munitions shortages only augmented the problem, but when the Russians were well equipped they did fight well, though they were badly hampered by unimaginative commanders and poorly served by inadequate supply services hamstrung by the lack of an efficient transportation network. Interestingly enough, Russian soldiers often felt a sense of their own superiority over the Austrians, even though the latter were generally as well equipped as the Germans, if not as well led. The first Russian defeats during the East Prussian campaign were due more to the failure of Russian intelligence, backed by incessant pleas from the French to hurriedly engage the enemy, than to any particular German tactical superiority, yet it was on the foundations of these early campaigns that the myth was perpetrated. Many Germans, of the Hitler mold, were probably victims of their own propaganda, and began to see themselves as somehow genetically above the ill-armed, ill-fed, often illiterate enemy troops. They began to believe that it was their destiny, perhaps even their right, to bring all the benefits of German culture to the underdeveloped, backward East, and herein lay the problem. Russia's poor performance in the First World War convinced many Germans—including Hitler, who never fought on the Eastern Front—that any future campaign against Russia would be a walkover. Without the slightest consideration for any notion that the new government in Moscow might possibly have had any beneficial effect upon the nation and certain of an inherent superiority of Teuton over Slav, German leaders would, a generation later, once more hurl their forces against the giant to the east. And the consequences of this later struggle would be far more bitter than any German could have imagined, given the experience of the first war. It was all so tragic, the more so if one remembers the traditional friendship of Russia and Germany for most of the 19th century and the Russo-German Pact of 1939. In both cases, had these nations strengthened their ties instead of allowing themselves to drift apart, there was no coalition in all the world mighty enough to have defeated them. That they needed each other but did not care to admit it, is history. That the world, because of their conflict, could never again be the same, is a tragedy which will always be borne by all humankind.

Bibliography

Abbot, Willis J. *Pictorial History of the World War* Leslie-Judge Co. New York 1919

Allen, George H. *The Great War (5 Vols.)* George Barrie's Sons Philadelphia 1915-1921

Asprey, Robert B. *The German High Command at War* William Morrow & Co. New York 1991

Banks, Arthur *A Military Atlas of the First World War* Leo Cooper republished 1989

Beckett, Ian F.W. *The Great War 1914-1918* Pearson Education Limited 2001

Brusilov, General A.A. *A Soldier's Notebook 1914-1918* Macmillan & Co. London 1930

Buchan, John *A History of the Great War (4 Vols.)* Houghton-Mifflin Co. 1922

Bull, Dr. Stephen *World War I Trench Warfare* Osprey Publishing London 2003

Bull, Dr. Stephen *Trench Warfare* PRC Publishing London 2003

Bunyan, James and H. H. Fisher *The Bolshevik Revolution 1917-18* Stamford University Press (2nd printing) 1934

Cameron, James *1914* Rinehart & Co. New York 1959

Chant, Christopher *Austro-Hungarian Aces of World War I* Osprey Publishing 2002

Charles, Daniel *Mastermind: The Rise and Fall of Fritz Haber* Harper-Collins 2005

Cornish, Nik *The Russian Army 1914-18* Osprey Publishing 2001

Dallas, Gregor *1918: War and Peace* Overlook Press 2001

Drury, Ian *German Stormtrooper 1914-1918* Osprey Publishing (reprint) 1996

Ellis, John and Michael Cox *World War I Databook* Aurum Press London 2001

Esposito, Vincent J. (Ed.) *The West Point Atlas of American Wars* Praeger New York, Washington and London 1959

Europe at War (various authors) Doubleday, Page & Co. 1914

Farmborough, Florence *With the Armies of the Tsar* Stein and Day New York 1975

Fedyshyn, Oleh S. *Germany's Drive to the East and the Ukrainian Revolution* Rutgers University Press 1971

Ferguson, Niall *The Pity of War* Basic Books 1999

Fischer, Franz *Germany's Aims in the First World War* W.W. Norton & Co. (English translation) 1967

Fitzsimons, Bernard (Ed.) *Tanks and Weapons of World War I* BPC Publishing Ltd. Beekman House New York 1973

Forty, Simon *Historical Maps of World War I* PRC Publishing London 2002

Fosten, D.S.V. and R.J. Marrion *The German Army 1914-1918* Osprey Publishing (reprint) 1993

Fülöp-Miller, Rene *Rasputin- The Holy Devil* Viking Press New York 1928

George, David Lloyd *War Memoirs* Ivor Nicholson & Watson London 1934

Gilbert, Martin *Atlas of the First World War* Dorset Press 1984

Gilbert, Martin *The First World War* Henry Holt & Co. New York 1994

Golovin, General N.N. *The Russian Army in the World War* New Haven 1931

Goodspeed, D.J. *The German Wars* Houghton Mifflin Co. Boston 1977

Gorky, Kirov and Others *The History of the Civil War in the U.S.S.R. (2 Vols.)* Academic International Press 1974, 1975

Halpern, Paul G. *A Naval History of World War I* Naval Institute Press Annapolis 1994

Halsey, Francis W. *The Literary Digest History of the World War, Volume Seven: Russian Front* Frank & Wagnalls Co. New York and London 1919

Hirschfeld, Dr. Magnus *The Sexual History of the World War* Panurage Press New York 1934

Hoffman, General Max *The War of Lost Opportunities* Battery Press 1999

Hogg, Ian V. *The Guns 1914-18* Ballantine Books 1971

Hogg, Ian V. *Gas* Ballantine Books 1975

Hook, Alex *World War I Day by Day* Grange Books 2004

Horne, Charles F. (Ed.) *The Great Events of the Great War (7 Vols.)* The National Alumni 1920

Howland, Colonel C.R. *A Military History of the World War* General Service Schools Press Fort Leavenworth, Kansas 1923

Hoyt, Edwin P. *The Army Without a Country* New York and London 1967

Ironside, Major General Sir Edmond *Tannenberg The First 30 Days in East Prussia* William Blackwood & Sons London & Edinburgh 1925

Johnson, Douglas W. *Topography and Strategy in the War* Henry Holt & Co. 1917

Jukes, Geoffrey *Carpathian Disaster-Death of an Army* Ballantine Books 1971

Jukes, Geoffrey *The First World War-The Eastern Front* Osprey Publishing 2002

Jung, Peter *The Austro-Hungarian Forces in World War I (2 Vols.)* Osprey Publishing 2003

Jurado, Carlos C. *The German Freikorps 1918-1923* Osprey Publishing 2001

Keegan, John *Opening Moves August 1914* Ballantine Books New York 1971

Kennan, George F. *Russia and the West Under Lenin and Stalin* Little, Brown & Co. Boston & Toronto 1960

Kihntoph, Michael P. *Handcuffed to a Corpse: German Intervention on the Balkan and Galician Front 1914-17* White Mane Books 2002

Knox, Major General Sir Alfred *With the Russian Army 1914-1917 (2 Vols.)* Hutchinson & Co. London 1921

King, W.C. (Ed.) *King's Complete History of the World War* The History Associates 1922

Leites, K. *Recent Economic Developments in Russia* Clarendon Press Oxford 1922

Lewis, Jon E. (Ed.) *Eyewitness World War I* Carroll & Graf Publishers New York 2003

Life Magazine, By the Editors of *The First World War* Time, Inc. 1965

Lincoln, W. Bruce *The Russians Before the Great War* Oxford University Press 1993

Lincoln, W. Bruce *Passage Through Armageddon-The Russians in War and Revolution* Oxford University Press 1994

Lincoln, W. Bruce *Red Victory-A History of the Russian Civil War* Da Copa Press 1999

Livesey, Anthony *The Historical Atlas of World War I* Henry Holt & Co. New York 1994

Lockhart, Bruce R.H. *British Agent* G.P. Putnam's Sons New York 1933

Ludendorff, Erich Von *Ludendorff's Own Story (2 Vols.)* Harper Brothers New York and London 1919

Manchester, William *The Arms of Krupp* Little, Brown Co. Boston and Toronto 1968

March, Francis A. *History of the World War* United Publishers of the U.S. and Canada 1919

Martin, William *Statesmen of the War* Milton, Balch & Co. New York 1928

Massie, Robert K. *Nicholas and Alexandra* McClelland & Stewart 1964

McEntee, Girard L. *Military History of the World War* Charles Scribner's Sons New York 1937

Mirouze, Laurent *World War I Infantry in Color Photographs* Windrow & Greene London (reprint) 1995

Mollo, Andrew *Army Uniforms of World War I* Aero Publishing New York 1978

Moorehead, Alan *The Russian Revolution* Harper & Brothers New York 1958

Nagel, Fritz *Fritz-The World War I Memoirs of a German Lieutenant* Der Angriff Pubs. W.V. 1981

Newman, Bernard *Balkan Background* Macmillen New York 1945

Orton, William *Twenty Years Armistice* Farrar & Rinehart New York and Toronto 1938

Palmer, Svetlana and Sarah Wallis *Intimate Voices from the First World War* Harper-Collins Publishers New York 2003

Pares, Bernard *The Fall of the Russian Monarchy* Phoenix Press edition 1988

Parkinson, Roger *Tormented Warrior: Ludendorff and The Supreme Command* Stein and Day New York 1978

Perry, John C. and Constantine Pleshakov *The Flight of the Romanovs* Konecky & Konecky 1999

Pipes, Richard (Ed.) *Revolutionary Russia* Harvard University Press 1968

Reed, John *The War on All Fronts, Volume V The War in Eastern Europe* Charles Scribner's Sons 1918

Reynolds, Francis J. and Others *The Story of the Great War (8 Vols.)* P.F. Collier & Son New York 1916-1919

Robertson, Bruce (Ed.) *Air Aces of the 1914-1918 War* Harleyford Publishers Limited, Aero Pubs. Inc. 1964

Rolt-Wheeler, Francis and Frederick E. Drinker (Eds.) *The World War for Liberty* National Publishing Co. 1919

Russell, Thomas *The World's Greatest War* L.W. Walter 1915

Shaw, George Bernard *What I Really Wrote About the War* Brentano's New York 1932

Showalter, Dennis E. *Tannenberg-Clash of Empires 1914* Brassey's Inc. 2004

Simonds, Frank H. *History of the World War (5 Vols.)* Doubleday, Page & Co. 1919

Stevenson, David *Cataclysm: The First World War as Political Tragedy* Basic Books New York 2004

Stone, Norman *The Eastern Front 1914-1917* Charles Scribner's Sons New York 1975

Strachan, Hew *The First World War* Viking Press 2003

Strachan, Hew *World War I-A History* Oxford University Press New York and London 1998

Sweetman, John *Tannenberg 1914* Cassell & Co. London 2002

Taylor, A.J.P. (Ed.) *History of World War I* Octopus Books London 1974

Taylor, Edmond *The Fall of the Dynasties* Doubleday & Co. New York 1913

Thomas, Nigel *The German Army in World War I (3 Vols.)* Osprey Publishing 2003

Titler, Dale M. *The Day the Red Baron Died* Walker Publishing Co. edition 1970

Treadwell, Terry C. and Alan Wood *German Knights of the Air 1914-1918* Barnes and Noble 1997

Tuchman, Barbara *The Guns of August* Macmillan Publishing New York 1962

Tuchman, Barbara *The Zimmerman Telegram* Macmillan Publishing New York 1966

Turczynowicz, Laura De *When the Prussians Came to Poland* G.P. Putnam's Sons New York 1916

Vinogradoff, Sir Paul (Ed.) *Economic and Social History of the World War* New Haven 1930-32

Westwell, Ian *World War I Day By Day* MBI Publishing Co. 2000

Willmott, H.P. *World War I* DK Publishing Inc. New York 2003

Zaloga, Steven and James Grandsen *Soviet Tanks and Combat Vehicles of World War II* Arms and Armor Press 1984

Zeman, Z.A.B. *The Break-Up of the Habsburg Empire* Oxford University Press 1961

Endnotes

Chapter Two

[1] After the war the area as a part of Finland achieved its independence from Russia. Stalin re-annexed the area after the so-called "Winter War" of 1939-1940. It has been a part of Russia ever since, the local Finnish populace choosing to relocate over the new frontier after 1940. The town is now known by its Russian name, Primorsk.

[2] Some sources claim it was the newer Imperial yacht *Standart*.

[3] Keegan, Opening Moves, August 1914 Page 22

[4] Tuchmann The Guns of August Pages 41-42

[5] Goodspeed, Page 59

[6] Of course, a comparison of size of the two nations quickly reveals that Germany possessed the more complete system, with far more mileage per capita than Russia.

Chapter Three

[7] Allen Vol. II Page 343

[8] Jukes The First World War Page 17

[9] The order of size of army units (in most armies) was smallest to largest: squad, section, platoon, company, battalion, regiment, brigade, division, corps, Field Army, and Army Group.

[10] Guns and howitzers differ in that a gun shoots a projectile in a fairly flat trajectory, similar to a rifle. A howitzer lobs a shell high into the air so that it can return to the ground at a sharp angle.

[11] Lincoln, Passage Through Armageddon page 203

[12] Stevenson, Cataclysm Page 193

[13] Ibid page 194

[14] Knox Page 217

[15] Brusilov Page 281

[16] Zaloga Page 9

[17] Zaloga Page 26-27

[18] Reynolds Vol II Page 368

[19] The full story of the wayward Czech soldiers is best told by Edwin P. Hoyt The Army Without a Country N.Y. and London 1967. Excellent reading.

[20] Jung Vol I Page 21

[21] Ibid Page 45

[22] Ellis and Cox Page 227

[23] Jung Vol II Page 24

[24] Stevenson Page 194

[25] Stone Chapter 4 for the complete story.

[26] The other three being Great Britain, the Netherlands and the United States.

[27] Hogg The Guns Pages 28 and 31

[28] Fitzsimmons (Ed) Page 12

[29] Drury Page 17

[30] Fosten/Marrion Page 13

[31] Manchester Page 279

[32] Ellis and Cox Page 256

Chapter Four

[33] Halpern Page 184

[34] The Russians referred to Army Group as a Front. The term should not be confused with a battle front or front line.

[35] Brusilov Page 46

[36] The 17th of August cannot be a date which the residents of Schirwindt, East Prussia cared to remember. Longitudinally the easternmost town in all Germany, it was the very first German town to fall to hostile forces in World War II, on the 17th of August 1944. Since the latter capture it has remained in Russian possession. It is unclear whether it or Eydtkuhnen was first to be occupied on August 17, 1914.

[37] Die Letze Reiterschlacht der Weltgeschicte, von Hoen and von Waldstaetten, Amalthae-Verlag, 1929

[38] Tuchman Page 293
[39] As the story goes he shot himself, having lost his way in the woods at night. The Germans found and buried the body, which was repatriated two years later.
[40] Stone Page 67
[41] Reynolds Vol II Page 385
[42] The Illustrated War News (London) September 9, 1914, Page 5
[43] Robertson Page 152; Reynolds Vol. II Page 393
[44] Ironside Pages 266-268
[45] Lincoln, Passage Page 84
[46] Halsey Page 34
[47] Perry and Pleshakov Page 124
[48] Russell Pages 221-226

Chapter Five

[49] Knox Vol I Pages 134-135
[50] Halsey Pages 77-78 describe this action
[51] Pares Page 207
[52] Halpern Page 186
[53] Esposito Map 25
[54] Kihntopf Pages 34-35
[55] Palmer and Wallace Pages 76-77
[56] Abbott Page 80

Chapter Six

[57] Jukes The First World War Page 30
[58] Stone Page 113
[59] Banks Page 283
[60] Turczynowicz Pages 98-99
[61] Knox Vol I Page 253
[62] Stone Page 114
[63] Reynolds Vol III Page 176

[64] Buchan Vol I Pages 526-527

[65] Reynolds Vol III Page 261

[66] Russell Page 374

[67] Turczynowicz Page 154

[68] Russell Pages 371-372

[69] Stone Page 121

[70] Most of the units captured in the fortress were brigade sized or smaller, hence only one division, the 23rd Infantry, was lost and never reformed, despite the enormous number of prisoners (119,600) taken.

Chapter Seven

[71] Lincoln Passage Page 125

[72] Farmborough Page 33

[73] The situation may not have been as bad as the commanders liked to believe. See Stone Pages 130-132

[74] Farmborough Page 37

[75] Horne Vol III Page 181

[76] Reed Page 99

[77] Reed Page 129

[78] Hogg Gas Page 32

[79] Knox Vol I Page 276

[80] Farmborough Page 189

[81] A general retreat so soon after Italian intervention would have shocked the allies, and it was still hoped that Romania was about to intervene as well. Also the main "fortresses" that Sukhomlinov had wanted to scrap would necessarily be lost, thus proving his point, a situation which at the time few in Russia would have wanted to bear witness to. By then the War Minister was very much in disgrace, and was finally arrested in June, on a host of charges, much to the delight of his many enemies.

[82] Farmborough Page 72

[83] Ibid Page 75

[84] Chant Pages 81-82

[85] Palmer & Wallis Page 105

[86] Farmborough Pages 86-87

[87] Stone Pages 174-175
[88] Robertson Page 155
[89] Farmborough Page 92
[90] Lincoln Passage Page 151
[91] Robertson Page 157
[92] Titler Pages 47-49
[93] Halsey Pages 150-151
[94] Farmborough Page 111
[95] Stone Page 187
[96] Farmborough Page 117
[97] In time, the hungry Germans slaughtered many of the bison for food, and placed the species on the verge of extinction. They have since, under careful management, made a reasonable comeback.

Chapter Eight

[98] Pares Page 277
[99] Massie Page 322
[100] Knox Vol I Pages 338-339
[101] Horne Vol III Pages 318-319
[102] The German "South Army" had long since ceased to be German, except in name. After the September withdrawals, only one German division remained, under Bothmer, south of the Pripet.
[103] Halpern Page 203
[104] Halsey Page 192
[105] Knox Vol I for a complete account Pages 385-387
[106] Fülöp-Miller Pages 158-159
[107] Reynolds Vol IV Page 466
[108] The number of Russians actually dispatched was not particularly large—less than two divisions—and some of these were diverted to the Salonika Front.
[109] Jukes Carpathian Page 120
[110] Farmborough Page 173

Chapter Nine

[111] Jukes Carpathian Page 102
[112] Stone Page 228
[113] Hogg Guns Page 126
[114] Estimates of Russian losses for the Northern Fronts in March run as high as 122,000.
[115] Fülöp-Miller Page 342
[116] It was Austro-Hungarian practice to credit both men in a two-seat airplane with a victory for each enemy unit destroyed.
[117] Chant Page 76
[118] Lincoln Passage Page 178
[119] Brusilov Pages 214-216
[120] Jukes Carpathians Page 86
[121] Halpern Page 208.
[122] Taylor Page 146, Jukes Page 113
[123] Farmborough Page 192: an *arshin* equals 71 centimeters (28in)
[124] Ibid Page 194
[125] Linsingen already theoretically controlled the Austrian Fourth Army, and from mid June, the Second. This left only Pflanzer-Baltin's army still directly subordinate to Hötzendorf in the East.
[126] Buchan Vol III, Page 72
[127] Stone Page 254, Buchan Vol III, Page 77
[128] Farmborough Pages 201-202
[129] Knox Vol II Page 451
[130] Robertson Page 153
[131] Kihntopf Pages 86-87
[132] Farmborough Page 210
[133] Lewis Page 228
[134] Ibid Page 229
[135] Farmborough Page 222
[136] Ibid Page 227
[137] Hogg Gas Page 113

Chapter Ten

[138] For an excellent understanding of circumstances behind the turbulent Balkan politics of 20th century Europe, see Balkan background by Bernard Newman, N.Y. 1945

[139] According to Buchan (Vol III, page 139), "On the basis of population the Romanians should have had 69 representatives in the Hungarian Parliament; they never had more than 14, and in 1910 were reduced to five."

[140] Esposito, opposite map 37.

[141] The Szeklers were a compact group of Magyar people inhabiting the southeast corner of the province of Transylvania. Their unique ethnic area, surrounded by Romanian speakers, was often called the Szekler "island." The people considered themselves traditional guardians of the mountain passes.

[142] Farmborough Page 232

[143] It was in fact the last airplane shot down by the Austro-Hungarian ace. His last and final victory came on December 18th of the same year against a Russian observation balloon. Jindra's total: 9 confirmed "kills."

[144] Knox Vol II Page 487 A verst is roughly equal in length to a kilometer.

[145] An internal explosion of great magnitude caused the ship to blow up and roll over and eventually sink. There were roughly 900 casualties. Sabotage was suspected, but not proven.

[146] Halpern Page 248

[147] Stone Page 265

Chapter Eleven

[148] Stone Page 125

[149] The figures are from Golovin, General N.N. The Russian Army in the World War, New Haven, 1931

[150] Knox Vol II

[151] Jukes Pages 85-86

[152] Britain alone supplied 750 guns, 27,000 machine guns, one million rifles, 300 airplanes, 6,000 motor vehicles, 260 mortars, and vast amounts of ammunition and parts during the years 1914-17.

[153] Gilbert Atlas See map on Russian war debts.

[154] Vinogradoff See chart page 311.

[155] Vinogradoff See Russian Agriculture During the War. Livestock of all species actually increased in numbers during the war.

[156] Initially, for every man at the front, Russia required two men in her supply and transport services. Later this was reduced to a one to one ratio.

[157] Vinogradoff See charts Page 394

[158] Knox Page 426

[159] Vinogradoff Page 213

[160] Actually only about 2 million troops manned the front lines in the spring of 1916. The remainder were either occupied in transport and communications, were in reserve units, or had yet to arrive in the order of battle.

[161] Massie Page 388; Pares Page 416; Lincoln Passage Page 325

[162] Lincoln Passage Page 316

[163] Ibid

[164] Farmborough Pages 254-255

[165] Lloyd George Vol III Pages 1102-1103

Chapter Twelve

[166] Reynolds Vol IX Pages 3379-3380

[167] Robertson Page 160

[168] Lincoln Passage Page 323

[169] Lincoln Passage Page 344

[170] Ludendorff Vol II Page 35

[171] Lewis Pages 279-280

[172] Farmborough Page 264

[173] Farmborough Pages 268-270

[174] Brusilov Page 310

[175] Ibid Page 291

[176] Ibid Page 310

[177] Robertson Page 158

[178] Farmborough Page 275

[179] Or, "no fight no loan"

[180] Halsey Page 298

[181] Knox Vol II Page 493

[182] Farmborough Page 275

[183] Halsey Page 306

[184] Knox Vol II Page 666 The savagery is described in some detail. Apparently the Russians soldiers' behavior in Germany in 1944/45 had some precedent. But like most crimes committed by the enemies of Germany, such incidents have typically been ignored by most historians.

[185] Robertson Page 158

[186] Horne Vol V Pages 256-257

[187] Jukes Carpathian Page 156

[188] Ludendorff Vol II Page 41

[189] Farmborough Pages 286-287

[190] Halsey Page 309

[191] Knox Vol II Pages 668-669

[192] Hogg Gas Page 120

[193] Hogg Guns Page 127

[194] Not to be confused with the Aa of Courland. Neither is a tributary of the Dvina, but both empty into the Gulf of Riga within a few kilometers of the larger stream.

[195] Halpern Page 213

[196] Bunyan and Fisher Pages 24-26

[197] Ibid Page 27

[198] Ibid Page 33

[199] Halpern Page 215

Chapter Thirteen

[200] Farmborough Page 328

[201] Gorky and others Page 144

[202] Ibid Page 520

[203] Farmborough Page 336

[204] Robertson Page 156

[205] Gorky and others Page 501

[206] Gorky and others Page 648 (First, Second, Third, Fifth, Eighth, Tenth and Twelfth Armies)

[207] Hoffmann Page 197

[208] Farmborough Page 363

[209] Hoffmann Page 209

[210] Bunyan and Fisher Page 486

[211] Thomas Page 5

[212] Thomas Page 6

[213] Fedyshyn Page 91

[214] Perry and Pleshakov Pages 191-192

[215] Dallas Page 379

[216] Kennan Page 41

[217] Fischer Page 515

[218] For a complete account see Fedyshyn Chapter XII

[219] Fedyshyn Page 239

[220] Halpern Page 257

Chapter Fourteen

[221] Lincoln Red Victory Page 156

[222] Reynolds Vol VIII Page 82

[223] Hungary at the Paris Peace Conference Page 115 Francis Deak, Columbia University Press 1942

[224] Jurado Page 19

[225] "Drive to the East" Many Germans long believed their future lay in the vast expanses of Eastern Europe. Visions of "Lebensraum" (space for living), a future pet phrase of the Nazis, originated with the earlier sentiments.

[226] See Military History Magazine March 2006. "Bloody Lances and Broken Sabers" by Simon Rees

[227] Deutscher Soldatenkalender München-Lochhausen 1960 Page 148

About the Author

G. Irving Root became interested in the First World War during the 1960s when he lived in New England and was a collector of war relics. Later he published an illustrated collector's guide to the steel helmets used in that conflict, and today he chronicles the results of many years of careful research into the battles and campaigns of the "War to end Wars." He now resides in Western Texas.